# China's peasants

## The anthropology of a revolution

*by*

### Sulamith Heins Potter

*Research Associate, Department of Anthropology,*
*University of California at Berkeley*

*and*

### Jack M. Potter

*Professor, Department of Anthropology,*
*University of California at Berkeley*

CAMBRIDGE
UNIVERSITY PRESS

Published by the Press Syndicate of the University of Cambridge
The Pitt Building, Trumpington Street, Cambridge CB2 1RP
32 East 57th Street, New York, NY 10022, USA
10 Stamford Road, Oakleigh, Melbourne 3166, Australia

First published 1990
Reprinted 1996, 1997

Printed in Great Britain at the University Press, Cambridge

*British Library cataloguing in publication data*

Potter, Sulamith Heins
China's peasants: the anthropology of a revolution
1. China. Guangdong. Villages. Social change, 1949–1985
1. Title   11. Potter, Jack M.
307.7′2′095127

*Library of Congress cataloguing in publication data applied for*

ISBN 0 521 35521 4 hard covers
ISBN 0 521 35787 X paperback


Transferred to digital reprinting 2000
Printed in the United States of America

# China's peasants

*To Elizabeth and Noah*

# Contents

# Illustrations

## Maps

# Tables

# Preface

This book is the first comprehensive anthropological study of a rural Chinese community to be carried out by foreign anthropologists in the People's Republic of China since the Revolution of 1949. It is a diachronic investigation of rural Cantonese village life, with the pre-revolutionary period as its starting point. The major theme of the book is the analysis of revolutionary efforts to bring about social reform and economic development. Since 1949, such efforts have taken many forms, and have created diverse consequences. We examine the initial processes of reform, the Maoist period, and the post-Maoism of the present day. The pre-revolutionary period is reconstructed from personal accounts by the villagers, from historical documents made available locally, and from comparative material gathered over two decades of studying Cantonese peasants. The portrayal of the Maoist period is based on personal accounts by the villagers and on our fieldwork in Maoist rural China in 1979–80. The account of the transition from Maoist to post-Maoist society is based on return field trips in 1981, 1983, 1984, and 1985.

We have attempted to understand the local significance of one of the largest and most important events in contemporary world history by using the methodological and theoretical repertoire of the discipline of anthropology. Our fieldwork took place in Chashan district, located in Dongguan county, about half way between Hong Kong and Guangzhou. In 1979, Chashan was called a commune, and included the town of Chashan, with a population of 4,000, and 15 production brigades in the surrounding countryside. The population of the district was approximately 35,000. Our research site was Zengbu brigade, a cluster of three natural villages and two hamlets, with a population of approximately 5,000.

Zengbu was divided into 17 production teams. These teams made a living partly by working the land, and partly by rural industrial enterprises. The brigade owned approximately 5,000 *mu* (about 350 hectares) of agricultural land, including fishponds.

1. Lane of Lu's Home village, 1979

We had requested a field site with the general characteristics of Zengbu, in order to have the possibility of making a fruitful comparison with the villages of Ping Shan, in Hong Kong's New Territories, previously studied by Jack M. Potter (1968). Zengbu and Ping Shan share custom, culture, and regionalism, broadly speaking, so it is possible to use the comparison to clarify the changes the Revolution has produced.

The authors and their two children, aged seven and two, were provided with living accommodation in four small rooms in the brigade headquarters building. This building was customarily used as living-accommodation by brigade cadres and other visitors, as well as ourselves. The brigade headquarters was a center of Zengbu social life: brigade-level governmental transactions were carried out there; meetings were held and decisions were reached. The building is located where the three villages meet. The brigade headquarters is not isolated from village social life, in which we participated freely. There were no official restrictions placed upon our research.

Fieldwork in the People's Republic of China presented certain special problems. The Chinese had hesitated to admit anthropologists. For 30 years they had excluded all outsiders, and they were clearly sensitive to the process of being observed. China was a country where social reality was explained in terms of a shared public morality expressed in ideological form; the understanding and interpretation of such explanations makes demands on the anthropologist's capacity for insight. However, anthropological understanding is based on the development of empathy with what is initially perceived as alien, rather than on taking an ethnocentric or adversarial position. The task is to understand the people of Zengbu in their own terms, insofar as possible, and then to make those terms intelligible to outsiders.

Change has by no means ceased in Zengbu; rather the reverse. Our period of field research encompasses both the final year of Maoist practice in the countryside and the dramatic redefinition of rural economic life under the present policies. We have also been able to observe the relationship between ideology and social reality in the context of an extraordinarily wide range of ideological formulations. The length of time we have known Zengbu, and the range of policies we have seen put into effect, provided perspective and context.

Three chapters of this book are based upon previously published work by Sulamith Heins Potter. "The Cultural Construction of Emotion in Rural Chinese Social Life" won Honorable Mention for the Stirling Award in 1986, and has appeared in the journal *Ethos*. Versions of "Chinese Birth Planning: A Cultural Account" have appeared as Working Paper on Women No. 103, Office of Women in International Development, Michigan State University, East Lansing (1985), and in Nancy Scheper-Hughes' *Child Survival* (1987). "The Position of Peasants in Modern China's Social Order" was originally presented to Columbia University's Modern China Seminar on April 9, 1981. It later appeared in *Modern China* (October 1983, pp. 465–499); a shortened version was published in Dernberger *et al.*, (eds.), *The Chinese: Adapting the Past, Building the Future* (1986).

We wish to thank the villagers and cadres of Zengbu, the cadres of Chashan district, Dongguan county, and Guangdong province, and the Chinese Academy of Social Science, for their help and kindness. We wish to thank Professors Elizabeth Colson, Norma Diamond, and Eugene Cooper for reading our manuscript and making constructive comments. Adrienne Morgan drew the maps and illustrations.

Our research has been funded by the Committee for Scholarly Communication with the People's Republic of China, the Center for Chinese Studies of the University of California at Berkeley, and a Wang Institute Fellowship in Chinese Studies.

# Notes on the text

## Table for conversion of Chinese units of measurement

**LENGTH**
1 *li* = 0·5 kilometer
1 *chi* = 0·333 meter

**AREA**
1 *mu* = 0·077 hectare
1 *li* = 0·01 *mu* = 0.1 *fen*

**WEIGHT**
1 *dan* = 50 kilograms
1 *jin* = 0·5 kilogram

## Official Exchange Rates, U.S. dollars and Chinese yuan

1979–80 1 U.S. dollar = 1·5 *yuan*
1981 1 U.S. dollar = 1·7 *yuan*
1983 1 U.S. dollar = 2·8 *yuan*
1985 1 U.S. dollar = 2·7 *yuan*

## Romanization

Most Chinese names are written in Mandarin, romanized according to the pinyin style. Cantonese names and words are romanized in the United States Department of State Foreign Service Institute's modification of the Huang-Kok Yale romanization.

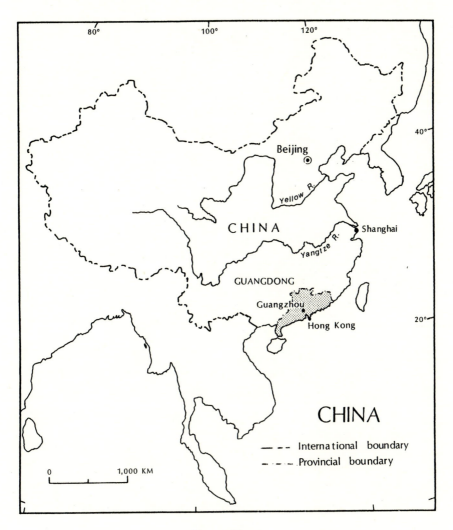

Map 1 China

# I

# The old "feudal" order: Zengbu before Liberation

Prior to Liberation in 1949, Sandhill, Pondside, and Lu's Home, the three major villages of Zengbu, were organized as single-surname lineage villages. Such settlements are very common in this part of China, where the old Chinese lineages ("clans," or *jiazu*) were especially strong (see Freedman 1958, pp. 1–8). Two separate Liu lineages inhabited Sandhill and Pondside and, as the name indicates, a Lu lineage inhabited Lu's Home. Groups of people with various other surnames, interspersed with colonies of families from the dominant lineages, inhabited Upper Stream and New Market, Zengbu's two smaller villages, satellites of Lu's Home and Sandhill, respectively.

The Lius of Sandhill and Pondside first settled in Zengbu over nine hundred years ago, in the Song Dynasty, when many of the old established lineages of Guangdong province were founded by Chinese migrating from central and northern China. The Lius first settled in Pondside village next to a Zhong lineage, which at that time lived in the present Lu's Home village area. The founding ancestors of the Liu lineages were half-brothers, sons of the same man by different wives. The Pondside Lius are believed to be descended from the son of the first wife, the Sandhill Lius from the son of the second. These two men founded two lineage villages, each with its own separate ancestral hall. As the present-day villagers put it in their own ritual idiom, "the two groups did not share sacrificial pork," which they would have done if they had considered themselves members of one group. The two Liu lineages of Zengbu have not had very good relations over the generations, being in continuous competition with one another for wealth, power, and prestige in local society and maintaining an uneasy coexistence as rival groups. Occasionally they have fought one another and engaged in lengthy feuds; open battles between the two have occurred within the memory of the older villagers.

The Lus of Lu's Home village settled in Zengbu 400 years ago, some five centuries or so later than the Lius. Initially they settled next to the Zhongs,

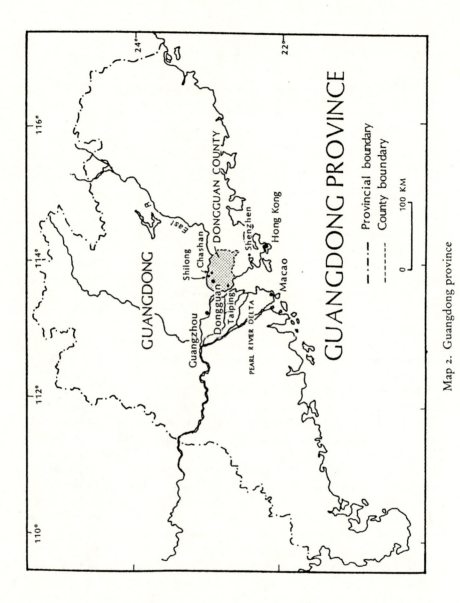

Map 2. Guangdong province

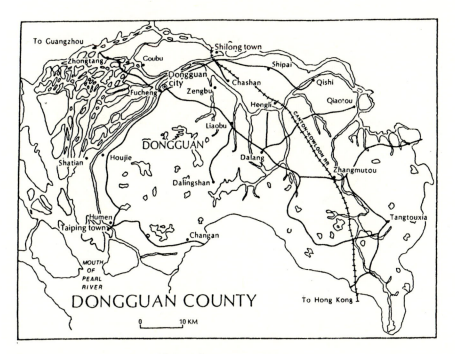

Map 3. Dongguan country

but as time went on the Lus waxed and the Zhongs waned. To avoid being bullied by the Lus, the Zhongs finally moved away. Lu's Home village was first settled by two families who came to Zengbu from Hobei province in northern China. Although they shared a common surname, they were not brothers and, like the Lius, did not found a common ancestral hall. Instead, the first-generation men or their descendants built two ancestral halls in Lu's Home village, one for the descendants of each founder. Today one of the halls serves as a brigade school and the other as the brigade kindergarten. Over the centuries the descendants of the branch that built the school prospered and grew in numbers, and they now form over 90 percent of the village population. Descendants of the kindergarten hall branch did not increase in wealth or numbers to such an extent and consequently were dominated by the larger branch.

Before Liberation each of the three major Zengbu lineage villages constituted a very complex social unity. Each was a localized residential unit, clearly separated, if only by a narrow village lane, from the two adjacent lineage villages. There was unity derived from kinship in that the core of each lineage was a group of men descended in a direct line, traced through males only, from a known common ancestor. A written genealogy (*zupu*) was kept by

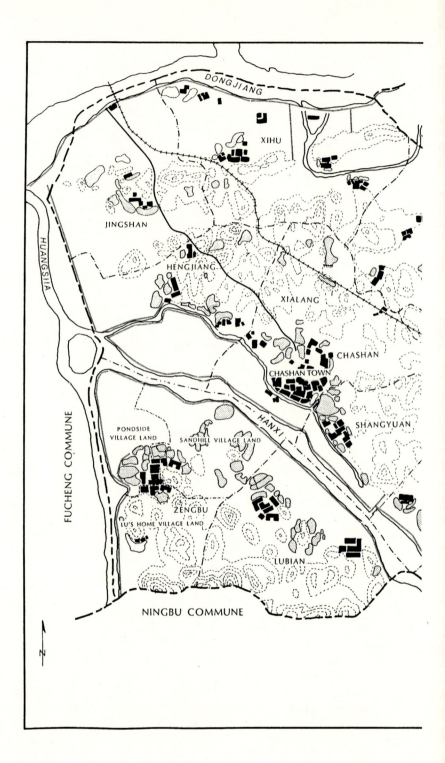

DONGJIANG

XIHU

JINGSHAN

HUANGSHA

HENGJIANG

XIALANG

CHASHAN

CHASHAN TOWN

SHANGYUAN

FUCHENG COMMUNE

HANXI

PONDSIDE
VILLAGE LAND

SANDHILL VILLAGE LAND

ZENGBU

LU'S HOME VILLAGE LAND

LUBIAN

NINGBU COMMUNE

N

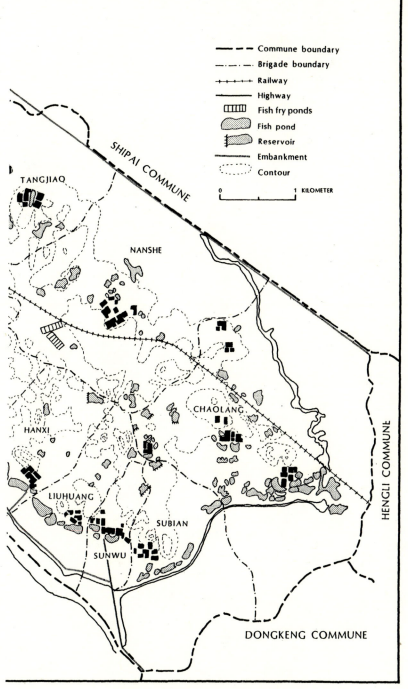

Map 4. Chashan commune (district)

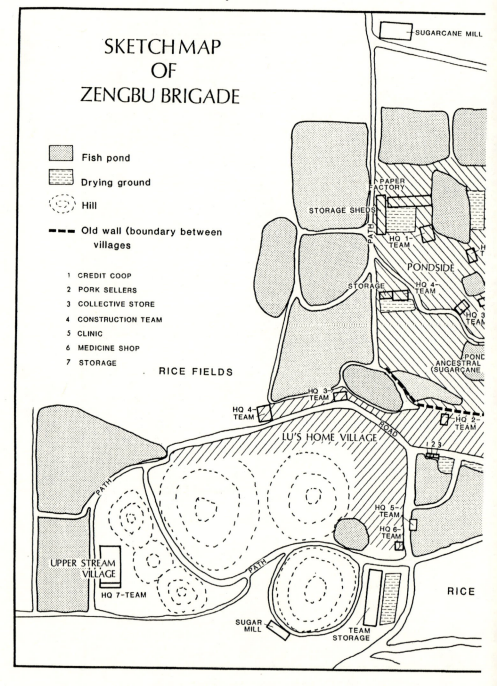

SKETCHMAP
OF
ZENGBU BRIGADE

Fish pond

Drying ground

Hill

--- Old wall (boundary between villages

1 CREDIT COOP
2 PORK SELLERS
3 COLLECTIVE STORE
4 CONSTRUCTION TEAM
5 CLINIC
6 MEDICINE SHOP
7 STORAGE

SUGARCANE MILL

PAPER FACTORY

STORAGE SHEDS

PONDSIDE

HQ 1-TEAM

STORAGE

HQ 4-TEAM

HQ 3-TEAM

POND
ANCESTRAL
(SUGARCANE

RICE FIELDS

HQ 3-TEAM

HQ 4-TEAM

ROAD

HQ 2-TEAM

LU'S HOME VILLAGE

1 2 3

PATH

HQ 5-TEAM

HQ 6-TEAM

UPPER STREAM VILLAGE

HQ 7-TEAM

PATH

SUGAR MILL

TEAM STORAGE

RICE

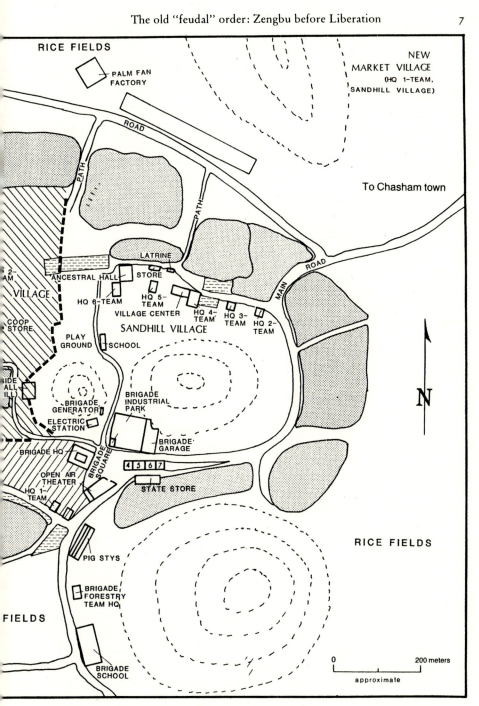

Map. 5 Sketch map of Zengbu brigade

the elders of each lineage which included the names of all the male members of the group down through the generations. These registers served as legal documents which defined the exact membership of the lineage and its various subbranches and specified which people had shares in the ancestral estates owned by the lineage and its subbranches. When a man was adopted as an heir of a lineage member (the common solution to having no sons), he first had to secure the permission of the elders and his close adoptive male relatives (who would have to give up their share of the potential inheritance); then the adopted man's name was entered into the genealogy and his position legalized.

All male members of the same generation within a given lineage considered themselves to be brothers and used appropriate fraternal forms of address. All women members of the same generation (excluding wives who had married in) considered themselves to be sisters and employed the same terms of address as those used by real sisters. The different generations, in the same way, used appropriate kinship terms, calling one another uncles and nephews and aunts and nieces, so that everyone within the Zengbu lineage villages was incorporated linguistically into a family-like group. However, the lineage was not an expanded family: it was a corporate group with economic, ritual, political, judicial, and military functions.

Zengbu lineages were economic corporations based upon the collective ownership of ancestral estates attached to ancestral halls. The ancestral hall elders (the oldest men in the most senior generations) rented out their halls' land, orchards, and fishponds, and used the income to pay the land tax, to keep the fields in good condition, to hire classical tutors to educate the young men of the lineage in the Confucian classics, to give charity rice to widows and orphans who were in need, and (if the estates were wealthy enough) to divide among the lineage's constituent families on a *per stirpes* basis as private income. Before the fall of the dynastic system in 1911, lineages also gave stipends to lineage members who had passed the imperial civil service examinations, to reward them for their accomplishments. Such men were useful to the lineage because they belonged to the prestigious group of scholars who staffed the imperial bureaucracy. Local graduates used their positions to represent their lineages' interests to the government.

Ancestral trust property was the foundation of the lineage, and the strength of a lineage was directly related to the size of its estate (Freedman 1958). Zengbu ancestral estates were quite modest in size compared to those of the powerful Yuan lineages who lived in and near the market town of Chashan. The Yuans owned large ancestral estates, which they rented to men from dependent tenant lineages in the surrounding countryside. Many of the Yuans were wealthy merchants with shops in the market town. The Yuans had a long tradition of scholarly accomplishment with many examination graduates among their members, who gave them prestige and official connections. After 1927, many of the Yuans became officials in the new Guomindang ("Nationalist") government. The Yuans controlled the market town as well as the local government administration, filling the important official posts. They hired local mercenaries, some of whom were little better than thugs, to protect themselves and their property against bandits and as instruments to dominate local society. Combining landlordism, commerce, and official careers in the same group, the Yuans were typical representatives of the bureaucratic gentry class which dominated the local levels of Chinese society. Together with the leaders of other wealthy and important lineages in the Dongguan countryside, they ruled local society and exploited it for their own profit (see Fei 1953 for a discussion of this class, especially its character after 1911). After the Qing government was weakened by foreign intrusion and rebellions, beginning in the middle of the nineteenth century, these local gentry had gained increasing autonomy from the national government and their power increased in the early twentieth century as China almost disintegrated into territories controlled by warlords and political armies.

Elders of the Zengbu lineages used the rental from lineage property to finance the ancestor-worshipping ceremonies held twice yearly, in the spring and autumn. In the fall, the male members of each lineage assembled in their spacious and imposing central ancestral halls, beautifully decorated with carved wooden and porcelain panels and hung with wooden plaques on which were written samples of the calligraphy of famous scholarly ancestors, to carry out the rituals of the ancestral sacrifices. Women were not allowed in the halls, but sometimes they crowded in the doorway so that their infant sons could observe the proceedings. Offerings of cakes, wine, chickens, and golden roast pigs were placed before the ancestors, on altars surrounded by burning ritual candles and ritual vessels. The men of the lineage, dressed in floor-length blue and gray robes, came up in order of their generation – first the 27th, then the 28th, followed by the 29th and so on – to bow before the ancestors and pour out libations of rice wine, being guided in the ritual by the director of ceremonies, who stood at the side barking out instructions. The air was filled with the intoxicating smoke of burning incense and candles. These, together with the smell of the burnt offerings, the sound of the ritual oboes with their high, mournful, whining notes, and the noise of the firecrackers set off outside to signify the end of the ceremony, all contributed to the overwhelming atmosphere. Afterwards, the sacrificial pigs (whose essence had been consumed by the spirits of the ancestors) were chopped up on the floor of the hall, and one share was given to every male member of the lineage, with the elders getting additional shares in accord with their dignity.

In addition to their unified nature as an economic corporation and a religious body, each lineage had internal political mechanisms for making decisions for the group as a whole and for enforcing lineage customs and regulating sex, marriage, and inheritance. Leaders of the Zengbu lineages were of two kinds.

The "elders" (*fulao*) of the lineage, the oldest men in the most senior generation, were the ritual leaders in the ancestor-worshiping ceremonies in the halls and at the ancestral tombs scattered in the countryside; they also helped manage the ancestral property. Recruited on the basis of age and seniority alone, the elders might be poor and inconsequential men.

The really powerful lineage leaders, however, were always wealthy men of high status. Before the fall of the Qing Dynasty, in 1911, the leaders included the gentry graduates of the nationwide civil service examinations, which qualified them for official office and for membership in a privileged stratum of society; and in the Republican period, from 1911 to 1949, they were rich landlords and local despots, with ties to the warlord regimes and later to the Guomindang. In cooperation with the lineage elders (whom they controlled by bribes or intimidation), they dominated lineage affairs, and frequently used lineage property for their own interests, renting it for small sums from the ancestral halls which they controlled and then subletting it to others at a profit or exploiting it for their own benefit.

Powerful leaders of the lineages of Zengbu organized village guards, young armed men who supposedly protected the village against bandits, but who actually served as thugs of local landlords and bullies, offering "protection" and "insurance" to weaker lineages for a yearly fee. The right to operate the village guards in this area of China was frequently auctioned off to local bullies by the central ancestral hall of each wealthy and powerful lineage. In return, the gang leaders agreed to pay so much to the ancestral hall each year and to furnish a banquet of fixed specifications for the lineage elders.

The lineages of southeastern China were notorious for their quarrelsome and warlike character. They often fought among themselves – sometimes in well-publicized pitched battles fought by the young men of different lineages on neutral ground, and sometimes in treacherous sneak attacks at night. Their fortified villages, complete with walls and moats, were not purely decorative. Confucian officials from Northern China looked upon these troublesome people as barbarians.

Lineage leaders also served as a judicial body because each lineage preferred to solve its own disputes rather than take them outside to the government courts, which could prove to be costly and humiliating. In cases of sexual transgressions – premarital sex, adultery, or premarital pregnancy – lineage leaders punished offenders by having the village guards whip them, drive them from the village, or place them in a woven bamboo pig-carrying basket and drown them in the fishpond, a place where the bedding of dead people and other polluting things were thrown, the symbolism being explicit. In some cases of flagrant transgression against lineage sexual mores, the elders ordered all the pigs in the village to be slaughtered and eaten in a communal feast, with the bill being given to the offending families, who sometimes had to sell their houses and land to pay it, or else leave the village.

Thieves were punished by the village guard and elders with fines or a whipping or, in more serious cases, were handed over to the government court with a recommendation for punishment. In some cases where a thief stole chronically from members of his own lineage (stealing from outside was not considered so bad), after consulting with the offender's closest relatives and getting their permission, the thief was simply taken out and killed.

Although to the outside each lineage presented a unified social front, internally each lineage village was crosshatched with groups who competed with one another for dominance. Lineages were subdivided into competing branches by a traditional practice, whereby a rich and successful man could leave part of his accumulated wealth and property in an ancestral trust, usually attached to a branch hall, for the benefit of his sons and their direct descendants only. Unlike ordinary family property, which was divided among the sons and thereby fragmented in each generation, the ancestral estates were permanent property of the trust founder's descendants. These groups, defined in special relations to the branch ancestral halls and their associated property, were set off from other people in the village who did not have a share in the group. Branch ancestral estates and branch halls theoretically could have been founded in the name of any of the several hundred ancestors of the Zengbu lineages who had lived over the centuries, but only a few of the ancestors of the lineage became successful enough as officials or merchants to accumulate the necessary property. Some subsidiary branches of each Zengbu lineage had produced many successful and wealthy ancestors, who founded estates and were elaborately subdivided into branch halls; others were unsuccessful and were not subdivided. The branch halls remained a part of the lineage; a member of a wealthy and differentiated lineage branch had membership in many halls, while still remaining a member of the lineage as a whole.

The crucial points of internal lineage segmentation, around which subsegments of the lineage were formed; were precisely those points at which wealthy ancestral estates were located. Sublineage A for example, separated itself off from sublineage B because sublineage A had joint rights in the ancestral property and the branch ancestral hall left in the name of the ancestor of group A. Sublineage B, in turn, later separated from the remaining groups in the lineage because its members were a corporate group holding ancestral property B in common.

In each Zengbu lineage village the major sublineage segments were the groups that owned the largest estates in the village or had the most members, or both. It was in the large and wealthy segments that most of the landlords were located. The concentration of wealth and power within particular subgroups of each lineage village enabled these groups to dominate the rest of the lineage and control the property in the lineage's ancestral estates. So, although each lineage was a unity when in conflict with the outside, internally it was rent by factions who were in continuous competition and conflict with one another.

To take an example, figure 1 shows the internal divisions in Pondside's Liu lineage. All members of the lineage – the men and the unmarried women – belonged to the central ancestral hall, to which was attached a few *mu* of property to keep the oil lamps burning eternally in front of the ancestral altar and to pay for the yearly sacrifices. Of the three major branches of the lineage – A, B, and C – A and C were very weak, with only a few living representatives and little or no collective property. Branch B contained almost all the people in the village, and was internally divided intro five subbranches, each with its own branch hall and property (except branch 2, which had died out). Branch B1 was weak, divided into two subbranches (B1a and B1b), with only 15 and 30 living representatives, respectively, and only a little land in their ancestral estates. Branch B3, with its 300 people, 100 *mu* of land (approximately 7 hectares) and 17 *mu* of fishponds, was the second most powerful subbranch in the lineage, with two of the village's six landlords coming from it. Branch B4 was the richest and most powerful in the lineage, with over 300 members and 120 *mu* of ancestral property. Three of the people classified as landlords at land reform came from this branch. It was further subdivided into four groups (B4a, B4b, B4c, and B4d), which were rather evenly matched in size, with about 80 members each. Because of this balanced division within branch B4, this group was rent by internal competition and unable to unite solidly so as to control the lineage as completely as it theoretically should have been able to do with its preponderance of wealth and numbers. It is because of this, or so some of the living Pondside people claim, that one branch was not able to dominate Pondside as happened in Lu's Home and Sandhill villages. Branch B5 was small in numbers, without property and, therefore, of little significance.

Sandhill's Liu lineage was less evenly balanced than Pondside's, with one subbranch of the lineage containing most of the people, most of the collective property, and most of the landlords. Lu's Home village's Lu lineage was also asymmetrically segmented, with one subbranch, the second richest, dominating the rest of the lineage because of its numbers and its strength of will (see figures 2 and 3.

Class divisions between rich and poor, within the lineage as a whole and within each separate subsegment, split the lineage horizontally, just as the lineage segmentation split the group vertically. Prior to Liberation, each Zengbu lineage contained a few wealthy men as well as many extremely poor tenant farmers and laborers. As pointed out above, within the lineage as a whole and within each subsegment, the wealthy landlords and merchants dominated the group's affairs and controlled the collective property for their own benefit, reinforcing their power by controlling the village guard. The vast majority of poor people in Zengbu benefited from membership in their

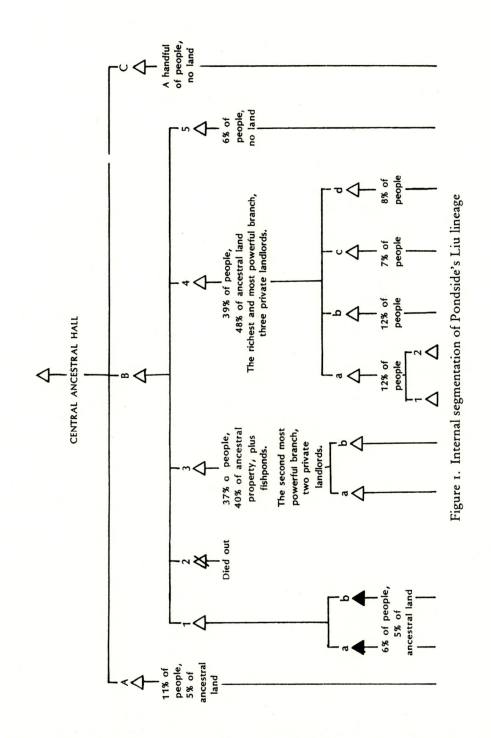

Figure 1. Internal segmentation of Pondside's Liu lineage

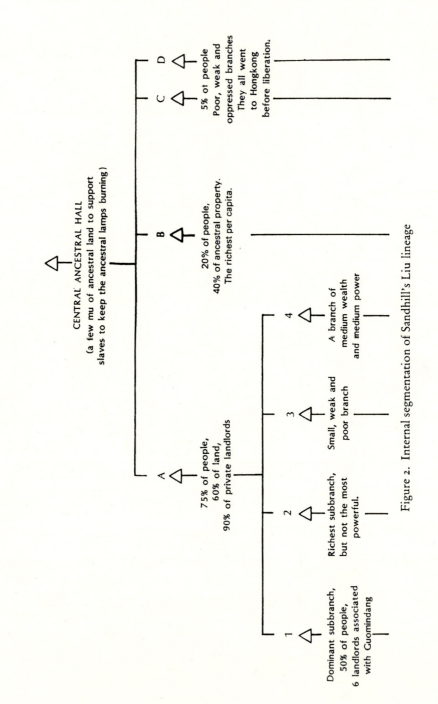

CENTRAL ANCESTRAL HALL
(a few mu of ancestral land to support
slaves to keep the ancestral lamps burning)

A
75% of people, 60% of land,
90% of private landlords

1
Dominant subbranch,
50% of people,
6 landlords associated
with Guomindang

2
Richest subbranch,
but not the most
powerful.

3
Small, weak and
poor branch

4
A branch of
medium wealth
and medium power

B
20% of people,
40% of ancestral property.
The richest per capita.

C    D
5% ot people
Poor, weak and
oppressed branches
They all went
to Hongkong
before liberation.

Figure 2. Internal segmentation of Sandhill's Liu lineage

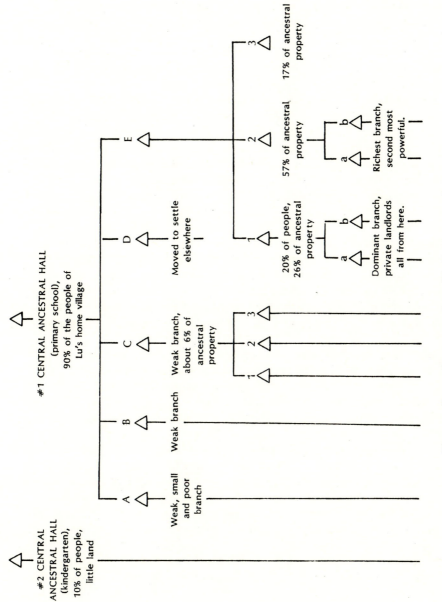

Figure 3. Internal segmentation of Lu's Home Lu lineage

group when facing the outside world, but they suffered the domination of rich and powerful segments led by landlords within their own group. These class antagonisms were keenly felt. The poorer members of the lineage and its branches hated the richer members for their arrogance, envied their wealth, and resented their domination of the lineage and their use of its collective property for their own private interest. Elders who were controlled by the powerful and wealthy were hated symbols of corruption.

In addition to class divisions between gentry families and peasants of varying degrees of wealth, Zengbu villages also contained slaves. Each lineage village prior to Liberation owned five or six slave families, the descendants of men who had been purchased by wealthy ancestors in the past and were later left as property attached to an ancestral hall. Called *ernanzai* ("second male servant or second male child") in Zengbu, these families were literally the property of ancestral halls and could not leave the lineage that owned them. The original slave boys who were the ancestors of the slave families had been purchased by wealthy Zengbu families from poor families in other lineages. These slave boys were servants to the families that had bought them and later to their descendants, keeping the oil lamps burning before the ancestral altars in the halls and assisting them at ritual occasions. When there was a funeral, a wedding, a grave-worshipping ceremony, or a ceremony to expel "dirty" (ritually impure) things from the village once a year, the slave families carried the things out of the village and burned them. When the lineage members dug up the coffins of their recently deceased family members in order to wash their bones before burying them in a ceramic funerary vessel (for more on this, see below, pp. 24–25), the slave families washed the bones.

The slaves were endogamous, forming a separate lower caste. They were married to slave women from other lineages or maidservants owned by wealthier families. No respectable family would marry their daughter to a slave, nor would they take a slave as a wife, except as a concubine or second wife if the slave was especially beautiful. Married male slaves were given land to farm as tenants of the lineage. Slave families had to live at the rear or the edge of the village in inferior houses apart from those of regular lineage members, who would not set foot in the slave quarters of the village for fear of social defilement. When addressing members of the dominant lineage, the slave families had to use kinship terms that were elevated one generation from normal usage. If a slave man was addressing a Liu or Lu of his own age, he would have to call him uncle instead of brother. If the man of the dominant lineage was of the slave's father's generation, the slave would have to call him by the term for grandfather's older brother rather than father's older brother. When members of the dominant lineage addressed slaves, they did not use kinship terms at all, as ordinary politeness usually required, but instead addressed them by name, even if a free child was addressing a slave sixty years old.

Slave families were sadistically bullied by the Lus and the Lius. Although theoretically, in the last two or three decades before Liberation at least, they could own land like anyone else, slave families did not actually buy any because it could have been taken from them at any time or they could have been driven from the village and their property confiscated. They owned their own small mud-brick houses but not the house lots on which they were built. They were not allowed to have the usual wedding trappings; they could not have music played nor could they bring their brides into the village in a sedan chair. Other members of the dominant lineage deliberately provoked incidents in which the slave families were accused of a breach of etiquette because they did not show proper deference to a free family, and were forced to apologize by giving money to the offended party. Sometimes they were falsely accused of theft and their property confiscated. The children of slave families were humiliated and bullied by the children of the regular lineage members, and if they dared to fight back or protect themselves they would simply be taunted and beaten. Slave parents cautioned their children to be deferential to other children because they were afraid that a quarrel between children would be used as a pretext for beating the entire slave family. Thus from an early age the slaves were taught the kind of submissive and deferential behavior that would most effectively keep them out of trouble.

Slave status was hereditary in the male line. Slaves were considered property of the dominant lineage and were not allowed to leave the village. However, under certain circumstances, they were allowed to purchase their freedom by paying back their purchase price. In Ping Shan, a settlement of the Deng lineage in Hong Kong's New Territories, 80 kilometers or so to the south of Zengbu, there is a story about a man surnamed Soo who left the Deng lineage as a slave, and rose to become a military official of the Qing Dynasty. He returned to Ping Shan in his official robes, accompanied by his retinue. Outside the village he dismounted from his sedan chair, removed his official robes, and went in to bow before the Deng lineage elders. After this obeisance he bought back the contract that had been drawn up when his ancestor was purchased, and thus he attained his freedom. He then put on his official robes, mounted his sedan chair, and was conveyed back toward Guangzhou preceded by flags, with cymbals clashing and oboes playing. (For more about the Cantonese slaves and their status, see J. L. Watson 1976, 1977, 1980.)

In addition to the slaves, Zengbu villages contained another lower-status group of families called adopted heirs (*lisizai*). This group was descended from families of poor men adopted into the lineage to serve as heirs of men without children. Their position was higher than that of the slaves – they were free and they did have shares in their adopted father's ancestral hall, but they were forced to go through a humiliating ceremony of being adopted into the lineage at New Year. The adopted heir, who was often a grown man with

a family of his own, was considered to have been born at the time of the
ceremony incorporating him into the lineage and had to take the social role
of an infant, using the kinship terms appropriate to his adoptive age all his
life. The children of adopted heirs were bullied and abused by the children of
regular lineage members, being taunted with the epithet "one-year-old
babies," referring to their father's adoption into the lineage, which was
considered shameful. Thus, the poor tenant farmers, the laborers, and
especially the slaves and the adopted heirs were all subject to ritual
humiliation.

As can be seen, traditionally in rural China the strong and rich oppressed,
exploited, and bullied the weak and poor. Of the lineages settled in one locale
one would grow stronger, wealthier, and more numerous over the generations; and then the weaker groups would either have to suffer the hegemony
and bullying of the stronger group or move away to settle in a frontier region
or place itself under the protection of another strong lineage somewhere else.
The Lu and Liu lineages dominated the two smaller mixed-lineage villages,
Upper Stream and New Market, but they, in turn, were under the local
hegemony of the Yuan lineages of Chashan. Between more evenly matched
groups – such as the three lineage villages of Zengbu – a precarious balance
was maintained, with constant jockeying for power among the three. Within
each of Zengbu's lineage villages strong and rich sublineage segments dominated the other members of their lineage. Horizontally, each village was
divided into different classes, with the gentry landowners at the top, land
owning peasants in the middle, and poor tenant farmers and laborers near the
bottom. At the very bottom were the adopted heirs and the separate caste of
slaves. The hatred and envies and conflicts in such a structure of inequality
formed a reservoir for violent class conflict.

The pre-revolutionary Zengbu peasant family was a male-centered and
male-controlled institution which depended upon the subordination of the
young and the domination and exploitation of women for the preservation of
its structure. Marriages were arranged. The bride and groom came blindly to
their marriage bed without having previously seen one another. Marriage
was considered the family's concern, not the concern of individuals, and
young people were married without giving their consent and often against
their personal wishes, which were not considered relevant. Marriage was
often referred to as "taking a daughter-in-law" instead of taking a wife,
indicating that the primary purpose of the marriage was to benefit the
groom's parents and continue the family line rather than to furnish a
companion for the son.

Marriage ceremonies were as elaborate and expensive as the families
concerned could make them, for they were one of the primary means of
displaying status. The groom's family gave cakes, gifts, and a cash brideprice
to the bride's family; both sides gave banquets for their own kinsmen and

relatives; and the bride's family sent her to her husband's home with a dowry, which often included gifts of gold jewelry and furniture.

Residence after marriage was patrilocal, a bride moving to live with her husband's family. Authority was in the hands of the eldest male, who was usually the family head. Membership in the Lu and Liu lineages of Zengbu and shares in the ancestral estates at all levels were passed down from father to son. Private property in the form of land, houses, orchards, and fishponds was inherited only by males through males, women having no right to inherit.

The ideal traditional prestigeful household in Zengbu, in theory at least, was a large and complex group of people consisting of four generations – grandparents, several sons and wives, grandchildren, and great-grandchildren – all living together under the headship of the oldest man, who controlled the family property and the earnings and labor of all family members and took from this common purse to provide for every one's needs.

In practice, however, in Zengbu as elsewhere in China, these large extended households were extremely rare. At most, only those landlords and merchant families who constituted (according to brigade records) 5 percent of Zengbu's population would have had the economic resources to support such a large number of people, the status and power to effectively govern them, and the property to motivate sons to stay together under their father's authority to await their inheritance. Only wealthy households could afford such an expensive display. Poorer people tried to approximate at least the spirit of the large-family ideal by settling their sons and sons' families around them in the same village neighborhood.

Most of Zengbu's peasants lived in small households composed of nuclear families (a married couple and their unmarried children) or stem families (a married couple and one married son's family). The stem family household was a necessary means of providing care for elderly parents in a society without old-age pensions.

Eighty-two percent of Zengbu's residents at the time of Liberation were poor peasants, laborers in the countryside or nearby towns and cities, small peddlers, and floating elements (vagabonds). These families were often separated because the men of the family had to go to Hong Kong or elsewhere in a desperate attempt to eke out a living. Zengbu's cropland in pre-revolutionary times was unproductive and in short supply; the countryside was overpopulated and people could not rent enough land to make a living. Many people from Zengbu went to Hong Kong or Singapore to work in unskilled trades. Those that remained behind carried grass for the fishponds owned by the landlords and ancestral halls, dug mud from the river bottom for local brick and tile kilns, or worked as coolies or shrimp fishermen. Most of Zengbu's people were so poor that they often could not manage even to hold the nuclear family together in a stable and permanent fashion, let alone support the four-generation extended family which was the most prestigious Chinese family.

The typical cycle of the pre-Liberation Zengbu peasant family began with the small nuclear family formed by a marriage. When the children resulting from the union grew to maturity, the daughters married out and became members of their husbands' families; the sons married in order of seniority, bringing their wives to live with them in their fathers' household for a short time and then dividing the household and establishing a separate residence. Sometimes parents would not divide their property until they retired or died. Usually, however, those families in Zengbu who owned landed property gave each son in turn a house and a share of the land after he and his wife and children had lived with his parents in a joint household for a number of years. The parents remained in their own house with the youngest son or lived alone, being cared for by the sons jointly.

Often parents kept back a share of the property from their sons to ensure that they would have some means of subsistence in their old age and not be completely dependent upon the dutifulness of their children. If the parents lived with the youngest son permanently, he often inherited their house and their share of the property to repay him for taking care of them; if not, the eldest son usually inherited the extra share. In case of a dispute over inheritance among the sons (a not infrequent occurrence), the mother's brother, considered a neutral party, would be invited in to resolve the dispute. Since so many of Zengbu's people before Liberation were either propertyless or owned only a few *mu* of land and a house and shed or two, most families were not able to give their sons much of an inheritance at all.

Zengbu women fared badly under the traditional family system, and tears still run down the cheeks of the older women when they describe their situation before Liberation. Initially under the authority of their own parents, upon marriage they passed under the authority of their husbands' families. Women were of low status and were not considered as economically valuable or as socially important as men. They were not regarded as permanent members of their family of birth because they would eventually marry out and become members of their husbands' families. In their traditional songs, Zengbu women lament the lot of women who, "like birds, grow up only to fly away from their parents' home." They were called "goods on which one loses" because after raising them to maturity their parents had to provide an expensive wedding banquet and dowry, the cost of which exceeded the brideprice given by the groom's family. Women were not educated, because the benefits of a woman's education would pass to her husband's family, rather than being of use to her parents. In any case, there were no positions for educated women in Chinese society. Daughters were not in a position to earn money for their natal families. Rather, they helped care for their younger siblings and the children of their older brothers, and did housework and farm-work under the direction of the head of household, until they married, usually in their late teens.

In traditional Zengbu, women were considered dangerously polluting and unclean beings whose menstrual blood could spoil a religious ceremony or a happy event like a wedding. They could not escape from an unhappy marriage, for divorce was frowned upon and almost impossible to obtain. A woman had no place to go if she left her husband's family. Her own father's family had no place for her (a daughter's tablet could not be placed upon her father's altar); she could not take her children with her, for they belonged to her husband. Occasionally driven to desperation and with no other escape, unhappy married women committed suicide, hoping that their angry ghosts would come back to take vengeance upon their mothers-in-law, who were frequently the agents of most of the unhappiness of young wives. The only other alternatives were to escape to the city and become a servant or a prostitute.

Widows were not supposed to remarry, no matter how young. If they did remarry or were married off, they had to move into their new husband's village in the dead of night to conceal the shame of it. Men, however, were permitted to take more than one wife, to ensure the birth of a male heir or simply as status symbols. Wealthy men had multiple wives inhabiting separate households in Zengbu and concubines in the town as well.

The crucial relation in the traditional family was the relationship between parents and sons, and not the relationship between husband and wife. Sons continued the family line, inherited the property, and owed their parents respect and obedience while they were alive. They had the duty of caring for and honoring them in their old age, and the religious duty of worshipping their souls after death. Next to their parents, men owed loyalty to their brothers and to their lineage brothers (their patrilineal cousins). In a dispute they automatically supported members of their own family and kin, if at all feasible; nepotism, far from being a transgression against accepted social norms, was considered an ethical obligation.

The basic goal in traditional Zengbu society was first of all survival, which for many of the poorest people meant a struggle that consumed almost the totality of their lives. If subsistence was assured, the Cantonese engaged in the active pursuit of wealth, power, and prestige, with emphasis on the former. The traditional Zengbu villagers had a this-worldly and materialistic ethic. Their intense drive for success was the mainspring of a dynamic and highly competitive society. Before the fall of the imperial system, in 1911, the ultimate goal was to obtain a traditional Confucian education, pass the civil service examinations, become a high official, and then enrich oneself during an official career. This was an unattainable goal for ordinary peasants. An indirect, long-range alternative route was to become a businessman. Once a man became wealthy through commerce, he could buy land, educate his sons, and hope that they could become officials. Alternatively, it was possible to become a military official or to seek power as a bandit or warlord. Few traditional Zengbu people actually gained conspicuous success through any of these routes. However, the myth of the peasant boy who started reading Confucius on the back of his water buffalo and ended up as a great scholar and a high official persisted in the face of observed reality, as did the myth about the peasant who started business peddling firewood and salted fish and finally became a wealthy gentleman merchant.

With the fall of the Qing Dynasty in 1911, and with it the imperial system as a whole, the route to success through the civil service examinations (eliminated even before the fall of the Qing) was no longer open. Modern education, at home and abroad, was still regarded instrumentally – as giving one a better-than-average chance for official advancement and wealth – but degrees from modern universities never had the prestige and significance of the old examination degrees, and the local lineages refused to give modern graduates the stipend that they had once given to the old Confucian scholars for obtaining their degrees.

As a result, the major route for social mobility was as a merchant. Zengbu before Liberation was filled with would-be shopkeepers. A very large percentage of the men had attempted to start some kind of small business – peddling, drying litchi, opening a store – at some time or another in their lives.

The basic achievement values of Zengbu villagers, reflected in their struggle for success in this world, were intimately related to their cosmology, their world view, and their supernatural beliefs and practices (see J. M. Potter 1970a). The supernatural forces and beings which Zengbu people believed to inhabit their world had profound consequences for their lives and fortunes. If people were able to bind these supernatural forces to their will, or enlist their aid, they could achieve a long life, physical and mental well-being, success, and fortune. If they did not deal with these forces and beings properly, thus alienating or disturbing them, and if they did not receive supernatural aid in their worldly affairs, life could be a continual series of disasters and failures. Those ordinary persons who simply "lived along" with average success had achieved a kind of neutrality in their relations with the supernatural: they succeeded in passing through life without incurring the ill effects that would have resulted if they had alienated or disturbed the supernaturals, but nevertheless they had not obtained supernatural aid; their mediocrity was mute testimony to this failure.

Traditionally, from the villagers' point of view, all success was the result, ultimately, of luck or fortune, and all failure – including death, the ultimate failure – was due to bad luck and ill fortune. That everyone would exert maximum effort to succeed was taken for granted; but success in this world could not be assured by hard work and effort alone. For no matter how hard one tried – and the Cantonese villagers worked very hard indeed – one could not succeed unless one was lucky, and one was lucky only if supernatural power was successfully utilized in worldly affairs. Consequently, most religious and magical behavior was an attempt to avoid the unlucky elements of the universe and to control or enlist the aid of those forces and beings that could bring luck.

In a sense, Zengbu villagers believed that their fates were sealed by the concatenation of astrological forces present at birth. These forces were described in a person's "eight characters," which expressed the exact time of birth and the astrological influences that determined the person's fate in life. But Zengbu villagers attempted to modify fate by enlisting supernatural aid and protection, and by magical manipulation. Thus, the Zengbu world view was neither completely fatalistic nor optimistic. The universe was seen as a stage on which human beings, impersonal supernatural power, and supernatural beings interacted in a constant drama of life and death, success and failure. People's fortunes were determined by how they fared in this complicated drama of life.

At the base of the villager's traditional cosmology was a belief that the world contained an impersonal supernatural power called "wind and water" (fengshui), which pulsed or flowed over the land configurations and bodies of water forming the earth's surface. Fengshui was believed to be a primary source of luck and efficacy. Success was associated with the control of good fengshui, and lack of success with inability to control it. Like high-voltage electricity, fengshui could be a beneficial force if properly handled, but it could also be extremely dangerous and destructive if used improperly or clumsily. Since ordinary villagers could not hope to understand the finer points of this intricate system of geomancy, practiced and trained experts who had read the classical books on the subject, called fengshui teachers (fengshui xiansheng), were consulted in important matters. These teachers were employed to design villages, houses, tombs, ancestral halls, and all other structures so that they would draw maximum power from the invisible currents flowing over the earth, while avoiding the bad influences. If the concentration of fengshui upon a house or a village was too powerful and direct, it might lead to the death or impoverishment of the inhabitants; if it was too weak, the inhabitants would at best have only mediocre luck. To direct the flow of magical power into useful channels and ward off unpropitious currents, retaining walls were erected in front of buildings, magical mirrors were hung to deflect bad influences, and entire villages were designed to fit fengshui specifications. Within each village the ancestral halls and even the doors and windows of houses and the shape of their roofs were determined by advice from fengshui specialists.

The ancestral cult was another central component of the villagers' world view. Family ancestral spirits, enshrined on household altars in wooden spirit tablets or on orange altar paper, were the foci of the family ancestral cult.

More distant lineage ancestors from earlier generations, enshrined in tablets on the altars of the central and branch ancestral halls, were the foci of lineage and subsegment worship. Family ancestors were worshipped daily with incense, with special observances on the first and fifteenth of every lunar month, on the major holidays (with offerings of food), and especially during the *Qingming* grave-cleaning ceremony in the spring. More distant ancestors were worshipped in ancestral hall rites twice yearly and the tombs of the lineage ancestors, located in the surrounding hills and mountains, were worshipped collectively by groups of direct descendants during a period of several weeks in the autumn.

In ancestral rites the descendants honored their ancestors and furnished them with the food, drink, and money that they needed for their life in the afterworld of Hell, where they were believed to go after death to be judged by the King of Hell according to the morality of their behavior in their lives. After a period in purgatory, where they were tortured for the bad things they had done in their previous life, they were reborn as animals or humans, depending upon their accumulated virtue (these ideas are clearly the result of Buddhist influences on Chinese folk religion). Ancestral spirits on the family altars, as far back as four generations, were remembered as individual personalities and were considered to be basically benevolent beings who watched over and protected their descendants. If, however, they were not treated with respect and supplied with appropriate offerings, they could be malevolent. The spirits of remoter lineage ancestors were not remembered as individual personalities, because most of them had lived and died generations ago. Ancestors so far removed were regarded almost as deities, resembling in function the temple deities of Buddhist or Taoist origin enshrined in the village temples and in the temples in the surrounding mountains.

The ancestral cult of Zengbu and the rest of Guangdong was characterized by elaborate and distinctive burial practices. A Zengbu person who died was first buried in a wooden coffin on a special geomantically neutral burial hill near the village. There was one for each lineage. After a period of five to ten years, family members of the deceased would consult a spirit medium (found in almost every Cantonese village), who would contact the dead person's soul and ask whether it was the right time to dig up the remains and bury them in a more permanent location. If the deceased person's soul, speaking through the spirit medium, agreed, the coffin was disinterred and the skeletal remains of the ancestor were ritually washed. They were then placed in a glazed ceramic funerary vessel, about sixty centimeters high and 30 centimeters in diameter, called a *jinta*. These *jinta* were placed in neutral *fengshui* spots on hills surrounding the village.

Even the *jinta* were theoretically only temporary resting places for the ancestral bones. The ideal was ultimately to bury them in elaborate circular masonry and brick tombs; these were the preferred final resting places for the villagers' ancestral spirits. However, the ceramic funerary vessels were the final resting places of most ancestral bones. Only wealthy families could afford to hire a *fengshui* teacher to undertake the complex process of locating a tomb site with excellent *fengshui*. Consequently, most *jinta* were left permanently exposed on the hillsides, where they were worshipped every spring by their immediate descendants. Eventually, most of the *jinta* would be lost, and the ancestral spirits they contained forgotten. The *jinta* might be overgrown with vegetation or kicked open by a stray water buffalo, and the bones scattered. Even if the *jinta* were not lost or broken, most descendants discontinued the yearly worshiping and grave-cleaning ceremony in the spring after a period of time. Ancestral property was seldom attached to a *jinta* burial and the villagers attached more importance to burials that carried an endowment to pay for the worshiping expenses and to purchase roast pork to be divided among the male descendants.

Only the wealthier villagers could expect that their families would be able to establish a permanent tomb endowed with property, so that their descendants could come to worship down through the generations. Only the wealthy could have the tomb located in an excellent *fengshui* spot that would tap the earth's supernatural power and would favor succeeding generations. The *fengshui* teacher was expert in tracing out the flow of magical currents in the surrounding countryside so that he located the tomb on the exact spot where the luckiest influences were concentrated. Such care was taken because the fortune of the dead person's descendants was believed to depend on the character of his and his lineage's ancestral tombs. If the *fengshui* of a grave was good, a person's descendants were more likely to become wealthy, achieve high official position, or increase in numbers. On the other hand, ancestral graves with neutral or poor *fengshui* might result in the impoverishment or even the actual extinction of a lineage. The differential success of lineages and of different branches of the same lineage over long periods of time were attributed to the quality of the *fengshui* of their ancestral tombs.

In addition to the complicated magical system of *fengshui*, the Zengbu peasants had a well-developed system of beliefs involving anthropomorphic supernatural beings. The spiritual world of the villagers was inhabited by gods, ghosts, and devils who profoundly affected their lives. Although the supernatural beings were endless in their variety, in the eyes of the villagers they fell into a limited number of functional categories defined on the basis of how they affected human fortunes.

The first category of supernatural beings were ancestral spirits and temple deities of Buddhist, Taoist, or Confucian origin. These were believed to be powerful and basically benevolent beings from whom the villagers could expect aid in the form of supernatural intervention. They were spoken of as "bright" and "lucky" beings.

The second category of supernatural beings were malevolent spirits of the dead, people who had lived unfulfilled lives or had died unnatural deaths because they had been executed or murdered, had committed suicide, or had died in childbirth. People who had died without male descendants to worship them, and provide them with the food, clothing, and money necessary for life in Hell, also became malevolent spirits. These malevolent spirits preyed upon humans by causing illness and bad luck, so that offerings of money and food would have to be made by their victims. These supernatural beings mirrored the villagers' view of human beings in the real world: a few were beneficent patrons to be supplicated in the hope that they would use their superior power helpfully, but most were understood as envious, malevolent, and harmful creatures to be propitiated if they could not be avoided.

There were also household ancestors and deities (such as the kitchen god, the door gods, and the guardian spirit of the house), and local guardian deities of the village land area. The traditional religious system included a complex and full religious calendar in which all of these deities – the Buddhist and Taoist deities in the village temple and other local temples, the malevolent spirits, the ancestors in the halls and tombs and the household and localized deities – were worshipped. The aim was to obtain the aid of the beneficent deities in maintaining the villagers' health and security and in helping them to prosper. The malevolent spirits were bribed with offerings to make them leave the village without harming the inhabitants by possessing their bodies, kidnapping their souls, or causing them illness, death, or misfortune. The central purpose of all religious worship was to obtain power and help from benevolent supernatural beings and to ward off the attacks of malevolent ones.

An integral element of the complex religious and magical system of the pre-Liberation people of Zengbu was a set of beliefs about the human soul (*linghun*). A person's fortune in this life was closely related to the quality of his or her *linghun*, which represented a person's life force and vital spirit. Illness was believed to be caused by the temporary loss of one's soul, and death was believed to result from the permanent separation of the soul from the body.

The state of a person's soul was said to be either lucky or unlucky, bright or dim. A person with a bright soul succeeded in everything he or she attempted. Since persons with luminous souls were imbued with the bright *yang* principle, the malevolent spirits (*gui*), dark creatures from the underworld, shrank back from them in fear and were unable to cause them harm. Most villagers were afraid to wander out at night because this was the time when the *gui* returned from Hell to wander over the earth, and an accidental brush against one could cause illness or death. Persons with bright souls, however, could wander out at night unafraid, since the *gui* were repelled by their soul light. Persons with bright soul lights had, in effect, captured a portion of the vital *yang* spirit of the universe (equivalent to the magical power in *fengshui*) and could use it to accomplish anything they wished. The *gui* were almost as much afraid of such people as they were of the powerful temple deities.

On the other hand, persons whose soul lights were dim were unlucky persons, who failed in almost everything they attempted. Their families were continuously beset by the *gui*, and they were visited with sickness, poverty, and death. People with dim soul lights actually attracted *gui*. Such individuals had to be continuously careful and had to employ every magical means available to guard against supernatural attacks.

The traditional Zengbu peasant world view and philosophy of life had certain internal contradictions. People were achievement-oriented; on the one hand, they worked hard and tried to become wealthy and successful, and there was believed to be a definite connection between effort and achievement. On the other hand, success was believed to depend upon people's fate at birth and later upon their relations with supernatural agencies and powers. Thus, in addition to hard work, the villagers actively attempted to manipulate magical and religious forces and beings in their quest for success and security. Their world view was a complex mixture of rationality and magic. The contradictions in the traditional culture were no more inconsistent, however, than the Calvinist ethic, which held that a person's fate was predetermined but that the only way one could know whether he or she was saved was one's achieved success in doing God's will in one's calling on this earth.

Living under a family system in which people valued nothing so much as children to support them in their old age, and a lineage system in which branches sought to increase their political power by increasing the number of male descendants, created an inherently unstable pattern of social process. These systems were suited only for historical conditions under which excess numbers could expand into exploitable territory. Once the southernmost part of China was fully populated, there was nowhere to go but abroad. The system produced, within China, an agriculturally involuted countryside, where there was not enough land for everyone or even for most people, to make a decent living. The old mode of family production in rice agriculture was no longer viable by the beginning of the twentieth century; population pressure was too great. Contact with the West undermined the crumbling old political order, leading to a situation of anarchy, which the Western countries exploited for their own economic and political advantage.

The city of Guangzhou had always been a center of foreign trade and it was here that the earliest and most sustained contact between China and the West occurred, starting with the Portuguese arrival in 1517. The Portuguese were allowed to settle at Macao, across the Pearl River from Zengbu, in 1557.

Like most of the other villagers in this part of China, the people of Zengbu knew about the coming of the British to trade at Guangzhou in increasing numbers and with increasing frequency at the end of the nineteenth century.

Men from Zengbu went to Guangzhou to take the imperial examinations or
to trade, and may have sold tea, silk, or sugar to the British. The villagers were
only 40 kilometers away from Tiger Gate (*Humen*) on the western coast of
their county, where the Pearl River flows down from Guangzhou. From
Tiger Gate the foreign ships were plain to be seen sailing up the river to
Whampoa harbor, just south of Guangzhou, where they could unload their
cargoes of textiles, glass, and later opium.

When the British decided to intensify their policy of illegally trading
Indian opium into China, beginning in the late eighteenth century, it is
probable that Zengbu people, located as they were on the river network
extending into the delta, participated in the lucrative opium smuggling into
China, in defiance of the Chinese government. They certainly bought opium,
and some of the Zengbu villagers took up the debilitating and ruinous
opium-smoking habit. Even today several of the larger houses are described
as former opium dens. When, between June 3 and 25, 1839, Commissioner
Lin publicly slaked in lime pits the 20,000 chests of opium he had confiscated
from the British and American merchants in Guangzhou, this event was of
local interest to the villagers. It is not unlikely that some of the Zengbu people
went with the thousands of Chinese and foreign observers to witness the
remarkable feat. Currently, the event is regarded as a significant assertion of
ethical Chinese government practice, so that present-day Zengbu junior high
school students speak of their admiration for Commissioner Lin, and the
story of the opium burning on the beach at Humen is a favorite chapter of
history.

During the hostilities surrounding the Opium War (1839–42) and its
aftermath, mercenary "braves," or soldiers, from Dongguan county were
prominent among the Chinese militia gathered by the Qing government and
the local gentry to fight the British (Wakeman 1966, pp. 22–23), and it is
possible that some Zengbu men were among them. (Dongguan county was
noted for its mercenary soldiers.) During the Opium War itself, when British
men-of-war tacked their way up the Pearl River toward Guangzhou,
bombarding the Chinese forts, Zengbu men may well have been part of the
militia forces that tried to stop the attackers by stretching a line of fireboats
and other barriers across the mouth of the river.

After China's defeat and the establishment of the British colony of Hong
Kong, about 45 kilometers to the south, the history of Zengbu became more
directly tied to the history of this famous treaty port. During the second half
of the nineteenth century, Hong Kong's population grew as Chinese from the
economically-depressed and overpopulated countryside, including Zengbu
people, went to the colony to find work. As a result of the introduction of
crops from the New World by the Europeans in the sixteenth century – sweet
potatoes, peanuts, and maize, crops which could be grown on the highland to
supplement the rice grown in lowland irrigated fields – population pressure

gradually increased until by 1812 the situation in Guangdong was similar to that of Hunan and other heavily populated provinces. The amount of cultivated land per capita in Guangdong in that year was only 1.67 *mu*, one of the lowest in China (Wakeman 1966, pp. 179–180).

Since theirs was one of the poorest settlements in the area surrounding Chashan, Zengbu residents were some of the earliest people to go to Hong Kong to work in the latter half of the nineteenth century. (Dongguan county has always been one of the major sources of Chinese emigration to Hong Kong.) Many of the Zengbu villagers also used Hong Kong as an embarkation port for Southeast Asia and other parts of the world. By the late nineteenth century, 120,000 people from Guangdong were leaving China each year (Wakeman 1966, p. 180).

Travel to and trade with Hong Kong and Guangzhou was made much faster and more convenient with the completion of the Kowloon–Canton railroad in 1924. This railroad passed through the outskirts of Chashan town, only about an hour's walk from Zengbu. The coming of the railroad facilitated the extension of Hong Kong's economic influences into the interior of the province.

A traumatic period in the history of the people of Zengbu began in 1938, when the Japanese invaded and captured Guangzhou and Dongguan city. Conditions worsened in 1941, just after Pearl Harbor, when the Japanese armies took Hong Kong. The British there were interned in prisoner-of-war camps for the duration of World War II, and, as the economy could no longer support emigrant villagers during the Japanese occupation of the colony, thousands of Chinese residents returned to their native villages to sit out the period of hardship. Many Zengbu people returned to reclaim land they had rented to tenants when they went to Hong Kong. They began to work it themselves, causing much hardship for the former tenants and increasing the pressure on the land. (The rules of land tenure in this region of China separated ownership rights to the subsurface of the land from tenant rights to rent the surface of the land, with the tenant being secure unless the landowner wished to work the land himself or sell it.) The Japanese occupation, from 1938 to 1945, was a nightmare of hardship, near-starvation, and physical insecurity for the people of Zengbu as for many others in China. The Guomindang government had retreated to northern Guangdong and to western China to escape from the Japanese, leaving the people at the mercy of the invaders.

The coming of the Japanese troops is still remembered vividly by some of Zengbu's older people. Conditions during the Japanese occupation and the subsequent civil wars between the People's Liberation Army and the Guomindang form their model of what China was like prior to Liberation. When the older generation measures the success of the new system, their universe of comparison is the social and economic conditions in Zengbu during the 1930s and 1940s as against the 1980s.

When the Japanese troops first appeared on the narrow road across the rice paddies from Chashan town, the people yelled to relay the news ahead, shouting from field to field until the message reached the villages that "the Japanese dwarfs" were coming! Those villagers that could gathered up their belongings and hurriedly escaped into the southern mountains by road or sampan. The Japanese bivouacked on Fruit and Flower Hill, which formed an easily defended vantage point overlooking Zengbu. Setting up machine guns, they sprayed bullets over the village roofs, scattering roof tiles into the streets and down into the houses below and frightening everyone. The invaders stayed this first time for only three days, looting the village and taking all the pigs, chickens, and rice that the villagers had not securely hidden. They did not kill anyone on this first visit, nor did they burn the Zengbu villages, for the villagers did not offer them any resistance.

On their second visit to Zengbu the Japanese shot and killed several people: two villagers who were rowing away in a boat, and another man who happened to be rowing by on his way to market some shrimp. They also killed an old beggar woman from Sandhill village who was a deaf mute and did not hear their orders to halt. The villagers had to deal with the Japanese using the village headmen as intermediaries, and communicated across the language barrier by tracing mutually intelligible Chinese characters on the palms of their hands.

What the people of Zengbu remember most keenly about the occupation is how close they came to starving. In poorer families rice was reserved for the men of the family because the lives of the entire family depended upon the men's ability to labor. The women and children and old people ate sweet potatoes, rice bran, and wild herbs from the mountains, cooking these things in thin gruel, when they had it. In 1944 alone, villagers remember that 150 people starved to death in Zengbu's five villages. Some poor families were entirely wiped out. More female children than males died because the male children, considered more valuable to their parents, were given more and better food. Villagers say that bands of wandering beggars from even less favored places starved to death on the outskirts of Dongguan city.

When people in Zengbu speak of this horrible time, tears stream down their cheeks with the pain of the memories. As Secretary Lu put it, "When we got up in the morning we did not know if we would still be alive at the end of the day; a man's life was not worth a *jin* of sweet potatoes." Bandits roamed the countryside, bands of desperate men who tried to survive by preying upon other poor devils who were only a little more fortunate than themselves. Hungry beggars wandered through the countryside. Many Zengbu families were forced to sell their children in order to survive – first the daughters and then the sons. Those who could not sell their children took them to the crossroads between Shilong and Dongguan and gave them away to anyone who would agree to feed them and save their lives. After Liberation many Zengbu families succeeded in tracing some of these lost family members and reuniting their families. But most of the sold children could never be found.

One Zengbu woman recalls what happened to her, a girl of six, during the occupation:

In 1938 the Japanese invaded my home village and took everything we had, including all our food. We had to go begging to other villages. My mother became ill and there was no money to take her to the doctor or to buy medicine, so she died; she was only 23 years old. My younger brother was then only two years old and still nursing. After my mother died, there was no one to take care of him and he became ill. We had no money to treat him; his illness became more serious day by day. At that time, the Japanese isolated and quarantined any family that had a death from illness and would not let anyone live nearby. In order not to trouble the other neighbors who had no place to go, we quietly buried my brother before he had completely died and did not register his death. This was so horrible that I shall never forget it as long as I live.

The villagers' recollections are not political myths about the old days before Liberation; they are, unfortunately, true and accurate, and can be confirmed by outside observation. Graham Peck, that acute observer of pre-Liberation China, personally traveled through Guangdong during this time. He describes graphically what happened there during the Japanese occupation, when the Guomindang government turned a sustained drought into a disaster infamous throughout China, by selling rice from the unoccupied areas to the Japanese, even though this meant that their own people, like those in Zengbu, would starve:

If the bad harvest had been the autumn one, and the leaves soon fell and turned inedible, the peasants would begin eating bark or clay, or selling their farm tools and land to buy back more grain. Now they sell their land, destroying their hope of ever farming again without new debts ... One mark of this stage of the peasants' descent into despair would be the period when they began saving for grain by burying their dead naked, without coffins ... The numbers who turned bandit would increase, and in their need and the haste brought by increasing competition, they would begin killing before they robbed ... By now, many peasants would be too weak or uninterested to bury their dead at all, and would simply drag them into the fields away from their homes. Some would begin prowling for other families' corpses, driving away the dogs and ravens while they cut off their own food. Some would begin selling the less useful members of their families in the hope of saving the rest. Women and children were sold by the pound even when they were sold as slaves, not food, and the day the price of a pound of living human flesh sank below that of a pound of grain could be taken as the point at which the famine settled into its final stretch. More than a million and a half people are believed to have perished in Guangdong during the 1943–44 droughts. (1950, pp. 21, 23)

Throughout the Japanese occupation and the ensuing period, between the Japanese surrender in 1945 and the establishment of the People's Republic in

1949, the Zengbu countryside was in a ferment of political and military instability. The only organization to hold power effectively was the East River Guerrillas, a Communist-led, united front organization established by Guangzhou students in 1938, just after the beginning of the Japanese occupation. The East River Guerrillas had their greatest success in the mountainous region of eastern Guangdong, which included Zengbu (Vogel 1971, p. 35). The poorer people of Zengbu enthusiastically supported the guerrillas, both during the occupation and later in their fight against the Guomindang. Many Zengbu men fought with the guerrillas, and some of the women took supplies to their base camps in the mountains. By means of a schoolteacher in Zengbu, who worked in the underground, the guerrillas kept the villagers informed about the progress of the People's Liberation Army in the north of China. The farming people hid the guerrillas in their homes and kept them supplied with intelligence information about the activities of the Japanese and, later, the Guomindang. After the war, the villagers split over the support of the Communist guerrillas, with the landlords supporting the Guomindang and the poor and landless peasants supporting the guerillas.

In the period just before Liberation – the late 1930s and the 1940s – the economy of Zengbu was based upon two crop rice agriculture, fishpond farming, and the growing of litchi, various other fruits, sugarcane, hemp, peanuts, taro, beans, and vegetables of all kinds. Pigs were reared at home for sale in the market. Sugarcane was processed in village mills into a course brown sugar for home consumption. Peanuts were pressed for cooking oil; litchis were dried for export; and cassava was ground into powder and then exported. Bamboo shrimp traps, the traditional Zengbu handicraft, were woven and sold to delta fishing villages to supplement family income.

In spite of the many crops grown or attempted, Zengbu was the poorest area in the Chashan region before Liberation. Located at the confluence of two large rivers, Zengbu's low-lying, marshy paddy fields flooded nine years out of ten and produced essentially only one crop of rice a year. The yield of the land was only a fraction of what it is now. People from the surrounding villages used to taunt the people of Zengbu with this jingle:

*Zengbu lao, Zengbu lao, Bu chi ni, jiu chi cao!*
[Old Zengbu people, old Zengbu people, If they don't eat mud, they eat grass!]

The jingle refers to the fact that Zengbu's land was so unproductive and their crops so unreliable that Zengbu people often subsisted by digging up river-bottom mud to sell to the nearby brick kilns, or else by carrying grass from the mountains to feed the fish in the fishponds owned by the local landlords.

Other villages also mocked the isolation of Zengbu. Its villages were surrounded by unbridged rivers that had to be crossed by ferry. The saying went that if you lived in Zengbu you had to pay a 20 cents' fare to the ferry man every time you stepped off your doorstep!

Before Liberation, most of the land in Zengbu was owned not by individuals but by ancestral halls which acted as collective landlords. This kind of concentration of ownership was not uncommon in this part of China (see Wakeman 1966, p. 110). The elders of the halls had the authority to lease the ancestral lands to tenant members of the group and to outsiders. To keep on good terms with the elders, it was the custom for tenants to give them small gifts of "black money" when a lease was signed, and a chicken, duck, or goose at New Year. After each rice harvest long lines of tenant farmers could be seen trudging into the courtyards of the Zengbu ancestral halls with sacks of unhusked rice on their backs to pay their rent. Each hall had a manager. Usually a wealthy man was chosen, since it was believed that he would be less likely to embezzle money from the hall. The manager would record the rice that the tenants brought him, and store it during the year. Crafty managers lent out the rice at interest to non-members of the hall and pocketed the interest, gambling that they would have the cash to clear the accounts before the elders met at the annual meeting in the ancestral hall at the end of the year.

Five percent of the people of Zengbu were classified as landlords at the time of land reform. However, most of these did not have large holdings by any standards except the standards of the very poor. The largest individual landlord in Zengbu owned 40 *mu* of land and fishponds (a little less than 3 hectares), and the next largest owned only half of that. (There were much larger landlords among the nearby Yuans of Chashan.)

Land was so scarce and competition for it so keen that rent for rice land was always very high. In years of flood or drought the landlord and the tenant simply split the harvest. Normally tenants paid from 40 to 60 percent of the rice crop as rent to private landlords, and 66 percent to the more rapacious ancestral halls. Sixty-three percent of the people of Zengbu farmed at least some land prior to Liberation, but only about 10 percent were able to make a living farming their own land. Eighty-two percent of Zengbu's residents at Liberation were rural proletarians – farm laborers, coolies in the nearby towns and cities, small peddlers, or vagabonds. The wages for a farm laborer, hired on a yearly basis in the 1930s and 1940s, consisted of his food, one suit of ordinary cotton clothes, and 100 *jin* (50 kilograms) of unhusked rice a year. Young boys from poor families helped fill the family coffers by hiring out to watch the buffaloes of richer farmers; few attended school.

Before Liberation poorer women did work in the fields but not as much as they were to do after the Revolution. They spent most of their time at home tending the children, taking care of the household, raising the family's pigs and chickens, and weaving bamboo shrimp traps to earn extra cash.

Nearly two-thirds of the nonagricultural workers were unskilled coolies in the towns and cities. Both men and women hired themselves out to carry goods from the railway stations in Shilong town and Chashan, to Dongguan city, which was not served by the railroad. Many of the older men and women tell of carrying shoulder-pole loads of more than 100 *jin* from Chashan to Dongguan, a distance of 16 kilometers, for a few grams of rice a day. To supplement their wages they stopped in other villages on the way back from Dongguan to pick up a load of firewood to sell in Chashan when they returned. Over one hundred people from Zengbu were coolies engaged in this type of work.

Men and women from Zengbu also worked in Hong Kong as coolies and servants. Married men sent money back to support their wives and children in the village, returning to visit them only on special occasions. Some local men were labor contractors for Hong Kong business. Known as "Number One boys," they recruited gangs of laborers from the village and took them to work in Hong Kong, receiving a commission from the employer.

The way of life in Zengbu during the two or three decades before Liberation was not viable for the vast majority of the people. The Zengbu countryside, like most places in rural China, was overpopulated and poverty-stricken. There was little or no modern medical care and no decent schools. The death rate was appalling, with many people dying of what would now be considered minor illnesses. Women were exploited and downtrodden, serving the male half of society who controlled the family and the lineage. Slavery still existed in Zengbu, with the outright buying and selling of people – sons, daughters, slaves, maidservants, concubines, and even wives during famine. There was no national disaster relief agency to prevent people in Zengbu from starving to death.

There was not enough agricultural land to support all the people of Zengbu, and what land was available was largely in the hands of private and collective landlords who extracted from one-half to two-thirds of the rice crop as rent, leaving the tenant farmer very little to feed himself and his family. Eighty percent of the Zengbu people just before Liberation were poor peasants, farm laborers, or semi-itinerant unskilled workers who went between jobs like coolie work on the Hong Kong docks and shrimp trapping in the Pearl River, desperately seeking to make a living for themselves and their families. The jobs made available by the development of Hong Kong actually eased the harsh situation for the many Zengbu people who found work there. Those who could not find work in Hong Kong emigrated to Singapore or even further afield.

Local Chashan society was dominated by the wealthy Yuan landlords who controlled the market town and the local administration, and were supported by other wealthy landlords and lineages in the surrounding countryside. These landlord-gentry officials also controlled the local militia, which they used to enforce rent payments and to preserve their class hegemony. Beginning with the Opium War in the middle of the nineteenth century, the

Chinese central government's hold on the Zengbu countryside began to crumble, a process hastened during the warlord period which began after the fall of the Qing Dynasty, in 1911. Then, later, the Guomindang government was not able to protect the Zengbu people against the Japanese invaders who occupied Zengbu and raped, murdered, and exploited the people at will. The Guomindang could not make any meaningful reforms in local society because its power rested upon the local landlord-bureaucratic class, whose interest it was to preserve the existing order.

Agriculture was very backward, and its technology was primitive. Irrigation works and flood control facilities were in poor repair. There was no local agency capable of mobilizing the peasant farmers on the large scale needed to carry out the building of reservoirs, levees, and canals necessary to increase the amount of irrigated land and to protect against floods or droughts. Farms controlled by the peasants were extremely small, and individual farm units were divided into numerous small plots that were inefficient to work. Like most traditional peasant societies, Zengbu's economy did not rest upon agriculture alone. Commerce and decentralized rural industries and household handicrafts were well-developed. But long-distance transportation facilities were so primitive and marketing so inefficient that economic development was inhibited. Most of the capital accumulated in the countryside was siphoned off by the landlords in the form of rents, and the rest was spent by village families on expensive life-crisis ceremonies to enhance their social status. Economic conditions in the countryside were made intolerable by the endless civil wars that swept over it and by the terrible experience of the Japanese invasion and occupation during World War II.

In short, life in Zengbu on the eve of Liberation in 1949 was nasty, short, brutish, poor, and – most important – without hope. The old Chinese "feudal" society, economy, and polity that had existed since the founding of the imperial order centuries before and which had once supported a brilliant civilization was nothing but a bloated, festering corpse. A new order was needed. The Chinese Communist party promised the establishment of a new order, and the overwhelming majority of Zengbu peasants had nothing left to lose and everything to gain by trying it.

# 2

# Establishing the new order

Guangdong was one of the last parts of China liberated from the Guomin-dang. It was not occupied by the People's Liberation Army until the end of 1949. Several weeks earlier, in Tiananmen Square in Beijing, Chairman Mao had already declared the establishment of the People's Republic of China. In the "old revolutionary bases," where the new government had ruled for a long time, and in the "early liberated areas," such as northeastern China, tasks such as establishing the new government in the cities and the country-side, recruiting and training a reliable group of cadres, propagandizing the peasants and organizing them to overthrow the landlords and local bullies, and carrying out land reform, were already well under way; in Guangdong they had not yet been undertaken (Vogel 1971, p. 42).

In Dongguan county, the East River Guerrillas had occupied Dongguan and Shilong prior to the arrival of the People's Liberation Army, which took over from them. District governments were established in these towns, which were important to Zengbu because of their proximity, but for a period of two years between Liberation and the end of 1951, little of structural significance happened in Zengbu itself. The old landlord-gentry officials, although restless and uneasy, remained in power. Rice-purchasing contingents from the new government came out to Zengbu in 1950 to buy rice for the cities. The new government organized song and dance propaganda troupes which came to Zengbu to explain the Communist party and its programs to the peasants, but there were no other changes of consequence.

This period of two years was a time of calm before the storm that was to break out with the beginning of land reform. The majority of the people in Zengbu (at least 80 percent by most accounts) supported the new govern-ment, which had established order in the countryside – in itself an important accomplishment from the point of view of people who had suffered decades of anarchy and war. Wealthier people, landlords, and those who had family connections with the former Guomindang government, were understandably nervous about what was to come. Those who felt most imperiled by the new regime left for Hong Kong. The peasants were also uneasy. Although they were generally in favor of the new government, and knew that they hated the domineering landlords and local bullies, they were also afraid that the Guomindang might come back into power. In such a case, peasants who had openly opposed the landlords and local elite could expect to be destroyed in revenge. Both the rich and the poor of Zengbu felt uneasy, uncertain, and endangered.

This period of balanced tension ended late in 1951, when Lu Zhongzhu, (later secretary of the Zengbu Communist party branch, but then a young man in his late twenties) gathered a small group of radical young men together, arrested the worst of the landlord-despots in Lu's Home village, and turned them over to the district government for trial. This was the first active step toward the achievement of structural change in Zengbu itself, and Lu's arrest of the landlords has become a part of Zengbu's revolutionary mythology.

In order to understand the significance of Lu's actions, it is necessary to understand his position in the village. Lu Zhongzhu was a member of the adopted heir group (*lisizai*) of Lu's Home village. His family had been ritually humiliated when they were adopted into the lineage. They had suffered repeatedly from the arrogance of the dominant lineage leaders, and had good reason to hate them. They had been driven almost to desperation by economic circumstances. Lu had come of age as a poor and landless peasant who had worked as a farm laborer, a tenant, a shrimp fisherman off a sampan in the Pearl River, and as a coolie carrying the luggage of Western ships' passengers on the Hong Kong docks. None of these occupations provided reliable subsistence. He returned to his native village after Liberation but found that the same oppressive village power structure, manned by the same people, was still firmly in place – as though the Revolution had never happened.

The landlord-bullies who held power in Lu's Home village all came from the strongest branch of the Lu lineage. They ruled the village by virtue of their sizable ancestral property, their numbers (15 to 20 percent of the village population), and their reputation for fearlessness. They were supposed to be willing to fight to the death in any dispute. They had controlled the village for generations, and it took an almost foolhardy courage to face them down in a struggle.

Lu and a small group of other young activist friends felt that a revolution which left this dominant group in place was incomplete. They planned in secret to arrest the landlords and turn them over to the district government for trial. However, the landlords were informed of these plans and decided to kill Lu and his fellow conspirators first, as an example to the other villagers. But Lu was informed of the landlords' intentions, as they had been of his. This is how he tells the story:

I owe my life to a poor village man from the most powerful landlord's branch of the lineage, who came to warn me that the landlords were planning to murder me. This man was a hired laborer in the landlord's family. One evening the landlord invited the village schoolteacher [who had at one time been progressive, but later sided with the landlords] to his house for a dinner of roast goose. The landlord told the schoolteacher that they planned to shoot me and the other activists. The schoolteacher was alarmed because the laborer had overheard the conversation, and the teacher was afraid that he would reveal their plans. But the landlord told him not to be afraid because the laborer was a close lineage brother of his and would not betray them. The landlord was mistaken. Later, about nine that night, the laborer sneaked over to my house and told me of the landlords' plan to murder me at midnight. The hired laborer was a poor person, and his class solidarity was stronger than his kinship allegiance to his landlord lineage brother.

Lu and his small group of activists slipped from their houses and slept in the hills that night. The next day they proceeded by boat to the district office of the revolutionary government. In the boat to the district office, Lu Jia, a group member who was a Taoist priest, panicked, and tried to make the others turn back, but Lu Zhongzhu threatened to throw him overboard if he would not continue with the enterprise. At the district office, they told the cadres there what had happened. The district government sent three militiamen back with them to arrest the landlords.

Lu's party first caught the schoolteacher and tied him up, threatening to kill him if he escaped and warned the landlords. They decided to catch the landlords asleep in their own houses, at 4:30 a.m. It was clear that a frontal attack would not be easy, because the landlords were well-armed, and Lu's party had only two rifles among them. Lu Jia, the Taoist priest, began shaking with fright and refused to go on with the others. "After all," the priest said, "the landlords have guns and might shoot us, or they or their families might take revenge on us later." After Lu Zhongzhu threatened to tie up this reluctant revolutionary, he agreed to continue with the others.

This incident delayed the group, and news of the planned attack spread through the village like wild fire. Lu Chenjia, one of the landlord-bullies, was warned, and enabled to escape. He fled to Guangzhou and hid there for two years until he was caught and sent to prison.

Lu Zhongzhu told of his confrontation with the most ruthless landlords:

We went to Baiqong's house and asked him to come out. He refused. Then he ran part way up the stairs toward the loft of his house. We knew he had grenades and guns hidden up there on the second floor. When we shouted to him that we would shoot if he went any farther, he stopped; if he had gone one step farther then we would have shot him. After Baiqong had surrendered, the other four landlords gave up without a fight.

The five landlord-despots were delivered to the district government. Lu's actions were the first and most dramatic step in overturning the old order in

Zengbu. Lu himself later became a most successful leader in Zengbu and served as the party branch secretary for many years. However, the Taoist priest was so unnerved by what he had done, and so terrified that the landlords would return with the Guomindang and kill him, that he went mad a few days later, and never recovered. It is easy to mock these fears in retrospect, but at the time they proved so overwhelming as to destroy a man's reason.

After the overthrow of the landlords in Lu's Home, a new administration was elected and Lu Zhongzhu served as deputy village head. This administration had the support of 80 to 90 percent of the villagers, who were generally very much in sympathy with the arrest of the local tyrants.

Since the new government was already established before its leaders began to tear down the old order and fashion the new one in Guangdong, there was a debate in the party about the proper policy to follow in carrying out land reform there. Some thought that since the party was no longer fighting for its life in the midst of an anti-Japanese war and a bloody civil war, land reform could be carried out more slowly and peacefully. This was the initial policy, but very quickly a more radical policy was insisted upon, especially by the northerners who came down to take key positions in the Cantonese government; consequently, the ensuing land reform in Guangdong was also violent and turbulent, emphasizing political struggle and class war (see Vogel 1971, pp. 95 ff.).

In the winter of 1951–2 land reform work teams from the district government came to Zengbu. Their aim was to raise the class consciousness of the peasants by helping them recognize the exploitative nature of the pre-Liberation social order, to organize peasant associations and militia units that would wield power during land reform, and to assign all Zengbu families a class status. Then land would be taken from the rich and given to the poor peasants. Over thirty persons came to Zengbu, some young, some old, a few ex-guerrillas, but mostly from middle schools and universities.

The first act of the work team was to ask all the villagers to surrender their weapons and to dismiss the officials who were holding office when the land reform team arrived, on the assumption that these officials were either reactionaries themselves or tools of the landlords and local bullies. This caused no problem in Sandhill and Pondside villages, where the old village heads were still in power, but in Lu's Home village, where Secretary Lu and other activists had already taken power after overthrowing the bullies, a difficult situation was precipitated. Secretary Lu and the other activists were forced to leave office and prevented from participating in any of the important and crucial activities surrounding the formation of the peasants' associations and the militia. In 1979, Secretary Lu recalled:

The work teams met with us, and they told us they could not trust us. They declared that we were not to participate in any of the activities of land reform and that we should stay at home and keep out of things. They even required us to ask permission if we wished to leave our homes. In some other villages the local officials were actually locked in their houses; they did not try to do that with me. The work team people were outsiders and did not understand local conditions.

Secretary Lu recognized that the team was simply following national policy, but nevertheless he was embittered by this ironic decision. Only later, in the midst of land reform, when the work team realized that he was the most literate and most capable of the poor people in Zengbu, was he asked to return to active political life.

To locate reliable leaders for the peasants' association and the militia, the work team asked the villagers for the names of the poorest, the most oppressed, and the most persecuted in the villages of Zengbu, people who previously had no social position at all. They were given the names of slaves, adopted heirs, poor peasants, and landless laborers. They then investigated these people very thoroughly, checking with their neighbors to see if they really had been poor and exploited. They did not want landlord elements to infiltrate the peasants' association because they might blunt the force of the Revolution and turn it to their own purposes. Once the poorest people were located, the work team honored and dignified them. The very poorest were chosen as the first "backbone elements" (*guganfenzi*), persons of unyielding proletarian integrity, to lead the peasants' association of Zengbu. In the winter of 1951 the work team first chose 12 members for the peasants' association in Lu's Home, among whom was one of Secretary Lu's younger brothers, a farm laborer.

The person chosen as the first effective chairman of the Zengbu peasants' association (each village had a vice-chairman) was a young man of 22 named Liu Erbiao of Sandhill village. He was a landless laborer and poor tenant whose father and older brothers had deserted him and his mother during the Japanese occupation. His father's older brother, an opium-smoking local despot, stole his inheritance and left him penniless. His mother helped eke out their living by weaving shrimp traps and working as a servant for a family in Chashan. For living quarters they had only one-quarter of a dilapidated house. The family was exploited further by the uncle, who was manager of the branch ancestral estate in which they all had a share. The uncle rented land cheaply from the ancestral hall and then sublet it to Erbiao's family, profiting from the difference. Liu Erbiao was the poorest member of the richest branch of Sandhill village's Liu lineage.

Once they had located Liu Erbiao as a likely prospect for leadership, the work team visited and talked with him, educating him and explaining to him that the root cause of his poverty was the exploitation of the landlord classes in Zengbu. In 1979 Liu Erbiao explained what had happened to him:

The work team explained why I worked all day long and could not make enough for two meals. They told me that the reason I was poor and had no money and could not make any was because the landlords – the local bullies who served as the managers of the ancestral halls – stole the ancestral land for their private use. They said that the ancestral lands and fishponds were plentiful but that they had been appropriated by the rich who used them for their own benefit. I believed them.

The work team asked Liu Erbiao to become the vice-chairman of the peasants' association in charge of Sandhill village. Liu Erbiao was reluctant to accept the position because, like most of the backbone elements, he was illiterate and had never taken part in public affairs, but, at their urging, he agreed to try.

Lu Dengku, a man from Lu's Home village, had been chosen as the first chairman of the all-Zengbu peasants' association. The work team asked him to give them the names of other potential backbone elements, formerly downtrodden men and women who would be suitable as the initial members and leaders of the peasants' association. Lu recommended 12 other persons who, after investigation, were accepted. It became clear, however, that Lu was an ineffective leader, since he was incapable of public speaking, which is an essential qualification for a cadre, and Liu Erbiao, who spoke well, assumed the post of chairman. As the winter of 1951 wore on, more and more people were recruited into the peasants' association by the same method; they were personally recommended by the backbone elements, investigated carefully, cleared, and then invited to join. One hundred joined in the first wave, then almost another hundred, so that within a period of three months there were over 170 members in Lu's Home. Finally, at least 70 percent of the people in Lu's Home were members. The same process took place in Zengbu's other villages.

Those in the villages who had stood and watched while other villagers were recruited into the association, felt isolated and grew more and more apprehensive as time went on. The work team and the association had not assigned villagers to their official class status categories but they had begun to discuss what people did for a living and whether they were exploiters or not. The poorest peasants were relatively secure, being the most favored group under the new system; but even they were apprehensive about the magnitude of the changes that were being discussed. Religious practitioners like the terrified Taoist priest who had accompanied Secretary Lu when he arrested the Lu's Home landlords, and the local spirit medium (guipo), were apprehensive because the new government said that their religious practices were nothing but superstitious means of tricking and exploiting people. There was so much propaganda against the landlords that families who thought they might be placed in that category were beset with worry and suffered from extreme and constant anguish. Some tried to give property to their relatives or tenants in hopes that they could escape being classified as a landlord. Everyone knew by then how important the classification of one's family would be for the future; they began to hear stories of land reform in other areas where landlords had

had their property confiscated, or had been imprisoned or shot. These stories added to the apprehension. Middle peasants were afraid of being classified as rich peasants, and rich peasants worried lest they be classified as landlords.

As well as organizing the peasants' association, the work teams set up armed militia units of 10 or 12 members in each of the villages, to guard against any attempt by the remaining landlords and bullies to threaten people who spoke out against them, and also to be available to arrest landlords or anyone else on the peasants' association's orders. Power in the villages of Zengbu was being transferred to the peasants' associations, and the militia units were to enforce and support this.

While the peasants' associations and the supporting militia units were being set up, the work teams, with the help of the peasants' association leaders, held meetings explaining to the people the theory behind the Revolution, and exhorting them to follow the socialist road. There were many, many meetings during this time. The message taught was essentially a simple one. The work team members asked the peasants "Why are peasants poor?" "Why do the peasants nurture the landlords?" "Why do the landlords get fat without working?" They pointed out to the peasants that the root cause of their misery was the feudal exploiting class. Work team members reminded their listeners that although land and fishponds were plentiful in the ancestral estates of Zengbu the local bullies who served as managers had rented the best property themselves at a low rental, exploiting the common land for their own private interests. They pointed out that the landlords and moneylenders had impoverished the poor peasants by charging them rents so high that peasants could not pay them and feed their families, and then by charging double interest on the loans of money and grain that the peasants were forced to take out to stay alive.

There was so much bitterness among the poor peasants and landless laborers toward the landlords and local bullies that these ideological seeds fell upon fertile ground. The work team was providing a form of expression for pre-existing sentiments that were deeply felt. Even kinsmen of the same lineage branches hated their richer lineage brothers, who exploited them as tenants and debtors and stole the income from the ancestral estates. Some of the poorer villages had had their property taken by landlords; others had been beaten by them. The slaves and the adopted-heir groups in the villages found in the repeated public humiliations they had known, reasons to hate the dominant lineage's landlords with a white-hot intensity. The class divisions in the society made it easy for the land reform work team to organize opposition to the landlords. The hatred and envy of the rich by the poor, and of the free villagers by the slaves, which already existed, fueled the revolutionary movement in Zengbu.

Once the peasants' association and the militia had been organized and had been given the reins of power in Zengbu under the guidance of the work team, they carried out the analysis of classes. Each family was assigned to one of the rural classes, ranging from landlords to poor landless laborers, that had been defined by the Chinese government in its "Agrarian Reform Law of the People's Republic of China" (1950). The guidelines used by Zengbu cadres for assigning class status followed in general the guidelines of the national classification but had some local peculiarities. These categories are an attempt to measure the relationship between property, work, and social relationships, rather than an attempt to measure property without reference to the social relationships it implies.

According to local cadres who actually carried out Zengbu's classification of families, the criteria used were as follows:

1. Landlords (*dizhu*). Landlords were defined as those families which, in the three years before Liberation, had received 70 percent (or by some accounts 75 or 80 percent, memories differing) of their income from exploiting others. Exploitation came from the renting out of land by private landowners, by lending out money at exorbitant rates of interest, and by hiring long-term farm laborers to do the work of production with the landlords' families doing little or no farm-work themselves. Another form of exploitation was the use of ancestral hall property for the private benefit of a manager, an important factor in Zengbu because most of the land and fishponds were owned by ancestral estates, and managed by individuals who had opportunities to use them for their own profit.

Local cadres distinguished two kinds of landlords. There were the landlords proper, who met the above criteria, and then there were landlords who were at the same time local despots and bullies, men who used force to dominate their villages. Ordinary landlords were resented as exploiters. Landlord-despots were hated figures who were to be denounced and punished.

In addition, during land reform the local people also spoke of "dead landlords" (*si dizhu*). These were the ancestors of living sublineage members in whose name were held the ancestral halls and estates which made up most of the land and fishponds in Zengbu. The dead ancestors were the formal property owners, and in their name small sublineage branches within the larger lineage villages of Zengbu corporately owned a high proportion of village land and fishponds. A few of these lineage subbranches were owners of such wealthy ancestral estates that they distributed money yearly to individual families as personal income after all the necessary expenses of the estate had been paid. Theoretically (and actually, in the eyes of local people) these wealthy families could have been classified as landlords, but they were not, even though their sublineage groups were far more significant exploiters than some individuals classified as landlords because of their private holdings. Most of the land in Zengbu (as much as 70 percent in Pondside, for example) was in the hands of sublineage corporate owners. Sublineage collective owners thus escaped the punishment meted out to private landlords for their exploitation of others. This loophole in the land reform law spared many people whose wealth was derived from "dead landlords" from being classified as landlords themselves and suffering the consequences of that label.

The only members of the powerful and wealthy corporate kin groups who were classified as landlords were those who had mismanaged ancestral estates and those who had rented land from the estates and then sublet it to tenants at a sizable profit. The managers became in a sense scapegoats for the wealthy groups as a whole. The corrupt extortion of money from the ancestral estates, a traditional crime, was also corrupt exploitation according to the new class definitions. Profiting legitimately from an ancestral estate, however, was not thought of as a way of being a landlord, even under the new regime.

On the other hand, it was possible for a man to be classified as a landlord even if he owned no property at all. One example was a man from Sandhill village who was a traditional Chinese doctor. He rented fishponds from Sandhill ancestral halls at a very small rental and then hired laborers at low wages to work them for him. Neither he nor any of his family did any appreciable amount of physical work. He was the wealthiest and the most powerful man in Sandhill village because his brother was a district head in the Guomindang government. He used this connection for local influence, and he was classed as landlord, for these reasons, although he owned no land.

2. Rich peasants (*funong*). Rich peasants were those who obtained a large share of their income from exploiting hired workers or tenants. The major difference was that rich peasants and their families took part in productive labor alongside their hired workers. Although the rich peasants were not hated like the landlords, they were publicly criticized and had land and fishponds confiscated during land reform. There was only one family in all of Zengbu classified as rich peasants.

3. Middle peasants (*zhongnong*). These owned enough land to make a living and did not exploit people except for hiring a few days' short-term labor during the busiest part of the agricultural year.

4. Poor peasants (*pinnong*). Families were classified as poor peasants if they had to sell their labor power to make a living, thus differentiating them from the middle peasants. Some poor peasants owned small amounts of land, but not enough to live on. Others owned no land at all, renting their entire farms from landlords or ancestral halls. Their lives were not so secure as those of the middle peasants. "In good years they had enough to eat; in bad years they did not know where their next meal was coming from," as one person put it.

5. Farm laborers (*gunong*). These families had no land or property of any kind, except for a house or a part of one, nor were they able to obtain any land to rent. They had to support themselves by hiring out as agricultural laborers,

usually for the long-term, and over 90 percent of their meager income was derived from these labor contracts. They were the poorest and most oppressed members of the agricultural community.

In addition to these major classes of people, to be found in most rural Chinese villages, there were the following additional categories:

6. Small landowners (*xiaotudichuzuzhe*). These were families that owned a little land which for various reasons (poor health, a job in the town, the death of the husband) they could not work themselves and so they rented it to others. Although theoretically they were landlords and exploited their tenants, their special circumstances and the small amount of land they owned made it ridiculous to place them in that category.

7. Workers (*gongren*). Families that owned no land at all but usually did not participate in agricultural production were classified as workers. In Zengbu most of these people dug mud for the local tile and brick kilns, worked as coolies, or worked as unskilled laborers in a town or city.

8. Small peddlers (*xiaofan*). These were people who hawked merchandise, going from market to market and from town to countryside to buy cheaper and sell more dearly.

9. Handicraft workers (*shougongyizhe*). These were people who supported themselves from their own small handicraft establishments, making bamboo baskets and brooms, furniture, and such. They worked themselves and, except for occasional apprentices, they did not employ workers and therefore were not exploiters.

10. Small merchants (*xiaoshangye*). These people did not work on the land at all; they lived off small shops or had other enterprises like drying and selling litchi.

11. Professionals (*juanyerenyuan*). These were people such as teachers, medical practitioners, and doctors, who depended upon their independent professions for their living. They did not hire workers or exploit others.

12. Religious practitioners (*mixinzhiyezhe*). People like Taoist priests, Buddhist monks, spirit mediums, and geomancy specialists obtained most of their livelihood from their religious activities.

13. Vagabonds or "floating elements" (*youmin*). These were unemployed vagrants or vagabonds who had no discernible source of income. They usually made a living working in illegal occupations such as the opium business.

14. Poor people (*pinmin*). These were poor citizens who did not farm or work; they stayed alive by begging.

15. Former bureaucrats (*jiuguanliao*). This category was applied to one person in Zengbu who formerly worked as an official in the Guomindang government. He was punished with imprisonment.

Every head of household in Zengbu was classified into one of these family class background (*chengfen*) categories. All the members of a household were assigned to the *chengfen* of the father, which became a permanent description of a person and was entered next to his or her name in the household registers kept by the government. It was to be very important in determining one's future in the new social order.

Later, class background status was inherited patrilineally from one's father like a surname; if one's father was a landlord, the children's class status would also be landlord. If a daughter of a landlord family married a poor peasant, their children would inherit the family class status of their father. If the son of a landlord married a poor peasant woman, the children would be landlords too. The notion of the inheritability of class status, which seems on the face of it very strange in a Marxist society, is an important principle in Chinese cultural thinking. (See chapter 15 for a full discussion.)

The assessment of class status, according to the cadre in charge of land reform in Zengbu, was carried out smoothly and with no real problems. The criteria for placing families in one class or another was explained publicly so that everyone understood. Each family was considered in turn. The family members themselves would suggest what class they thought they belonged to, and then the other villagers would agree or disagree and make counter suggestions. According to the cadres who carried it out, the assessment was democratic, with the principles of classification in the Agrarian Reform Law being followed closely.

In the midst of land reform Secretary Lu was asked by the work team to step in and help, since the team had found that most of the poor peasants they had chosen as the backbone elements of the peasants' association were illiterate and hence incapable of keeping written records or understanding the regulations governing the assignment of class status. The poor, uneducated peasants and landless laborers knew the world of their village very well, but they did not understand Revolutionary theory and could not put it into practice. Lu, although still smarting from being summarily thrown out of office, agreed to help, but he refused to take a formal office in the peasants' association.

The result of the classification of all the Zengbu families was as shown in table 1. Of the three Zengbu villages, the class distribution of the population in Pondside and Lu's Home villages were quite similar, with 38 percent in Pondside and 41 percent in Lu's Home classified as poor peasants. Twenty-four percent of Pondside villagers and 26 percent of Lu's Home villagers were classified as nonagricultural workers. Sandhill differed from the other two villages in having 66 per cent of its population classified as poor peasants, and only 13 per cent as nonagricultural workers.

Most of the people accepted their class assignments without much protest because they were placed in the lower categories where people had everything to gain and nothing to lose. It was those classified as landlords or rich peasants who would later have their excess property confiscated and redistributed to the poorer people.

Table 1. *Percentage of Zengbu families in each class status*

| Classification | Percentage |
| --- | --- |
| Landlords | 5 |
| Rich peasants | 0 |
| Middle peasants | 8 |
| (Poor and) Lower middle peasants | 3 |
| Poor peasants | 52 |
| Farm laborers | 4 |
| Small landowners | 1 |
| Workers | 20 |
| Small peddlers | 4 |
| Handicraft workers | 0 |
| Small merchants | 0 |
| Professionals | 0 |
| Religious practitioners | 0 |
| Vagabonds | 2 |
| Poor people | 0 |
| Former bureaucrats | 0 |
| | Total 99% |

*Source*: Household registration books of Zengbu brigade. The classifications with 0% (due to rounding off) actually contain at least one household

In Chashan commune as a whole, about 7·4 percent (393) of the households were classified as landlords and 2 percent (92) as rich peasants. Some of those classified as landlords vigorously objected to being placed in that category. Even though they formally fitted the criteria for membership in the landlord class, they felt that they had never done anything wrong and that they had never exploited people. One of the landlords succeeded in getting his classification changed to rich peasant, and a few were changed from landlord to merchant, but generally the classifications were upheld.

Once the villagers had been classified, the work team and the peasants' association began the "struggle against the landlords," (*douzheng dizhu*) initiating a period of revolutionary terror.

To prepare for the struggle against the landlords, the cadres held further meetings to educate the peasants about the exploitative nature of the landlords and rich peasants and how these classes were responsible for their misery in the old society. At first the poor peasants were loath to speak out directly against the landlords, and it was only with difficulty that the cadres were able to convince them that they would not endanger themselves by speaking out, and that they would actually receive expropriated land from the wealthy.

But finally the peasants began to discuss their local situation in class terms. There was a resonance between the way local villagers traditionally saw the world as divided between the rich and the poor and the ideology of class exploitation advanced by the party cadres. It was not at all foreign for the peasants to look at their social world in this way, since resentment of the wealthy by the poor was never far beneath the surface of Zengbu's traditional social life. Even the supernatural world of the pre-Liberation Zengbu peasants reflected the class structure, containing hungry wandering ghosts, usually from poor families, who kidnaped the souls of living humans and held them for ransom (J. M. Potter 1970). All the appropriate emotions – envy, hatred, resentment, and greed – were already present. Only the terminology was new, and the sense that the social world might be modified for the better.

When struggle meetings against the landlords were held, the militiamen were sent out to arrest them and take them to the open field at the intersection of the Zengbu village territories, where the brigade headquarters now stands. The landlords' wives and children under 18 were not required to come to the meeting unless they had personally financially exploited or physically beaten the poor peasants. Zengbu and the nearby villages that now comprise adjoining Lubian brigade (see map 4) participated jointly in the struggle meetings. Over three-quarters of the entire population of Zengbu and Lubian – several thousand in all – gathered to criticize and denounce the landlords as exploiters and class enemies and to speak bitterness against those who had committed crimes against the common people. The guiding slogan of the struggle sessions was "The poor and middle peasants are one family; the enemy are the landlords." This slogan symbolically redefined the landlords, excluding them from the category of kinsmen (to whom the villagers owed loyalty), and placing them in the category of class enemies and outsiders towards whom harsh treatment could be morally justified.

The landlord families stood with heads bowed, and quivering with fear, on a temporary stage built in the open field from tables, while the chairmen of the peasants' associations sat at desks, and peasants crowded around. At first the poor peasants were reluctant to speak out directly against the landlords because these people were kinsmen. They were also inhibited by the remnants of paternalism; some of these people had been their patrons. They were accustomed to deferring to them; they were accustomed to fearing them. But the work team urged the peasants to come forward, and the leaders of the peasants' associations were the first to speak out, setting the example, so the peasants began to tell how they had been beaten and robbed by the landlords, overcharged in rent and interest, and had seen their families destroyed by the landlords' rapaciousness. With tears streaming down their faces, they angrily shouted accusations at the landlords and came up to the stage to beat them. Nephew spoke out against uncle, and members of the same lineage branch spoke out against their close kinsmen. "Lineage branch membership did not matter anymore," as several witnesses put it. All the old structural oppositions in the traditional society between slave and free, rich and poor, and strong and weak lineage branches, were expressed in the struggle meetings. Feelings ran very high and the crowds screamed at the landlords and struck them.

Emotions rose even higher when the most hated landlord-despots were brought before the crowd. Five of the Lu's Home village landlords from the most powerful subbranch of the Lu lineage were especially hated and detested. One of these was Lu Wensing. He had controlled a gang of armed thugs whom he had paid to commit murders for him. Wensing was a supporter of the Guomindang, and one victim had been a member of the East River Guerrillas. A second victim had been one of his own hired laborers, whom he had ordered beaten to death for stealing 10 *jin* (5 kilograms) of unhusked rice to feed his hungry family. A third victim had been a friend from another village. This man had lost money gambling, and to pay his debts he had stolen and sold Wensing's pistol. For this theft, Wensing had ordered him beaten to death. In addition to being responsible for three murders, Wensing had been a moneylender. He had charged desperate people such high interest that they could never repay their loans. He took the land which they had given as security. The sense of the struggle meeting was that the confiscation of debtors' land indirectly killed people by impoverishing them beyond all hope, so that they had to sell their sons and daughters as a last resort, and then very likely starve to death.

Lu Wensing was also denounced as an oppressor by Lu Futian, a former beggar from Wensing's own lineage branch. At the struggle meeting, Lu Futian told how Wensing had coveted a house site and litchi trees with a yield of 500 *jin* a year which had been inherited by Futian's uncle. Lu Wensing had wanted to build a house on the site and to have the trees for his own. With his pistol, Wensing had beaten Futian's uncle until he agreed to give up the property. Futian was only 12 years of age at the time. He had shouted to his uncle to let Wensing have the land and the trees, and vowed that they would get them back someday. When Wensing heard this, he had beaten Futian, and Futian had picked up a rock to throw at the landlord. The infuriated Wensing shot at the boy, narrowly missing him. Futian had had to flee the village and become a wandering beggar. At the struggle meeting Futian angrily told his story while Wensing was on stage. Others told how Wensing had raped a local woman. Futian, who was a member of the militia, and who had earlier been restrained by the work team from shooting Wensing, gathered 500 signatures on a petition to sentence the despot to death.

The second hated bully from Lu's Home village was Lu Yaotang. Yaotang was called a "termite of the ancestral hall" because, with the support of his two brothers and many uncles and cousins, he had swindled money from the ancestral estates which he controlled. His eldest son worked as a Guomindang official, and a relative by marriage of his son was also a Guomindang official in Guangzhou. These official connections gave Yaotang local power and influence, which he used to control the village. He was said by the cadres to have "indirectly killed" people by taking their property and destroying their families. He was so powerful in his ancestral hall that he took as many as 18 shares of pork from the ancestral sacrifices, even though elders were usually entitled to only 2 shares.

Of the five landlord-despots from Lu's Home village, the people's court at Wentang sentenced Wensing and Yaotang to death and they were taken out and shot. The others were sentenced to prison terms.

The only landlord-despot in Pondside village was Liu Ken, nicknamed "Big King Ken," because he was powerful enough to dominate the entire village. Big King Ken did not own property of his own, but he rented a vast amount of land from a Pondside ancestral hall and then sublet it to others, charging high rents and pocketing the difference. Ken was a local bully who headed a gang of thugs and was an opium addict besides. The villagers were much afraid of him. Seeing the writing on the wall, he fled to Hong Kong before land reform, and thus escaped the peasants' wrath.

Two of the eight Sandhill village landlords on the stage that day were considered especially oppressive. Liu Chan had tyrannized his fellow villagers when he served as village head under the Guomindang government. Knowing that he was much hated and that the new government would not look favorably on a man who had served the previous one, he ran away to Hong Kong after Liberation. Apparently even his Hong Kong relatives would have no part of him and refused to take him in. So, to keep from starving, he had to return to the village. He was accused of "indirectly" killing people by using his official position to exploit them and steal their property, thus causing many to sell their children and starve to death.

Liu Wenhao was the second most widely hated of the Sandhill landlords. A local bully, he had personally ordered his thugs to kill several villagers. Both Liu Chan and Liu Wenhao were convicted of being guilty of direct or indirect murder by the Zengbu peasants' association and sent to the district government at Dongguan. The people's court there upheld the Zengbu decision, and the two men were taken out and executed.

In these meetings, final decisions about a case were left to the higher-level people's courts. The purpose of the meeting was to express bitterness against hated people in a public context. Some landlords were less hated than others; if the amount of their property was less enviable, and if they had acquired it without overt rapaciousness or the use of physical force, they did not draw the same level of resentment. In pre-revolutionary China, however, one did not usually acquire and maintain property by gentle means, and villagers had enormous arrears of resentment to make up. The most hated landlords were beaten as they stood before the crowd and some were ritually humiliated by the defilement of having to kneel while menstruating women stepped over them. In this extraordinary setting, with its explosive expression of emotions that had been dangerous or impermissible, people acted from many motives. Some relished the opportunity to receive validation at least for the grievances they felt from longstanding injuries. Some used the chance to gain vengeance against old enemies. Some saw in these specific landlords examples of the exploitativeness of the ruling class; leaders encouraged this depersonalized and comparatively idealistic way of thinking about it. As in any political movement, many wishes and emotions were swept along together in the social momentum, and the political movement was used to serve a variety of ends.

After the struggle meetings, the peasants' association cadres confiscated all the landlords' land and excess housing, as well as fishponds, orchards, farm animals, and farm tools. The cadres calculated the degree to which each landlord was deemed to have been exploitative, and ordered that a proportionate amount of grain be delivered to the poorer peasants; this was called "settling accounts" (suanzhang) with the landlords. The amount asked of each landlord was arbitrary, based on the peasants' association's assessment of what the landlord would be able to pay. Many landlords, however, had to borrow from friends and relatives to make up the required amount.

This penalty precipitated an incident which sobered everyone. A widow named Jinxing who lived in Pondside village had owned over 10 mu of land and 1 mu of fishponds, plus a flock of geese that she raised to sell commercially. She had worked this property with the help of one son and a hired laborer. Her husband had died just before land reform. Although she had never oppressed anyone and was not a hated figure in the village, she fitted the criteria of a landlord and was so classified. Left to face the villagers by herself, she was ordered to deliver a large amount of grain to the peasants' association for distribution to the poor and landless peasants. She did not have enough money to buy that much grain herself, and her husband's relatives and friends refused to lend her as much as she would need. In despair, and half-mad from fear of what would happen to her if she failed to come up with the "exploited grain," she committed suicide. The cadres consider this incident a tragic and unnecessary mistake, and speak about it now with sorrow, saying that there was certainly no need for her to kill herself. But clearly the struggle against the landlords, the execution of some, and the general confiscation of landlord property, produced an extremely frightening social setting in which some, like this widow, could not bear the strain and were driven to suicide.

To make sure that the landlords were not hiding anything, the peasants' association and the militia ransacked their houses, taking "surplus" furniture, clothes, money, and whatever else they could find. Things got out of hand during the frantic and disorganized searches, as members of the militia and the association argued among themselves about who should get the things taken from the landlords. However, Secretary Lu, who had resumed an active leadership role in Zengbu, took a strong stand against mindless looting and restored the association's actions to a creditable level.

The violation of accepted mores implied in the ransacking of the landlords' houses terrified the ransackers as well as the landlords. Lu Yongbao's older brother was a member of the militia and participated in the searches of landlords' houses in his village. The experience so upset him that he became mentally deranged, paralyzed by the fear that the landlords would somehow regain power and take revenge on him.

The peasants' association confiscated all the property that had been the landlords', all the land and property that had belonged to the ancestral estates, and all the property attached to the village temples (of which each village had at least one). It was then given to land distribution groups representing different sections of the Zengbu villages for redistribution. Each group calculated how many people in its section were entitled to shares (everyone who was willing to work was), how much property there was to distribute, and how much each share would be worth.

In order to do this, the value of the estimated yield of land and fishponds was expressed as a quantity of unhusked rice, which was regarded as the most useful standard for measuring value. Land was divided into four grades, each of which was estimated to yield a certain number of *jin* of unhusked rice per year, the lower grades yielding less. The absolute quantity of land was not so important to the peasants as its expected yield. The estimated yield of fishponds was also converted into a value of unhusked rice; 1 *mu* of the best fishponds was expected to yield the value of 800 *jin* of unhusked rice per year, and 1 *mu* of the less productive fishponds was valued at 400 *jin*.

Each land distribution group calculated the total value in unhusked rice of the property for which it was responsible. Then the total was divided by the number of people who were to be given a share. This showed the value of each person's share, and allowed the group to calculate each household's allotment. (Property was distributed to households rather than individuals, although calculated on a per capita basis.) The groups also decided which households were to be given first choice and more of the better grades of land in their allotments and which were to be given later choices and more of the worse grades. Poor peasants who had always farmed in the village for their living were given first choice. Middle peasants were allowed to keep the land they had farmed and to supplement their holdings with additional land to bring them up to the average. Workers who returned from towns and cities to get a share of land were given the third choice. Finally, landlords were given their share, but they received the worst-quality land and had the lowest priority.

The average amount of land distributed to each person in Zengbu was

2. A branch ancestral hall, distributed to private households during land reform and later cut in half for building materials

about 1 *mu*, in parcels of different quality. In Pondside village, for example, one person's share consisted of either rice land or fishponds, or a combination of the two, that yielded the value of approximately 1,000 *jin* of unhusked rice per year; figures for the other two villages are comparable.

Since fishponds could not be physically divided as easily as plots of land, the ponds were given to groups of eight to ten families per pond, to manage jointly. The households owning shares in a pond formed what was in effect a small agricultural production cooperative, which foreshadowed the cooperatives organized a few years later. Each household shared the labor and management of the ponds, and they shared the fish produced.

The total expected production of the litchi trees was also divided by the number of persons who were to receive shares in them. This yielded a figure for the weight of litchis per share. Then enough trees were distributed to each household to produce the weight of litchis to which the household was entitled. The rice, farm tools, animals, and clothes of the landlords were distributed as equitably as possible. Families with no farm animals or farm tools to use in working their newly acquired land, were given confiscated animals and tools, or the money to buy them.

The branch ancestral halls, the village temples, and the extra houses confiscated from the landlords, were divided up as housing for the poorest peasants who had no homes of their own, the larger halls and houses being divided by adding interior walls. Some families dismantled their shares of allotted dwellings and rebuilt using the old materials in new arrangements. This resulted in a few half-buildings that still stand in the villages.

Land reform was completed in Zengbu by the end of 1952. It was a period with two interrelated kinds of consequences: the consequences for those who received more than they had ever had and the consequences for those who now had less than before, and had been redefined as a stigmatized class. Eight out of ten Zengbu families received at least some property during the general distribution at land reform. The family of Lu Yongbao is one example. Before Liberation he had farmed 5 *mu* of rented land and 1 *mu* of his own with his father and older brother. As rent, they paid 40 percent of their crop to the landlord. They were so poor that his mother had to go to work in Hong Kong as a coolie to make ends meet. At land reform Yongbao and his extended family were given 9 *mu* of land in addition to their 1 *mu*. Yongbao told of his feelings after he had been given his land:

Our lives were much better then. Now we had land of our own and we did not have to pay rent. Everyone in the village was pleased. Before, only 30 or 40 households in the village owned any land at all, and most of them owned only small bits and pieces. Now many people had land; and 50 households received houses too, including some private ancestral halls which the cadres had divided up as dwellings for those who had no houses.

The redistribution of wealth eliminated the landless tenants and workers at the bottom of the Zengbu class hierarchy, making them into poor or lower-middle peasants with land and dwellings. The economic circumstances of the poorer people of Zengbu, whose lives had been miserable during the two decades before Liberation, were much improved, and they were pleased.

Former landlords were not so well pleased with the new order. Not only had they been subjected to struggle meetings and the confiscation of most of their property, but they had become a despised group, subject to many restrictions. They could not continue in school past the primary grades. They could not join the Young Communist League or the Communist party, nor could they serve as cadres or enter the army. Thus all avenues of social mobility in the new society were closed to them. Under the team system of ensuing years, the number of "voluntary workpoints" which each team member was supposed to donate to the collective for public works was doubled for landlords. Landlords were subjected to periodic harassment by being called before meetings as representatives of the old "class enemies." The cadres watched them closely to see that they were not engaging in sabotage or acting as Guomindang spies. Every spring, from 1953 to 1976, they had to clean the villages before the Spring Festival (the old New Year's festival). A similar job (clearing the village of polluting materials) had been performed by the former slave caste, so it was a humiliation as well as a task. In short, the landlords had become the new embodiers of despised status in the village, and served the social function of witches and scapegoats.

One landlord from Pondside village was in his mid-twenties at the time of land reform; his father had died earlier, leaving him, his mother, and several younger siblings. They owned about 20 *mu* of land (about 1 ½ hectares), most of which they worked themselves, and 10 *mu* (just under a hectare) of fishponds, which they rented out. The family also owned two to three hundred geese, which they raised with the aid of three hired laborers. At land reform the family was classified as commercial landlords. The peasants' association and the work team said that they had exploited the labor of other people and had extracted rent from their tenants. According to this landlord, he did make money from the geese but very little from the land and the fishponds, and since he paid fair wages he never felt that he was an exploiter. He says now that the main reason they classified him as a landlord was that he had hired the three laborers.

The peasants' association confiscated his family house and one of the sheds, in which he stored firewood, leaving him with three sheds which he had used to house his geese. He rebuilt one of them to serve as his family house and kept the other two for his geese. They confiscated all his land and fishponds, leaving him only his geese, from which he has made a living ever since. The association assigned him a quota of 350 *dan* (17,500 kilograms) of rice to deliver to them in symbolic repayment of the grain he was supposed to have exploited from poor villagers in the past. By selling most of his geese and borrowing money from friends and relatives, he managed to raise enough money to purchase the requisite amount from the rice shops.

At least one of the landlords from Lu's Home village, a man arrested by Secretary Lu, was impenitent. He was sentenced to ten years in prison for his crimes, but was released after serving only five years. In 1957, after he returned to the village from prison, this man is said to have threatened to kill Secretary Lu, and to have attempted to rape a neighbor woman. For this he was again sent to prison where he stayed for many years. Emerging from prison, he returned to Lu's Home, where he made a living growing vegetables. Soon after his return he either became mentally unbalanced or (in the opinion of some of the cadres) pretended that he had, and went around the village saying that Chiang Kai-shek (the leader of the Guomindang) was going to return to eat moon cakes in Zengbu and would kill all those who had destroyed him. Because of his incorrigibility and their fears for the life of Secretary Lu, the local cadres restricted him to his house, where he remained until he died in the early 1970s.

The former landlords of Zengbu were pleased when in 1979 the government finally decided to "take off the caps of the landlords" and end the discrimination against them that had been in force since Liberation. Originally, the class labels were supposed to have been lifted after five years if the class enemies had practiced good behavior, but in fact the labels had remained in place for 27 years. In the future, landlords were to be like everybody else; and their children were to have the same educational opportunities. The party branch secretary said, in 1979, that it would be permissible for the children of landlords to become cadres now that the policy had changed.

The social effects of land reform can hardly be overemphasized. Traditionally, and increasingly after the middle of the nineteenth century when the power of the Qing dynasty began to weaken, Chinese villagers had been accustomed to organizing their own affairs in the context of their families, lineages, and villages – under the control of the local landlord-officials. The direct power of the imperial government had rested lightly on the countryside, with a bureaucracy so small that for all practical purposes government did not interfere at the local level as long as order was maintained and taxes were paid. It was the direct power of the landlord-gentry, which assisted the state in keeping order, and, in this part of China even collected the taxes, which rested heavily on the villagers. The peasants, in direct contact with the landlord-gentry, and only in indirect contact with the government, were always suspicious of the latter, and had as little to do with it as possible. Now a new concept of China as a nation state, with a government embodying and representing the interests of the entire Chinese people and responsible for their welfare had arisen, and was being set in place. The landlord-bureaucrat-local despot class which had dominated Zengbu before Liberation had been eliminated, and power, prestige, and wealth forcibly stripped from them. They had traditionally been a Janus-faced buffer group, mediating between the peasants and the state and obstructing any reform that threatened their class interests. But with the elimination of the landlord group, the state was free to extend its power directly into the villages in a way that had never been done in the old society.

During land reform, the power vacuum created by the destruction of the landlord class was filled by the new cadres and by the cooperatives, women's associations, and other state organizations under cadre supervision. These were structures that enabled the state to control the peasants more directly, rather than via the landlord-gentry class, and to carry out with as little hindrance as possible its rural social and economic development program. This was an important structural change.

Simultaneously, other major structural changes were taking place in Zengbu society. With the disappearance of their property base, the lineage and lineage branches effectively ceased to exist as corporate groups. Their economic, political, legal, military, and religious functions were taken over by the state and its local cadres. Slavery as an institution was also eliminated at this time. The Zengbu slaves, who had previously been singled out by their different surnames, all changed their surnames to Lu and Liu, the names of the dominant lineages in the villages where they lived, and from that time forward held the status of ordinary members of the community.

It is important to note that land reform in Zengbu was a creative rather than a destructive movement. The peasants were welded into a coherent power-holding community. The work teams assisted them to organize themselves anew, without the interference of those who had ruled the community in the past, educated them to raise their consciousness, and then insisted that they actively participate in the class struggle against the landlords and the despots. The idea was that only through revolutionary praxis could the peasants truly emancipate themselves from the values and ideas of the old society and learn to think of themselves as potent social actors. The leaders of the new government did not send in soldiers to arrest landlords and confiscate property, but insisted that peasants carry out these acts themselves, so that they would become active participants in the revolutionary drama. The peasants were to have a material stake in the new social order, and they would have to organize themselves to play their new parts.

The momentous structural changes inaugurated by land reform meant dramatic changes for other groups as well as peasants. The new cadres, formerly the poorest and most downtrodden members of the old society, now had position, status, honor, and power; they ruled over those who had once humiliated them. The cadres were people who had every reason to help destroy the social order which in times past had oppressed them. They had every reason to see that this old order was neither preserved nor resurrected. The Zengbu cadres gained confidence during their successful struggle against the landlord-despots and their successful implementation of land reform. In these cadres the state now had allies within the villages who owed everthing to the new social order and would therefore seek to defend it, preserve it, and advance its interests.

The human costs of revolutionary change were, of course, most evident among the landlords, whose social and personal worlds were completely destroyed. As a despised pariah group scapegoated by the rest of the community, their position was not enviable. Over the ensuing decades their self-confidence would be completely eroded and they would become mostly broken people.

The effects of the structural upheaval upon villagers other than the landlords were sometimes severely traumatic, too. The Taoist priest who went mad from fear after he helped Secretary Lu arrest the local despots; the man who lost his mental stability after ransacking the houses of the landlords in his village; the landlord widow who committed suicide because she could not meet the peasants' association's demands; and the landlord who went about the village muttering that Chiang Kai-shek would return to eat moon cakes and avenge him – all are evidence of villagers breaking under the social strain of the Revolution, and there must have been many more who came near the breaking point.

During land reform a new symbolic order was created and legitimized by the work team and the peasants' association. It was an egalitarian social order which honored those who had suffered most from class domination. It replaced a social order in which the strong and the rich had bullied the poor. Landlords who had reflected in their higher levels of living and in their leisurely lives as *rentiers* the highest values of the old order were condemned; hard working cadres and peasants became the honored members of the new order. It now became a sin to exploit others and to have more than others. Egalitarianism in the social world of the village and hard work for the creation of a new, modern China became the official values and goals; nationalism was to supersede familism at the center of the new order.

Yet, examined more closely, the new egalitarian social order of the Zengbu lineage villages, in which distinctions of rich and poor had been eliminated and in which all men could now truly be brothers, was merely one manifestation of the dialectical structuring of the traditional southeastern Chinese lineage order. The old structure had rested on the interaction of two contradictory principles – one emphasizing the equality of lineage brothers, and the other the inequalities inevitably produced by competition in an enconomically and socially differentiated wider society. The new order was a manifestation of the ethic of equalitarian fraternalism of the lineage, subtly and unconsciously merged with the equalitarian ideals of socialism. In this sense, then, the new order was not so new as to be unfamiliar to the Zengbu villagers, encompassing as it did one pole of their traditional values.

In any case, however, the old power relationships had been replaced by a new order controlled by agents of a strong new state, with an ethical mandate for economic change. The stage was set for a uniquely Chinese pattern of rural development and modernization that was to astound the world.

# 3

# The ordeal of collectivization

Land reform had created a new poor and lower-middle peasant economy and society, which gave most peasants a basic means of livelihood, and certainly secured peasant support for the new government. But it was not a final solution to Zengbu's agrarian problems. If land reform were implemented merely as a clean start for private ownership, and if private ownership as an institution were allowed to continue, within one generation there would be a re-emergence of economic inequality, with rich peasants at the top of the rural economic class structure, and poor and landless peasants at the bottom, depending on the differential economic success of each family. And success would not necessarily be the result of competence: demographic variation alone would produce a re-emergence of classes, since some families would have to divide their small allotment of land among six sons, turning all of them into poor peasants in the second generation, while others would leave all their land to an only son, making him automatically a rich peasant.

At the higher levels of the Chinese government – "higher levels" being the term the peasants use to refer to the bureaucratic echelons rising above them – there began a debate over agricultural policy which has continued up to the present. Some more orthodox Marxists believed that the attainment of a collectivist socialist or communist society in rural China would not be possible until the technological and economic base was developed and modernized. Until then a peasant economy, with some rich and some poor, would have to be allowed, or else the lack of incentive for people to work hard would lead to economic stagnation. Chairman Mao, a less orthodox Marxist, who still held to the Yenan revolutionary spirit that had brought him and the Communist party to power in China, believed that the Chinese could not wait for mechanization and the creation of a scientific agriculture before they collectivized. If they accepted the existing institutional arrangements, classes would re-emerge in the countryside and a new conservative rich peasantry would arise to oppose further reform, moving China back toward the system that had existed before the Liberation, and defeating the Revolution. Mao and his supporters believed that by using ideological appeals and by manipulating rural social organization, they could successfully move forward to a new egalitarian and collectivist form of rural society; later they could develop the scientific agriculture and technology that would maintain the new social forms. This struggle over the appropriate strategy for rural development went on continually over the 24 years between the end of land reform and the death of Mao in 1976, and has by no means been finally resolved.

Initially, Mao won out, and soon after land reform, the people of Zengbu and the rest of rural China's hundreds of millions of peasants were started on a collectivist road that in 1958 would culminate in the Great Leap Forward and the agricultural communes. (See Chao 1957, Hinton 1966, Myrdal 1965, Schurmann 1966, Selden 1979, and Shue 1980, for general descriptions and comparative examples of collectivization.)

The decision to collectivize the Chinese countryside was formally announced in December 1953 (Fairbank 1979, p. 394). Mutual aid groups (*huzhuzu*) were to be the initial structural form for the implementation of collectivization. Zengbu's first mutual aid group was established by Secretary Lu Zhongzhu in Lu's Home village only one year after the conclusion of land reform. Although other mutual aid groups in the Chashan area tended to be only three or four households in size, the Lu's Home group included ten households and 40 persons. They cooperated in planting and harvesting and shared their tools. Secretary Lu was elected chairman.

The organizational processes of these early mutual aid groups were based upon the pre-existing traditional labor exchange institutions. Customarily, kinsmen, friends, and especially close patrilineal relatives had helped one another during the busier parts of the agricultural year. In Zengbu, this had meant helping with the labor of the midsummer plowing and transplanting, and the late fall harvest. Hosts traditionally furnished a meal for their labor exchange partners. Although labor was supposed to be donated voluntarily, careful informal records were kept so that the exchange between households would balance over a period of a year or two, with one full day's adult male labor in plowing or one-half day's adult female labor in transplanting seedlings, for example, being repaid by the same quality and duration of work. Chinese peasant socialism drew on the cultural background of traditional rural China. Although the government was responsible for formal ideology and policy announcements, actual implementation came from Chinese peasants working on the basis of their own experience and using solutions that seemed appropriate to them, in their own cultural context, when problems arose. This is a point that cannot be made too strongly; Chinese socialism is not a culturally rootless system without a history, but is thoroughly integrated into pre-existing cultural patterns as it is implemented.

In Sandhill and Pondside villages, mutual aid groups were not started until the close of 1954, a year later than in Lu's Home. Under Secretary Lu's leadership, Lu's Home was always more progressive and collectivist-minded than the other villages in Zengbu. The two more conservative villages of Lius always trailed a year or so behind and were more resistant to collectivization. (They were also quicker to adopt the post-Mao production responsibility system; see chapter 8.)

Sandhill village activists set up ten mutual aid groups, which averaged six or seven households each. Most groups included a balance of households, in the sense that some had a surplus of land compared to household labor power and others had a surplus of labor compared to land. Careful records were kept of how many hours of a certain quality of labor were contributed to the group by each household and this labor was paid for at the harvest. This was a reasonable way to gain mutual advantage in a system that did not permit the renting of land or the hiring of labor; and it worked well. Also, some households that did not have draft animals or tools benefited from cooperating with households that did have them.

In Pondside village Liu Puijin was the first person to organize a mutual aid group. Liu Puijin had been given some money by his sister, who had just returned from Hong Kong, and he wanted to use his money to demonstrate in some dramatic way the superiority of the socialist collective road in agriculture. He chose three other men with high political consciousness as the members of Pondside's first mutual aid group. The four households of the group owned 20 *mu* of land between them, but they had no draft animals and had great difficulty getting their rice fields plowed. Liu Puijin took money from his sister and bought a female buffalo, giving it to the poorest of the group's households to care for. The other members of the group were to pay for this service at the end of the year. The arrangement was designed to benefit the group as a whole, as well as to give additional employment to the poor family. The group later paid back Liu Puijin for his initial investment. The buffalo gave birth to a calf, which was sold, and each household of the group received more than 30 *yuan* from the sale. The buffalo was used to plow everyone's fields and the group was an economic success.

Although mutual aid groups collectivized work on a temporary basis they did not alter the structural primacy of the household as the basic unit for agricultural planning and production. During this period, the private ownership of the newly distributed land remained in force. Zengbu's peasants were free to join the mutual aid groups or not. Later, however, it became increasingly difficult to remain aloof from collectivization, as the upper levels started to put more pressure on village officials to implement collective forms.

Meanwhile, as conservative Pondside and Sandhill were slowly and tentatively taking their first steps on the collective socialist road in agriculture, Secretary Lu, in 1954, had already started operating Zengbu's first lower-level, semi–socialist, agricultural producers' cooperative (*chuji nongye shengchan hezuoshe*) in Lu's Home village.

In 1979, he described this process:

Using my mutual aid group as the backbone element, I organized a cooperative with 55 households, over 200 people, and 100 labor power units [i.e. one worker or the equivalent]. We had problems initially because, having no experience, we did not know how to assign labor properly or how to apportion the group's income equitably. These problems were solved after much hard work and after I carried out ideological education. We held meetings every night to discuss the cooperative and its problems, and the meetings often lasted well until midnight. Then we [the leaders of the cooperative] had to get up the next day, exhausted, to assign work to the collective's members. It was very arduous and time-consuming work.

Lu's lower-level agricultural cooperative was one of the first 14 established in Dongguan county and quickly became famous. Cadres were brought to Lu's Home village from all over the central and eastern parts of Guangdong province to hold on-the-spot meetings at which they discussed how they could take Secretary Lu's cooperative as an example for establishing or improving their own.

In such "lower-level cooperatives" as these, land was still privately owned. In addition to their land, each household entering the cooperative had to put up 35 *yuan*, which went into the cooperative's capital fund. If a household had no money, its members could contribute water buffaloes or farm tools instead.

A major difference between lower-level cooperatives and mutual aid groups was that, in this more highly socialized unit, the members put all their land at the collective's disposal, along with their farm equipment, cattle, and labor. Then the land was cultivated on a collective basis. The cooperative was divided into small work groups, each with a head to direct the group's efforts and keep track of the amount of labor contributed. The leaders of the cooperative, together with the leaders of the small work groups, met in the evenings to plan work for the following day. Planning of the year's crops was also done collectively, on the basis of a unified plan.

Approximately 30 percent of a household's income was calculated on the basis of the land it had contributed to the collective. The remainder of a household's income was determined by the work its members performed, measured by the number of workpoints (*gongfen*) they accumulated during the year. Workpoints were the measure of labor performed for the collective; they established the relative proportions of each individual's contribution in labor to the collective. The specific value of a workpoint could not be fixed until the collective's income had been calculated; then the total number of workpoints earned by all members were divided into the profit of the collective, to establish the current worth of one workpoint. Thus, work-

points were the basis for the distribution of the collective's income in cash
and kind at the end of each year. There was (as there has been consistently
since 1949) a sense that labor should be rewarded according to capacity to
work. However, it also seemed important to reward actual production by
paying piecework rates. Secretary Lu experimented for six months with the
organization and assignment of work on a collective basis (rather than the
household basis used in the mutual aid groups); then every worker was
assigned a workpoint rating (*difen*), which was supposed to measure the
amount of work performed in a day and the skill with which it was
accomplished. For example, an adult male laborer in his full strength might be
rated at 10 points, an older man at 8·5, and an adult woman at 8. A full day of
work was paid with the rated number of workpoints. Thus the worth of each
person as worker had a measured value.

Simultaneously, a piecework system was set up. The accomplishment of
every task in the agricultural production process was rewarded with a specific
number of workpoints; thus the worth of each task had a measured value.
The peasants knew from long experience how onerous a given task was, so
they could assign it a proportionate workpoint value. For example, varying
numbers of workpoints were given for plowing 1 *mu* of rice fields, for
transplanting 1 *mu* of seedlings, for weeding 1 *mu* of rice, or for carrying
100 *jin* of weeds to the fishponds.

Reward was calculated according to two systems simultaneously, in order
to recognize two principles at one time: the principle that inherent capacity
should be rewarded, and the principle that willingness to apply one's capacity
should also be rewarded. As the peasants saw it, strength was worth
something, and diligence was worth something: the factors might exist
separately or together, and there should be a system to calculate the value to
the collective of each factor.

Paying partially on the basis of piecework ensured that people did not get
all their possible workpoints simply for putting in time. There was, however,
a problem: neither the reward for capacity nor the reward for piecework was
directly related to the quality of the work done: an intrinsically strong person
might produce the full quantity of work as quickly and as carelessly as
possible, and be fully rewarded both for strength and for quantity produced,
yet the quality of the work might be poor. Apparently, during the initial
period of collectivization, there was a sense of enthusiasm for the new system
which tended to prevent the problems with quality that were to recur later. A
solution to the problem of the best way to reward quality remained elusive
under a wide range of economic policies.

The lower-stage agricultural cooperative was treated as the basic accounting unit. This is an extremely significant social category; it is the level on
which profits are calculated, taxes paid, and payments for land and labor
distributed. Its organization must be workable and effective. Its success

determines the success of its members. The smaller agricultural work groups, into which the cooperatives were divided, were not accounting units in this sense. They were merely record keepers, recording the amount of labor the members performed, evaluating this in members' workpoints, and reporting workpoint earnings to the leaders of the cooperatives.

The situation in Zengbu in 1955 was as follows. Lu's Home was divided into three lower-level cooperatives modeled on the original one Secretary Lu had founded in 1954. Sandhill village had amalgamated its ten smaller mutual aid groups into three larger and more permanent groups called "United groups" (*lianzu*), which incorporated about 80 percent of the Sandhill villagers. However, organizationally, these groups were not lower-level cooperatives, but an intermediate form. Pondside village had followed Sandhill's lead, combining its mutual aid groups into two large "united groups." Pondside and Sandhill were at an intermediate stage between the original small mutual aid groups and the lower-level cooperatives.

Then, in the latter part of 1955, there was an accelerated collectivization campaign at the upper levels, and Zengbu responded with a surge of activity. In November 1955, the entire village of Pondside was organized into two lower-level producers' cooperatives, based upon the existing united mutual aid groups. Similarly Sandhill turned its united mutual aid groups into three lower-level cooperatives, enlarging them and increasing the degree of collectivization.

At this point Zengbu was engulfed by the "high tide of socialist collectivization" that swept over the country. Accounts of the latter half of 1955 are as confused now as the situation must have been then. Pondside and Sandhill, which had moved from small mutual aid groups to larger mutual aid groups and then to lower-level cooperatives in less than a year, were hurried on and told to organize higher-stage agricultural producer's cooperatives by the end of 1955. The lower-level cooperatives organized by the people of Sandhill and Pondside existed for less than two months and largely on paper; they were never really put into operation. The process of collectivization was hurried and untidy but the direction was clear: the Zengbu villagers were moving to higher and more collectivized forms of agricultural cooperation.

At the end of 1955 three higher-level, fully socialist agricultural producers' cooperatives (*gaoji nongye shengchan hezuoshe*) were established in Zengbu. Each of the three largest villages was made the core of an advanced cooperative. The small hamlet of Upper Stream was incorporated into the Lu's Home cooperative. New Market, the hamlet east of Sandhill, was made a part of that village's organization.

The fact that the traditional village became the social unit of the higher-level cooperative had important implications. It meant that the new wine of social reform was being poured into the old bottles of the traditional lineage village structure. As a result, the economic and governmental power of a traditional unit would be reinforced, and familiar traditional assumptions about village governance would be invoked. The village was a larger social unit than the previously tried cooperatives; a cooperative on this larger scale might not be organizationally effective. When the cooperative unit was the whole village, it would perforce include the unwilling as well as the willing. Putting the old structure to new uses might be construed as intrinsically inimical to change. However, other dramatic reforms were introduced simultaneously. It was at this point that private ownership of land and other resources of production were finally abolished. Placing property at the collective's disposal was no longer a private decision to be rewarded with income. Land, large farm implements, buffaloes and cows, fishponds and litchi orchards, all became collective property. The sideline industries of Zengbu, (consisting at that time only of digging mud for brick and tile kilns, weaving shrimp traps, and raising flocks of geese) were taken under the cooperatives' management. The income of members was to be derived from the labor they performed.

The vast majority of the villagers – some 80 percent – were willing to join the collectives. However, households with few able-bodied workers, such as households of retired couples, or widows, or households with many small children, were afraid that their incomes would drop under the new plan. Households owning more land, more draft animals, or more farm implements than average also objected. They wanted compensation for their greater material contribution to the collective's productive means. Objections to joining the new cooperatives were not made on ideological grounds, in terms of private versus collective property: they were based upon purely practical concerns as to whether the new arrangements would increase or decrease a family's income.

The Zengbu cadres visited these reluctant families every night after work. They spoke of the superior strength that the new higher-level cooperatives were expected to have, and tried to explain the benefits of taking "the socialist road" to modernize the countryside. They said that the cooperatives would result in increased production, higher incomes, and greater security for everyone. These peasant cadres phrased their presentations not in terms of general ideological principles, for the peasants were not interested in discussing ideology, but on the immediate practical advantage of increased income to the Zengbu households.

The arguments were new, but the process of persuasion using repeated visits by local leaders was a traditional process, not an innovation of the new order, as many outsiders mistakenly suppose. To meet the objections of the families who would have to contribute a disproportionate amount of property, the cadres agreed that the collective should pay cash for tools and animals over the average amount and that the workpoints of those who contributed more than the average amount of land should be augmented over a period of several years. Thus, loss of property was compensated. Households with fewer workers were not compensated, but had to make the best of the situation. However, the cooperative promised to set aside funds to care for households of those in real need who could not support themselves.

Families were allowed to retain the ownership of the plots on which their houses were built, and small farm implements. They were allotted small garden plots on which to grow vegetables and other crops such as sugarcane and peanuts for their own consumption.

The Zengbu leaders divided up their landholdings so that each higher-level cooperative would have contiguous land, clearly separated from the land of the other village cooperatives. Previously the land of the villages had been interspersed through the countryside. Now fields of comparable grade were exchanged by the villages so that the holdings of each cooperative would be amalgamated and be discrete. The cooperatives made maps showing these holdings, with their territory demarcated into sections and all the fields in each section numbered. This consolidation was more convenient, more efficient to manage, and avoided disputes over irrigation water, since the problem of different owners of adjacent fields competing for the use of a single stream did not arise. Also, the responsibility for the building and repair of irrigation and water control works was now clearly divided among the separate village cooperatives.

The high-level cooperative was now the basic unit of agricultural management, production, and accounting. This change required the selection of leaders to shoulder the responsibility of managing the collectives. They had to plan the year's cropping patterns, assign work, keep yearly records of the workpoints earned, and manage the financial affairs of the unit. They also had to manage the industrial sidelines (fuye).

The village-wide scale was perceived as cumbersome from the point of view of management. The cadres divided each higher-level cooperative into smaller production teams, more suitable for the flexible organization of day-to-day agricultural work. Pondside divided into 4 production teams, Sandhill into 21, and Lu's Home into 18. The teams were formed on the basis of location, by dividing the village map into equal areas, rather than on the basis of kinship. There was a deliberate, conscious, and effective effort to avoid reproducing the old lineage segments and the neighborhoods associated with them. The teams were numbered in sequence from east to west.

Each team had a leader and deputy team leader, selected in general mass meetings, sometimes with nominations shouted from the floor. Most of the new team cadres were former leaders of mutual aid groups. Every evening the leaders of all the teams decided what agricultural tasks had to be done the following day. Then the leaders of each separate team went around to the houses of their members and gave individuals (not households or married couples) their assignments – some to transplant rice, some to carry fertilizer, some to repair irrigation ditches, some to dig mud, and so on. There were no separate team headquarters and no team committees, as there would be later on. Each team had only a leader and a deputy leader. Although the teams were not accounting units, they kept day-to-day records of workpoints earned, which they passed on to the accountant of the cooperative. Distribution was carried out by the cooperative as a whole.

Rewarding individuals' labor remained complicated and the state gave only general guidance. Zengbu continued to use a labor reward system (*difen*), which rewarded capacity, and the reward continued to be calculated in workpoints.

The cooperatives divided their fields into equal portions, one for each team. Each team was also given an equal amount of fertilizer, tools, draft animals, insecticides, and a grain quota to be delivered to the cooperative after harvest. If team members delivered more than their quota, they were praised; if not, they were criticized.

The cooperatives were attempting to become economically viable under inherently adverse conditions. Population was large in relation to arable land, and most of the land only produced one rice crop a year. So the problem was twofold: many mouths to feed, and many people to employ, with inadequate resources for either. No cooperative could survive on rice agriculture alone, yet local-level industrial enterprise did not exist to take up any of the slack. Two important and related changes took place in the pattern of employment at this time.

By a stroke of good fortune for the cooperatives, temporary construction laborers were needed in nearby towns and cities, and contingents of male collective members were sent to do this work. They labored not as free agents, but as continuing cooperative members. The labor of a cooperative member was defined as the property of the collective; a person was not considered as an economic entity outside the context of the economic group of which he was a part. (This rests on Chinese cultural assumptions that the self is not an isolated self, but exists most importantly in the fact of its relationships to a group.) These laborers were paid in cash, which they turned over to the cooperative, and they received credit in the form of workpoints in return. The cooperative, not the temporary employer, provided rice and other rations. Each laborer was expected to turn 3 *yuan* over to his cooperative per day, and was credited with 12 workpoints. Should the laborer manage to earn more than 3 *yuan*, he was paid a bonus equivalent to fifty percent of the extra sum earned, and 50 percent of the bonus was paid in workpoints, while the other 50 percent was paid in cash. This respected two principles: the laborer's primary obligations to the collective (shown by retaining 50 percent of his earnings over 3 *yuan* and by paying him partly in workpoints) and the extraordinary effort involved in earning more than 3 *yuan*, which was rewarded in cash. The purpose of the bonus was to motivate people to work harder, both for the benefit of the collective, and for themselves. The availability of jobs outside the cooperative provided a level of prosperity that would not have been possible on the basis of resources within the cooperative alone.

Within the cooperative, a second important change in employment patterns was taking place. The women of Zengbu began to participate in agricultural labor on a full-time basis, motivated by the workpoints offered by the collective. One important social consequence of this was that their work became of measured economic value, and the workpoints they earned demonstrated their economic worth; by contrast, work within the household, or agricultural field labor on behalf of the household (which had occurred traditionally) tended to be unmeasured, minimized, or thought of as socially invisible, when carried out by women. Making the measured value of women's work public tended to enhance their status, both within the family and in the community as a whole. When women undertook full-time field agriculture in the higher cooperative period, it was significant because for the first time, their contribution was a matter of public record; this had never been the case before, and marked an important change.

The Zengbu cooperatives operated from 1956 to 1958. Like the mutual aid teams, they did not remain in place long enough to make it possible to understand or evaluate their effects over the long term, or to allow peasants to count on them as stable economic or social structures. From the point of view of the upper levels, the cooperatives were merely an intermediate step toward larger and more collectivist forms. Chairman Mao was attempting to move rural China directly to a communist stage of society, without waiting for the establishment of the economic and technical base that Marx had always considered a prerequisite to such a development. Using ideological appeals and political power, Mao hoped to build the social and cultural superstructure first and then to create the substructure that would support it.

In order to achieve these aims, China's peasantry was collectivized into 26,000 communes. These were to be the key organizational units that would enable China to pass from socialism to communism. Communes were formed by combining many higher-level cooperatives into larger units. In China as a whole, the average population of a commune ranged from 20,000 to 30,000 people. Zengbu, however, became part of a much larger commune. In October 1958, the people of Chashan, together with over 100,000 others from four districts on both sides of the East River, were incorporated into Shilong (Stone Dragon) commune, named after the town at the intersection of the East River and the Kowloon–Canton railroad, which was to be its administrative headquarters.

Shilong commune was a social organization of an entirely different order from the Zengbu cooperatives. It contained more than twenty-five times as many people as the three Zengbu villages together. It was highly consolidated and multifunctional, in contrast to the cooperatives, which were primarily agricultural production units. As well as being responsible for agricultural production, the commune managed virtually all other administrative functions: political, social, educational, commercial, and industrial. For ease of management, the commune was divided into specialized production brigades. The agricultural brigades were generally equivalent in size to the older higher-level cooperatives, and thus, in effect, based on the village.

It is a consistent feature of Chinese administration to emphasize the importance of a particular administrative level, giving it primacy at a particular time over other levels, either larger or smaller. Levels not being emphasized remain in existence, subordinate, temporarily functionless, or null from the organizational point of view, and are available to be reactivated as it seems appropriate under ensuing policy. In this case, the new commune levels had primacy and the village/higher-level cooperative, now called the brigade, continued to exist as a structure, but at a greatly reduced level of importance.

Greater size and multifunctional administration were combined with an organizational ethic more purely and absolutely collective than the cooperatives had been. The peasants' domestic animals and private garden plots were redefined as collective property to be maintained and used by the commune. Peasants were to own only their houses, and to depend for their livelihood solely on their labor as administered by the collective. Work itself was redefined, to be thought of in military terms. Both men and women were mobilized for work in the fields. (The term mobilized, in this context, means that they went to work each morning in squads, with military drums and with red flags waving, and returned in the same military formations in the late afternoon: every able-bodied man or woman had to participate in labor.)

The effort to consolidate social functions at the highest possible level meant the implementation of new institutions, such as nurseries and kindergartens, collective dining halls, and old people's homes, which were designed to take over such traditional functions of the family as food preparation, socialization of the young, and care of the aged.

It was hoped that this highly consolidated commune would be an intrinsically efficacious form of social structure, capable of solving a wide range of problems. Large-scale planning was expected to result in more rational agricultural management, producing not merely a sufficiency of food, but the surpluses required for the provision of improved social services and industrialization as well. In preparation for this, fields were enlarged and regularized, and boundary strips were removed to facilitate mechanization. The commune began to build schools, hospitals, opera halls, and movie houses, on the assumption that they could be funded by the expected agricultural surplus. A large-scale decentralized light industry was to be developed as well. (Heavy industry remained an urban concern.) Productive labor was to be organized more efficiently, and surplus labor would be directed to large-scale capital improvements which would benefit the commune as a whole. Irrigation, flood control, and reforestation projects were planned, and a range of agricultural improvements and innovations were to be carried out efficiently under the centralized management.

The commune as a whole was the accounting unit. The former higher-level cooperatives, now brigades, served merely as units for the assignment of labor. Thus, the brigades had the same relation to the commune as the teams had had to the higher-level cooperatives. Workpoints were eliminated as measures of labor performance. Instead, men and women were divided into labor grades, with men receiving a fixed monthly salary of 4 to 5 *yuan*, and the women 3 or 4 *yuan*. Meals, medical care, and education came under the free supply system, so salaries paid for clothing and extras. People were supposed to be motivated to work hard out of loyalty to the government and out of a desire to serve the people and help build a new China. Since the commune was the basic accounting unit, Zengbu delivered its records to Shilong, where the accounting took place, and the commune's income was distributed equally to all 100,000 members. Zengbu and other former higher-level cooperatives were assigned production targets; if they over-fulfilled them they were given bonuses and recognition.

The belief that these reforms could actually be implemented effectively was based on several important assumptions. The first was the very Chinese idea, rooted in Confucianism, that appropriate social structure and appropriate administration will produce prosperity by a natural and inevitable process. The commune was to be the appropriate structure, appropriately administered, and prosperity was to be its natural result. The idea that the ideal community in rural China should be based upon a unit which included a rural town and its surrounding tributary villages, incorporating rural industry and agriculture, was not new; it had been at the basis of much Chinese thinking about the appropriate organization for rural social and economic development since the 1930s (see M. C. Yang 1945, pp. 229–249). The second assumption was that with this new appropriate administration, there would be agricultural surpluses sufficient to fund the social programs that were envisioned. This rested on a corollary assumption that peasants, if left to themselves as they had been during the cooperative period, were incapable of managing agriculture as well as higher-level administrators would be. In fact, although the new program was not implausible, on the face of it, it is clear that it embodied deeply held Chinese values suggesting that appropriate social structure would have a virtually magical efficacy in producing a prosperous social order.

Hopes ran very high indeed as the new program was introduced. People were encouraged to participate both at the level of thought and the level of action: the slogan was "Dare to think and dare to act." People were urged to break from their old defeatist ideas, and to gain confidence in their own ability to improve their lot through hard work. This invoked Chinese assumptions about work and social relationships with profound symbolic significance, and increased the level of belief and hope that accompanied the introduction of new system. Idealism ran extraordinarily high.

One villager remembers:

The people's consciousness was so high at the beginning of the Great Leap Forward that we wanted to do everything in a collective manner. There was no need even for clerks in the stores because people could be trusted to leave the correct amount for the goods they had taken.

Prosperity and appropriate social order were to bring a symbolic benefit with a profound hold on the Chinese imagination. Food was to be provided by the group to everyone in it, as needed. This meant that people were to be fundamentally taken care of and valued for their work on behalf of the collective. No longer would people go hungry after a day's exhausting labor; the familiar possibility that one might work and yet not eat was to be ended once and for all by the new social order. An important symbolic focus for these ideas was the collective dining hall, which seemed like the realization of an impossible but longed-for ideal. (For more general discussions of the symbolic significance of food, see Solomon 1971 and E. N. and M. L. Anderson 1977.) The normally cautious and withholding villagers donated building materials for new dining halls in Pondside and Sandhill in 1958. They built imposing structures, larger than the traditional ancestral halls, which still stand today.

One villager described the initial euphoria in the dining halls:

In Pondside we had a common dining hall with 12 cooks. Everyone could and did eat three, four, or even five or six times a day if they wanted. To eat as much as one wishes, in bustling company, is a very desirable circumstance.

Unfortunately, the initial euphoria did not last long, and serious problems began to emerge. For one thing, the commune did not work well as an accounting unit. It distributed a basic equal income to all the brigades under its control, regardless of their previous income, the amount and quality of their land, the effectiveness of their leadership, or how hard they worked. This was perceived as unfair by the people of Zengbu, who saw their surplus rice, fish, litchis, and other produce being hauled away to the commune. They felt they should benefit from their own surplus, rather than sharing it and only receiving free rice and food and a few *yuan* per month to meet all their living expenses. They knew that they were hardworking and well-organized and they did not want to divide the fruits of their labor and their land with other villages in the countryside. They suspected that the members of other units were not as well-organized or as hardworking as they were: if this were so, others were benefiting unfairly from Zengbu's labor and resources. Old lineage suspicions and antagonisms were re-expressed in these terms. A cooperative based upon a single lineage or, as in Zengbu, on three neigh-boring lineages, was understandable, but not a unit which included all the other lineages in the surrounding countryside, with whom there had been a traditional state of competition and even open hostilities. Land reform had not eliminated the fact that some villages were richer than others. Now these richer villages, were brought down to the same income levels as the poorer villages. The commune's equalitarianism reduced Zengbu's circumstances. Furthermore, the intervening administrative levels mediating between the peasants and the implementation of policy had been removed. Distant commune-level cadres now controlled the peasants' wealth and labor, and they felt helpless, and dangerously exposed. Skillful and hardworking villagers saw that they were receiving the same food and the same meager salary as those who did not work hard or well. Resentful, they began to go through the motions of working, rather than putting forth their best. The general level of work effort fell to that of the least enthusiastic worker, and production dropped.

Another source of serious difficulty was that the upper-level bureaucrats, who assumed that their administrative methods were superior, intervened directly in agricultural production. They overruled the time-tested methods of the peasants, and imposed their own policies, based on theory rather than practice. The peasants call this "blind orders from above," and it was one of the most disliked features of the Great Leap Forward. At the midyear planting in 1958, for example, the upper levels ordered the people of Zengbu to transplant rice seedlings into the fields in an 8 by 8 centimeter pattern, instead of the 15 by 15 centimeter pattern that is most productive. (One peasant called this the "ants coming out of a cave pattern," because the seedlings resembled an army of ants.) Local cadres refused to implement this policy, knowing by experience that it would lead to a crop disaster. The party secretary of Shilong commune came down himself to enforce the policy, and the villagers were required to follow his instructions. As a result, rice production in Zengbu fell from a level of 600 or 700 jin a crop per mu to 300 or 400 jin per mu, in the last harvest of 1958. This would have been a sufficient disaster in and of itself, but for political reasons the disaster was compoun-ded. Because of pressures from above to show that the polices of the Great Leap Forward were producing extraordinarily successful results, the local cadres were required to report to the commune and the higher levels that they were producing 1,000 jin per mu per harvest. If the cadres had not reported increases in production they would have been seriously criticized or replaced; commune was competing against commune, county against county, and province against province, to show the increased production that would prove the success of the policy. Then, the quota for the amount of grain that Zengbu was required to sell to the state was set on the basis of inflated production reports rather than the real production, and to everyone's horror little was left for the Zengbu peasants to eat. Secretary Lu, seeing that real suffering was inevitable, ordered the people of Zengbu to plant their highland fields in sweet potatoes and cassava, the foods of poverty on which the villagers survive in hard times. His foresight prevented the people of Zengbu from starving to death, but they faced a disaster of the first order.

The extent of the disaster was exacerbated by the food policy which had been the focus of such high hopes. In the fall of 1958 the government had encouraged the peasants to eat rice at three meals a day to maintain their strength for production, in spite of the fact that there was no surplus grain in the granaries at any level. Hope and belief had triumphed over reason and moderation, and now it was time to reap the consequences.

The collective dining halls are remembered with a peculiar mixture of shame and horror. According to one peasant, everyone "irresponsibly" ate whether they were hungry or not, and in 20 days they had finished almost all the rice they had, rice which should have lasted six months. When the rice was gone, the villagers had only the sweet potatoes and cassava to fall back on, and finally people were once again reduced, as they had been during the Japanese occupation, to eating thin rice gruel and herbs. Their stomachs and bodies began to swell from malnutrition. During this terrible period, the state had little grain to give the villagers because the higher levels had based their planning on the inflated reports. The only bright spot for the villagers was that they at least had the protein from their plentiful fishponds, unlike some other villages that were even harder hit.

In the midst of this disaster to the economy of Zengbu, the traditional peasant markets were discontinued for all but the sale of vegetables. And since the peasant families' garden plots had been confiscated with the coming of the communes, there were almost no vegetables to buy. The entire system of petty private enterprise that had found itself a place in the interstices of the collective economy was destroyed, and levels of living plummeted. The dining halls had their own gardens, but they did not produce as efficiently as private gardens had. People complained that frequently the vegetables in the dining halls were yellow and hard, as well as often cold by the time they were eaten.

By the middle of 1959, the peasants and cadres of Zengbu were disillusioned, sullen, and resentful. Their initial enthusiasm for the communes had turned into feelings of disillusionment and hatred. As John K. Fairbank (1979, p. 415) aptly summarizes, "Seldom has faith been frustrated on so vast a scale."

Given this sequence of events, there are two important and interrelated anthropological questions to be asked about the Great Leap Forward. The first is, what was its meaning as an event with shared cultural significance, from the point of view of the peasants who were living through it? Second, what was its actual significance from the point of view of social structure?

The Great Leap Forward drew upon Chinese cultural assumptions about the meaning of the social order, assumptions that had a deep significance and a profound importance. According to these assumptions, there existed a perfect abstract social order; the problem in governing was to discover it by theoretically appropriate means, and to apply it in practice. It would then yield a perfect social life in a perfect society. This assumption, with its Confucian overtones, existed, and continues to exist independently of, and logically prior to, any specific party policy. Right thinking would yield right social life. This assumption is perhaps more clearly understood when considered in comparison with what it does not do: the alternative assumption that appropriate social structure could or should be gradually constructed, following on experimentation, and emphasizing praxis rather than theory, is *not* used as a basis for social action. (Paradoxically, the second assumption is not used even when the appropriate theory is believed to be pure pragmatism!)

The efficacy of the theoretically correct social structures of the Great Leap Forward was assumed, and they were introduced all at once, in their entirety and on a basis of faith rather than practical testing. Then, when it became clear that the policies of the Great Leap Forward were not the perfect policies that would produce the perfect social order, they were discarded in their entirety. From the anthropological point of view, this is to ignore the possibility that a structure might have advantages and disadvantages, that it could be modified to suit a series of social purposes, that good results will not be immediate, and that structure cannot be evaluated on purely theoretical grounds and rejected for lack of a quality that might best be described as magical efficacy. In Chinese thinking, the efficacy of a new structure is a question of belief. Previous structures are not thought of as data for analysis, or as useful experiments in the reality of planned change, but as magical failures. The Great Leap Forward drew so deeply and so intensely on these assumptions, that it assumed a millenarian quality, and people believed that they were going to have a perfect social order in actual reality. The untried new structures were introduced under conditions that amounted to an organizational act of faith. The fervor and high hopes as the policy was introduced make manifest and demonstrable the essentially magical potency that is attributed to social structure, and the quasi-religious implications of organizational form.

The question of the practical structural significance of the Great Leap Forward is an interesting one. The Great Leap Forward was another in a series of changes so continual and incessant that they had the quality of flux rather than of process. The period since Liberation had been characterized throughout by the imposition of innovative structure after innovative structure, with no pause to allow the consequences of any particular change to be played out to their full amplitude. Clearly, the Great Leap Forward itself partook of this quality of flux; new structural forms that remain in place for a mere six months can scarcely be called structure at all. The most significant aspect of the Great Leap Forward was its scale. Previous flux had been small-scale, face-to-face flux. The Great Leap Forward was flux on a grand scale. All of the short-term consequences of the new system were magnified, in proportion to the large size of the basic organization, just as larger waves are formed in the ocean than in a duck pond. Moving administration to a higher and larger level meant that problems were solved more slowly, at a distance, and in general terms, rather than particular ones. This was cumbersome from the point of view of local-level administration and daily life. It eliminated the intermediate levels which mediate between the upper levels and the lower ones, and forced a direct confrontation with the "blind orders from above"; such a confrontation can be mitigated and modified if intermediate structures exist to carry out these functions.

As a millenarian movement, the Great Leap Forward had encouraged people to believe that the time was right for the achievement of a promise with fundamental symbolic significance to the Chinese; the universal provision of food in the context of the perfect social order. The belief in the strength of the new structural order was strong, and the longing to believe was stronger yet. Had these attitudes not existed, the subsequent recognition that they were unrealistic would not have been so wounding. Had the policy not been so apocalyptic, it might not have been so sweepingly rejected, so soon. In rejecting the Great Leap Forward, people were acting upon a sickening sense of disappointment. In recognizing the failure of their beliefs, they experienced an emotion that appears to have been closely akin to shame. Yet, in spite of disappointment and failure, and the certainty that this had not been the perfect social order after all, the underlying assumption that there *was* an ideal social order, and that it would shortly be understood and implemented, remained unchallenged, and this assumption formed the basis for social continuity.

In late 1959, Chairman Mao addressed a letter to all the basic-level cadres in the country. The letter advised rural cadres to ignore impractical policies handed down by the upper levels, such as the close planting policy, which had led to disaster. He advised them to refuse to tell lies in order to meet impossibly inflated production quotas, and to take a long-term and practical view towards developing collective agriculture. He tried to bring an end to the ideological and utopian "communist wind," as the policies of the Great Leap Forward were called (see Selden 1979, pp. 511–514). There is a bitter irony in this disavowal of policies which had been carried out in loyalty to himself.

The first important modifications in Great Leap Forward social structure were modifications that attacked the problem of appropriate scale. The dining halls continued to operate but efforts were made to improve them. Rice rationing was instituted to guard against the kind of shortages that the villagers had previously experienced. In 1960 the Zengbu production teams established separate dining halls. These were an improvement on the village-wide halls because their smaller size made them more easily managed and the quality of food was more easily controlled. Later, a flexible policy was adopted which allowed team members to eat either in the collective hall or take their meals at home.

Reorganization in mid-1959 created Chashan commune to replace the gigantic and unwieldy Shilong commune. This reduced the size of the commune to 25 percent of what it had been. Brigades, in general equivalent in scale to the old higher-level cooperatives, were made the accounting units. Production teams under the brigades were the units for assigning and managing work. The commune was still large but its scale had been greatly reduced, and it was no longer the accounting unit.

Although the emphasis on large-scale structures characteristic of the Great Leap Forward was clearly unworkable for many social purposes, nonetheless, it was effectively suited for others. Large-scale capital construction, particularly of flood control and irrigation works, could be better organized on this large scale. Wittfogel (1957) has argued that the existence of such projects presupposes levels of organization large and complex enough to manage them. The Great Leap Forward provided such levels, and they could and did develop and administer hydraulic works.

The centralization and increase in scale of the collective, as the Great Leap Forward started, gave local and regional cadres control over sufficient human and financial resources to build reservoirs, canals, embankments, and pumping stations for drainage and irrigation. These were desperately needed to increase production and supply food, for the population was growing by leaps and bounds, since war had yielded to peace and improved medical care had become more widely and cheaply available. Shortly after the large-scale communes were formed in 1959, the Chashan cadres, together with other cadres in the county, began to plan the remodeling of flood control and irrigation works for Shilong commune. Ambitiously they decided to dam and redirect the Hanxi river. This enormous river meandered past Chashan town through many thousand *mu* of marshland. The river was to be confined to its main channel, and the worthless marshland was to be drained and reclaimed for rice agriculture. The leaders felt that they had learned appropriate methods and techniques on the projects of 1957–8, when canals had been dug, and reservoirs built, on the upper reaches of the Hanxi River, and people of Shilong commune had participated as laborers.

These plans were laid during the time when the commune level was Shilong commune, but they were not carried out until Shilong commune had been replaced with the more workable Chashan level, in 1959. In order to understand what the project entailed, it is necessary to understand what the situation was before it was undertaken. There were 30,000 *mu* of rice land in the new Chashan commune, but of these 18,000 were flooded "nine years out of ten," as the local people say, and could not produce early crop rice at any time. This marshy land was estimated to yield only 50 *jin* of rice per *mu* annually, in comparison with the dryer land which yielded approximately 600 *jin* per *mu*, and most people felt it was not worth working. While inundated, this land was used as a source of mud for the brick and tile kilns, or as fishponds. However, even the fishponds were marginal, for their banks were frequently breached by rising waters, and the fish swept away with the flood.

The water control project had to be timed so as to fit into the rice planting cycle. The rice crop of fall, 1958, had been a disaster because of close planting according to the "blind orders from above." The first rice crop of 1959 was a good one, and at the end of 1959, the Chashan water control project was started, and the people were mobilized to work on it. Since this was after the disillusionment, people participated not primarily for idealistic reasons, but rather because the state subsidized workers on the project with food rations of one *jin* (500 grams) of sweet potatoes and 0·4 *jin* (about 100 grams) of rice a day, and they had little choice but to accept. The disillusioned villagers went unwillingly, feeling that they themselves were not likely to benefit much from their backbreaking work. The project was to start by building the embankments on the Chashan side of the Zengbu peninsula, and would most directly benefit the brigades on that side of the river. The Zengbu villagers were told that, if they helped the brigades on the Chashan side, those brigades would later reciprocate. The villagers of Zengbu feared that the promised reciprocity would never materialize. However, they set to work, along with the residents of the five other brigades along the river. They constructed an enormous dam of stone and earth across the river to the south, at the point where it entered the commune, in order to hold the waters back temporarily. Then they built huge embankments along the course of the river, forcing its meandering streams into a single controlled central channel. This project was completed in the spring of 1960, and the 7,000 *mu* of newly reclaimed marshland were planted to rice. Many of the villagers who had worked on the project were skeptical about the newly reclaimed land, and did not believe that it would really be productive. However, the rice yield in 1960 was promising, and later, when large pumps were installed to assist in draining the areas behind the dikes, the land reclaimed by this project was dry enough to yield a bumper harvest in 1961.

The portion of the project that would benefit Zengbu directly was started in the winter of the following year, 1960. As the villagers had feared, the brigades on the other side of the river failed to reciprocate the help they had already received. They did not respond when Secretary Lu announced that he was mobilizing to complete the water control project, and the people of Zengbu were left to work alone with the people of Lubian brigade, which shares the Zengbu peninsula. The people of Zengbu were so furious at this betrayal by the other four brigades that, as one cadre put it, "They almost lost faith in the Revolution." With little labor, the project took two winters to complete, rather than one. It was necessary to build ten linear kilometers of high mud and stone embankment in order to protect the Zengbu peninsula from flooding (see figure 10).

Everyone from Zengbu worked on the project, and every adult was given a quota for moving rocks and mud. Men, women, and children went to the fields with their handcarts and their bamboo carrying-poles and baskets. Nursing mothers took their babies so that they could nurse them without leaving work. Food was brought to the fields and eaten there to save time. Children helped their parents fulfill their quotas. Stones were blasted from the fields and hills. Even the foundations of many of Zengbu's old temples and ancestral halls were dismantled to furnish material for the embankments. The work was almost unbearably arduous and, quite literally, backbreaking. The peasants, who worked for three appalling winters moving mountains of rocks and dirt to build the levees, paid a high price in exhaustion and lasting physical injuries, primarily back injuries from carrying. People speak of that time almost in awe of what they were able to accomplish. Secretary Lu's leadership in pushing the project through in spite of hunger, disillusionment, and the betrayal of the other brigades is remarkable. Zengbu brigade was given congratulatory banners from the upper levels commemorating their achievement.

The results were worth the effort and the sacrifice. As well as building the embankments, in 1961, with the aid of the commune and the state, Zengbu was able to install large drainage pumps to pump the rainwater from their enclosed rice fields into the rivers. At the same time, boundary ridges dividing the fields were removed and the fields were enlarged and made suitable for tractor cultivation. The old fishponds were dug out and leveled to make rice fields and new, secure fishponds constructed. Small roads for handcarts and tractors were built at regular intervals out into the fields to facilitate the transportation of crops, fertilizers, and the products of the kilns and other rural industries. The old meandering river courses that had flowed across the peninsula were either turned into controlled canals or freed from water and converted into rice fields. A three-level irrigation system, operated with electric pumps, was built. By 1962, the land was drained, irrigated, and completely encircled with protective embankments. Zengbu was no longer poor, marshy, and marginal, but fruitful land well-suited to rice agriculture and secure from flooding. Rice production rose dramatically.

As a whole, Chashan commune's capital construction and land reclamation yielded spectacular results. All 18,000 *mu* of its marginal rice land were reclaimed and turned into protected fields, which made possible the production of two and sometimes even three crops of grain a year. The commune was no longer a rice-deficient area, but an area with rice-surplus. The commune's total production of unhusked rice doubled, from about 100,000 *dan* (5,000 tonnes) in 1957 to 205,000 *dan* in 1962.

The Great Leap Forward was a paradoxical period, in combining the massive disillusionment following a millenarian movement with equally massive and significant capital construction. Working with heavy hearts and in bitterness of spirit, the peasants nonetheless managed to complete the projects that were to form the basis of their future prosperity. If the work and the high hopes had coincided, the process might be more easily understood, but much of the work was done after the peasants had been disillusioned. Perhaps they felt that ideology had failed them, this time at least, but toil would not.

Meanwhile, the shift and flux of basic structural forms had persisted, within the larger shift of commune size. The organizational principle that consistently recurs is that there must be at least one intermediate level between the actual administrators and the people who are required to carry out their orders. Thus, if the administrative orders come from a unit larger than the brigade, the brigade stands as a single entity between the administrators and the peasants. But if the brigade itself is administering directly, it tends to split. For the big Chashan water project of 1960, the brigade amalgamated into one, standing between the higher-level administrators and the villagers; when the impetus for the 1961–2 waterworks came from Secretary Lu at the brigade level, the brigade split into smaller units so that it did not administer its own project directly, but used the teams as administrative intermediaries.

This process resembles the segmentation of lineages in segmentary opposition. Lineage segments unite in the presence of an outside threat, and split again when the outside threat becomes less important than internal factionalism. In the Chinese case, the problem is a bureaucratic problem in a complex stratified society, rather than a purely kin-based problem. The process, which can be termed bureaucratic segmentation, occurs in response not to an outside threat but in response to an administration issuing orders from above. Being activated from above rather than from outside, the process may be thought of as vertical rather than horizontal, concerned with inequality rather than with a power balance among equals. It serves the social function of providing actual leeway between the orders and the way they are carried out, by separating the order givers and the order takers by an intervening administrative level. Thus, the lower levels do not confront the upper levels with their direct refusal to carry out orders directly as given, and the bargaining from level to level which characterizes Chinese administrative process (see also the discussion of birth planning in chapter 11) becomes possible. The nature of the task being carried out, and the level directing it, produce the activation or deactivation of available structural levels beneath the administrators, in order to maintain this pattern. Thus, structure responds flexibly to praxis, producing a fluctuating organizational process. The disaster the peasants suffered under the giant Shilong commune, when, as we have seen, all the protective structures between them and the direct orders of the bureaucracy were removed, makes the peasants' efforts to place structural buffers between themselves and the higher levels of the bureaucracy seem rational and understandable.

In 1961 and 1962 structure was redefined into a three-level system. Under the three-level system, the production team was the lowest level, and also the basic accounting unit. Each team was given a proportion of village land and its own draft animals, tools, and buildings, and controlled the labor of its members. The team members were paid in workpoints, (on a piecework rather than a labor-grade basis) which gave them shares in the team's profits, to be divided at the end of the year. The brigade, the next of the three levels, became a unit of administration, party organization, and rural light industrial management, intermediate between its constituent teams and Chashan commune. The income of the brigade's own enterprises was separately accounted and used to help the separate teams, or for joint projects which benefited the brigade as a whole, like extending irrigation works, or building the brigade headquarters complex. The commune was the third level of administrative, economic, and political organization. It organized and funded projects that would benefit the commune level as a whole. The commune was the highest of the three levels that dealt directly with peasants. It was, at the same time, the lowest level of organization to administer directly the laws and policies of the state. The leading cadres at the commune level were state cadres from the national bureaucracy, rather than rural cadres administering their own native locales (see chapter 13). The three-level system proved workable and flexible.

The four years from 1962 to 1966 are remembered by Zengbu peasants and cadres as a "golden period." There are two kinds of reasons for this: material reasons and policy reasons. The material reasons were the legacy of the Great Leap Forward. The amount of arable land in the commune had been increased by 18,000 *mu*. There was an effective irrigation system, and flooding was prevented by the new flood control system. These material improvements improved the ratio of land to population, made the land able to be cultivated more effectively, and protected it from the flooding which had been a major reason for agricultural losses. Rice production shot up, both per capita and per *mu* (see figs. 4 and 5), and this would have produced increased prosperity under a wide range of possible policies.

At the same time, however, policies that were comfortable for the peasants

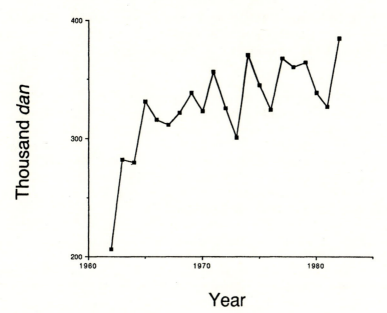

Figure 4. Chashan commune, rice production, 1962–82

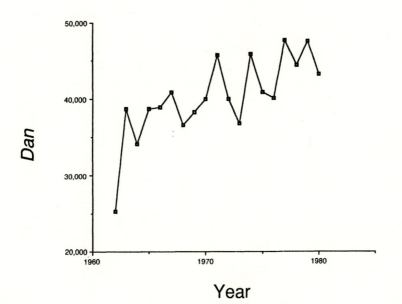

Figure 5. Zengbu brigade, rice production, 1962–80

were being implemented. Following the Great Leap Forward, Mao had lost some power and Liu Shaoqi had gained at his expense. The purist forms of collectivization which Mao preferred were no longer required. The dining halls were disbanded (like haunted houses they still stand in the villages) and rice rations were once again distributed to separate households, which prepared their own meals. Private garden plots were distributed to the peasant households, and now they could grow their own vegetables and raise their own pigs and chickens, with some hope of controlling the kind, quantity, and quality of their own food. Rural markets were once more allowed to operate. The peasants of Zengbu were told to diversify their economy, and advised to concentrate on growing commercial crops, for profit rather than subsistence. Local-level cadres had freedom to make economic decisions on the basis of their own understanding and experience. They were no longer to be subject to direct interference by the party bureaucracy. They were free to start industries on the team, brigade, and commune level.

It was clear that, given the pressure of increasing population in Zengbu and the limited supply of land, the villagers could not expect to make a really good living in the present or to improve their income in the future from agriculture alone. Local-level industry was not an adjunct, but a necessity. Under the restrictive policies in force from 1958 to 1961, villagers had not been allowed to pursue economic profit; under the new liberal rural economic policy they were encouraged to do so. During this period, Zengbu teams experimented with household responsibility systems, in which households were allotted land to work and each household could manage the land in its own way. (These experiments closely resembled the household responsibility systems currently in effect.) The peasants were happier and more prosperous. The heroic sacrifices and the nightmare ideological disappointments of the previous few years appeared to be over.

But then, in late 1966 and early 1967, another political and ideological storm descended from the upper levels and enveloped the hapless peasants once more.

# 4

# The Cultural Revolution

The Cultural Revolution was essentially a revitalization movement, a kind of millenarian movement designed to purify, intensify, and apotheosize. Its purpose was to restore the mystical vitality of the revolutionary process, which had been vitiated by practical disappointments, and to regain a lost sense of power. In its pure form, it lasted roughly from 1966 to 1969 in Zengbu. (See J. Chen 1975, Myrdal and Kessle 1970, Rice 1972, and Selden 1979, for general accounts of the Cultural Revolution; for a closer comparison with Zengbu, see the accounts of Chen village by Chan, Madsen and Unger 1984, and by Madsen 1984.) The initiative for this movement was Chairman Mao's. Ideologically, the issues at stake were similar to the issues of the Great Leap Forward: was China to strive directly for the most purely communist social forms, or would it be more expedient to temporize? The years 1962–6 had been years of temporization, under the influence of President Liu Shaoqi and his followers. Mao considered these policies to be "following the capitalist road." He thought that they would result in the re-emergence of economic classes, and that they were intrinsically counterrevolutionary for this reason. He opposed the routinization of the party's revolutionary charisma, which would take the mantle of power from dedicated Communist fighters and revolutionaries like himself and give it to professional specialists, technicians, and bureaucrats. Although his awesome prestige, authority, and charisma as China's leader had been weakened by the partial failure of his Great Leap Forward policies, it had by no means been destroyed. He wanted the Revolution to continue until Chinese society and the Chinese people were completely and irrevocably transformed and remade, a process that he knew had not yet been completed.

Supported by the politicized People's Liberation Army, Chairman Mao, in 1966, mobilized millions of youthful Red Guards and sent them all over the country. Their mission was to rekindle the messianic fervor of the Revolution in the minds of the Chinese people. The Red Guards were to attack the party apparatus and to prevent the people who supported Liu

Shaoqi from bringing about a counterrevolution. Purity of revolutionary thinking was to be restored by eliminating the feudal and foreign customs which had polluted the minds of the Chinese people, causing them to lose faith and preventing them from carrying their Revolution through to completion. With these profane elements removed, the purified revolutionary process would be able to create a truly communist society.

Since the process of purification required that evil and foreign influences be ferreted out, and since these influences were believed to be located in particular people, who were then punished for being the locus of evil, the Cultural Revolution was a scapegoating movement, or, in anthropological terms as well as more informal ones, a witch hunt. This scapegoating approach is not intrinsically inconsistent with traditional Chinese thinking, as expressed in Confucianism, which holds that for a society to be well-ordered, everyone's thinking must be harmonious with the true social doctrine; it is the enactment of the dark side of a belief system which values conformity of social thought.

In its scapegoating aspect, the movement cast the young in the role of the scapegoaters, and the routinized revolutionaries in the role of scapegoats. Party leaders were publicly denounced, humiliated, and removed from office, especially if they were foreign-trained intellectuals. Houses were ransacked; people were beaten, imprisoned, and killed. Many scapegoated people, in Zengbu and in the rest of China, committed suicide.

There was another aspect to the movement, expressing idealization, which provided a positive motivating force. This idealization consisted of the effective deification of Mao. Traditional Chinese thinking made no sharp distinction between humans and deities; successful men in pre-Liberation Zengbu were referred to as "living deities," and historical figures such as Guangong were deified after their death (see J.M. Potter 1970). Mao was made such a figure.

The Cultural Revolution is generally believed to have affected China's urban dwellers much more than it did the peasantry. However, in Chashan and Zengbu it certainly created great turmoil. From the local point of view, the Cultural Revolution began in November 1966, when a small work group was sent down from the "upper levels," to organize people to carry out the Cultural Revolution in Chashan commune. The work group organized committees in every factory in town and every brigade in the countryside, and in the town's middle school. Initially the cadres did not interpret the work group as a threat either to the social order or to themselves; it appeared that the Cultural Revolution was being carried out within the local party apparatus. When the local cadres read the "Sixteen points: guidelines for the Great Proletarian Cultural Revolution," issued by the Central Committee of the party in Beijing (see Selden 1979, p. 549–556), they believed that it would indeed be a good thing to purify the party of bad elements. They had no idea that in practice these guidelines would be used against themselves. After all, as some of them later said, everyone supported the principles of Mao's thought and was opposed to superstition. They had heard that Liu Shaoqi, the chief of state, was anti-Mao, and if he was, they believed that he should be removed. They had no clear idea of what was happening in Beijing.

The work group drew Red Guard leaders from among the leaders of the Communist Youth League, an organization which enrolled "advanced" youths between the ages of 16 and 25. The deputy secretary of each youth league branch became the head of the local Red Guards. In Zengbu, this was Lu Chuanpei, 21 years of age in 1966. He was given the task of recruiting members of the youth league, and others of poor and lower-middle peasant background, for the Red Guards. This was reminiscent (as it was intended to be) of the work of the land reform work groups in forming the peasants' association in the early years of the Revolution.

The Zengbu Red Guards, acting under the instructions of the work group, proceeded to attack the "class enemies of the people" – the former landlords, rich peasants, and "bad elements." In struggle meetings they again publicly reminded the people of the crimes of the landlords and also spoke of the landlords' possible "continuing actions against the Revolution." With a mandate to search for spies and saboteurs, the Red Guards made it a point to distinguish carefully between legitimate members of the social group and outsiders. People present in Zengbu who did not have a legal household registration in the brigade were sent back to their original villages or towns, to be investigated by their own Red Guards.

The Zengbu Red Guards went through the brigade, re-enacting a version of the revolutionary drama that had taken place over two decades previously. They were looking for remnants of the old feudal culture and for bourgeois influences. All "yellow" books, meaning those that were considered decadent and superstitious, were confiscated. Love stories were seized as immoral. Religious books were taken as symbols of superstitious feudal thinking. The old classical Chinese books, including the lineage genealogies, were also taken. These books were carried to the brigade headquarters, where they were thrown on a huge bonfire and burned.

The Red Guards held meetings to instruct the people of Zengbu about the pernicious influence of religious and magical beliefs from the old society. They took the position that there were two important objections to traditional ceremonial practices. First, the ceremonies were based on the fallacious reasoning of a superstitious view of cause and effect, and they bound people to carry out complex and useless procedures that would not ensure the health, harmony, and prosperity that were being sought. The more direct procedures of socialism might realistically be expected to accomplish the same goals as ritual, but in practical terms, and without resort to mumbo-jumbo. Secondly, the traditional rituals were expensive, as well as being useless in practical terms. This expense was defined as wasteful.

The leader of the Red Guards searched his own family's house and criticized their religious practices, in order to demonstrate commitment to his cause. He took out the ancestral tablets of his father and grandfather, believed to be the seat of their souls, and sacred, and burned them, to set an example. Had he not done so, the other Red Guards would not have followed him in destroying religious objects throughout Zengbu. Symbolically, it is clear that the activities of the Red Guards drew on resentment of parents which existed covertly but ran very deep, and were given expression in this context. There was particular concern at this time that local leadership should demonstrate its independence of family obligations and make it clear that concern for the common welfare superseded family ties.

One cadre from Lu's Home village said:

I escaped criticism during the Cultural Revolution from team members because as a team leader I always gave the heaviest, most difficult, and least remunerative work to members of my own family. I also gave them fewer workpoints than other members of the team. My wife and children frequently complained about this, but at least I was not as severely criticized as some of the other team leaders here.

Every building in Zengbu was searched, and all evidence of religious activity was destroyed or confiscated. Ancestral tablets in private houses were taken from their altars. Statues of Guanyin, the Buddhist goddess of mercy, Guangong, the deity and model of manly virtues, were also taken. The Red Guards stripped off the yellow-orange altar papers with the names of deities and the names of ancestors. The pictures of fierce guardian generals, pasted to the doors of houses in order to prevent evil spirits from kidnaping the souls of family members, were removed. The paper images of the kitchen gods, who watched over the behavior of the family, and returned to heaven at the end of the year to tell the Jade Emperor what they had seen, were torn from their places above the stove. Many houses had paper spirit seats for the *dizhu*, the guardian deities of the households. These were all removed. In the lanes, niches in the walls had held burning incense and papers inscribed "Spirit of Heaven." These were taken. Pasted on many village houses were yellow papers with the character for "luck" written on them. These were torn down. The guardian spirits of the village were removed from the altars. The ancestral tablets in the ancestral halls were taken away and the decorations were pulled down and destroyed. The village temples and their images were demolished. The village spirit mediums and the Taoist priest were ordered to stop exploiting the peasants by the practice of their false arts. The villagers were told that if they continued to burn incense and worship the gods, they would be denounced at public struggle meetings.

The efforts to eliminate traditional ritual were sweeping in scope. No longer did the young women sing the ritual songs they had learned at the women's houses, as they prepared to be married. No longer did they wear the elaborate colorful wedding costumes that had been customary. Their families and their husbands' families no longer gave the traditional ostentatious banquets. Brides no longer wore golden earrings because "in Tibet, those earrings are indications of slave status," and because money spent on earrings could be better used for more productive purposes.

The rituals surrounding death were also attacked as superstitious practices. The idea that the dead were dangerous and polluting, and that ritual specialists must be hired to deal with them, was now to be eliminated. In order to demonstrate that the dead could not harm the living by polluting them, the leader of the Red Guards and three older cadres from Lu's Home village themselves took on the performance of a funeral; they placed the body in its coffin, disposed of the ritually impure clothing and bedding associated with the corpse, and carried the coffin to the burial ground on their own shoulders. But the villagers thought that the leaders were mad to take such risks, and continued to utilize the services of funeral specialists for these polluting tasks. The cadres were not themselves entirely at ease with what they had done, and did not repeat the demonstration.

The Red Guards also carried out reforms in the commune schools. The work committee in Chashan organized Red Guards in the lower and upper-middle schools, and then the Red Guard groups took over the running of the schools. All progressive students joined. Lu Yiyong, from Lu's Home village, a boy of only 16 in 1966, was studying in Chashan middle school at the time. He was from an active revolutionary family, his father having fought with the East River guerilla group, and he became an active leader of the Red Guards in his school and even helped organize the schools in other brigades. He said:

I and most of my classmates joined voluntarily. At that time, all the newspapers wrote about the Red Guards as being an advanced organization; if you were a young person and did not join, you would have been considered backward. We criticized all the teachers for being arrogant toward the students. We criticized the teachers' family backgrounds as not being proletarian enough. We believed that nonproletarian backgrounds resulted in bourgeois influences in teaching. We investigated the family backgrounds of these people carefully, even communicating with Red Guards in their home areas to find the truth about their background. We stopped the schools and insisted upon not starting them again until all the old influences had been eliminated and a new revolutionary content had been infused into the system.

In Zengbu's schools the slogan was "Stop class and carry out the Revolution." The students criticized the teachers, especially the principal, because all persons in authority were supposed to be criticized severely. After the criticism, the principal's and the teachers' authority was no longer respected and the students disobeyed them with impunity. One woman teacher in Zengbu said:

When I first came here during the Cultural Revolution, the students would not obey the teachers. It was maddening to try to teach. No one had any heart to teach or learn. The students sang a song whose theme was "If we go to work for a few years, instead of school, we can at least earn enough money to buy a bicycle." Some said that "if you study too much you make your brain mad, and it is better to earn workpoints than to go to school."

The situation was anarchic. Textbooks and other instructional materials were burned because of their feudal and bourgeois content. The teachers were afraid to write new textbooks or develop their own teaching materials because they might be denounced; since this fear was general among educators at every level, no new materials were devised. The only safe text was the little red book of quotations from Chairman Mao.

Since the policies of the Cultural Revolution were to shorten the school term and combine labor with education, school was closed much of the time so that both the teachers and the students could carry out farm-work. The teachers were to be re-educated in revolutionary consciousness by the peasants. Teachers were transferred back to their own native villages, where their backgrounds were known, to be educated by their own peasants.

The national examinations for admission to institutions of secondary education and colleges or universities were suspended in favor of a policy of selecting worker and peasant youths, who had the proper proletarian background and the appropriate ideology.

At the end of 1966, the Cultural Revolution in Zengbu and Chashan took a new turn, changing from attacks on superstitious practices, former landlords, and educators, to an attack on the local party structure itself. This change was signaled in Zengbu when the original leaders of the Red Guard, who included the youth league leader and Secretary Lu's own daughter, failed to be invited to a meeting held by the work group in Chashan. Other, more radical leaders were selected to head Zengbu's Red Guard, and to attack the party branch committee, consisting of the old leaders of Zengbu who, in many cases, had held office since land reform. The party leaders were criticized for carrying out the "capitalist road" policies of Liu Shaoqi. The particular aspects of policy which the cadres were told they should not have carried out included Liu's Four Freedoms policy, of the initial land reform period. The Four Freedoms were the freedom to buy and sell land, to hire laborers, to issue loans, and to engage in business enterprises. Liu's later Three Freedoms and One Guarantee policies, which advocated more free markets, more private garden plots, more enterprises with sole responsibility for their own profits and losses, and fixing production quotas in agriculture on a household basis, were also defined as policies which it had been wrong to implement. The local leaders were denounced for having used incentive systems, having paid workpoints on a piecework basis, and having assigned production quotas with rewards for overproduction and fines for underproduction. These were practices that were intrinsic in the policies that had been implemented by Mao's opponents after 1961, in the effort to recover from the Great Leap Forward.

The Cultural Revolutionaries, in contrast, advocated a return to the true principles of socialism – the payment of workers by fixed daily workpoints, with no quotas and no payments for piecework. They urged an emphasis on grain production in order to make China self-sufficient, and denounced efforts to diversify local economies by establishing moneymaking local enterprises and light industries.

The veteran cadres were confused and angry. They had implemented Liu's policies in a spirit of party loyalty, under the impression that the prosperity of the overpopulated countryside would be enhanced. They felt that the criticism was unjustified. Liu Shaoqi had been the Chairman of the People's Republic of China, and they had acted as conscientious civil servants. Now they were being criticized retroactively.

The Red Guards criticized Zengbu cadres in public meetings. The cadres were interrogated during the day and forced to write out self-confessions during the evenings. They were forced to rewrite their confessions time and time again, until the Red Guards were satisfied. They were periodically required to dance the "loyalty dance" (this was a real dance, not a mere metaphor) in public, and to sing songs praising Chairman Mao before the villagers. The veteran cadres felt humiliated by the dancing and singing. Several Chashan cadres committed suicide under this pressure and loss of social face. Others were broken and never again participated in public life. Leaders were sent back to their teams to work, so that they might reform themselves through labor.

A Cultural Revolution committee was formed for the commune. It had a membership of about thirty. Party members who had previously played an active part in commune administration were excluded from the new committee, much as the existing village administrations had been excluded from village affairs by the land reform teams. Five formerly inactive members of the previous party branch committee sat on the new Cultural Revolution committee, and the rest of the members were young people elected by the brigades. For the first month of this period (in early 1967) the commune was in a state of virtual anarchy from the point of view of the practicalities of administration. The newly-elected young people lacked all practical experience in running the commune's affairs. They divided into factions, vying with one another to defend Chairman Mao, and to attack the impure still in power. As in the Great Leap Forward, they affirmed the primacy and value of thinking and theory over action and praxis, by devoting their time to these heated but abstract debates. Had they not believed that these discussions were of overriding importance, they would have distributed their attention in more practical directions. As in the Great Leap Forward, there appears the assumption that right thinking has a magical efficacy in producing right governance. The commune remained, for all practical purposes, ungoverned.

To resolve this situation, which was general throughout the country, an army committee was set up in Dongguan city, at the county level, to maintain order. In mid-1967 this committee sent an army cadre down to Chashan to establish a new leadership group for the commune. This group was dominated by the army cadre. It also included the Red Guard cadres, and some former party leaders of the commune who had been "rehabilitated."

According to cadres who participated in this group, the army officer held the real power. The day-to-day administration was carried on by a rehabilitated former member of the Party Branch Standing Committee. This cadre did his best to hold the commune together and keep production going, despite what he felt was interference from the army man, who knew nothing about local affairs and yet refused to take advice. The army man was resented as an outsider to such an extent that home-grown anarchy appeared almost preferable to the local leaders than imported order.

It was also necessary to administer while respecting the radical young Red Guards, who were badly factionalized. A committee to oversee production was established, but a permit had to be obtained from this group before any decision could be made, a very cumbersome process. The necessity to refer all decisions to a single valid decision-making body, which was believed to represent "the masses" more truly than lower-order decision-making levels, mirrored exactly the pattern of the Great Leap Forward, and produced similar administrative difficulties. The purest of right thinking, even when a single definition of this could be agreed upon, did not necessarily provide the most useful answers to routine administrative problems. Conditions continued to be chaotic and production suffered. Furthermore, the Red Guards continued to be deeply divided. They split into two groups, the East Wind rebels and the Red Flag faction, both of which split again into still smaller factions. These factions, in what must have been a triumph of unstable compromise, formed into an uneasy alliance, called the Chashan Commune Revolutionary Rebels' Federation (*Chashan gongshe geming zaofaanpai lianhehui*), rather than engaging in armed conflict, as happened elsewhere in Guangdong. For a year or more, these groups ran the commune with the army officer. This cooperative government by the Red Guards and the army lasted for about a year. In November, 1968, a revolutionary committee was set up on the county level, to take the place of the army committee of 1967. Then, in March, 1969, Chashan commune established its own revolutionary committee. This committee contained the same three elements as the 1967 leadership group: the army, the Red Guards, and a few rehabilitated cadres.

During this time, conditions in Zengbu itself were also unstable to the point of being anarchic. Most of the young leaders were too young to command the respect of the villagers, and some of them were actually unable to carry out their work; the new accountant, for example, did not know how to do the accounts on which the team organization was so heavily dependent. One successful young woman cadre organized boat races between the brigades, on the analogy of the traditional dragon-boat races, except that the boats were sampans instead of the traditional long-dragon-boats (see chapter 12), and women as well as men were allowed to participate; these were greatly enjoyed. But generally speaking, the leadership of the period was carried out in an atmosphere of moral recrimination, inexperience, and high abstract sentiment that left the villagers feeling inappropriately governed and at a loss.

The moral model which was supposed to inspire the villagers at this time was Dazhai, a brigade in Shanxi province in north China, and the slogan "In agriculture learn from Dazhai" was painted in large red characters over the walls in Zengbu. The Dazhai system stressed the importance of self-reliance for each local community, and emphasized that villagers were expected to overcome hardship and natural disasters on their own. Politics was to be in command of economics. People were supposed to be motivated to work hard for the collective because of their ideological commitment rather than by reason of material incentives. The collective interest was to come first. The labor reward system practiced by Dazhai became the model for Zengbu and the entire country. It was based upon "pacesetter workpoints, personal reporting, and public assessment" (Chen Yangui, in Selden 1979, p. 612). The hardest working, most skillful, and most dedicated workers were chosen as the pacesetter model workers for a month. They were awarded a certain number of workpoints for a day's work. At the end of each month, the other members, in democratic assembly, measured themselves against the model workers and suggested the number of workpoints (usually less than the model workers') that they should be paid per day. The assembled peasants discussed the personal reports, raising or lowering or agreeing with the number of workpoints suggested. Workpoints were then recorded on a monthly basis, which made it unnecessary for the cadres to record workpoints every day or to inspect everyone's work, thus saving administrative time. An advantage to this system was supposed to be that everyone's attention was not fixed upon workpoints (as it would be in a piecework system), leaving workers free to concentrate on doing their job well.

Under every economic system tried in Zengbu since 1949, quality had been a major problem. A range of solutions to this problem of quality had been attempted, from the ideological to the solidly material. This purely ideological solution was the most extreme. However, Zengbu peasants continued to think of measurable work in terms of quantity; quality struck them as less relevant and they did not strive for it, particularly if they had to reduce the quantity of output to do so. As a way of ensuring high-quality work, the Dazhai plan was ineffectual.

Another facet of the Dazhai system as practiced in Zengbu was a return to the emphasis on grain growing and de-emphasis on commercial crops. People concentrated on collective agriculture and not on private plots, household sidelines, and team and brigade-operated rural industry; all of which were defined as capitalist and frowned upon. Rural markets were discouraged, and during these years very little was offered for sale.

This policy was economically unworkable in Zengbu. A brigade with a growing population and only about one-half *mu* per capita could not make a good living from agriculture alone, but depended upon the development of team, brigade, and commune industries. Developing brigade and team industries in Zengbu was criticized on ideological grounds, yet without nonagricultural income, the brigade could not prosper. And even in terms of purely agricultural choices, the villagers were restricted in ways that seemed economically unreasonable to them. For example, they were required by the upper levels, which were emphasizing the importance of growing grain, to fill in some of their productive and profitable fishponds in order to increase rice production. The villagers thought this policy was another example of "blind orders from above."

In 1969, the Brigade sent up a request that Secretary Lu be restored to his position as brigade secretary. It is difficult to guess what lay behind this; he had already been denounced and humiliated, so there would have been no need to have him back, but he was strong enough, and had the fundamental respect of his fellow villagers to a degree that made it possible for him to govern effectively. Also, he was senior enough to command respect, and the villagers were uncomfortable with government by cadres who were junior to themselves in age. The commune agreed to Secretary Lu's return. From 1969, he ran the brigade, following the Cultural Revolution policies, but restoring demoralized former cadres to power, and emphasizing the importance of maintaining social order, "opposing anarchy," and emphasizing the importance of obeying the leaders, particularly with regard to work assignments and production.

By 1971, the party as such was once again the most significant organizational element in local government, with the army no longer an important factor. The party leadership had been seriously demoralized, and many former leaders would not return. Those who were still willing to serve began to regroup, however. Some of the former Red Guards had been assimilated into the mainstream party structure, and the Red Guard groups had been routinized into the regenerated party organization. Attention began to focus once more on production, rather than on revitalization and ideological purity. The people of Zengbu were tired of disruption and disorder; they were more interested in being governed than in expressing resentment against those governing them.

The Cultural Revolutiuon centered around issues of intrinsic political significance but it was importantly fueled by the socially sanctioned opportunity it provided to express malice, and to humiliate people who could not legitimately be humiliated or insulted under normal circumstances. It tapped the deep Chinese ambivalence towards seniors, the old, the leaders in power, and parents. The wish to express malice toward authority figures persists as an undercurrent, as does the ambivalent resentment of authority from which it springs. Chinese political movements, whatever their formal ideological aims, tend to offer such opportunities to denounce and humiliate, which are a continuing component of political action, whatever the specific content of current ideology may be. A dialectic persists between the wish for orderly administration and a resentment of those who have the task of carrying it out.

# 5

# Maoist society: the production team

The production team (*shengchan dui*) was the most significant social structure in Zengbu from the end of the radical Great Leap Forward experiment, in 1961, until the demise of Maoist society in the early 1980s. It provided the economic, political, and social framework within which Zengbu's peasants organized their lives, and a generation of young people grew up with the understanding that this collective form of society was the locus of their efforts to earn a living.

The production team, as a corporate group, collectively controlled the social organization of production. It had exclusive rights over its share of land, and it owned the instruments and means of production – tractors and other agricultural machines and implements, fishponds, orchards, drying floors, storage buildings, and team headquarters. The team also controlled the labor power of its members. The basic organizational principle of the team was that it should maintain strict economic equality among its members and its constituent households. Labor was rewarded as a proportion of the team's profits. After the team had paid its taxes, delivered its compulsory crop quotas to the state, and set aside funds for production expenses, welfare, and capital investment, it distributed its yearly net profits to its constituent households on the basis of their contribution of labor, as measured in the number of workpoints they had earned over the course of the year. The team was also the usual source of a minimal guaranteed food supply. It sold a per capita grain ration to its member households, with the ration varying according to the age, sex, and labor power of each household's members. Peasant food rations were fairly secure, even if the team suffered a poor grain harvest, since the state guaranteed that it would make up any shortfall of grain below minimum rations, by remitting state grain purchases or by bringing grain in from areas where the harvest was better. Zengbu peasants gained guaranteed employment, and freedom from starvation; they gave up the opportunity to strive for wealth using their own resources.

From the viewpoint of the revolutionary Marxist party state, the teams

3. A production team warehouse and rice-drying ground, Lu's Home village, 1979

were instruments of revolutionary change. They were to be a framework in which socialist praxis, an active process of living and working collectively, would produce social reform in and of itself. Social experience in a new framework would destroy the ideological pillars of the old culture: familism, sexism, nepotism, blind marriages, clannishness, and superstition. The new socialist collectives would provide the basis for a new socialist society in new kinds of economic relationships; this would lead to a new culture, with new values and a new ethical system. In this new ethical system, loyalty to the team would replace loyalty to kin, village, and lineage. Parochial kinship loyalties would give way to the moral categorical imperative to treat all members of the team alike. Brothers and even fathers would be treated just like other team colleagues: no special favoritism was to be shown to one's own family or kin. These new universalistic ethics were not merely utopian; they were functionally essential to the successful operation of the team. If families or groups of kin set themselves off from the other members of the team, the resulting suspicion and distrust would disrupt the team and make it inefficient or even inoperable.

Pre-Liberation society had acted on the understanding that men were lineage brothers, but that some lineage brothers were rich and others were poor. Fraternalism as an ideal was rendered unattainable by the forces of economic stratification. The team modified this. Men were to be as brothers within the team, and economically equal within the team as well. Maoist socialism built upon the ideals of traditional lineage fraternalism, but ideals that were now to be reinforced by economic equality, rather than undermined by economic differentiation. A traditional value was to become attainable in a more perfect form. No team member was to be permitted to advance himself economically apart from his team, for this would destroy the essential equality of households within the team. The masculine emphasis of peasant social thinking is reflected in speaking of fraternalism, and in using the masculine pronoun. According to the party's program, women were to be the social and economic equals of men within the team. They were to participate in team work and team political life on the same basis as men, and would receive equal pay for equal work, breaking down the inequality between the sexes that was so much an integral part of the old society. In spite of these professed ideals, however, the inequalities between men and women were cultural artifacts so built into Chinese thinking that they were defined as "natural," rather than as social constructs subject to revolutionary change.

The team was to provide the setting in which people would optimistically and confidently take rational command of their own destinies. They would use their own land, labor, and organizational ability, and the resources of modern science and technology, as these became available, to create better lives for themselves. Thus the team would make the old superstitious world view, in which people believed that their fate depended upon luck, geomancy, and the will of ghosts and gods, unnecessary, and these beliefs would give way to a modern socialist culture. The peasants of rural China would learn the essentially Marxist humanistic doctrine that they could succeed in creating a new, modern society through their own collective efforts.

In addition to seeing the team as a revolutionary instrument of change, the state also saw it as an instrument of social control and as a framework for extracting surplus value from the peasants, to finance the industrialization and modernization of Chinese society. The Zengbu peasants were bound for life to their team. They were obligated to carry out the tasks required by the team: they had to work the team's land, produce their own rations, and deliver the team's fixed quota of grain and other agricultural products to the state at fixed low prices. The peasants had no choice but to labor in the collective fields under the direction and authority of their team leaders and the local party cadres: if they did not work, they did not eat. The cadres had great control over the lives and fortunes of their fellow villagers. Their power over the team's collective economic life reinforced the political power they wielded as representatives of the state. A cadre could fine a peasant and collect the fine by ordering a team accountant to deduct it from the peasant's team account. If a peasant annoyed a local party cadre, he might well end up wearing "shoes that pinch," that is, the cadre might give him the worst work assignments, or ensure that he and his family members never received coveted opportunities such as joining the army or going outside the village for higher education.

As a result, from the point of view of social control, Maoist Zengbu was a kind of bureaucratic feudalism, with party cadres closely controlling peasants who had been structurally immobilized in their teams. Peasants were separated from urban residents by legal restrictions creating a caste-like barrier against both geographical and social mobility that was virtually impenetrable (see chapter 15). If one was born a peasant, one remained a peasant for life and was not free to leave one's team. The structural similarities between Maoist bureaucratic serfdom and the classical forms of European feudal serfdom are clear. The Maoist peasant was fixed as firmly in his team as the serfs of feudal Europe were fixed on the manor. By fixing peasants on the land, and having the team control their labor, the Maoist state created a set of serf-like conditions more classically "feudal" than the pre-Liberation society, in which peasants controlled their own labor, and could leave their villages. Zengbu villagers were inextricably suspended in the collective social and economic webs spun by the state.

Geographically, the team was a segment of a large village, or a single tiny hamlet. In 1962, the local cadres divided the villages of Zengbu into more or less equal residential districts, and the residents of each demarcated area were assigned to one production team. But team boundaries were deliberately drawn to avoid including only members of a single lineage segment within the same team. Each of the old lineage segments was scattered over more than one team, and each team contained more than one lineage segment. Not only were lineage segments deliberately deconstructed as sociogeographical entities, but close patrilineal relatives, such as uncles, brothers, and patrilateral first cousins, were assigned to different teams. Detailed investigation of these points in Zengbu indicates beyond the possibility of doubt that conscious, deliberate, and successful action was taken to ensure that the team did not reproduce the old lineage segment under a new name. Old ties were deliberately cut in forming the teams, and new ones established. On the surface, the resultant structural form was entirely new. At a more profound level, however, the team, like the lineage segment, was an essentially Chinese social form. Both team and lineage exhibited characteristics determined by Chinese assumptions about the nature of social organization. In both, a corporate group of patrilineally related men controlled land and resources by virtue of their kinship status, with women having legitimacy only by virtue of relationship to the line of males, as daughter if unmarried, or as wife if married (see chapter 12). The creation of the team was at one level a genuine change of social order, not a mere renaming. At another level, it perpetuated by its form the structural assumptions of Chinese culture.

The commitment to dismantling the old lineage segments in Zengbu came not from the party but from the cadres themselves. The cadres who created the teams were from former poor and landless families. Their lives had been dominated by men from powerful and wealthy lineage segments in the old days, and they actively sought to avoid replicating the old exploitative lineage structures in the new production teams. As one cadre said, "We thought that the two principles of organization would be incompatible; if we had organized the teams to correspond to lineage branches, the elders would have ended up as team leaders!" In some villages, such as Chen village (Chan, Madsen, and Unger 1984, p. 32) team boundaries are reported to have been deliberately drawn so as to include only members of a single lineage segment. In Zengbu, the process was rather the reverse. The two hamlets in Zengbu which remained geographically the same after team organization as before are New Market, a mixed surname group, and Upper Stream, a tiny group divided between two surnames.

Another deep structural continuity manifested by team organization was in terms of the relationship between the person, the team, and other corporate social groups in the wider society. A person was inherently and for life a member of a corporate group, and the person was not thought of in isolation from the group. The formation of production teams divided rural China into functionally unspecialized closed corporate units, reduplicated in the millions. Relations were between corporate "units" (teams, brigades, and communes), and not between individuals or households. Team members were merged with and subordinated to their group, just as individuals had been inseparable from family and lineage in the days before Liberation; the new social form was inherently Chinese in enacting the same assumptions as the old.

It took several years for the teams to solidify into collective units which seemed stable, reliable and permanent. There was some experimentation and fluctuation in the number and size of teams, but by 1967, the teams had taken the forms that they would retain throughout the Maoist period: Sandhill was divided into six teams, Pondside into four, and Lu's Home into seven, so that Zengbu brigade had seventeen teams in all. Zengbu's production teams were designated by prefixing the village name to the team number: "Lu's Home Number 1 team," "Pondside Number 4 team," "Sandhill Number 6 team," and so on. The residents of the two small hamlets that were attached to Zengbu, New Market and Upper Stream, formed separate production teams. However, they were designated as segments of larger villages. Sandhill Number 1 team was really the team formed by the people of New Market hamlet, and Lu's Home Number 7 team was actually Upper Stream. In 1979, the population of Zengbu's teams ranged from 92 people in the smallest team to 546 people in the largest, with an average of 292 people (or about 64 households) per team. The average population of the 109 production teams in Chashan commune was 271 people per team, so the Zengbu average population per team is slightly higher than the average population of teams in the commune as a whole.

A committee administered the affairs of each production team. The committee was elected democratically by all the adult members of the team using a secret ballot. Although the size and composition of the team committee varied with the size of the team, all 17 Zengbu teams, in 1979, had the following functionaries: team leader, deputy team leader, deputy team leader for women's work, deputy team leader for finance and economy, accountant, cashier, storehouse keeper, and workpoint recorder (sometimes this function was performed by the accountant). In addition to the above, seven teams had at least one head of a major team enterprise (such as a brick kiln) on their committee; five had fishpond management group leaders; and twelve included two or more leaders of small specialized agricultural groups (*xiao zu*) which were being experimented with in two of the Zengbu villages in 1979. In addition, the larger teams – such as the giant Sandhill Number 6 team, with over 500 members – also included several members-at-large to expand the representation. A few Zengbu team committees included representatives of poor and lower-middle peasants' associations, organizations dating from the Cultural Revolution. They were on the committees to see that the team cadres paid attention to the interests of the majority of poorer people. Some teams also had a security person who guarded the team's crops and fields from theft. The security people were the Maoist equivalents of the old village guard, formerly operated under the auspices of the central ancestral hall of each village, but now operated by the teams, under the supervision of the brigade cadre in charge of security.

The team leader had a dual function: economic management and political education. He had to be a competent agricultural manager. He received the credit if his team prospered, and took the blame if it did poorly. He had to deal with conflicts arising from his own leadership and conflicts between team members, so as to keep the team working in a harmonious and productive way. The process of team management presented great difficulties in the resolution of conflict, not only within the team, but also between the team and other bureaucratic levels. Sometimes the team was faced with a conflict or contradiction between the policies of the upper levels and the economic exigencies of team life, which were mutually incompatible. Examples of this occurred during the Great Leap Forward and the Cultural Revolution. In these cases, team management had to try to cushion the team from the ill effects of such upper-level policies as mandatory close planting, and to try to ride out the storm. Thus, the team leader was in the classic position of the foreman, with the task of mediating between the peasants, on one hand, and the brigade and commune cadres, on the other. The team leader had to have the formal stature to solve these conflicts, and this meant that he must be male, senior enough to command respect, and in full possession of his physical powers, with excellent capacity to perform agricultural labor. Furthermore, he had to have the capacity to withstand criticism without having his self-confidence and self-esteem destroyed.

The deputy team leader shared the responsibility for assigning work and had a special role in supervising agricultural production groups in the fields. Like the team leader he had to be an experienced farmer in order to direct agricultural operations. The team leader and the deputy team leader met every evening in the team headquarters to plan the next day's work. During the day, the team leader and the deputy supervised work in the fields, moving from group to group. During the Maoist period, the team leader and his deputy had to spend much of their time working in the fields alongside ordinary team workers, in order to establish their legitimacy through productive labor. They were not allowed to remain in their headquarters and set themselves off from the ordinary team workers by virtue of their position. Popular and effective team leaders were those who worked hard alongside the ordinary members of their teams.

The deputy team leaders in charge of women's work were the only team leaders in Zengbu who were female. Their job was to mediate the communication of women's conditions, such as menstruation and pregnancy, that influenced their capacity to labor; a woman would feel uncomfortable communicating such matters directly to a male leader. It was considered uncivilized to assign a pregnant or menstruating woman to any labor which involved standing in water, since this was believed to harm the health and fertility of women. Nursing women were assigned to tasks which enabled them to remain close to home, or tasks which would be carried out with a baby strapped to their backs. The team leader in charge of women's work was also responsible for helping to administer birth planning policy for her team. When a team member became pregnant, this information would be passed on from the team level to the brigade cadre in charge of women's work. The deputy team leader in charge of women's work distributed the supplies of birth control pills that were provided to the brigade by the upper levels. Also the team-level women's leader represented the women of her team at brigade meetings of the women's federation.

The deputy team leader in charge of finance and economy was responsible for the financial affairs of the team, acting as a sort of treasurer. He checked and oversaw the work of the accountant, the cashier, and the storehouse keeper, and he deposited team funds in the local credit cooperative. On some teams, this leader also supervised the team enterprises and rural industries.

The team accountant, although not powerful or responsible for making decisions, was a vital figure in team management. When the team rewarded labor, distributed workpoints, calculated the actual value of production, and sought to maintain economic equity among team members, these social actions were carried out on the basis of the calculations provided by the accountant. Team decisions stressed equity rather than simplicity of accounting. Frequently, for example, a task was rewarded half on a piecework and half on an hourly basis, in order to recognize the validity of both principles, making payment complex to calculate. The accountant added up the labor done by every team member, the profit and loss of the team, and all the subsidiary figures, and calculated the value of a workpoint by dividing the total net profit by the number of workpoints earned by all team members. Then he figured the money value of the total workpoints of each household. He also calculated the distribution of rice, oil, and fish to households according to their rations, and withheld the monetary value of these items from the final payment for workpoints. Each calculation was highly significant to the household involved, and a pattern of errors would make the daily life of team members unlivable. Teams without competent accountants were virtually unable to function. In fact, the extreme dependence of the team on accounting, and the consistent pattern of decisions which suggests that ease of accounting was not a relevant value compared with the inclusion of many factors considered critical to a definition of economic equity, are among the most striking features of team organization. Each team accountant was under the immediate supervision of the brigade accountant, and contributed his own team's records to aggregate reports which the brigade sent to the commune level.

The team cashier was the keeper of the team's money. Only he was empowered to draw money from the team's account at the local credit cooperative when it was needed. He received and handed over the actual cash, kept records, and provided receipts. He was responsible for cash transactions to and from team members, as well as cash transactions on behalf of the team as a whole.

The team storehouse keeper was in charge of the team's buildings and the grain, machines, fertilizer, and tools stored in them, and acted as keeper of the keys. He was also in charge of the team scales which had to be used in order to determine workpoints for weight hauled or carried.

The workpoint recorder validated and recorded the workpoints of team members as they earned them, and reported them to the accountant. He or his assistants went into the fields where people were working, observed the work, and noted down how many workpoints a team member earned each day. When women were carrying loads of fertilizer, for example, a workpoint recorder would stand by, checking and counting each load as it was dumped, and making sure that it was full weight and duly recorded. The responsibility of the workpoint recorder was to weigh, count, and measure every aspect of the work of team members that could reasonably be weighed, counted, or measured, so that team members could be assured that everyone was doing a full share of work and being rewarded appropriately.

In 1979 some of the Zengbu teams, encouraged by the government, were experimenting with a new "small group responsibility system" in agriculture.

The team's land, tools, and workers were divided up into two or more small groups. Each small group was a basic unit for production, to be penalized or rewarded as a whole. If a small group overfulfilled its quotas, it was rewarded with bonuses by the team; if a small group did not meet its quotas it was fined. The heads of these small groups, called the small group leaders, were also members of the committees of teams in which they were found.

All team leaders were elected in a written secret ballot by all adult team members over the age of 16. Government at the team level, the fundamental level where people labored to make their living, was democratically chosen: the peasants had the important right to elect their immediate work supervisors. The teams were encouraged to hold elections every two or three years, but did not always do so. Team elections were held in 1970, 1975, and 1979, in Zengbu.

Seeking election is constrained because it is culturally inappropriate to suggest that one thinks one's self a suitable candidate. Such a statement would be grossly and laughably immodest, for it would suggest that one regarded one's self as worthy, or even as superior. Anyone who made such a statement would be regarded as a figure of fun. Furthermore, any open admission that one wished to hold office would be followed by intolerable public humiliation if one were not actually elected. As a result, the prevailing political style is positively Gilbertian in its formal constraints, for the candidate for office can neither seek office publicly nor admit that he would serve if elected. The process must be carried out entirely in covert terms, never overtly. Even the most low-key of Western political campaigns would strike the villagers as grotesque, blatant, laughable, and inappropriate. When the election has taken place, it is possible to infer from the election tallies that there have been rivalries, and that some candidates have prevailed, while others have been disappointed, but such information is never made manifest in the form of a campaign before the election.

The election in 1979 was regarded as extremely important by the brigade cadres. On election day, team members gathered at the team headquarters. Men and women sat separately. Women held babies and many continued to weave bamboo into shrimp traps while preparations for the elections were being made. Brigade cadres addressed the team members on the importance of team elections, especially now that there had been a shift in the significance of the team leader. Previously, the first duty of a team leader had been to demonstrate his solidarity with the peasants by laboring among them "like a water buffalo." Now, however, there was to be a new emphasis on administrative and business skills, and the ability to plan and put into effect new ways of making money for the team. Team members were told that they were free to choose anyone they wanted for each space on the ballot. The voting was for the committee as a whole, rather than for specific offices. The team committee would be made up of the candidates who received the largest number of votes. Thus, if there were to be nine committee members, the nine candidates with the highest number of votes would form the committee. Voting for the committee rather than for the offices tended to ensure the representation of all powerful factions. The most powerful person in a given faction would not be eliminated from holding office by losing a specific position to the leader of an opposing faction; rather, both leaders would probably be elected to the team committee, while the less popular candidates from either faction would be eliminated.

Two different methods were used for assigning specific team offices to the newly elected committee members. According to one method, the committee members would caucus among themselves, and assign the team offices to one another as they thought best. According to the other method, after the committee members had been elected as a group, a second election would take place, in which team members would choose which elected team officer would take up each specific position. The latter method was more democratic, because it left a greater degree of choice to the team membership as a whole.

In order to prevent fraud, only ballots with the brigade seal on them were accepted as valid. Team members could leave the hall after voting, but they had to remain nearby until the election results had been officially completed, certified, and announced.

Inside the team headquarters, the cadres distributed ballots to the team members, who gathered in sex-segregated groups to mark them, often after carrying on long whispered discussions about the candidates. Illiterate members of the team were helped by the attending brigade cadres to mark their ballots. Completed ballots were carefully folded to keep the vote a secret, and dropped by the voter into a new bamboo fertilizer basket at the front of the room, which served as a ballot box.

After everyone had finished voting, the cadres chose several team members to open the ballots publicly and tally them. These team members opened the ballots, one by one, and called out the names of the candidates who had votes. The names were written up on large blackboards. Beside each candidate's name, the number of votes he received was recorded, not by four straight strokes with a line diagonally across them to represent five, but by a Chinese way of symbolizing the same thing: each vote was a stroke of the Chinese character *zheng*, which has five clearly differentiated strokes in its composition. People crowded around the blackboard as the tallying proceeded and the suspense grew. Then when all the votes had been tallied, the cadres announced the results of the election, and the team members dispersed.

Although most incumbents were returned to office in 1979, each team election showed results implying significant rivalry for office. For example, in Lu's Home village's Number 1 team, the voting results showed that, in addition to the 9 committee members elected, there were 7 people who were strong runners-up and 31 other team members who received at least four or five votes each. Ten women, for example, received votes for the position of team leader for women's work.

In Sandhill village's Number 3 team, with 400 members and 175 adult workers eligible to vote, 165 persons attended the team election to select 11 persons with the highest votes as the team committee, and 162 attended the afternoon session to assign the new members to their positions. In addition to the 11 successful candidates, there were 7 runners-up who received substantial numbers of votes, and many more who received one to five votes each.

Two cases in which the incumbents were not returned to office are of interest because they illustrate team level political process in more specific terms. The team leader of Pondside Number 1 was a man between 35 and 40 years of age. He had not served long, and villagers had concluded that his behavior was not appropriate to his position. He was regarded as "selfish," in the sense that he appeared to be favoring his own family members and relatives by giving them easy work assignments which yielded greater workpoints. Even if untrue, the mere appearance of favoring kin invariably created extreme hostility against a team leader. He had become embittered, and felt that team leadership was a thankless task. In purely economic terms, the previous year had not been a good one. In previous years, Pondside Number 1 team had consistently been as successful economically as the other teams in Pondside village, but in 1979 their distribution per capita was only 254 yuan, compared to figures of 370, 330, and 323 yuan for the village's other three teams. The team members held the team leader responsible for the team's economic failure, and he was voted out of office.

The leader of Lu's Home Number 3 team, in contrast, had been leading agricultural collectives and teams for 23 years, and had finally grown old in harness. His health was declining and he suffered from stomach ulcers. In the past year he had been growing more and more obviously embittered and unhappy, and would yell orders rudely at his team members. Some villagers believed that he had broken under the strain of his position. The brigade leaders spoke to him privately, and asked him not to run again. They felt it would be better to ease out their veteran colleague before the situation had deteriorated to the point where he might suffer the humiliation of being voted out of office by the team members he had served so long. They arranged for him to resign before the election, and suggested that a young party member from his team, whom they had been grooming for several years, should replace him. The old team leader resigned and the team members had no objection to the young man's taking his place, so the transition was accomplished.

This case illustrates brigade-level intervention in team leadership. Although the teams retained the final say in the choice of their own leaders, it was possible for the brigade to influence the process. The brigade would be most likely to intervene when a team was having such serious economic difficulties that it was unable to solve them on its own. The brigade cadres' own reputations depended upon the economic performance of the units under them. They preferred to intervene rather than to let a team deteriorate obviously.

Generally speaking, however, there was remarkable little change in the core of team committee personnel in the 1979 Zengbu elections. Of the 182 incumbent team committee members, only 6 were actually voted out of office. According to the brigade party secretary, this was the normal pattern in Zengbu. Team leaders served for extensive periods of time, and if they managed to keep the team's prosperity on a par with other village teams, and the earnings of team members up to the average, they were usually re-elected.

Scale was a factor in the returning of incumbents. Teams were small-scale organizations, and produced few potential leaders and managers with the requisite proletarian class background. Furthermore, the position of team leader was fraught with pitfalls and poorly rewarded. A team was not normally provided with more than one or two members who could run it competently, even if they were willing to try. Some qualified leaders and managers were entirely disheartened by the overwhelming criticism to which they were subjected in the Cultural Revolution period, and did not wish to expose themselves to a repetition of their public humiliation. In many teams, everyone who could usefully serve was already in office.

In 1979, Zengbu team leaders and the other team committee members were paid salaries in workpoints at a rate set just below the workpoint earnings of the best team workers plus an additional 10 percent to recompense them for their added responsibilities. They usually put in a ten-hour day instead of the eight-hour day (six hours for the team and two hours on the private garden plots) put in by most ordinary peasants. Time-consuming duties such as planning the team's operations, assigning work, supervising the work itself, and attending meetings, prevented the team leaders from working on their private garden plots as long as ordinary members. A frequent complaint of team leaders and their wives was that the leaders sacrificed their own economic interests to that of the collective.

After the team leader and deputy leader had met in the evening to plan the following day's work, they posted work assignments by listing the tasks on a blackboard, and displaying the bamboo name tag of each team worker opposite the assigned task. The following morning team members would find their assignments for the day.

One specific example of a team's work assignments are those made by the team leaders of Pondside's Number 4 team on the morning of August 5, 1979, as shown in table 2.

Table 2. *Pondside Number 4 team work assignments*

| Work assignments | Number of workers |
|---|---|
| 1. Pulling up seedlings | 23 (women) |
| 2. Transplanting rice in the east water field | 15 (men) |
| 3. Building up rice field boundaries | 1 (man) |
| 4. Plowing already harvested fields for transplanting | 5 (men) |
| 5. Pulling up rice seedlings in section 1 | 13 (women) |
| 6. Replanting yellow beans | 8 (mixed) |
| 7. Caring for team buffaloes | 13 (older women) |
| 8. Team workers in brigade enterprises (plastics factory, palm leaf factory, carpentry shop, repair shop, and so on) | 27 (mixed) |
| 9. Workers in team enterprise making plastic shoe bags for Guangzhou factory | 9 (women) |
| 10. Weaving bamboo baskets in team enterprise | 13 (mixed) |
| Total workers assigned | 127 |

Most of the work groups assigned to agricultural tasks were segregated into male work groups or female work groups, according to the culturally-defined division of labor in rice agriculture. Women did more of the agricultural field labor than they had before Liberation, but the structural distinction between men's work and women's work persisted.

The management of human relations within the team was a complex and continuing problem. Each production team contained members of the team leader's own household and some of his close patrilineal relatives, so accusations of favoritism would lose the respect of team members, and his authority would be diminished. Indeed, successful leaders often went to the opposite extreme. The wives and children of Zengbu team leaders frequently complained that, in attempting to avoid criticism, the team leader tended to give them the hardest and least rewarding work to do. In the old society it had been an ethical duty to favor one's family and kin. In the new society it seemed important that the reverse be demonstrated publicly. Yet a clear conflict remained, with obligations to kin at odds with obligations to the team, and the problems presented by this conflict could not be resolved without doing injury either to one set of values or to the other.

The management of labor was a complex matter. The strength and skill of each team member had to be matched to appropriate tasks. Each team member had an obligation to perform his fair share of the most difficult and onerous work, which was to be balanced with less burdensome or better rewarded work. Complaints about the fairness of work assignments were constant. In spite of, and because of, this context of inevitable daily dissatisfaction, it was clearly important to maintain a level of morale that would motivate team members to work enthusiastically and well. Yet the teams had little to offer by way of incentives. Furthermore, if one member received a higher reward, this reduced the amount available for distribution to others, since workpoints were shares in the limited collective earnings of the unit, and if one member received more there was inevitably less to be divided among the others.

Disagreeable tasks, such as carting the team's collectively raised pigs to market at the state livestock purchasing station in Chashan, were assigned according to a formal rotation. There was a clock-like circular wooden device, with a pointer in the middle and the numbers of the team households written around the circumference, which served to indicate which household was due for such tasks. The purpose of this was to ensure that the burdensome work of the team would be distributed evenly to each household. These arrangements suggest an atmosphere of mutual distrust and suspicion, with team members fearing that some households would try to avoid their responsibilities and shirk the less desirable forms of labor.

At reorganization, the cadres had provided each team with an equal share, figured on a per capita basis, of the land, orchards, fishponds, forests, and rural industries of its village. Prior to liberation, the separate villages of Zengbu had owned unequal amounts of land. The landholdings of villages were never redefined and equalized after the Revolution, but remained unequal. As a result, the land owned by teams from different villages arbitrarily reflected each village's pre-1949 holdings (see table 3). If the pre-Liberation village had been relatively land poor, the post-revolutionary teams of that village were relatively land poor as well.

Since the territory of each village included a variety of small ecological zones – good and bad rice fields, marsh, highland, hills, orchards, and forests – each team was given some of the land in each zone, in balanced parcels, including land of various grades. As a result, the permanent land allotments of a team were not concentrated in a single area, but scattered throughout the village and interspersed with fields owned by other teams. This scattered ownership pattern resembled the ownership pattern of individual peasant landholdings before the Revolution.

The actual amount of land owned by Zengbu teams, in 1979, varied from 92 *mu* per team to 345 *mu* per team, with an average of 235 *mu* per team (about 17 hectares, see table 4).

In 1979, *per captia* land ownership from team to team varied from 0·63 *mu* to 1·20 *mu*, with Pondside teams having the most land per capita (an average of 0·98 *mu*), Lu's Home next (0·85 *mu*), and Sandhill last, with only 0·68 *mu*

Table 3. *Land per capita, Zengbu teams, 1979 (including dry and paddy)*

| Village and team | *Mu* per capita |
|---|---|
| Lu's Home 1 | 0·85 |
| Lu's Home 2 | 0·94 |
| Lu's Home 3 | 0·94 |
| Lu's Home 4 | 0·88 |
| Lu's Home 5 | 0·75 |
| Lu's Home 6 | 0·75 |
| Lu's Home 7 | 1·00 |
| Sandhill 1 | 0·72 |
| Sandhill 2 | 0·70 |
| Sandhill 3 | 0·68 |
| Sandhill 4 | 0·63 |
| Sandhill 5 | 0·75 |
| Sandhill 6 | 0·63 |
| Pondside 1 | 0·88 |
| Pondside 2 | 1·20 |
| Pondside 3 | 0·91 |
| Pondside 4 | 0·94 |

Mean average *mu* per capita for Zengbu, 0·83
Mean average *mu* per capita for commune, 1·10
Mean average *mu* for commune (excluding the town population), 1·30
*Source:* Brigade records

per person. In spite of these discrepancies in land ownership from team to team, the land allocations were never changed. Original disparities in village ownership meant that the teams started unequal, and as time passed, differential population growth became another important factor. Teams whose populations had grown more rapidly were left to deal with the situation as best they could. Since land resources were fixed, the usual solution was to develop handicrafts and local industry. The practice of transferring families within the same village from one team to another to maintain equal ratios between population and land, as was done, for example, in Taitou in Shandong province (Professor Norma Diamond, private communication) was not followed in Zengbu.

Within the brigade, the richest team owned twice as much land per capita as the poorest. As a result, economic equality was maintained among the households within a single team, but not among the constituent teams of a village, brigade, or commune. The attempt to eliminate these wider inequalities by organizing large-scale radical communes which equalized incomes over a wide area, had been a failure; other, smaller-scale methods of

Table 4. *Zengbu production teams, statistics, 1979*

| Team | No. house-holds | Population | Number of laborers | Planted area (*mu*) | Annual per capita distribution | Labor day value |
|------|-----------------|------------|--------------------|--------------------|-------------------------------|-----------------|
| LH 1 | 51 | 229 | 104 | 195 | 325·5 | 1·30 |
| 2 | 48 | 215 | 95 | 202 | 281·4 | 1·04 |
| 3 | 64 | 300 | 135 | 282 | 371·8 | 1·18 |
| 4 | 70 | 314 | 140 | 277 | 265·3 | 1·06 |
| 5 | 54 | 271 | 120 | 204 | 356·7 | 1·31 |
| 6 | 70 | 324 | 150 | 244 | 305·7 | 1·15 |
| 7 | 20 | 92 | 45 | 92 | 322·8 | 1·35 |
| SH 1 | 56 | 247 | 115 | 179 | 312·5 | 1·00 |
| 2 | 45 | 195 | 85 | 137 | 212·1 | 0·85 |
| 3 | 97 | 407 | 184 | 277 | 278·3 | 1·10 |
| 4 | 115 | 453 | 198 | 287 | 218·7 | 1·02 |
| 5 | 75 | 315 | 143 | 236 | 245·3 | 1·02 |
| 6 | 118 | 546 | 226 | 345 | 281·1 | 1·05 |
| PS 1 | 62 | 268 | 120 | 236 | 254·4 | 1·17 |
| 2 | 51 | 224 | 108 | 270 | 370·2 | 1·02 |
| 3 | 64 | 285 | 128 | 260 | 330·7 | 1·10 |
| 4 | 60 | 286 | 129 | 269 | 323·4 | 1·00 |
| Total | 1,120 | 4,971 | 2,225 | 3,992 | 297·4 yuan (mean) | 1·17 yuan (mean) |

*Note*: One labor day value is equal to the value of 10 workpoints
*Source*: Brigade records

establishing economic equality between teams were not tried, and inequalities between teams were accepted rather than reformed.

The landholdings of each team were divided into two categories, based on two ways of dealing with the relationship between people and land. The two categories of land were governed by different rules of land tenure and worked by different modes of production. The working of approximately one-tenth of the land was delegated by the team to households. This land was referred to as private plot land. The cultivation of the private plots was by the household mode of production. Nine-tenths of the team's land was collectively worked: a collective mode of production was used on these collective fields.

Private plot land was distributed on a per capita basis to individual households for their private use in growing their own vegetables, sugarcane, peanuts, animal feed, and rice. Prior to 1976, the basic private plot allotment in Zengbu was 5 *li* (about forty square meters) of irrigated rice fields and 5 *li* of dry land per person. In order to maintain the size of private plots in spite of consistently increasing population, the committees took land away from the collective holdings, and reallocated it as private plot land. In 1976, it was recognized that the collectives could yield no more land for private garden plots. Population had increased so greatly that there was not sufficient land to provide the 5 *li* plots; the remaining collectively managed land would be insufficient to grow rice for the team's rations, or to meet the state purchase quotas for other crops. Following this recognition, the size of allotments was reduced, and, although there was significant variation from team to team, a typical distribution by 1979 was 4 *li* of irrigated land and 4 *li* of dry land per capita. But some teams, Lu's Home Number 2, for example, distributed as little as 2 *li* of dry land and no irrigated land in 1979. Additional private garden plot land was also distributed per household pig, to be used by the households for growing pig food. The size of pig plot allocations varied, with the largest being 1 *fen* per pig raised (about eighty square meters). However, many of the pig plots were actually surface areas of waterways, where water hyacinth could be grown, rather than land as such.

The allocation of productive area to feed pigs, on a per pig basis, parallels the allocation of land to feed people on a per capita basis in a way that is culturally suggestive. Raising pigs is clearly of more than merely economic significance; in religious contexts, as in the context of plot allocations, they are sometimes treated as the symbolic equivalents of people in kinship relations. Pigs were the ritual offerings to ancestors and deities, to be divided among all male lineage members as a means of transferring the magical power of an ancestral grave to living male descendants. Pigs are the prizes in ritual competitions between lineages, such as dragon-boat races. Violations of the incest taboo within the lineage were formerly punished by drowning the offenders in pig baskets. And after a marriage, pigs were sent back to the bride's family by the groom's family, in order to affirm that the bride was a virgin. The existence of private plots designated for pigs, as well as private plots designated for people, is not a mere quirk of economic organization, but an example of the importance of cultural assumption in economic decision-making.

Households change in size as they pass through the various stages of the household developmental cycle. It was necessary to adjust private plot allocations periodically, in order to take account of these changes in the number of people per household. Every three years the teams carried out intermediate adjustments, and every six years a major reallocation took place. Intermediate adjustments were carried out by a team committee consisting of the team leader, the accountant, and two team members at large. They took back plots from households which had lost members through death, or the marrying out of a daughter, and transferred these plots to households which had increased in size through a birth of a child or the marrying in of a daughter-in-law. A household relinquishing land allotments was not allowed to give up its worst pieces of land while retaining parcels of higher quality, nor was it forced to give up the best. In cases of dispute over the quality of land to be transferred, the team committee had the disputants draw lots.

The three-year adjustments were minor ones; small pieces of land were exchanged by a few households, but most people's private plot allocations remained unchanged. Every six years, however, there was a major redistribution of private plots. The team committee recalled all the privately used land, and redistributed it by having the households draw lots. This was so that the quality of allotment could not be monopolized; no household would be forced to work a particular piece of inferior garden land indefinitely.

The private plots were worked by men rather than women – in the late afternoon and early evening after their work obligations to their teams had been completed. The private plots were significant sources of household income. According to the careful calculations of the rural work department cadres of Dongguan county, peasant households in the county received an average of 21 percent of their yearly income from private plots. The plots were tended with care. The household's accumulated night soil was applied as fertilizer. Weeds were pulled meticulously, and insects lifted off leaves, so that each cabbage was a perfect specimen. Using these intensive methods of cultivation, Zengbu households managed to grow all the vegetables they ate throughout the year. Few vegetables were sold on the market; not only were markets limited and controlled, but also people were afraid that if they sold too much of their garden produce, they would be accused of capitalist tendencies.

The private plots of each household were located together as much as possible, but there was some scattering of household holdings. For example, the sugarcane plots of team members were grouped together. This was so that the tall growing cane plants would not deprive adjacent plants of sunlight, as would have happened had the growing of sugarcane been dispersed.

A specific example of the way private plots were utilized illustrates the actual operation of this important aspect of the Maoist economy. A household from Lu's Home village's Number 2 team consisted of seven persons: a man, his wife, and their five children. Each member of Lu's Home Number 2 team was entitled to 2 *li* (about sixteen square meters) of highland fields, and since the family had five members entitled to shares, they received a total of 10 *li* (approximately eighty square meters). The two youngest children, two-year-old twins, had not yet had private plots distributed to them in the triennial distribution. The team had adequate highland but insufficient paddy fields, and thus did not distribute paddy land in the form of private plots. The household raised four pigs, and received 4 *li* of private plot land per pig, for a total of 16 *li* of pig plots, the pigs receiving more area than the people. On their 16 *li* of pig land the household grew sweet potatoes intercropped with daikon radishes. The sweet potatoes and vines and the radish leaves, along with rice bran and rice water, were used as pig feed. On the people's plots they grew sugarcane from which they made brown sugar for their own consumption. They also grew 8 *li* of soybeans (which they ate in soup), vegetables to supply the household, and peanuts, which they either ate or pressed into cooking oil.

The crops grown on each family's plots varied according to their taste in food and the choices they made between the limited number and amounts of other crops they could plant. To supplement their diet most households raised a few chickens, a pig or two, and fattened several geese for New Year's feasting.

Providing garden plot allotments had a cumulative social effect on the relationship between the household and the collective. As population increased steadily, the economic resources of the team were diminished and reallocated to households. Thus, over the long run, the team was weakened and the households were strengthened, in direct contravention to the formal ideology of the team. Families had powerful economic incentives to have as many children as possible. The normal demographic disincentives to having large numbers of children were removed, since the team bore the burden of population increase, and the household reaped the reward in increased workpoint earnings, food rations, and additional garden plots. The fact that a household could obtain a larger share of the team's collective income by increasing its numbers was a point of resemblance between family strategy within the team and traditional family strategy within the lineage; traditionally, the strategy for increasing a family's political power within a lineage village was to increase the size of the family and the lineage segment. Yet the lineage did not subsidize the population increase of families continually and directly like the team.

In its structure and allocation of resources, the Maoist production team was one of the most pronatal organizations in human history. Ultimately, this pronatalism was to contribute to the demise of the team, and the reaffirmation of the household as the most important economic unit in rural Chinese society. Ironically, this result was created by some two decades of subsidies, provided to the households by the teams – in an institutional setting the formal purpose of which was to achieve just the opposite.

The basis of the team's existence as an agricultural entity was the 90 percent of team land which remained to be worked collectively, after the private plot distributions had been made. The team's rights over its collective land were not absolute, but limited. The team was not free to sell its land to other teams, or to divide either ownership or cultivation responsibility privately among team members. Nor did the team have much flexibility in choosing how to utilize collective landholdings; most of a team's landholdings had to be planted in rice to feed the team members and rice to meet the team's state purchase quotas. Emphasis was placed upon growing rice, in accordance with the policy, "Take grain as the main!"

The team also had to grow commercial crops such as jute and pond fish as required under state production quotas. Team cadres said that after the team had planted enough rice to feed its people, and delivered sufficient amounts of quota crops to the state, it had from only 10 to 20 percent of its yearly two-crop cropping area available for other uses. Thus, a team had little opportunity to exercise its own economic judgement: most economic decisions were made for the peasants by requirements of the state. The policy of "Take grain as the main," for example, prevented Zengbu peasants from planting the vegetable cash crops which were more lucrative than rice, or from digging additional fish ponds, another comparatively profitable use of land. Indeed, the peasants had had to fill in some fish ponds and convert them to rice paddies, in order to grow enough rice to meet the required quota. The policy of taking grain as the main had the aim of insuring that China as a whole would have sufficient grain to feed its people. However, utilizing land for the growing of grain, which had to be sold at the artificially low state purchase price, was economically irrational when considered from the point of view of Zengbu peasants. They could, in theory at least, have made much more money raising fish or producing vegetables for the market, had the market been an active entity – which it was not, being severely restricted.

Each team committee made an overall yearly plan for the team as a whole. They decided which crops to plant, in accordance with the production requirements imposed on them from the upper levels, and made choices about the allocation of resources: which fields should be used for each crop, how much of the limited supply of fertilizer should be applied, and what crop rotation patterns should be followed. They decided whether they should undertake commitments such as contracting to grow vegetables for export to Hong Kong. They also made decisions about the allocation of labor. Some labor was used in agriculture, but the teams also engaged in enterprises which required workers. Sometimes team labor was employed by the brigade or higher levels, and this was taken into account.

Rural industry was as important to the economic life of China's peasants in 1979, as it had been in 1939, when Fei Xiaotong, in his book, *Peasant Life in China*, first drew attention to its salience. In addition to their land, orchards, and ponds, Zengbu's teams owned and operated small rural industries. These remained a keystone of the rural economy, because the fundamental facts of China's rural economic situation had not changed: population was so high in proportion to land resources that it was impossible to make a living on the basis of agriculture alone. To supplement their agricultural income the peasants had to engage in small-scale industries, managed collectively by production teams and brigades.

In Chashan commune, in 1979, one half of the commune's 109 production teams operated team industries. Because of the local abundance of river clay suitable for firing, the most frequently found team enterprises were brick and tile kilns. Other industries were based upon traditional handicrafts, such as weaving bamboo baskets and plaiting articles of straw. Some teams processed small metal articles for urban factories located in Dongguan or Guangzhou. Others dug a special clay, exported to Japan for the manufacture of insulators, or saltpeter for the fireworks factories of Dongguan. Teams also dyed firecracker paper under contract, grew silk worms, and so on.

Each of the 17 teams in Zengbu depended upon rural industry for a large part of its income. The average Zengbu team, in 1979, received 36·6 percent of its gross income from agriculture (in the sense of field crops) and 48·65 percent from rural industry, the balance coming from fish farming, forestry, and raising livestock. However, some Zengbu teams earned much higher proportions of their income from rural industry than others. Pondside village's Number 4 team earned 66 percent of its income from rural industry, more than any other team in the brigade, whereas, at the other extreme, Pondside village's Number 1 team obtained only 30 percent of its income from that source. The comparative figures for Zengbu brigade's teams are set out in table 5, which shows the teams' gross income figures.

Exact *net* income figures for that year were not available. In agriculture, expenses were approximately 35 percent of gross income, but in rural industry expenses were only about 20 percent of gross income. As a result, a larger share of the net team income came from industry than these gross income figures show.

A specific example, from Sandhill village's Number 6 team, can serve as a basis for understanding this aspect of the teams' economy. Sandhill Number 6 was the most populous team in the commune, as well as being the poorest in land resources, proportionately, in the brigade. It controlled only 316 *mu* (22 hectares) of irrigated rice fields, 125 *mu* of fishponds, and 29 *mu* of dry land, for a per capita average of only 0·63 *mu* of cultivated land. The members of Sandhill Number 6 team had been forced by circumstances to develop rural industry.

In 1979 Sandhill Number 6 team earned 62 percent of its total team income from rural industries. Its per capita distribution for 1979 was 281·1 *yuan*, slightly below the 297·4 *yuan* per capita average for the brigade's teams as a whole. Of Sandhill Number 6 team's full-time workers, approximately 37 percent worked mainly in agriculture, and 63 percent worked mainly in industry. One-quarter of those working in rural industry worked outside the team in brigade-owned enterprises, for which the team was compensated by the brigade. (One person from the team worked in a commune-operated factory in town; the commune compensated the team for his labor.)

Sandhill Number 6 team's tile kiln was its most important rural industry.

Table 5. *Zengbu production teams' gross income by category, 1979* (In percent)

| Team | | Agriculture | Forestry | Animals | Industry* | Fisheries | Others | Total in *yuan* |
|------|---|-------------|----------|---------|-----------|-----------|--------|-----------------|
| | | | | Source of income | | | | |
| LH | 1 | 49 | 0 | 5 | 41 | 4 | 2 | 17,146 |
| | 2 | 45 | 0 | 3 | 42 | 4 | 6 | 107,682 |
| | 3 | 42 | 0 | 3 | 47 | 4 | 5 | 190,430 |
| | 4 | 41 | 0 | 4 | 42 | 8 | 5 | 149,794 |
| | 5 | 46 | 0 | 6 | 41 | 4 | 3 | 144,693 |
| | 6 | 43 | 0 | 3 | 46 | 5 | 2 | 167,140 |
| | 7 | 43 | 0 | 8 | 38 | 8 | 4 | 54,239 |
| SH | 1 | 25 | 0 | 2 | 63 | 9 | 1 | 68,639 |
| | 2 | 33 | 0 | 2 | 49 | 14 | 2 | 79,609 |
| | 3 | 25 | 0 | 2 | 58 | 14 | 1 | 216,249 |
| | 4 | 34 | 0 | 4 | 46 | 14 | 2 | 157,254 |
| | 5 | 34 | 0 | 2 | 48 | 14 | 2 | 133,581 |
| | 6 | 25 | 0 | 2 | 62 | 10 | 0 | 280,527 |
| PS | 1 | 41 | 0 | 12 | 30 | 12 | 5 | 110,285 |
| | 2 | 33 | 0 | 10 | 47 | 9 | 1 | 142,539 |
| | 3 | 25 | 0 | 7 | 61 | 6 | 1 | 168,949 |
| | 4 | 21 | 0 | 4 | 66 | 6 | 2 | 195,123 |
| Average gross income | | 36·6 | 0 | 4·64 | 48·65 | 8·53 | 2·59 | 151,992·8 |

* Includes income from team members working in brigade enterprises

The kiln produced curved roof tiles and large square flooring tiles, of the kinds used in local building construction. The kiln operated all year around, employing 52 workers, 38 men and 14 women. Work in the kiln was hot, filthy, and exhausting, and was so regarded by kiln employees. Men had the job of mixing the clay. There were two methods: using human labor and the hoe, or driving buffaloes round and round in the clay mud. The buffaloes were blindfolded to ensure that they would not take the line of least resistance by stepping into previous footprints. Whichever the method used, this work was so filthy that the workers regarded it as shameful. After the clay was mixed, the heavy wet mud was carried to the workyard and formed into large squares. Women cut off squares of clay with wire saws, molded the clay into cylinders around a wooden molding wheel, incised the cylinders so that they would split neatly into four curved trough-like tiles when dry, and set them to dry in the sun. After they were dry, the cylinders were separated along the incisions, and became shaped tiles. These were collected and placed in the kilns to be fired. The temperature maintained in the kilns was extremely high, and the workers who tended the fire by throwing in dry wooden branches suffered from their proximity to the heat. After firing, the finished tiles were stored until they were loaded onto the customers' boats. The team was able to sell all the tiles it could produce, since building material was much in demand.

The tile kiln was managed by a director and a deputy director, who supervised the work for the team committee. They received the basic salary of a kiln worker and additional workpoints to compensate them for their additional responsibility. The kiln employed a cashier to handle the kiln's money. The cashier doubled as kiln gardener by growing vegetables in a nearby field for the kiln's kitchen. A cook prepared the morning meal and lunch for the kiln workers. The kiln was located far from the village on the bank of the river, so as to be close to transportation, and it was considered inconvenient for the kiln workers to walk all the way home to eat. The kiln employed a purchasing agent, who bought the evergreen boughs, with which the kiln was fired, from the mountain communes where they were grown. The kiln also employed a salesman, who sold the tiles to customers.

In 1979, the kiln was operating on a production quota and bonus system, an early version of a production responsibility system. In previous years there had been no bonuses, only the workpoints earned. In 1979, in an effort to encourage production by rewarding greater output, the kiln was allocated 20,000 workpoints by Number 6 team (based on the previous three years' usual expenditure of workpoints on kiln labor) to pay the labor costs of the kiln. The production quota was set at 8·5 kiln loads of tiles a year, each kiln load containing 135,000 pieces, which would yield an expected profit of 38,000 *yuan* for the team. If the kiln workers produced more than this, the kiln distributed 50 percent of the profit from the overproduction to the workers as a cash bonus; the other half went to the team to be distributed to all its members at the end of the year in the general distribution.

Men employed by the kiln were able to earn about 15 workpoints per day for mixing and piling the clay up in mounds. They worked on a piece-rate basis, receiving 1·3 workpoints for mixing enough clay to make 1,000 tiles. The women workers, who performed the comparatively skilled job of shaping the tiles on the wheel, received 2·10 workpoints per 100 tiles. They could make about 550 tiles a day, and earned on the average about 11·55 workpoints. This was less than men earned, even though women worked seven hours a day, rather than the six hours per day worked by the men. In addition, the women received a bonus of 0·17 *yuan* per 100 tiles, or about 0·39 *yuan* per day. The kiln had begun to pay this bonus in 1978, as part of the settlement agreed upon after the women kiln workers went on strike. Kiln work was conventionally given to young unmarried women when they left school at the age of 16 and first began to work for the team. The young women worked in the kiln for about three years before their places were taken by new school-leavers. If there were not enough replacements, women who had already completed three years at the kiln had to draw lots to see who would be allowed to leave the kiln and who would have to remain. Young unmarried women were believed to be the most malleable and most easily exploited group of team workers. Taught to be submissive to their elders and to men, they would tolerate much more difficult and humiliating working conditions than their brothers, without causing difficulties for managers. Since these young women would eventually marry out, they were not regarded as permanent members of the team, just as young women were not considered permanent members of their families or lineages in the old days.

However, in 1978 the young women kiln workers of Number 6 team rebelled, and refused to work unless their conditions were improved. After "ideological education" by team leaders failed to change the position of the young women, the team granted the bonus. In addition, the team gave all kiln workers, male and female, 0·10 *yuan* for breakfast, 0·06 *yuan* additional per day to help pay for their meals in the kiln kitchen, and free fish and vegetables with their rice. As an additional concession, the team gave the women kiln workers the right to take two-hour meal breaks for half of the year. During the first half of the year the young women worked from 6:30 in the morning until 3:30 in the afternoon, with an hour off for each of their two meals. In the second half of the year, the women worked from 7:00 a.m. to 4:00 p.m., with two hours off for meals. The workers, especially the women, were still not satisfied with their pay and working conditions, which seemed small in comparison with the magnitude of their daily drudgery.

Teams distributed income to households according to the number of workpoints earned by the members of each household. The recording of workpoints was a fundamental process in team management. Team accountants, with the help of workpoint recorders, noted down each person's work and how many workpoints he or she had earned, and entered this in their record books. The process was made complex by its dualism; intense concern with the nature of appropriate reward for labor had resulted in a system which rewarded labor according to two principles at once. The first principle was that each task was rewarded as a task, by a task rate. The second principle was that strength and inherent capacity to labor were rewarded. Thus, in 1979, team workers were paid workpoints on two systems simultaneously, the task-rate system and the basic labor-grade (*difen*) system.

According to the task-rate system, a set number of workpoints rewarded a given task, and completion of the task was the prerequisite for the reward. A workpoint book had been drawn up by the brigade cadres in 1978, based on earlier efforts going back to the 1960s. It listed every single task in the Zengbu repertoire of work that was administered by teams or by the brigade, including tasks in agriculture, rural industry, animal husbandry, and transportation. (It did not list housework; the omission reflects the sexist assumption that the tasks of housework, traditionally done by women, lack economic value and significance.) When completed to a specified standard, each task was rewarded with a specific number of workpoints. Each team accountant had a copy of the current workpoint book.

The Zengbu book started with types of plowing, the standards according to which the work should be completed, variables to be taken into account, and the workpoints to be earned for completing the task. Thus, plowing paddy fields for the first time (as opposed to later plowings), in order to plant the first rice crop, was rewarded with 4 workpoints per *mu*, if the field was near the village, and 4·5 workpoints if the man had to carry his plow and take his buffalo to a distant field. The standards for plowing were that the field should be plowed 3 Chinese inches (approximately 9 centimeters) deep, with no furrows skipped. Furthermore, the corners of the fields had to be finished to the same depth with a hoe. However, for doing this the plower could add 0·01 of a *mu* to the area when calculating his workpoints. The first plowing of a field of 1 *mu* prior to planting jute, wheat, and green manure (azolla), would be rewarded with the same number of workpoints as the reward for plowing a rice field. The plowing of unusually hard fields after the second harvest, to prepare them for fallowing during the winter, required more effort and time, so the workpoint payment was increased to 10 workpoints per *mu*, if the field was near and 11, if it was distant. Plowing the fields for the second rice crop was valued at 4·5 workpoints per *mu* for fields near the village, and 5 for distant fields. This allowed for the fact that the fields for the second crop were often under water, or muddy, and more difficult to plow.

There were further conditions for plowing set forth. To protect the water buffaloes from over use, it was specified that each buffalo should not be used to earn more than 12 workpoints, for working two three-hour shifts a day, or 15 workpoints, if three shifts were worked. No workpoints would be given if earned by abusing a tired, overworked animal, which was an expensive piece of team property. This applied to first-grade water buffaloes; second- and third-grade animals (i.e. older, smaller, and weaker ones) had more stringent restrictions on their use. Plainly, these complex and detailed descriptions covered almost every contingency.

In some cases, team members objected to the rewards stipulated by the workpoint book, and team leaders could negotiate with team members to reward labor with some flexibility. For example, Pondside's Number 4 team needed to haul bamboo from a neighboring commune to supply the team's handicraft industry. A group of team members declined the assignment, saying that it was too late in the day to travel such a long distance, too hot for such heavy work, and that in any case the standard workpoints for the task were too low. In response, the team leader increased the number of workpoints to be shared by the group, and gave them a small amount of cash from the team to buy fish and rice to eat along the way. By this means, he succeeded in having the work completed.

Another variation from the workpoint book occurred in midsummer, the busiest season of the agricultural year in Zengbu. Pondside Number 4 team had to harvest the first crop of rice, plow the fields, and transplant the second crop, all within a very short time, and it began to seem likely that the team's crop of peanuts would be left standing in the ground. The peanuts had to be harvested before they rotted in the wet soil, and the fields in which they stood plowed, so that other crops could be planted. The team leader of Pondside Number 4 team offered a bonus of workpoints to divide among the team members assigned to a peanut work group, if they would uproot the peanuts at faster than the normal rate; working at the normal rate would mean the loss of the team's peanut crop. The group succeeded in harvesting the peanuts three days earlier than they would otherwise have done. Workpoints worth 90 *yuan* were shared among the peanut harvesters, who divided the bonus according to their own estimates of the worth of each person's work. (Sometimes such work groups would divide the lump sum received from the team according to basic labor grades and sometimes on a task-rate basis, or a combination of the two, thus adding an informal sector to workpoint distribution.)

Workpoint recorders went to the field to check the work accomplished by team members. At the end of the day, the workpoint recorder noted down on a slip of paper the tasks each worker had performed. The workers kept their own records as well, in small handbooks. The accountant received the slips from the workpoint recorder and entered them into the team's account books. The total points each member earned were posted on a monthly basis. Workers could then check the accountant's figures against their own records. Often there were disagreements between worker and workpoint recorder over the proper reward for a particular task. In spite of the specificity of the workpoint book, team members could generally find a point of contention. Perhaps the fields had been especially hard, or the buffalo weaker than usual. Team officials had the authority to make minor adjustments in awarding workpoints; they had to do so frequently.

Under the basic labor-grade system, by comparison, each team member was rated according to intrinsic worth as a worker, at so many workpoints per day. The rating depended on the team leader's assessment of the worker's skill, ability, and willingness to work. A standard workpoint rating for a first-class male worker was 10 points per day. Younger and older men received fewer workpoints for a day's work, as did women. A person rated as a ten-point-a-day worker received 10 workpoints for working a standard day, as a salary. Every worker on a team had an assigned labor grade. In 1979,

Table 6. *Workpoint values of Zengbu labor grades*

|  | Men | Women |
|---|---|---|
| GRADES |  |  |
| First | 10 | 8·3 |
| Second | 9·7 | 8·0 |
| Third | 9·4 | 7·6 |
| Fourth | 9·1 | 7·3 |

most Zengbu teams rewarded from 70 to 80 percent of their work on a task-rate basis, but odd jobs, or work that could not be easily measured was paid according to the workers' basic labor grade.

The Zengbu standards, although variable from team to team, were generally as shown in table 6. More women were classified into lesser grades, as shown in table 7, an example from Sandhill Number 6 team. It is evident that women were discriminated against in the awarding of basic labor grades. Eighty-three percent of the men were rated as first grade workers, compared to only 25 percent of the women, who fell mainly into the second grade. This form of discrimination against women had been even more blatant during the Cultural Revolution, when labor was rewarded primarily by labor grade rather than by task-rate. Women's pay was more equitable when they were paid on a task-rate basis. According to the leaders of the Women's Federation of Dongguan county, women much preferred the task-rate method of reward that was being used predominantly in 1979. Even under the task-rate system, however, women were still discriminated against: traditional jobs of men continued to be defined as intrinsically of greater value than traditional jobs of women, so women's jobs were more poorly rewarded.

A specific example will serve to show how labor was rewarded in practice. An old woman of Sandhill Number 6 team had the basic labor grade rating of a third-class woman worker, so her labor was valued at 7·6 workpoints per day. On December 1, 1979, she planted winter wheat for her team and earned 18 workpoints, on a task-rate basis. On December 2, she weeded fields with a hoe for the entire day, and was paid 7·6 workpoints, according to her basic labor grade. On December 3, she carried water for one-half day and made 3·8 workpoints, one-half her basic rating. During the afternoon she collected dried straw from the second harvest rice fields on a task-rate basis, and earned 7·8 workpoints. On December 6, she selected seed garlic, and was paid 7·6 workpoints, according to her basic labor grade. On December 7, 8, 9, and 10 she cultivated arrowhead by basic labor grade and made 30·4 workpoints over the four days.

The Sandhill Number 6 team accountant entered her daily earnings in his

Table 7. *Labor grades of Zengbu men and women*

| Labor Grades | 1 | 2 | 3 | 4 |
|---|---|---|---|---|
| Men | 83% | 6% | 10% | 1% |
| Women | 25% | 60% | 7% | 8% |

workpoint book, on the account page of her household, beside the earnings of all the other members of her household. He subtotalled her earnings every 10 or 11 days. She earned 75·2 workpoints from December 1 to December 10.

The careful team workpoint records allowed an exact measure of the economic contribution of Zengbu men and women to their teams and to the incomes of their households. Men earned more workpoints on the average than women. Figure 6 displays workpoints earned per year by men in the three Zengbu villages. Figure 7 shows women's workpoint earnings. These figures are consistent with local rule-of-thumb estimates that the men usually earned from 4,000 to 5,000 workpoints a year, and women from 3,000 to 4,000.

Figures 6 and 7 show clearly the patterns of workpoint earnings for workers of both sexes at different ages. Men began work at the age of 16, and their earnings quickly rose to the height of their earning power, 4,700 points per year (517 *yuan* per year or 43 *yuan* per month) by their middle forties. After that they remained at an earning plateau of around 4,000 workpoints a year, gradually declining in earning ability, until their mid-sixties, when their earnings declined precipitously until they reached the age of 75. After the age of 75 their earnings remained at a plateau of about 2,800 workpoints per year (26 *yuan* per month) until they died. Both men and women in Zengbu continued to work as long as they were physically able to do so, and did not usually retire. Their self-esteem depended upon their ability to contribute economically to their households and to support themselves so as not to be a burden on others.

Women's life pattern of workpoint earnings was different. Unmarried women, from their mid-teens to their early twenties, earned more work-points on the average than their unmarried brothers – a remarkable finding, since it suggests a level of effort so great as to overcome a consistently unequal reward structure. (For a psychological explanation of this phenomenon, see chapter 9.) These women married out of their families in their mid-twenties; at the same age, other women married into Zengbu. These new brides tended to give birth to a child as soon as possible, usually within the first year or two after marriage. However, their workpoint earnings rose sharply throughout their late twenties and early thirties. In spite of being classified into lower labor grades, laboring at tasks which were defined as less valuable, and having

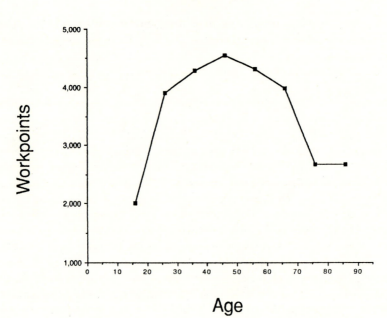

Figure 6. Male workpoints, by age, Zengbu brigade, 1978

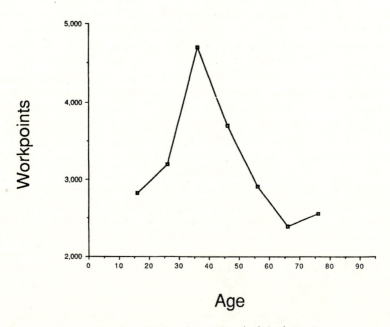

Figure 7. Female workpoints, by age, Zengbu brigade, 1978

to bear and care for young children, the earnings of Zengbu women continued to rise, reaching a peak in their mid-thirties, at an average level of almost 5,000 workpoints per year (46 *yuan* per month), surpassing the average earnings of men of that age group. Beginning around the age of forty, the workpoint earnings of women sharply declined and continued to decline through their fifties and sixties. One reason for this was that these women took over child care duties and housework for their daughters-in-law, freeing the younger women for work in the fields. In their late sixties and seventies the workpoint earnings of Zengbu women rose once more. In spite of the moral pressure for sons to care for their aged parents, many old women were left to live alone and support themselves.

Since peasants did not have control of their own labor power, they were not allowed to work outside of the team framework without permission from team leaders. In such cases, the outside unit employing the team member (most often the brigade or the state) would remit any wages earned directly to the team. The team member received team workpoints according to labor grade; the only exceptions to this were small piecework incentives. When outside units rewarded labor at a higher rate than the team, the higher reward was not the property of the person who earned it, but was divided among team members. Team members with outside employment did not increase their own income, except insofar as they increased the income of the team as a whole. Team members who had skills, such as sewing clothes, for which they might be paid by fellow villagers, were supposed to turn the money over to the team, and to be credited with workpoints. Thus, it was impossible to increase one's own income relative to other team members. To sell goods or services for private profit was to risk being denounced as capitalist. Only by maintaining strict economic equality among team members, and promoting economic development through collective action, was the old class-differentiated society to be prevented from re-emerging. Under the team, the Zengbu peasants lost the opportunity to strive, as individuals, to become wealthy – their major life goal in the old society.

Zengbu peasants did not receive rations from the state, as urban residents did; production teams were responsible for distributing rice rations and other collective benefits to team members. If the harvest was good, team members could eat well; otherwise they could not. When rice yields were so low that peasant rations would fall below the starvation level (41 *jin* per person per month of unhusked rice), the state took the responsibility of selling enough additional grain back to the team to bring rice rations up to the minimum necessary for subsistence. In Zengbu, this had most recently been necessary after the fall harvest of 1978.

In Guangdong province as a whole, there were at least three systems in use for the distribution of rice to households by teams. In some areas, rice was distributed in proportion to workpoints earned. In others, a ratio was

Table 8. *Rice rationing guide, Sandhill village, 1978*

|  | Summer distribution | Fall distribution |
|---|---|---|
|  | *Jin* per month | *Jin* per month |
| **Ages** | | |
| 1 | 17 | 12 |
| 2 | 19 | 13 |
| 3 | 21 | 15 |
| 4/5 | 24 | 17 |
| 6/7 | 27 | 19 |
| 8/9 | 31 | 22 |
| 10/11 | 35 | 24 |
| 12/13 | 40 | 28 |
| 14/15 | 45 | 35 |
| 16 | 50 | 35 |
| Male (middle school) | 53 | 37 |
| Female (middle school) | 50 | 35 |
| Old man | 50 | 35 |
| Old woman | 47 | 33 |
| **Grades of male laborers** | | |
| 1 | 72 | 50 |
| 2 | 66 | 46 |
| 3 | 60 | 42 |
| 4 | 56 | 39 |
| **Grades of female laborers** | | |
| 1 | 66 | 46 |
| 2 | 62 | 43 |
| 3 | 56 | 39 |
| 4 | 52 | 36 |

established between age, sex, and labor grade, and total workpoints earned. This ratio was then used as the basis for rice distribution. Zengbu used a third system, according to which rice was distributed on the basis of the age, sex, and labor grade of each member of the household, and workpoint earnings were not taken into account. Zengbu's system affirmed the importance of the consumption needs of the household, emphasizing the principle, "to each according to his need." Systems which based rice distribution on workpoints, by comparison, emphasized the principle, "to each according to his work."

One teams's rice distribution guidelines were as shown in table 8. One household in this team (Sandhill Number 6) had children aged eight, ten, twelve, and fifteen. The father was a first-grade male laborer, and the mother a second-grade female laborer. For the eight-year-old daughter, the family was entitled to receive 31 *jin* of unhusked rice per month at the summer rice distribution; for the ten-year-old son, 35 *jin*; for the twelve-year-old son, 40 *jin*; and for the fifteen-year-old daughter, 45 *jin*. The father was entitled to 72 *jin* per month; and the mother, 62 *jin* per month. The members of the sample household were therefore entitled to 285 *jin* of unhusked rice per month as their grain ration. At the first rice harvest, Sandhill Number 6 team, according to custom, distributed rations for five months, which were to last from August through December, when the second rice harvest would be distributed. The sample household, then, took home a total of 1,425 *jin* for five months. The rice was stored at home, and taken to be milled as needed at the brigade mill.

Rice rations were paid for by team members, who were charged the state quota sales price. When rice was distributed, the cost was debited from the household's account. The costs of other commodities distributed by the team, such as oil, peanuts, and fish, were also debited from the household's workpoint income. The electricity bills of team members and the contributions of each household to the brigade's health cooperative system were similarly handled. The team made periodic cash advances (in effect, advances on workpoint earnings) to its households to cover their needs between harvests; these were also debited against workpoint income. If any family found itself in dire financial straits because of an illness or some other good reason, and did not earn enough workpoints to cover its debits, the team committee could waive the balance or give the household another year to pay its debt to the team. The household account, shown in table 9, from the pages of the Sandhill Number 6 team account book, in 1979, is representative of a medium-sized household of six persons, containing three workers.

At the end of each half-year's operation, the team accountant prepared a detailed report on the economic performance of the team as a collective enterprise. He recorded the team's gross income from agriculture, forestry, domestic animals, tree crops, fishponds, and rural industry, with records of expenses paid, taxes paid, state purchase quotas filled, and the amount set aside by the team for capital expenditures (such as new tractors, threshers, and winnowers, of which each team had several), and to purchase seeds, fertilizers, and insecticides for the team's fields. He also kept records of the amount set aside by the team for charity, to care for old people of the team who had no sons to support them in their old age.

The production team tended to weaken the force of Chinese familism. As Mao (1954, p. 45) had pointed out, the closed framework of the traditional repressive family system had provided no escape from the formal authority of the senior male who was head of household. The team diluted the authority of the male head of household by subordinating junior family members to the authority of elected team leaders. The work of the young and of women was

Table 9. *A household account*

|  |  | Yuan |
|---|---|---|
| April 30 | 1. White sugar, 1·7 *jin* per person, totals 10·2 *jin*, at 0·38 *yuan* per *jin* | 3·88 |
|  | 2. Wheat, 77 *jin* at 0·14 *yuan* per *jin* | 10·78 |
| June 30 | 1. Rice equivalent of wheat ration, 130 *jin* | 15·08 |
|  | 2. One half year medical coop fee | 10·80 |
|  | 3. One-half year rice straw, 107 *jin* | 5·35 |
|  | 4. Electricity fee, half-year | 2·33 |
|  | 5. Rice ration, five months, 1,555 *jin* | 180·38 |
| August 31 | 1. Money distribution | 318·00 |
|  | 2. Peanut oil, 4 *jin* per person | 26·40 |
| November | 1. Money distribution | 160·00 |
| December 30 | 1. Rice straw | 4·50 |
|  | 2. Coop medical insurance fee, second half-year | 10·80 |
|  | 3. Share of team's sale of pigsty to private people | 19·00 |
|  | 4. 5 goslings to fatten for New Year | 7·50 |
|  | 5. Rice distribution, 16·45 *dan* | 190·82 |
|  | 6. Electricity fee, second half-year | 4·23 |
|  | Total debits to household | 969·85 |

evaluated publicly. Independent reputations for hard work could be earned outside the context of the family. Young men could achieve financial independence more quickly, since a young man could make almost as many workpoints as his father only a year or two after he began to be a full-time team worker.

The status and independence of rural women were enhanced under the production team, although women never achieved equality with men, either economically, socially, or politically. However, their position in all these areas was somewhat improved. With the public posting of workpoint earnings, women's capacity to work was socially validated and affirmed. Women's workpoints were tangible indicators of their economic contribution. The problem was that it was the male household head, and not the woman worker, who received the cash value of her workpoint earnings from the team at the end of the year. Women were seen to earn, and the value of their earnings was socially acknowledged, but nonetheless, they did not control their earnings themselves. In terms of their participation in village-level governmental process, women took part in the voting for team committee members. In former times, they had not even been allowed into the ancestral hall to observe the deliberations of the lineage leaders. This was a significant change.

The team acted to establish and maintain social and economic equality among peasant households over the course of their life-cycle. With private ownership of the means of production and private inheritance eliminated, and employment and entrepreneurship outside the team context greatly restricted, the team was a force in opposition to the re-emergence of economic inequalities and class stratification.

The team guaranteed a certain minimum of security. Members had the right to work, the right to receive their rice rations, and the right to their share of the income of their team, in proportion to their work. Such safeguards against unemployment, lack of availability of grain, and the possibility that one's labor might be unrewarded, were significant contributions to the welfare of the peasants, who, under the old society, had been at the mercy of these contingencies.

Since the team drew on a large pool of available labor, the presence of weaker laborers did not endanger the economic welfare of the group as it may do in a household. The team had enough strong labor for its needs, and could make allowance for those whose capacities were less. The needs of pregnant or nursing women could be considered in work assignments, so that they were not asked to do jobs that might endanger their own health or the health of their infants. Elderly couples without sons or kin were not required by force of circumstances to perform the heaviest tasks of rice agriculture by themselves. In the forestry team, for example, old people could maintain self-respect while earning workpoints at jobs that were not too heavy for them. When the household is the organizational unit of production, its small size and vulnerability at certain stages of the household cycle create hardship, because the lack of available labor power forces the weak to struggle at tasks that may be beyond their ability. The team provided a scale of organization that made this unnecessary.

The teams permitted a scale of farming large enough to make mechanization economically feasible. Households, working separately on small-scale farms, would not have been able to afford large equipment; it would not be economically feasible for one household to buy a tractor or a diesel thresher or winnower. The teams provided an essential framework for mechanizing Chinese agriculture and easing the labor burden on the peasants. (For the demechanization of the countryside under the post-Mao household responsibility system, see chapter 17.)

In some respects, the teams perpetuated fundamental qualities of the existing order. Where Chinese cultural assumptions ran deep, the team enacted them. Thus, the team was a kin-based, patrilineal organization; groups of men controlled the means of production. The team was a peasant organization in a stratified society, controlled by a bureaucratic elite. But in other respects, the production teams provided an effective organizational basis for the implementation of planned social change. They could control and modify the social organization of agricultural production on a scale large enough to be workable, but not so large as to be unwieldy. They were the framework for a set of working relationships that maintained an improved level of egalitarianism and social justice, at least within the team. They guaranteed the peasants an assured food supply, and the opportunity to work, where there had previously been unemployment and starvation. These were significant changes.

# 6

# Maoist society: the brigade

The production brigade was a social, economic, political, accounting, and industrial management level intermediate between the teams below and the commune above. Brigade administration was the job of the Zengbu Party Branch Committee, and brigade leaders were all party cadres (see chapter 13). In their capacity as intermediaries, brigade cadres represented the teams and the peasants to the commune, and the commune to the teams and the peasants. Brigade cadres were responsible for supervising the teams and their productive activities. They mediated between the teams when there was conflict over such matters as irrigation water. The brigade also administered economic enterprises of its own, both agricultural and industrial, and social services, such as schools and the health clinic. The brigade was a corporate group with its own property, income, budget, and administrative staff.

The brigade's operations were centered in the brigade headquarters building, which contained an auditorium for large assemblies, a smaller meeting room for the branch party committee, offices, dormitory rooms for brigade cadres and visitors, a kitchen staffed by two cooks and a cook's helper, a dining hall, showers, privies, and a well. Nearby was an open-air theatre belonging to the brigade, for holding mass meetings, or for viewing movies or the performances of visiting opera companies. (During the Cultural Revolution, the brigade cadres had been denounced in this theatre.)

Also belonging to the brigade was a large brick building which housed the Zengbu branch of the state trading and supply organization. This was a department store selling manufactured goods to peasants and buying local peasant products. Across from the state store was the brigade's health clinic, and an associated Chinese herbal medicine store. The brigade owned a slaughter house, for the preparation of pork to be sold in the small meat stalls in the villages. It owned an administrative center for brigade enterprises, a rice mill, a tractor and bicycle repair station, a sawmill and carpentry shop, a garage and gasoline depot where the brigade's small fleet of trucks was housed and a plastics factory. The brigade owned Zengbu's two primary

4. Zengbu brigade headquarters, 1979

5. Brigade office, 1979, with one of Zengbu's most experienced cadres

schools, a small library, and the Zengbu branch of the commune credit cooperative. It had fishponds, orchards, and a small vegetable garden, to supply the brigade's kitchen. It ran a palm-leaf fan and mat factory, brick kilns, and a jute-washing facility on the river. The brigade owned water pumping stations to control irrigation. It owned diesel generators to supplement the state-supplied power system, which went off every evening. The generators allowed the brigade to operate its plastics factory during the night as well as during the day.

Zengbu brigade was the largest of Chashan commune's fifteen brigades, with a population of approximately 5,000 in 1979. The smallest was Sunwu brigade, with 562 people, and the average population per brigade was 2,107 persons. Brigades in Chashan commune were larger, on the average, than other brigades in Guangdong province. In 1979, the average brigade in Guangdong province included 1,650 people, and the average brigade in China as a whole included 1,162 people (Xue 1982, p.965). Zengbu brigade had 17 production teams. This was more than twice as many teams as the average of 7·3 for brigades in Chashan commune. The average number of teams in a brigade for China as a whole was 7·4 (Xue 1982, p.965).

Land ownership per capita varied greatly from brigade to brigade. Among the Chashan commune brigades, Sunwu had the least, with only 0·79 *mu* per capita of farmland. Zengbu was next poorest, with 0·81 *mu* per capita. Chaolang, a rich brigade, had the most, with 1·88 *mu* per capita, over twice as much. Like the inequalities between teams in the same village, and villages in the same brigade, the inequalities between brigades had been carried over from before Liberation and no attempt had been made to equalize land ownership at the brigade level.

Chashan brigades varied in size from one to eight villages; the average brigade contained three villages. There was a correspondence between the Maoist brigades and the pre-Liberation lineages. Five of the Chashan brigades were territorially equivalent to one single-lineage village each. Six Chashan brigades were based upon single lineages which included more than one village. (These multi-village lineages resembled such previously described lineages as Ping Shan, in Hong Kong's New Territories, see J. M. Potter 1968). Only three of the brigades in Chashan commune included more than one lineage; Zengbu was one of these.

Thus eleven of the Chashan brigades, 80 percent of them, were based upon a lineage, either a lineage concentrated in one large village or a lineage comprised of several subbranches in different villages. This implied a structural continuity between lineage and collective at the brigade level: both were patrilocal residential communities made up of men descended patrilineally from a common ancestor, and both rested upon a material base of corporately owned landed property, in which each member had a share. (See chapter 12 for further discussion of the significance of this.) Lineage *seg-*

*ments* had been crosscut and replaced by the teams, but the corporate lineage *as a whole* tended to be preserved in the brigade.

The brigade was the level at which basic social services for the peasants were administered. The brigade's health clinic was the Zengbu branch of China's rural medical care system. Originally founded by the commune, the health clinic had been operated by the brigade since 1968. There were three barefoot doctors practicing in Zengbu. Two of them had been trained at Dongguan county's Public Health School (one for two years and the other for one), and one had studied at Zhongshan Medical School in Guangzhou for two years. The first two had also studied at the commune hospital in Chashan. All three attended a refresher course of clinical training at the hospital each year. They used both Chinese and Western methods in their treatment.

There was a midwife, who attended births in the homes of Zengbu women. Women usually gave birth to their first children at the commune hospital and to all subsequent children, assuming that there were no complications, at home under the care of the midwife.

There was a clinic nurse, who immunized children against communicable diseases, gave injections of antibiotics, and assisted the doctors. There were two Chinese herbal doctors, local practitioners whose skills had been passed down in their families. There was a cashier who collected fees and kept the books.

Members of the clinic staff were paid through their respective production teams. The brigade paid cash to the teams for the salaries of the health workers, and the teams credited the health workers with workpoints. They received the cash value of their workpoints at the end of the year. This meant that some of the doctors made more money than others for the same work; workpoint values varied from team to team.

In 1979 the cost of an average office visit to the clinic was 0·50 *yuan* (about 33 U.S. cents). The maximum charge for an office visit was 1 *yuan*. Medicine was extra, but very cheap. Patients paid directly for treatment, and were recompensed at the rate of 90 percent of the cost of treatment by the brigade health insurance. Health insurance cost Zengbu residents 0·30 *yuan* per person per month. This amount was deducted from household workpoints by the team accountants and forwarded to the brigade level. The health insurance and clinic fees were not enough to cover the cost of the clinic's operation; the balance was made up each year by the brigade from the profits of brigade enterprises. In 1981, the health cooperative's deficit, paid by the brigade, was 35,000 *yuan*.

The health clinic held office hours from 6:30 a.m. until 10:00 a.m., 12:00 noon until 2:00 p.m., and from 3:30 p.m. to 5:00 p.m. In the summer the clinic tended to treat stomach upsets and fevers; in winter, colds and fevers.

The brigade clinic's doctors were prohibited from treating major illnesses:

their role was to treat minor ailments and to screen cases for referral to the commune hospital. For problems defined as serious, such as broken bones, extensive burns, electric shock, or severe abdominal distress, the patient would be sent to the commune hospital in town. Patients were transported by means of a bicycle-tired handcart. (New fathers brought home their wives and firstborn children from the commune hospital on these carts.)

The health clinic placed great stress on preventive medicine. Children were immunized against tetanus, (informants described a number of deaths from tetanus), "infectious coughs," whooping cough, polio, and, the clinic workers claimed, meningitis. Responsibility for ensuring that each child in the team went to the clinic for injections at the appropriate time was delegated to a team representative.

In practicing traditional Chinese medicine at the health clinic, doctors acted on the belief that a healthy body was one in which the humors of the body – hot and cold, wet and dry – were properly balanced. Illness was caused by bodily imbalance brought on by improper eating and by changing weather. Illnesses with symptoms of a dry mouth, a sore throat, cracked lips, and a cough, were caused by an excess of dry heat in the body. Stomach-ache, constipation, diminished urine flow, and a yellow and white mouth were caused by an excess of wet heat. (Western cabbage was believed to be extremely "wet and hot," and this was why it was used only as food for pigs.)

To prevent illness, the people of Zengbu prepared their meals so that the body's balance between hot and cold would be maintained. In order to do this, they classified all foods either as "hot," or "cold." Illnesses were due to imbalance in the body caused by an excessive eating of either cold or hot foods, particularly the latter. Winter diseases were usually due to an excess of hot, because in winter people liked to eat deep-fried foods like *youtiao* (a long, deep-fried bread) and fried eggs. For an excess of hot, Chinese medicinal herbs were boiled down, according to prescription, into a tea, called " cold tea," which was supposed to restore the body's balance. In hot weather people tended to eat too much cooling food, leading to an excess of cold. For an excess of cold, the Chinese doctors at the health clinic prescribed a little ginger.

The people of Zengbu – both laymen and medical practitioners alike – believed firmly in the superiority of Chinese medicine. They said that Western medicine (by which they meant mainly the injection of antibiotics) cured quickly, but it did not cure completely. Furthermore, Western medicine had strong side effects. In contrast, Chinese medicine was thought to be slower, but the cure was permanent.

Given this preference for Chinese medicine, most of the prescriptions given by the doctor at the health clinic (and by lay practitioners in the village) were for Chinese herbs. The brigade operated a Chinese medicinal herb shop. The medicine shop contained drawers of herbs such as angelica root, the fruit of the Chinese wartberry, the root of the herbaceous peony, licorice root, and the root of the hairy asia bell. Prescriptions written by clinic doctors were paid for by the health cooperative insurance. Those written by unofficial local practitioners were paid for by the patients themselves. (See chapter 7 for a description of the commune's health insurance system).

The brigade was also responsible for local level defense, and ran the militia. The militia was divided into two categories, the basic militia and the armed militia. The basic militia consisted of all men aged 15 to 30, and all women aged 16 to 25. According to the commander, the functions of the basic militia were to actively take part in socialist revolution and construction, to complete their work actively and well, in order to set a good example, and to safeguard the fatherland and fight oppressors. In practice, the basic militia performed such tasks as repairing damaged levees in a flood.

The armed militia were party members, usually army veterans. They were under the control of the commune-level armed militia, and would be called out if it became necessary to stop fights between villages, to safeguard collective property, or to protect such installations as bridges and railway stations in the event of a national emergency.

The Zengbu Credit Cooperative (*Zengbu xinyong hezuoshe*) was run by the brigade in order to "concentrate the savings of the people and keep them safely, to loan money to people in case of emergency, and to help the brigade and the teams to improve their production." The brigade cadre in charge of finance was responsible for the credit cooperative at the brigade level. Structurally, the brigade credit cooperative was subordinate to the commune credit cooperative, which was, in essence, a branch of the state bank. (The employees of the Zengbu Credit Cooperative brought their money out to the brigade from the Chashan bank each morning, and took it back to the Chashan bank for safekeeping at the end of each day.) Each of the three villages had a separate branch office of the brigade credit cooperative, staffed by two employees – one a state cadre, paid by the state, and the other a brigade employee, paid by workpoints through his team. The brigade employee, classified as a peasant, made much less than his state cadre colleague, classified as a worker (see chapter 15), and did not have a retirement pension or any of the other perquisites that the state cadre enjoyed, in spite of the fact that the two did the same work.

Most Zengbu families kept an account in their village's credit cooperative. As one of the peasants said, "It keeps the money safe, and it prevents the children from stealing the money to buy candy, as they might do if it was left at home." Sometimes different family members had separate accounts. The credit cooperative officers were required by law to keep accounts secret. Two types of accounts were available. One was a "current deposit" account, which paid low interest (0·18% a month), but let the depositor draw out funds freely with no interest penalty. Time deposit accounts were also available. Money left for one year earned interest at 0·33% per month, money left for three years earned 0·375% per month, and money left for five years earned 0·40% per month. There were penalties for early withdrawal.

In 1979 the brigade cadre in charge of finance said that the savings accounts of Zengbu households could be divided into three categories. The largest deposits, from 3,000 to 5,000 *yuan*, were owned by only a handful of households, usually those with overseas relatives. Average deposits, from 400 to 500 *yuan*, were held by most of the Zengbu households. Small deposits of 1 to 10 *yuan* were held by the poorest families.

Money could be borrowed from the credit cooperative, under certain conditions. A cooperative could lend only 40% of its deposits, 60% being held in reserve at all times. Private people could borrow only for emergencies: to pay the expenses of an illness, to buy food to last until the next team distribution, or to cover minor expenses in the building of a house. (A maximum of 200 to 300 *yuan* was loaned for building expenses. In 1979, the cost of building a house was more than 10,000 *yuan*.) Borrowing to buy a new bicycle, for example, would not be accepted as a legitimate emergency.

Borrowing by villagers was ordinarily limited to 100 *yuan*; loans over this amount had to be approved by the brigade cadre in charge of finance. People could have more than one current loan as long as they did not exceed their 100 *yuan* limit. The director of the Lu's Home branch of the credit cooperative estimated that in 1979 about 10 percent of the village's members borrowed from the cooperative, usually small sums of 10 to 20 *yuan* at a time. They paid a flat interest rate of 0·36 *yuan* a month, or 4·32% per year, on these loans. No collateral was necessary. Households were held collectively responsible for any money borrowed from the cooperative, with sons having to pay off debts incurred by their father. If a family could not pay interest because of family difficulties, such as illness, the cadres reported this to the brigade; if the brigade approved, the family would be given up to three years to repay the loan, with no further interest being charged. The credit cooperative was assured, ultimately, of repayment. Since the brigade and team cadres controlled all income distributions to their constituent households, they could deduct the amount owed the cooperative from a household's income at the end of the year.

The Zengbu collectives, whether at the team or the brigade level, could borrow in order to increase production. The loans were at a special low rate of interest, 0·18% month. However, when the collectives made deposits, they received only 0·15% a month as interest, a lower rate than the 0·18% paid to private depositors.

These conditions for borrowing represent a reaction against the extreme usuriousness of pre-Liberation lending practices; there is no sense, here, that historical practice is being unconsciously perpetuated. Rather there is an insistence on low interest rates, remission of interest in cases of hardship, and reforms designed to provide some protection for the borrower.

It was also possible to borrow money privately, from friends and relatives, and many, perhaps most, people did so, rather than borrowing from the cooperative, since it was less embarrassing, and larger sums of money could be borrowed. Such borrowing was usually for the purpose of house building. There was no law regulating the amount of interest that a private lender could charge, but a lender found to be charging too much would be publicly criticized.

The brigade had a branch of the state supply and marketing organization, and this was a key unit in local commerce. Most large brigades in Dongguan county had their own branches of the state store, and in 1977 the brigade cadres of Zengbu applied to the state for permission to have such a store and for funds to build it. The commune and county levels approved the application and provided 26,000 *yuan* for the purchase of building materials. Zengbu brigade supplied the labor from the brigade's construction team, and the building was built.

The store was under the direction of the provincial purchasing and marketing organization for the countryside, and served a dual function, buying from the peasants and selling to them. It bought agricultural products and peasant handicraft goods from the people of Zengbu: bamboo shrimp traps, palm-leaf fans, peanut oil, dried litchis, dried longans, sugar, soybeans, and cassava. During the first 11 months of 1979, the Zengbu store purchased goods worth 280,000 *yuan* from Zengbu peasants, and sold them goods worth 260,000 *yuan*, so that the net balance of trade was slightly in favor of the peasants. The store was authorized to purchase unlimited amounts of foodstuffs, but only limited quantities of handicrafts that the provincial purchasing organization was sure of being able to sell. This reflected the operation of supply and demand under the state economy. When the store was buying bamboo shrimp traps, for example, there would be an announcement that a specified quantity of shrimp traps would be bought at a given price on a particular day. Then peasants would line up early, hoping to sell their shrimp traps before the store bought its quota.

The people of Zengbu purchased most of their durable goods from this store, which carried the same range of goods, purchased wholesale from the same state trading company, as other branches of the same organization, including the slightly larger one in Chashan town. An examination of peasant purchases and the prices paid for goods gives an intimate view of the quality of material life during the Maoist period.

Cloth was a significant item purchased by the peasants. Each person, in 1979, was allotted 13 *chi* (about 4 meters) of cotton cloth per year, or about enough for one adult's suit of clothes, including top and trousers. The villagers had several choices in using their cloth rations. They could buy 100%

cotton cloth in the amount specified, or they could buy larger amounts of cloth woven from 60% dacron and 40% cotton. A ration coupon good for the purchase of 3 *chi* (1 meter) of 100% cotton cloth could be used for 7·5 *chi* (2·5 meters) of dacron and cotton mixture. A third choice, at least in theory, would be to buy cloth made entirely of artificial fiber, but this was far too expensive.

Cotton cloth coupons were also necessary to buy mosquito netting, which was an essential item for villagers. A ration coupon good for 3 *chi* of cotton cloth could be used to buy 36 *chi* of mosquito netting.

Cloth prices in 1979 at the brigade store were 2·04 *yuan* per meter (U.S.$ 1·36) for blue 100% cotton cloth 75 centimeters wide. Checkered cloth of 100% cotton, 90 centimeters wide, was 1·50 *yuan* (U.S.$ 1) per meter. Dacron and cotton cloth 90 centimeters wide was 4·50 *yuan* per meter (U.S.$ 3). Completely artificial-fiber cloth was 4·65 *yuan* per meter; no ration coupon was necessary, since this cloth contained no cotton.

The cloth business quickened before New Year, because, in traditional Chinese fashion, people wanted new suits of clothes to mark the season. One store clerk commented that peasants bought the cheapest cotton cloth, even though the variety was small and the quality low, because that was all they could afford, and even then they did not have enough coupons to buy as much as they needed. He said that in his opinion, one of the best ways to improve people's lives would be to have more cloth of a better quality available.

The state store sold what the Chinese call supplementary foods, chrysanthemum wine at 1·80 *yuan* per bottle, and beer. There were high-quality cigarettes for 0·40 *yuan* per pack, medium-quality for 0·27 to 0·30 per pack (about 7 U.S. cents). Most local people smoked the medium-priced brands.

Zengbu peasants could purchase rice noodles, wheat noodles, cookies, and cakes at the store. However, since these commodities came under state grain rationing rules and peasants had no ration coupons for rice or wheat, a quantity of rice equal in weight to what was purchased had to be paid to the store in lieu of coupons. For example, peasants who bought 1 *jin* of cookies for 0·50 *yuan*, had to bring 1 *jin* of rice (for which they were credited 0·1 *yuan*) and pay an additional 0·4 *yuan* to the store in cash to cover the balance of the price of the cookies.

The store had a variety of manufactured goods. There were Shanghai-made mechanical alarm clocks, weak light bulbs to light the houses of the thrifty Zengbu peasants, thermos bottles of various colors and sizes, thread, Japanese-style thong sandals, cloth shoes, rubber rain boots, screwdrivers, electrical supplies, padlocks, fountain pens, ballpoint pens, plastic wash basins, towels and washcloths, stationery, toilet paper, ink, bicycles, made-in-China black-and-white television sets and electric fans. A 9-inch television set cost 240 *yuan* (about U.S.$ 160), a 12-inch set 410 *yuan* ($ 273), and a

14-inch set 470 *yuan* ($ 313). These were extremely high prices by world standards, and, given the fact that an adult peasant man had an income of only about 40 *yuan* per month, entirely out of reach of the peasants. No televisions were purchased by Zengbu peasants as individuals, although a few had been purchased collectively by the brigade and the individual teams. Private purchasers preferred to have a relative bring in a large-screen color television set from Hong Kong. (The villagers fixed antennas on top of bamboo poles and bought special tuners so that they might receive Hong Kong television.)

One of the major economic difficulties of Maoist China was the inability of the industrial cities to supply the peasants with manufactured goods of reasonable quality at reasonable prices. The peasants of Zengbu supplied rice and other foodstuffs to the comparatively privileged urban residents of China at artificially low prices. However the peasants did not receive in return the inexpensive and well-made goods that would have been necessary to improve their lives and to stimulate the growth of the economy; such manufactured goods as were available to peasants were shoddy and overpriced. Urban residents benefited economically at the expense of the peasants, who were in effect an exploited class.

As well as providing social services, such as the health post, and running economic organizations like the credit cooperative and department store in conjunction with the state, Zengbu brigade also acted as an economic entrepreneur in its own right, and ran a series of factories and enterprises. The income from these sources was used to pay for the expenses of running the brigade and funding its activities. In 1974–5, in one of the periodic shifts of administrative responsibility so characteristic of Chinese rural government, the brigade first took over the management of a number of local enterprises that had formerly been run by the villages. There was some argument at the time between those who thought that rural industries should continue to be managed at the village level and those who wanted to create larger, more efficient, and more highly collectivized enterprises at the brigade level, and the centralizers prevailed. Subsequently, the brigade developed new enterprises, like the plastics factory and the truck transportation unit. In 1979, Zengbu brigade operated 21 enterprises, all managed by brigade party cadres. Table 10 lists them, together with the number of their employees.

Workers in the Zengbu brigade enterprises were drawn from the production teams. Apart from the teams, the brigade had no constituents of its own; it was merely a management level. The brigade set its pay scale assuming workpoint values at about the average of the workpoint values of its seventeen production teams. If the brigade wages were set too high, the brigade would not make much profit, and if they were set too low, then the teams would not provide workers. The workpoint-day (the value of 10 workpoints) of the brigade from 1975 to 1978 was set at 0·80 *yuan*. This was about the average value of the work days of the teams during that period. In

Table 10. *Zengbu brigade enterprises and industries, 1979*

| | Workers |
|---|---|
| 1. Forestry team | 39 |
| 2. Farm tool repair shop | 13 |
| 3. Sawmill and carpentry shop | 13 |
| 4. Goose farm | 6 |
| 5. Pig farm | 2 |
| 6. Rice mill | 9 |
| 7. Palm-leaf fan and mat factory | 36 |
| 8. Jute processing plant | 35 |
| 9. Brick kiln number 1 | 14 |
| 10. Brick kiln number 2 | 14 |
| 11. Building and construction team | 16 |
| 12. Plastics factory | 104 |
| 13. Fish fry breeding farm number 1 | 10 |
| 14. Fish fry breeding farm number 2 | 13 |
| 15. Slaughter house | 6 |
| 16. Health clinic | 10 |
| 17. Chinese medicine shop | 2 |
| 18. Water transport team | 11 |
| 19. Truck transport team | 4 |
| 20. Agro-scientific research station | 4 |
| 21. Electric pumping and drainage units | 6 |
| Total | 367 |

1979, when the average work day value of the teams increased to 1·10 *yuan*, the brigade had to raise its wages to obtain workers from the teams.

Since the labor of team members belonged to the team, the team had to be compensated when its members went outside the team to work. The brigade remitted the wages of its employees to their teams, in cash, and the brigade employees were credited with team workpoints, the cash value of which varied from team to team. Thus peasants working in the same brigade industry and performing exactly the same job might be paid different amounts for their work, depending on the differing values of workpoints from team to team.

Two examples of brigade enterprises are the palm products factory, a traditional nonmechanized industry, and the plastics factory, a premodern industry with backward and outdated equipment.

The brigade's palm products factory was established in 1975 with 25 workers, mostly older women. It served a needed social function in giving light employment to older people. This factory made good profits in 1977 and

1978, because it received a contract for a particular type of mat, used as an adjunct in building construction, to protect pedestrians from falling material. The contract, an unenforceable oral agreement, was between the brigade and the Guangzhou Daily Life Necessities and Native Products Company. Like all agreements between peasant units and urban factories, it could be broken by the urban factory at any time with no penalties; the peasant unit bore all the risks. At the beginning of 1978, villages nearer Guangzhou began to make these mats; Zengbu lost its contract, and over 30 of the 50 people formerly employed by the factory had to be employed elsewhere.

In 1979 the factory was producing palm-leaf fans, palm brooms, and a small quantity of mats. The contract under which the fans and brooms were produced was with the same Guangzhou company that had previously contracted with the brigade for the mats. However, the fans and brooms were for export, rather than for use within China. The company furnished most of the raw materials and the factory processed them. The company paid a processing fee of 1 *yuan* per broom and from 0·11 *yuan* to 0·15 *yuan* per fan, with the rate varying according to quality. (This arrangement, according to which the collective accepted contracts for putting out work from urban Chinese factories, was used as the model when contracts were accepted from Hong Kong processing factories, starting in 1980.) The factory's yearly production was 2,500 brooms and 110,000 fans. After paying wages and management expenses, and buying some of the raw materials, the factory was left with a profit for the brigade of about 3,000 *yuan* in 1979. Without a good contract, the factory served more to provide work than to make profit.

The plastics factory had been established in Zengbu after a deliberate search for a new industry. Brigade cadres had sought help from the government trading company branch in Dongguan city, and other government units as well, in their efforts to develop a new local industry which would help to solve the serious problem of underemployment. Lubian brigade, adjacent to Zengbu on the south, ran a plastics factory which seemed to be doing well. Before investing in equipment such as plastic heaters, molds, and pressing machines, the brigade cadres sought to ensure a market for their products. They made an agreement with a Dongguan city fireworks factory (through a cadre there to whom they had personal ties) for the manufacture of plastic stands for fireworks. They made another agreement, with a Dongguan state export company, to manufacture plastic bottle caps for medicine bottles. Having assured themselves of a market as best they could, they purchased used plastic-molding machines for 120,000 *yuan* cash (about U.S.$ 79,000 at the time), which they installed in Zengbu. To do this was to undertake a sizable entrepreneurial risk.

The machines were old, inefficient, and dangerous. Raw plastic chips were put into a hopper and melted down by an exposed heating element which became red-hot. Then the operator of the machine was required to jump high up into the air, holding the end of a long lever which, on the downswing, exerted sufficient force to squeeze the melted plastic into the mold. The worker then opened the mold, removing hot plastic firecracker stands and bottle caps which had been molded into connected sheets. Other workers sorted and finished the firecracker stands and bottle caps and packed them. The work was exhausting, hot, and dangerous.

The life trajectory of the brigade plastics factory was spectacular but short. At the end of 1977, when the factory was being built and the machinery set up, the brigade requisitioned a work force of 100 from the production teams. In 1978 the factory continued to employ these workers, and during the first half of 1979 the plastics factory did extremely well. The customers were buying as many fireworks stands and bottle caps as the workers could produce. The factory began to operate 24 hours a day, with three shifts, and employed 154 people. The factory workers were offered new incentives; they could make cash bonuses of 10 to 16 *yuan* per month by producing over their quota on a piece-rate basis.

These bonuses had the effect of disturbing the collectivist and equalitarian framework of the Maoist teams. Money to pay the workers' regular workpoint earnings was sent back by the brigade to the teams, but bonuses were paid directly to the workers themselves, in cash. This altered the structure of team equalitarianism: factory workers had the opportunity to earn more than other members of the team.

However, this did not last long. In the latter part of 1979, the brigade's bottle cap contract was discontinued, and the production of stands for fireworks was reduced; the cadres of the factories which had been buying these products had transferred their patronage to other sources of plastics. The plastics factory drastically reduced its labor force to 40 workers. By the beginning of 1980, the cadres had succeeded in recouping the initial capital expenditures on the building and machinery, but the situation was discouraging, and worse was to come. By mid-1981, the factory was producing only a small number of fireworks stands, and the work force had been further reduced to 20.

The attempt to establish a rural industry that could improve the livelihood of the Zengbu peasants had failed. The brigade cadres had no modern machinery, no framework of business contracts within which to work predictably on a long-term basis with urban factories, and no contact with or knowledge of the world export market for which they were producing. Zengbu's rural industry was not a dependable source of income for the underemployed peasants. The traditional rural industries, such as the brick and tile kilns and the palm-leaf factory, were severely limited by the availability of raw materials; these, whether mud, palm leaves, or the evergreen boughs used as kiln fuel, were soon depleted or exhausted if exploited too vigorously, and the industries were not sustainable. The depletion of native raw materials was ecologically damaging. The lack of an assured market for local products with the state trading companies and the factories of the provincial and county towns was another problem. There was no stable legal framework protecting and enforcing contracts between peasant industries and state units. The peasant industries depended upon the urban factories and state export units to buy their products. However, the state units could discontinue their orders at any time, with apparent impunity, bankrupting the small peasant industries which depended upon them. The peasant units bore all the risks in the relationship.

Peasant industries like the brigade's suffered the combined deficiencies of socialism and capitalism, without the advantages of either. Peasant agriculture was rewarded at artificially low rates to subsidize the urban food supply. The brigade was forced to take entrepreneurial risks in an effort to improve the livelihood of the peasants, which was unsubsidized. Yet brigade enterprise was not planned for or protected by the socialist urban economy of the state, which, theoretically at least, could have assigned production quotas to industry and assured the sale of its products. Thus, the brigade was required to absorb serious failures and economic losses. Yet risky brigade industry was an increasingly important aspect of Zengbu's economic life: the underemployed peasants had little choice.

# 7

# Maoist society: the commune

The commune in Maoist society must be understood in terms of its structure and organization, its role as a point of articulation between rural and urban levels of stratification, and its social significance in relation to the theoretical concept of the standard marketing area.

Chashan commune includes an area roughly 7 by 8 kilometers, and contains the old market town of Chashan and 45 surrounding villages (see map 4). In July 1979, Chashan commune had a population of 35,929 people: 4,000 lived in Chashan town, and the remaining 32,000 inhabitants were peasants who lived in the outlying villages and were organized into Chashan commune's 15 production brigades. The residents of Chashan town were legally urban residents, and constituted a caste-like status group distinguished legally from the peasants (see chapter 15). But the townspeople were not socially homogeneous. Town residents were differentiated by finely-graded prestige and status privileges. At the top were the state cadres and state workers who staffed the commune administration and state branch units in town. This category included the leading party functionaries, the managers of the grain purchasing station, the bank, and all other major state units. These state cadres and state workers drew higher salaries and enjoyed better health and retirement benefits than the local people. They could travel and be transferred to other towns and small cities, whereas the residence of ordinary town citizens who were not state cadres or workers was fixed in Chashan. The presence of state bureaucrats at the commune level implies that the state bureaucracy is much larger than the old imperial bureaucracy, and penetrates down much farther; by comparison, the old imperial bureaucracy had stopped at Dongguan, at the county magistrate's level.

Beneath the state cadres in terms of prestige and privileges were the collective cadres. These were local people who had managed to achieve supervisory positions in the commune administration or in factories or other enterprises operated by the commune. They were followed by ordinary town citizens, employees in commune-owned and operated collective enterprises and factories, or in collectively-owned cooperative stores. As collective workers (to be distinguished from state workers), they had pensions and benefits paid for by the commune units in which they were employed, but these benefits were not as good as those of the state cadres and workers.

All town dwellers legally classified as urban residents, whether state cadres, state workers, collective cadres or collective workers, regarded themselves as superior to the peasants and looked down upon them. However, not all the people who actually resided in Chashan town were legally urban residents. Some of the residents of Chashan town were from households that had farmed prior to Liberation, and they had been classified as peasants. The houses of these people were mostly located on the edge of town, but some were interspersed with the houses of urban residents. So the location of one's residence did not determine classification as peasant or urbanite. These peasants were administered as a brigade, called Chashan brigade, rather than by the town apparatus.

In some respects, commune organization and brigade organization were analogous. Both commune and brigade were run by the party, as political entities (see chapter 13). Both levels were responsible for the implementation of upper-level policy. Both levels were responsible for the provision of certain social services to their constituents, especially schools and health care. Both levels supervised subordinate levels: the brigade supervised the teams, and the commune supervised both the town and the brigades. Both levels acted as economic managers, and were responsible both for providing employment and for funding their own activities, through enterprises and industries. However, there were also significant differences. Where the brigade was administered by leaders drawn from among its members, the commune was administered by outside cadres, who were, in a new version of the old Confucian governmental forms, brought in from elsewhere, so that they would not be biased by local ties and local sentiment. Where the brigades administered peasants only, the commune administered both peasants and urbanites. Its administrative process served to maintain stratificational differences.

The affairs of Chashan commune as a whole were managed by a number of interpenetrating bureaucracies. The state, as an agent of bureaucratic action at the commune level, the town as such, and the commune as such, all had administrative, political, and economic organizations. Many bureaucratic functions were duplicated and reduplicated in this complex structuralization. The resultant pattern can be characterized as sociological involution, a proliferation and elaboration of social (in this case bureaucratic) form, in which structure appears almost as an end in itself, rather than as a logical prerequisite to function. This involution of social organization may be attributed, in Weberian terms, to the tendency of bureaucratic units to develop and use the administrative apparatus in a self-perpetuating way. Or,

6. Chashan State Grain and Oil Purchasing Organization

it may be that Chinese culture is a fertile seedbed for administrative proliferation; traditional lineage organization presents a number of structural parallels. In any case, such proliferation was a prime characteristic of commune-level organization.

The bureaucracy of the state administered a number of organizations within Chashan commune. These organizations were a mixed and miscellaneous group; state organizations were not distinguished from the organizations of other levels by superior importance or particular function. The units administered by the state bureaucracy included the state purchasing, supply, and marketing organization (which supplied all wholesale goods to local state and collective stores), the grain and oil station, a state-owned Chinese medicinal herb shop, a supplementary foodstuffs store, a credit cooperative, a foodstuffs station (which purchased and slaughtered farm animals and poultry to supply the urban population), a town market administrative office (which ran the small town market, where both the state and private peasants sold produce), a water and marine products organization (which purchased local fish, by quota, for sale to the cities), the post office, and the state vegetable export station, located at the railroad station just outside of town.

In some of these cases, it is an oversimplification to speak of the organization's being state-owned and staffed by state cadres and state workers. The credit cooperatives were jointly owned by the commune and the county, although partially staffed by state cadres, and these two levels shared both the responsibility for the payroll and the profits. Although managed by state cadres, local branches of county and provincial state units were said to be ultimately under the control of the local commune party authorities. The exact division of authority and rights in such units remains unclear, with state and commune interests intertwined. It is as if no degree of bureaucratic complexity or division of responsibility were regarded as too complex or fragmented to implement.

One representative state unit, the State Grain and Oil Purchasing Organization, serves to illustrate the functioning of these organizations. The physical plant of this unit included a warehouse, storage silo, and mill complex at the edge of town (see plate 6). The staff of 56 state employees was under the direction of several state cadres. This unit was responsible for the purchase of grain, peanuts, and beans. These commodities were purchased from the commune's 109 production teams. (Following decollectivization, purchases were made directly from individual peasant households.) This unit did not merely purchase, however; it was also responsible for collecting tax grain, and commodities of which a quota was required to be sold to the state. Tax grain and state purchase quota commodities were brought to this unit to be turned over to the state. This was no straightforward administrative process, but required the implementation of a series of regulations of great complexity.

Rice was perhaps the most important commodity dealt with by this unit, and the process of collecting rice is illustrative. The commune produced, on the average, 39,000,000 *jin* of unhusked grain. The State Grain and Oil Purchasing Organization received a total of 15,000,000 *jin*, or about 38 percent of total production. The grain received by this organization was divided into three categories. The first category was tax grain (*gongliang*). This was a tax in kind, and there was no payment given for it. Teams brought grain to the grain purchasing station according to their obligations. The second category of grain was called "surplus rice" (*yuliang*). This was rice which the teams were required to sell to the state after the delivery of the tax in kind. The quantity required from each team was fixed by quota, and the price paid for this rice was state-regulated and artificially low, 9·80 *yuan* per *dan* in late 1979, after reform of rice prices. After the team had sold its required quota of "surplus rice" to the state, its quantity of remaining rice was assessed in relation to its population. If a team did not have enough remaining rice to provide minimal rations for team members, grain would be sold back in proportion to the team's needs. The term "surplus rice" is thus a misnomer, since this rice had to be sold to the state by quota even if the team was suffering a deficit.

A third category of rice was called "over-quota grain" (*chaogouliang*).

This was grain which remained after the delivery of tax grain, the sale of "surplus rice" to the state, and provision for rice rations for team members. Such grain could be sold to the state at a higher price; in early 1979, "over-quota grain" was purchased at 13·2 *yuan* per *dan*, in late 1979, after reform, at 17·95 *yuan* per *dan*. To encourage sales of "over-quota grain," teams were allowed to purchase 28·4 *jin* of chemical fertilizer per *dan* of rice sold under this heading, over and above their usual fertilizer allotment. Teams were always short of fertilizer. Normally, they could only purchase about 40 percent of the amount they felt they needed, so this was an important inducement.

Thus, the State Grain and Oil Purchasing Organization acted as buyer, storage agent, seller, fertilizer purveyor, and tax collector, and its organization reflected this complexity. It was divided into several subunits. One subunit tended the vast storage bins. Another managed the purchasing section, with its scales and storage rooms. The purchasing subunit received the three categories of grain twice yearly, after each rice harvest. A third subunit was the supply station, a state store which sold rice, oil, beans, and noodles to the people who were legally defined as urban residents of Chashan town. (Peasants received rations from their teams, and were not allowed to purchase these commodities from the state store.) Another subunit was the rice mill and fodder processing factory, which milled rice and processed rice bran into pig fodder. A fifth subunit sold the rice bran to production teams and brigades for use in feeding their collectively-owned pigs. A sixth subunit processed the peanuts sold to the state under mandatory quotas, and produced pressed oil. In addition, there was a seventh subunit, the financial group, whose job it was to "assist the commune's peasants with agricultural production" and supply them with seeds. In 1979, this subunit contracted with the teams to grow a high-quality rice – different from the usual varieties raised – to be sold in Guangzhou and exported to Hong Kong. Under this contract, the state furnished the teams with seeds and fertilizer at low fixed prices and purchased the special grain after the harvest. (Since this export rice yielded much less per *mu* than the ordinary rice grown by Chashan peasants, and normal incentives encouraged quantity, not quality, special arrangements had to be made to motivate the teams to grow it.) The activities of these subunits are so multifarious, and their realms of responsibility so diverse and complex, that it strains the logic of structural analysis to describe them under a single organizational heading.

The state administrative apparatus for collecting taxes at the commune level was not confined to the purchasing organization. The Dongguan County Financial and State Revenue Tax Bureau had a branch office in Chashan. As the name implies, the main task of this unit was to collect taxes from state, commune, and brigade enterprises. Two major principles seemed to govern the exceedingly complex tax rules administered by this office. From commercial shops, the cadres collected a tax on the basis of total sales; and from the factories they taxed the value of the goods produced. However, the rates varied from enterprise to enterprise. The commercial tax, in 1979, was 3 percent of sales in the sweets and wine shop; 5 percent of sales plus 20 percent of the profits of the restaurant and hotel; 3 percent on the selling and buying of livestock; and collective stores were taxed from 20 percent to 55 percent of the profits, the tax being graduated according to the size of the profits, ranging through nine grades!

The tax bureau also taxed the sales of peasants and teams. If a pig sold to the state weighed less than 130 *jin* (a rule apparently made to encourage the peasants to raise fatter animals), the peasants had to pay a sales tax of 3·50 *yuan*. If they sold brown sugar from their private plots, they paid a 30 percent tax; and on rice wine (a government monopoly) they were taxed 60 percent. If the peasants consumed any of the above items themselves there was no tax. This discouraged peasants from selling these commodities, and protected the state's monopoly.

In 1979, in the absence of market mechanisms, the state tax bureau used its taxing powers differentially, to encourage the creation of small commune and brigade enterprises and to stimulate the enterprises favorable to agricultural production. To encourage the growth of commune industry, the state did not tax the commune's cement plant, its lime factory, or its power station. The commune brick kilns were not taxed if their output was used for public building and construction. The farm tool and machinery repair factory was not taxed because its operation was necessary to agricultural production. The bamboo ware factory of the commune was not taxed on those baskets designed as shipping containers for commune products, but it was taxed on items produced for export. All the other commune factories not directly supporting agricultural production were taxed in accordance with further complex rules.

The tax station also supervised the collection of the tax in kind upon land, although the grain itself was actually collected by the State Grain and Oil Purchasing Organization. The land tax had been set at the time of land reform at a flat quantity which was then 12·8 percent of the average yield of the land over the three years before the tax was set. This quantity remained the same over the years, although production increased greatly. Because of this, the land tax in 1979 was only about 1·65 percent of production, and had, in effect, fallen considerably since 1953. An additional 0·7 percent was collected for emergencies and for lending to disaster areas. The total land tax for the commune in 1979 amounted to 378,452 *jin*, which was about 2·6 percent of the year's production.

The commune level was an important locus for the provision of social services. The state was responsible, jointly with the commune, for running the Chashan Commune Hospital, located inside a large compound through an arched gate off the main street of the town. People from the surrounding brigades, with illnesses that could not be treated by the barefoot doctors, came to this hospital. In 1979, the commune hospital's staff was headed by a director (a woman doctor) and two deputy directors (both male doctors.) These were all state cadres. The medical staff consisted of 25 doctors, including some who emphasized the treatment of patients with Chinese medicine and others who used mainly Western medical techniques. There were also 30 nurses and other medical personnel.

Like the other organizations, the hospital was organized into subgroups: the pharmacology group, which manned the hospital pharmacy; the logistics group, which included the accountant and the cashier, plus all the cooks and janitors; the rural health group, which was in charge of preventive medicine and women's and children's care; and the medical treatment group, including the doctors and nurses. This last group, the core of the hospital, was subdivided into an outpatient clinic, a nursing unit, a Chinese medicine unit, a dental clinic, an inpatient department, a laboratory, an x-ray room, an acupuncture facility, a cardiograph room, and an operating room.

Chashan hospital had the job of supervising the 63 barefoot doctors who served in the outlying brigade clinics, and the medical health workers of the production teams, who could treat the simplest medical problems. As well, the hospital administered the cooperative medical insurance system of the commune. Started in 1967, the medical insurance plan covered 99 percent of the commune members by 1979. The fee for insurance was 0·30 *yuan* per person per month, or 3·60 *yuan* annually. In 1978 the medical cooperative insurance fund had an income of 211,698 *yuan*, with 112,075 *yuan* paid from the income of families, and the rest contributed by the brigades, acting collectively. Members received medical treatment and medicine almost free of charge. Fees varied by brigade; some brigades paid 90 percent of the cost, and some the entire cost of care.

Here again, from the point of view of administrative organization, the hospital at the commune level provided a range of services and took on a range of responsibilities that were by no means narrowly defined.

The affairs of Chashan town as such were managed separately from the affairs of the state at the commune level, or the affairs of the commune as a whole. The administrative organization responsible for the town was the town management committee. This had an administrative structure analogous in some respects to that of a brigade. The party secretary was the head, and there was also a head of the town militia, an accountant, a cashier-treasurer, a head of the town branch of the youth league, and a woman cadre in charge of women's work. (These offices were also found in brigade committees.) The town committee also organized street leaders for each of the town's major streets. (Street organization was not found in brigades.) Street leaders were normally retired people. They were charged with reporting any suspicious activities, and informing the commune security people if there were strangers present. The town management committee employed street sweepers to keep the town free of litter, and had every house inspected to ensure that the rules of appropriate sanitation were followed. The town management committee operated child-care facilities for the benefit of workers in the town's enterprises and factories and their children. The town management committee also staffed the town civil affairs office. It funded its own activities by the management of an enterprise, the manufacture of beeswax forms which attract honeybees to hives. From the profits of this traditional local activity, the town management committee drew most of its operating expenses.

The commune level, as a third level distinguished from the state organization, and from the town committee, like the other levels, administered a diverse range of economic enterprises, social services, and civil service units. Commune-level industries were administered by a senior vice-director of the commune's office of industry and communications, who was under the titular authority of the vice-chairman for finance of the commune revolutionary committee. Although theoretically in charge of all rural industry in the commune, whether at the team, brigade, or commune level, this office was almost solely concerned with commune-level industry, operated independently from the team, brigade, and state levels. As the owner and manager, or joint owner and manager, of economic enterprises, Chashan commune was involved in 31 local industries, as set out in table 11.

A representative commune factory illustrates the structure and operation of a commune-run unit. The Chashan Commune Farm Machinery Repair Shop employed 194 staff and workers. The basic functions of this factory resembled those of the farm machinery repair stations operated by the brigades, except that more difficult and major repairs were attempted here. It also included a number of other miscellaneous production tasks under its rubric, some of them surprisingly unrelated. This factory made furniture, manufactured hoes, harrows, spades, and plows in its steel forge, repaired electrical equipment, such as pumps, and ran an iron foundry, where many different parts for farm machinery were produced. Lathes and grinding machines turned these products into finished parts.

The factory had a complicated administrative structure with a director and two deputy directors. Each separate workshop had its own head and assistant head. Large workshops were divided into small groups, each of which had its own small group head. The workers in this commune factory, like those in other commune enterprises, were divided into five grades, through which they moved according to their length of service. A person started as an apprentice and worked for three years for a salary of 20 to 22 *yuan* (1979). Then he or she went to grade one, at 30 *yuan* per month. After four years, workers moved on to grade two and then up through the grades to grade five,

Table 11. *Chashan commune enterprises and industries, 1979*

1. Brick and tile kiln
2. Farm machinery and tool plant, manufacturing plows, harrows, and threshing machines
3. Chemical factory, manufacturing tar paper
4. Cement factory
5. Food processing factory, making pickles, dried food, noodles, and cookies
6. Rubber factory, manufacturing conveyer belts
7. Arts and crafts factory, weaving bamboo and reed brooms, baskets, and mats
8. Bamboo ware factory, making bamboo brooms and baskets
9. Lime factory
10. Clothing factory, sewing children's clothes for export: a joint venture with Hong Kong investors.
11. Ship building and repair yard
12. Hardware factory, a machine and metal casting shop
13. Peanut oil pressing plant
14. Scrap steel works, manufacturing metal implements and iron reinforcing rods
15. Plastics plant
16. Honeycomb making plant, delegated to Chashan town
17. Rock quarry, a joint commune-brigade enterprise
18. Forestry center
19. Flower nursery, growing flowers for export to Hong Kong
20. Fish farm, producing fish fry
21. Chicken farm
22. Carpentry shop, sawmill, and lumber transport station
23. Power supply station, running generators to operate commune machinery when the state power supply failed
24. Farm machinery repair shop, repairing tractors and other farm machinery
25. Agro-scientific research station
26. Veterinary station
27. Building construction
28. Truck teams, transporting goods and passengers for commune
29. Water, irrigation, and electricity management group
30. Bicycle tire factory, making tires for local and regional sale
31. Glove factory, a joint enterprise with Hong Kong investors

which had a salary of 54 *yuan* plus an average bonus of 10 *yuan*, or about 64 *yuan* a month. Collective workers in commune units usually spent their entire career with one unit, so promotions tended to correspond to the age of the employee, with rank and salary rising as he or she got older. Workers had guaranteed jobs and assured rations and medical care, but little chance to transfer.

The working lives of the townspeople contrasted with those of the peasants. Instead of becoming a member of a production team by inherited right, as peasants did, young townspeople of an age to start work were appointed to positions as collective workers in the town's factories. Although they did not inherit work unit membership, nonetheless they had limited choice, or no choice at all, as to their life's work. The procedure was that each year the education office of the commune listed the names of students leaving school. School-leavers were asked what jobs they preferred, and enterprises were asked what openings were available. Decisions were made in terms of administrative convenience and the needs of factory managers, not in terms of the potential job satisfaction of individuals. (Job satisfaction is not a recognized Chinese cultural category, and those aspects of Marxism which tend to imply it, such as the analysis of alienation, are de-emphasized in Chinese political thinking.) The commune committee did not consider the intelligence, school record, or special aptitude of the school-leavers when making work assignments. These qualities were irrelevant for most jobs, which could be learned by anyone. If young people objected to their job assignments, the party assigned cadres to carry out "ideological education work" to convince them that they should be satisfied with their jobs. Usually people did not object to their assignments. There was little chance that an assignment could be changed, and an objection might attract the unfavorable attention of their factory superiors, under whom they would probably have to work for the rest of their lives. If a worker proved unable to perform the job satisfactorily, or if a health problem dictated a change of work, the commune could ask the opinion of the factory head as to whether a transfer was warranted. If the factory head agreed and another unit could be found to take the worker, a transfer was sometimes possible.

To avoid the complications of mixing family relationships and work relations, the commune avoided assigning members of one family to the same enterprise. However, as in state-owned industry, when a person retired, one of his or her children was permitted to inherit the position.

Income from the commune's own industries constituted a sizable portion of commune income from all sources in 1979 (see figure 8). The commune administration used the profits that they made from their industry for projects to benefit the commune as a whole, the brigades as well as the town. The profits of the commune industries have been used to widen the town's streets and to build factories to attract Hong Kong processing industries. The commune administration has built a large new party and commune government complex. The water purification plant, which serves the entire commune, was built using these monies.

The commune level serves a function as an administrator of taxation. In this it overlaps with such units as the State Grain and Oil Purchasing Organization and the State Revenue Tax Bureau, which also collect taxes.

The commune level runs a unit with the specific job of overseeing aspects of taxation that are not already the responsibility of other units.

The commune level is of intellectual interest because it is the only realistic referent for the theoretical category of the market town level, a concept which has been the focus of much scholarly speculation at a distance. Chashan commune happens to be centered around a traditional market town, and the commune, with the old market town surrounded by 45 villages, conforms to the definition of the standard market town area (Fei 1939, p. 115; C. K. Yang 1944; Martin C. Yang 1945, pp. 244–249, 1969, pp. 100–141; Skinner 1964–5, and others following Skinner, e.g. Skocpol 1979, p. 69). Local and county-level administrators consistently comment that this is by no means the norm. In fact, less than half of the communes in Dongguan county, in 1979, were formed on the basis of a traditional marketing area with a traditional market town at its center. Of the 29 agricultural communes in Dongguan county, only 14 were based upon established market towns, like Chashan. Three of the other 15 communes had no market town centers at all; these three communes were adjacent to Taiping, a large county town, and the commune members went to Taiping (see map 3) for urban services and marketing. Four communes near the town of Dongguan, the county seat, and one near Shilong, another large county town, had no market town centers for the same reason. In these eight cases, very large commune populations are centered upon towns which are in effect small cities, and which serve as centers for several communes at once, as well as for their own population of urbanites. Another commune divides its loyalty between two adjacent market towns, showing no strong preference for either. In four communes, residents go to market towns in neighboring communes, rather than to the small and underdeveloped commercial areas at their own commune administrative centers. And two of the Dongguan communes have no commune commercial centers at all. So the commune does not necessarily have its own market town, and commune members (including those whose own commune includes a town) carry out their marketing activities at a range of extra-communal locations.

The process of establishing and developing new markets has taken place without reference either to the commune as an organizational level, or to the traditional market town area. According to county-level cadres, sixteen new markets were developed by the county administration during the 1960s, and established independently of either commune or traditional market town location.

The argument has been made that the most important social unit of rural Chinese society, superior in importance to the lineage or to the village, was the composite social unit comprised of a market town and its surrounding tributary villages (see Huang 1985, pp. 24–26). G. William Skinner (1964–5) has been considered a main proponent of this view, the essence of which is as follows:

Chinese marketing systems have important social as well as economic dimensions ...
Anthropological work on Chinese society, by focusing attention almost exclusively
on the village, has with few exceptions distorted the reality of rural social structure.
Insofar as the Chinese peasant can be said to live in a self-contained world, that world
is not the village but the standard marketing community. The effective social field of
the peasant, I will argue, is delimited not by the narrow horizons of this village but
rather by the boundaries of his standard marketing area. (Skinner 1967, p. 85)

The idea that the standard marketing area is the most significant traditional
unit has led to the inference that the basic-level communes were probably
formed using the standard marketing area as a structural basis; but plainly this
was not necessarily the case in Dongguan county.

What, then is the relationship between present-day Chinese social order in
the countryside, and the theory that the face-to-face community of Chinese
peasants is the standard marketing area (Skinner 1967, pp. 87–89)? Chashan
commune, at least, in spite of being centered on a traditional market town is
clearly not a face-to-face community. One reason for this is that the Chashan
market town area is, and has been, too large in scale for such an idea of
community to be applicable. The population was 20,000 in 1950, and 36,000
in 1979. This is too large for mutual recognition. From the village point of
view, it is assumed that one does not know by sight the people who live in the
immediately adjacent neighboring villages, let alone the residents of more
distant villages, or townsfolk. It is actually improper for a woman to claim
recognition of unrelated villagers from adjacent villages in the same brigade.
(This traditional form of propriety must surely have tended to emphasize the
importance of relationships within the village at the expense of relationships
in the standard marketing community in any case.) Zengbu villagers recognize only the most prominent party cadres from other villages or from the
town at sight; they are not acquainted with others. The process of forming
extra-village relationships is impeded.

One important reason for this is the rigid quality of the social stratification
that serves to divide and separate commune dwellers. Urban residents and
peasants are on opposite sides of a caste-like social distinction, and their
relationships continually reflect this social disjunction. The townspeople of
Chashan are greatly advantaged economically, socially, and culturally. Their
status is markedly superior to the peasants, who have none of these
advantages. In theory, a stratified community might be more united by
community sentiment than divided by stratificational differences, but this is
not the case in Chashan. Townsfolk have an interest in maintaining their
superior status which divides them very effectively from the peasants.
Historically, for example, one of the problems encountered during the efforts
to consolidate and create larger commune organizations at the time of the
Great Leap Forward, was the opposition of the townspeople to being
included in the same accounting unit as the peasants. The standard marketing

community is split, caste-like, into townspeople and peasants, whose interests and community loyalties are mutually at odds.

Thus, relations between peasants and town officials are distant and impersonal. Townspeople tend to be extremely rude to villagers, as is consistent with their view that villagers are inferior. When village children from Zengbu attend upper-middle school in Chashan town, where they might be supposed to acquire wider social ties, they find that these ties, even with other peasant children, are tenuous and do not survive the necessity to return permanently to their separate villages after graduation. And ties between young peasants and young townspeople are not easily formed, because of the importance of the status difference.

In former times, according to Skinner, the local gentry were significant in linking peasants and officials to create community across the social hierarchy. He says that the primary significance of the market town "pertains to the relations between peasantry and 'gentry'" (1967, p.96):

The concept of the local elite as an intermediary and a buffer between the peasantry and the bureaucratic elite is – though the terminology may seem peculiar – a familiar one. And so is the view of the petty trader as a middleman between the peasantry and the merchants in higher-level central places. Both functioned as 'brokers' [E. Wolf 1956, p. 1,076] who at once shielded the peasant from an outside world which he distrusted and selectively filtered and transmitted to him its products ... My point here is simply that these Janus-faced 'brokers' – whether cultural, political, or economic – operated at the level of the standard market town, not the village. It was the standard marketing community which they linked to or ... isolated from the institutions of the larger society. (1967 pp.96–97)

With the Liberation, the gentry ceased to exist as a social group connecting peasants and officials in the standard marketing area, and petty traders were also a category of the past. Instead, the peasant and the state official confronted one another directly, and the process was not an integrative one. Cadres and workers who staffed the state units in Chashan town were strangers to the peasants. They were the servants of an ethic which made the utilization of social ties and the formation of patron–client relationships a violation of official propriety. They were outsiders, deliberately chosen for their lack of local commitments, and they were transferred before they could form an extensive network of local ties. Villagers had no way to gain sufficient wealth or power to establish systems of mutual obligation during an official's tenure in Chashan. From the villagers' point of view, the town was a place from which government orders and policies were issued, the place where their taxes, rice, pigs, fish, and vegetables were taken for the consumption of others, and the place where they went to obey orders and fulfill obligations. The town was a much more alien and impersonal setting than the familiar world of the brigade or the village: in effect, it was not a community at all.

The economic organization which divided team, brigade, and commune town into separate production, ownership, and accounting units, also acted to diminish the economic unity of the town with its surrounding villages, and reduced the importance of town shops, markets, and services for the peasants. The brigades were largely self-sufficient units, with their own branches of state stores, credit cooperatives, and clinics; this reduced the need to deal with the town. Peasants were not employed in the town, because the commune-owned and managed industries employed urban residents only. Such industries did not employ peasants even to work in the branch stores located in brigades; rather, urban dwellers commuted to the countryside for this employment. This segregation of employment opportunity further separated the people of the villages from the people of the town. There was no vertical integration between team, brigade, and commune town industries.

In dealing with kinship organization, the theory suggests that the standard marketing area forms an endogamous kinship unit, in which affinal bonds give structure and solidarity to the whole (Skinner 1967, p. 90). This view is inconsistent in many respects with the data from Chashan commune. Over the period 1979–81, the people of Zengbu brigade formed 26 percent of their marriages with people living in villages outside Chashan commune, and hence outside of the traditional standard marketing area. (A large number of these Zengbu marriages were with people from Wentang. This is a brigade in an adjacent commune, across one of the rivers which forms Zengbu's border. The river must be inconveniently crossed by ferry, and it is easier to get from Zengbu to Chashan than from Zengbu to Wentang.) Over the same period, 39 percent of their marriages were endogamous, i.e. in the same team, the same lineage village, or the same brigade. Traditionally, such marriages could have taken place between the separate villages of the brigade, but marriages within a village (and marriages within a team are also within a village) would have been thought of as incestuous; it would have been necessary to marry out. Marrying out would tend to reinforce relationships with people outside of the village. Thus, social reform appears to have produced a decline in the number of marriages formed outside the village, but within the standard marketing area. Marriages which serve, rather, to reinforce ties within the brigade, the village, or the team are more likely to be made. Only 35 percent of Zengbu marriages in 1979–81 were outside the brigade but within the standard marketing area. This is a substantial minority, but not enough to support an argument that such marriages and the affinal kinship ties resulting from them create a sense of cohesion sufficient to make the commune into a genuinely face-to-face community. Marriages with the urban residents of Chashan are out of the question because of the caste-like stratificational distinction; this further reduces the number of potential affinal ties formed within the commune. Significant social integration continues to be more likely to occur at lower and smaller levels of social organization. The Chashan data suggest that such scholars as Maurice Freedman, who stressed the importance of the village and the lineage as the most significant social units in southeastern rural Chinese society, were correct in their emphasis. They also suggest that post-Liberation reforms in social structure and social organization have reinforced the importance of these levels further, at the expense of the standard marketing community.

On the basis of his recent research in northern China, Philip Huang (1985, pp. 219–246) has also raised objections to the model of the importance of the standard marketing community for that region. His work indicates that the model is inapplicable to the less commercialized villages of the north. The Chashan data suggest that it is equally inapplicable to the more commercialized villages of central and south China. Firsthand observation in north and south China alike indicate, then, that the standard marketing area is of lesser significance as a social community than has been hypothesized. Regional variation cannot be an adequate explanation for the deviation from theoretical expectation, and the theory itself must be re-examined.

If the standard marketing area is of less importance than has recently been supposed, then some secondary interpretative constructs developed to explain Chinese social process require re-examination as well. Skocpol, (1979, pp. 148ff.) for example, explains the slow pace of the development of a revolution in China, as being due to the Chinese peasants' lack of "the kind of structurally preexisting solidarity and autonomy" possessed by village communities in France and Russia, with which China is being compared. Skocpol bases this conclusion on Skinner's argument that "the basic unit of community in traditional China was *not* the undivided village ... but the marketing community ... Though they resided and worked in undivided villages, the marketing community was the significant local world of the peasants" (Skocpol 1979, p. 149). If the assumption underlying this interpretation is incorrect, as it now appears to be, then new explanations for the pace of historical process must be found.

# 8

# Impatient aspirations: transition to the post-Mao period

The decollectivization of rural China took place over five years (1978–83), during which the work of three decades of revolutionary Maoism was undone, and a new, non-Maoist manner of rural development was substituted. The change had its roots in longstanding intraparty disagreement and struggle over China's rural development policy. The party had historically included advocates of two different roads to rural development, the collectivists, or "socialist roaders," led by Chairman Mao, and an opposing group represented by Liu Shaoqi and Deng Xiaoping. The party was trying to achieve two goals simultaneously: rural prosperity, on the one hand, and revolutionary reform and social equality, on the other. The Maoists wanted both, but they were willing to sacrifice immediate prosperity to achieve more radical and fundamental social transformations; the Liuists de-emphasized revolutionary change and were willing to sacrifice completeness of social reform to immediate prosperity. The Liuists were willing to go with the grain of peasant familism and conservatism; the Maoists wanted to change these once and for all.

From the Maoist point of view, a permanent and radical revolutionary modification of China's familistic peasant society and culture was necessary. This was to be achieved through collective forms of social organization. The collectives were characterized by a constructed moral economy, a moral economy imposed deliberately from above, where none had been indigenously present. Without the collectives, an amoral competitive familism would lead to the re-emergence of socioeconomic stratification among peasants. The class inequalities that the Revolution had sought to eliminate once and for all would be recreated. A rural class society would re-emerge, and with it the old feudal culture, which was its symbolic expression. The Revolution in the countryside would indeed be defeated.

The Liuists, by comparison, believed that prosperity could best be achieved by families working hard to assure their own material welfare within a paternalistic state structure. Implicit in the Liuist view was the assumption that the ideal rural society for China was merely the old one with some of its worst defects – landlords, bullies, bandits, and political disorder – removed. There was a willingness to risk a return to the old familistic household mode of production, if prosperity was to be the result. They minimized and discounted the connection between this system and the sufferings of the vast majority of the peasants prior to Liberation in 1949 which was so apparent to the Maoists (see chapter 1).

Mao initially won the intra-party debate on rural development policy following Liberation, and his policies prevailed until his death in 1976, but he never succeeded in eliminating either his opponents or their point of view. The Liuists had attempted to implement their own policies in agriculture during the early fifties, the early sixties, and the seventies, at times when Chairman Mao's political strength was weakened by obvious policy failures. In 1979 they gained the ascendancy. The Maoist polemic against this group, which had been ethnocentrically interpreted as mere rhetoric by the outside world, was shown by events to have been a matter of substance.

The critique of Maoist collectivism, which was just beginning to be stated openly by Guangdong cadres in 1979, cited a number of economic failures. The Great Leap Forward, the Cultural Revolution, and the Gang of Four periods were denounced as economic disasters because of their ultraleftist "peasant socialist" tactics. The economic egalitarianism of the Maoist collectives (the "Eat from the same big pot" policy) was denounced as having dampened all individual initiative and enthusiasm. The emphasis upon growing grain (the "Take grain as the main" policy) was denounced as having prevented the peasants from prospering, by preventing them from growing crops that might be more profitable or better suited to local conditions, and rewarding them with artificially low state purchase prices. The government's tight bureaucratic control over peasant economic decisions and lack of flexibility (the "Blind orders from above" and the "Cut with one big knife" policies) were denounced because they prevented the peasants from pursuing their own economic interests in the most effective ways. The Maoists were also criticized for having dismissed both peasant industrial enterprise and the production of crops for sale in the market as capitalistic practices.

Guangdong cadres did not take the position that Maoism had been entirely harmful. Rather, they maintained that substantial rural economic progress had been made following Maoist policies. (This opinion is shared by many economists: see Amin 1981; Gurley 1976, p. 13; and Rawski 1980, table 30.) Their position was that the creative potential of Maoist collectivism for the increase of production had been exhausted by the early sixties; later, the collectives had become fetters on production, and had created economic stagnation and poverty. New policies were urgently needed to bring this situation to an end.

Proponents of the new policies advocated the increased use of material

incentives to motivate and reward labor. They favored a more commercialized agriculture, with rural free markets outside the state purchasing and
supply system. These modifications would create a basis of rural prosperity
which was a prior condition for the establishment of socialism. Attempts to
establish socialism more directly, without building on a foundation of rural
prosperity, would result in the collective sharing of rural poverty, as before.
The idea was that rural China would have to go through the crucible of rural
capitalism in order to create the economic conditions that would at some
future time make socialism possible. In this, the Marxism of the anti-Maoist
group was more orthodox than the Marxism of the Maoists, who had thought
it possible to create socialism without rigid adherence to the stages in the
Marxist historical sequence. The Maoists had tried to bypass the stage of
capitalist development and move directly to socialism. They had failed:
economic prosperity had not been achieved, and without it, the goals of the
Revolution could not be achieved either.

It was clear to local-level cadres that the Maoist pattern was saturated, and
that its ideology had been carried as far as was possible. Basic-level cadres had
always justified the socialist collectivism of Maoist thinking to the peasants
most effectively by claiming that it would create wealth and prosperity for all,
and was "a way to make China rich." But the peasants were not wealthy and
prosperous. And the idea of contributing to the world revolution or to the
renaissance of China struck no responsive sparks.

What are the actual facts of the economic situation in the countryside in
the late 1960s and 1970s? And how are Maoist policies to be evaluated?

When the war-torn, impoverished, famine-prone, insecure, and anarchic
existence led by the villagers of Zengbu before Liberation is compared with
their lives under Maoism, it is plain that important strides had been made.
Peasants had food, clothing, housing, and access to basic medical care and
education. The average life expectancy had risen to 69 for men and 67 for
women. Levees and irrigation works had been built. Such capital construction as this had produced increased yields and security of production, and had
created a valuable agricultural infrastructure. The Revolution had brought
improved social justice. Economic stratification in the countryside had been
virtually eliminated, and slavery entirely so. No longer were the peasants
required to deliver from 40 to 60 percent of their rice crop to landowning
ancestral halls. No longer did they have to fear bandits, criminal secret
societies, marauding armies, or local thugs. The means of production were
owned by the peasant collectives, and peasants were paid, roughly, according
to the actual work they performed. The position of women had been
improved; their work was visible and valued, and they filled a few leadership
roles; marriage reform had eliminated a number of cruelties and abuses.

Some economic statistics provide more detailed and specific evidence of
the gains made during the Maoist period. For example (as figure 4 shows),

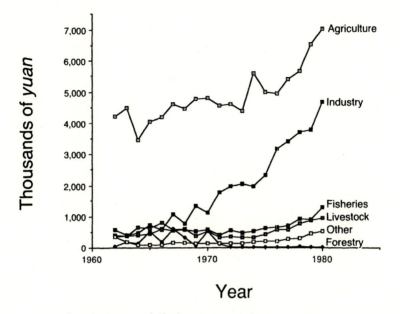

Figure 8. Sources of Chashan commune's income, 1962–80

total rice production in Chashan commune rose dramatically. In 1962, just following the completion of the commune's flood control and irrigation works, 210,000 *dan* per year were produced. A high of about 360,000 *dan* was produced in 1974, with somewhat less than that level being produced from 1974 to 1979. There was a substantial growth in the gross income of industries operating in the commune, from a value of about 600,000 *yuan* in 1962, to over 3½ million *yuan* in 1978 (see figure 8). The net income from all sources in Chashan commune rose from a little over 4 million *yuan*, in 1962, to about 6½ million *yuan* in 1978 (see figure 9).

These were significant achievements, yet they were not enough to prevent the Maoist period from being regarded as an economic failure. The reasons for this become apparent when per capita figures, rather than gross production figures, are examined. The following summary of the economic performance of Maoist collectives in Chashan from 1962 to 1978 (no records were available for earlier periods), is compiled from commune and brigade figures.

The average per capita distribution (i.e. income from workpoints) in Chashan commune fell from a high of about 180 *yuan* per capita, in 1962, to a level just over 100 *yuan* throughout most of the sixties and the seventies surpassing the 1962 level only in 1979, after the first post-Mao reforms (see figure 10). The people of Chashan commune gained little in per capita income between 1962 and 1978. (Zengbu brigade fared a little better

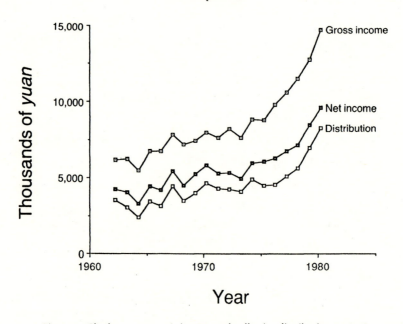

Figure 9. Chashan commune's income and collective distribution, 1962–80

[see figure 11].) Rice production per capita in Chashan from 1962 to 1978, (figure 12), and in Zengbu brigade, (figure 13), also showed a decline during the 1960s and 1970s. The level of living of the rural peasants had remained stationary or had declined throughout the sixties and seventies. Overall production had increased under the collectives, but per capita production, peasant incomes, and the living levels of the peasants had remained at a level far below the expectations of the Revolution. That this could be the case, in spite of years of toil and struggle, was disheartening even to the most dedicated of local cadres.

The apparent contradiction between significant overall growth in rice production and total income, on the one hand, and stagnant or declining per capita rice production and income, on the other, is explained by population growth (see figure 14). The commune's population increased from about 24,000, in 1962, to 35,522, in 1978. Chashan had pursued the tragically familiar agricultural involutionary path (Geertz 1963) into rural poverty: more and more Zengbu peasants labored to make a living from a fixed amount of land, until they reached a point of diminishing returns, where each additional input of labor led to a smaller increase in production, resulting ultimately in a declining per capita income.

Maoist agrarian policies had encouraged population growth so explosive that it absorberd all increased production, and there could be no growth in per capita rice production or per capita income. Secure food rations, adequate

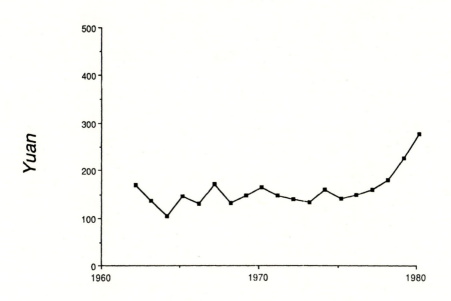

Figure 10. Average per capita distribution, Chashan commune, 1962–80

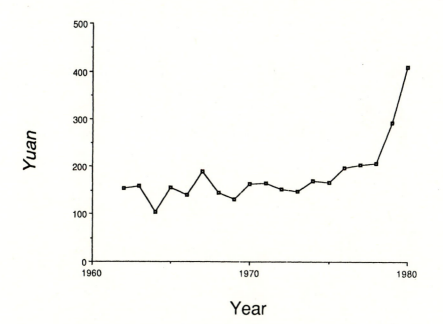

Year

Figure 11. Average per capita distribtion, Zengbu brigade, 1962–80

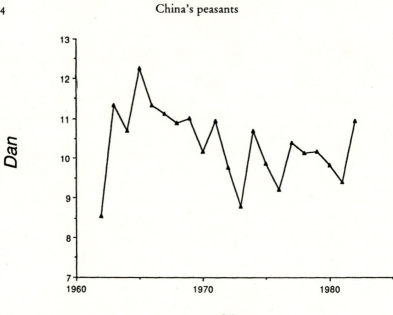

Figure 12. Per capita rice production, Chashan commune, 1962–82

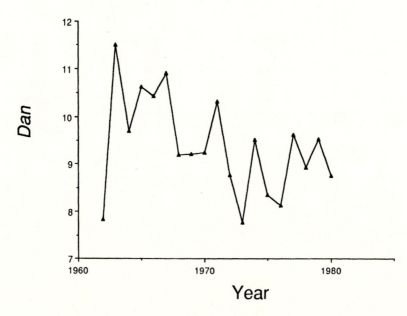

Figure 13. Per capita rice production, Zengbu brigade, 1962–80

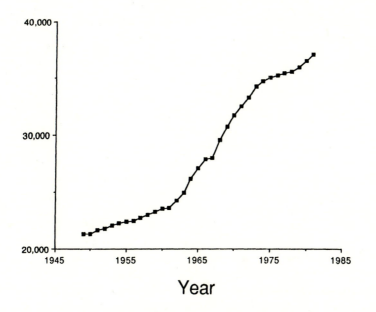

Figure 14. Population, Chashan commune, 1949–81

medical care, assured work for everyone, and private plots in proportion to the number of family members, provided systematic economic rewards to families for population increase, while costs of increased population were paid by the collective, rather than the family (see chapter 11). The fundamental defect of the Maoist system was not its inability to motivate labor, as Chinese economic thinkers tended to fear. Rather it was that the Maoist system, in conjunction with Chinese familism, created one of the most pronatal societies ever instituted. It would have been difficult for any rural social and economic system to raise the level of living of the rural population in the face of such population growth.

Another factor in the cumulative failure of the collectives was the ideologically rigid Maoist "anti-capitalist" policy, which inhibited the development of rural industry and rural markets and commerce. The pre-Liberation peasant market economy, based upon handicrafts, peddling, brokerage, and small retail shops and stalls, had been destroyed in the mid-fifties, when all commerce was taken over by state purchase and supply companies and by town cooperatives. This deprived the Zengbu peasants of traditional jobs in rural commerce and forced them to rely more heavily on agriculture. But the amount of land per capita was small, and constantly decreasing as population rose. The collectives could not absorb any excess labor into agriculture; rather the contrary. Unemployment and underemployment became a major problem. Some cadres estimate that in Guangdong, in the late 1970s, 60 percent were unemployed or underemployed. This was not the result of an intrinsic structural defect of the Maoist collectives, but the effect of an interaction between population, policy, and resources.

Another contributing factor in rural economic stagnation was the favoritism shown by the Chinese government, from Liberation on, to the workers living in the cities, at the expense of the peasants. As Frank Leeming (1985, p. 49) remarks, agriculture was the "pauper of the whole economic system." He says: "Chinese farming has been systematically starved of investment in order to support the greedy heavy industry sector" (p. 18). The priority in investment in Maoist China was urban industry. Xue Muqiao (quoted in Leeming 1985, p. 16) cites figures which show how much more rapidly the urban sector of the economy grew than agriculture. The total output value of urban industry increased by 700 percent between 1952 and 1980, while the total output value of agriculture increased only 236 percent. If the Maoist collectives had received a larger share of the state's capital investment, their production levels would have been much higher than they were. Furthermore, by maintaining low purchase prices for grain and agricultural products and high prices for industrial goods sold in the countryside (see chapter 6), the state indirectly extracted surplus value from the peasants and delivered it to the higher status urban residents. The state's extraction of surplus value to finance urban industrial development and to subsidize the higher living levels and greater benefits of the urban population was probably as important a cause of rural economic stagnation as the deficiencies of collective labor reward systems. Whyte and Parish (1984, p. 54) estimate that the average per capita income of workers was three times that of peasants in 1977. Extraction from, rather than investment in agriculture, exacerbated Zengbu's agricultural involution.

For all these reasons (the population explosion among the peasants, the decommercialization of the countryside, the extraction of surplus by the state for the benefit of urban industry and urban workers, and the lack of capital investment in agriculture by the state), the economic situation in rural China was desperate when measured against the Zengbu peasants' and cadres' impatient aspirations, and their knowledge of the development and economic prosperity of Taiwan, Hong Kong, and Singapore. Immobilized in their collectives, with no opportunity to migrate to towns or cities, the only possible avenue of change was change in policy.

The process of decollectivization in Zengbu began in Chashan commune in the winter of 1978, when the commune cadres persuaded some brigades to experiment with a household responsibility system. Under this system, the responsibility for growing certain commercial crops, such as peanuts and cassava, was transferred from the team as a whole to the individual laborer or individual household. (Rice was not to be produced under a household responsibility system at this stage, since removing responsibility for grain production from the collective was still regarded as too fundamental a negation of socialist principle to countenance.) This experimental system was voluntary. The production brigades and teams which chose to participate in the experiment gave individual and household contractors a quantity of land and a production quota. The quota was based upon the team's previous three years' production of the crops in question. The team provided a fixed amount of fertilizer and seeds, and an allocation of workpoints to reward labor. If the contracting individual or household produced more than the quota set by the team, the team rewarded this with a bonus of workpoints worth a certain percentage of the overproduction. The contracting peasant or household was responsible for cultivating the entire crop, from planting to harvesting, using only household labor. There were important differences between this and the collective mode of production under the team. Team members cultivated crops on collective land under the supervision of team cadres, who planned production and assigned labor (see chapter 5). Team members were responsible only for single steps in the growing of a crop, transplanting or plowing rice, for example, but never for the entire process or the final product, as they were under the new experimental system.

The point of contention in implementing the reform of the Maoist system centered initially around modes of reward for labor. (This was logical in its cultural context, given the symbolic importance of work and rewards for work in Chinese society. See chapter 9.) What percentage of the overproduction should be given to the producer as a bonus, and what percentage should be retained by the team? The larger the percentage of overproduction given as a bonus, the more the collective production system was symbolically threatened. Cadres who saw the changes as dangerous to the collectives, and opposed them on those grounds, favored awarding a minimal bonus. Cadres who favored stronger reform also favored awarding most of the profit of over-quota production as a bonus. These cadres were probing the limits, testing how far they could diverge from the principle that production and labor reward should be under collective control. And as they found that the limits receded, the bonuses became larger, until, finally, they included all production over the quota.

In Zengbu itself, as opposed to the commune as a whole, the first post-Mao changes began in 1979, and related production, not to the individual or to the household, but to the "small group," still an essentially collective entity. The small group production responsibility system was called variously *lian chan dao zu, bao chan dao hu,* or *wu ding yi jiang:* "connecting production to the group," "fixing production to the group," or the "five fixed and one bonus system." Under the small group production responsibility system (which had been tried previously, as early as 1957, in Guangdong [Vogel 1971, p. 339]), each team divided its labor force into semipermanent, specialized, small groups, which were given total responsibility for certain of the team's production tasks. For example, participating teams might form their members into a fishpond management group, a brick- and tile-kiln group, a pig-raising group, a vegetable-growing group and several rice-growing groups. Each specialized rice-growing group was allot- ted a share of the team's rice fields, buffaloes, threshers, insecticides, fertilizer, and tractors. The team guaranteed each group sufficient labor power and production expenses to produce the crop or product. Each group was given a production quota by the team – so many kiln-loads of bricks, so many *jin* of fish, so many *dan* of unhusked rice, or so many *jin* of vegetables. The division of the large Zengbu teams into smaller functionally-specialized groups would, it was hoped, result in a more rational and effective division of labor.

After each group had delivered its specified quota amount to the team, the team redistributed the profits from all the groups to all team members, still on the basis of workpoints. However, there was a significant change in reward in that, if a small group overfulfilled its quota, its members were awarded a percentage of the profit from the production in workpoints, as a bonus. If a small group did not meet its production quota, the team would not award a bonus, and might deduct some workpoints.

The assumption behind the post-Mao reforms was that the peasants would work only if they could see immediate material rewards for themselves and their families. Small scale was supposed to create a more direct and visible relationship between a person's work and the reward for it, and this was one supposed advantage of the small group production responsibility system; it broke down the large and unwieldy teams into smaller units. It was also supposed that the small groups were more easily managed than the larger teams. As some of the cadres put it, "A small boat can turn more easily than a big one."

The small group was responsible for the entire production process, and not simply for each disconnected step in the process. It was hoped that this would instill a sense of responsibility for the final results. If people were working for a bonus based upon their actual final production, they would be motivated to work carefully throughout the entire process of producing the crop. Working collectively for the team – by piece-rate or by the day – no one felt responsible for final production and no one had an immediate material interest in performing the work well; their immediate interest was only in accumulating workpoints.

As the teams which experimented with this system in 1979 discovered, however, the small group production responsibility system also had dis- advantages. It transferred the disadvantages of team organization onto a smaller scale, and created the necessity for organizational reduplication. For example, the reward for labor within each small group was still made in terms of workpoints, on either a labor grade or a piecework basis; the fact that labor was rewarded as a proportion of actual profits remained. Since separate accounts had to be kept for each small group, the book-keeping was increased. The new system created more leaders, further increasing the size of the bureaucracy and the management overhead costs. The old team leaders and the new younger small group leaders began to vie with one other for power: team leaders sought to retain control, while small group leaders wanted independent authority.

Since small group members were rewarded in relation to their small group's production, their material interest in the welfare of the team as a whole was reduced. Team leaders had more difficulty mobilizing team members to cooperate on projects requiring participation by the entire team. In 1979 and 1980, the small group system was seen to undermine the solidarity of some of the Sandhill village teams which had adopted it. For example, at the fall harvest of each of these years, some small groups completed their rice harvesting early. When the team leader asked the members of these groups to help other small groups who were harvesting later, and were under time pressure to complete the harvest quickly or lose part of it to inclement weather, they refused, saying that it was not their responsibility. Instead, many of them secretly went into Chashan town and hired themselves out privately as construction laborers in the emerging private economy. The fixed responsibilities of the small group became a rationale for evading the team's control of labor.

Methods of assigning individuals to small groups created further inequalities. Some teams had assigned members to small groups as families rather than as individuals, with all members of one family being in the same group. Families in successful groups earned multiple bonuses, but families in less successful groups earned none. Teams which had deliberately assigned workers from the same family to different small groups had avoided this pitfall, by creating a situation in which each family was likely to have at least one member who had earned a bonus in a successful group.

There were conflicts between the small groups, as well. The members of rice-growing groups envied the members of rural industrial and other specialized groups: transplanting and harvesting rice was considered to be the hardest and dirtiest work in the agricultural cycle. Members of other groups could work under shelter, away from the rain and sun, while the rice growers did the dirty work, or so the envious rice growers perceived the situation. Variations in pay and bonuses among the specialized production groups also undermined the economic equality of the team. Members of rice-growing groups made fewer workpoints and bonuses. The rice-growing groups quarrelled among themselves when some made bonuses and some did not, for reasons beyond the group's control, such as having been assigned at random to cultivate slightly less productive fields.

The advantages and disadvantages of the small group production responsibility system were argued heatedly, and the brigade was deeply divided. Adoption of the system was voluntary. All seven of the Lu's Home teams, and four of the six Sandhill teams experimented with the small group system in 1979. The four teams of Pondside and two of the Sandhill teams declined to organize into small production responsibility groups. Pondside depended heavily upon collectively operated team industry for a livelihood. The village's rationale for refusing to try the small group system was that division into groups would weaken the solidarity of the teams, which would, in turn, threaten their economic base. The two Sandhill teams made an egalitarian argument, rejecting small groups on the grounds that all team members should participate in the heavy work of the rice harvest, rather than leaving this work to the members of the rice-growing groups.

The economic results of Zengbu's experiment with small groups were inconclusive: some teams did better and others worse than before. The most successful team in Zengbu, Pondside's Number 4 team, had not adopted the system at all. Peasants were uncertain about the system's rationale and confused about its operation. As a system, it had certainly failed to lift Zengbu out of economic stagnation. Rather, the small groups had continued the familiar process of "sociological involution" by reduplicating structure and modifying scale, with marginal economic results. During the fifties, a series of modifications in scale producing larger and larger production units, had been tried, with the transitions progressing from the household to the mutual-aid group, and then to subvillage, village, and brigade-scale collectives, culminating with the enormous communes of the Great Leap Forward. Following this, the sequence was reversed, moving toward smaller and smaller scale production units: commune to brigade to production team. The teams had seemed to represent a reasonable compromise between scale and manageability, and had persisted from 1962 to the end of the Maoist era, although by 1979 the teams were larger and less manageable as a result of population growth. The next smaller unit of production was the small group. But at the small group level, the Zengbu teams had reached the point of diminishing sociological returns; the small groups cost more in terms of reduplicated leadership, increased accounting costs, and conflicts and dissatisfaction among the team members, than they were worth in terms of whatever minimal increased production they might have facilitated. The failure of the small group production responsibility system in Zengbu indicated that attempts to fine-tune the social organization of production by reinvoking the same structural solutions at ever smaller structural levels could not solve the problems of the Maoist collectives.

More fundamental changes were soon to follow. Experiments with fixing production responsibility to households had already been made, but only for commercial crops, since the collective cultivation of rice had so important a symbolism. The harvesting of rice by households rather than teams had never before been permitted by the upper levels. At the fall harvest of 1979, the harvesting of rice by households was permitted for the first time. Pondside and Sandhill team leaders adopted this alternative, justifying it with the argument that members of agricultural small groups were refusing to harvest unless all team members participated. Under the new system, this work would be shared.

Cadres from Lu's Home opposed the harvest of rice by households on ideological grounds, and accused the other villages of abandoning the socialist road. They argued that rice harvesting should be done collectively by the small agricultural groups whose special job it was. When jobs in brigade and team industries were set aside so that all team members could participate in the harvest, the result was a loss of income from industry; more money would be earned for the team as a whole by continuing to work in specialized occupations. Secretary Lu, of Lu's Home village, described the new way of harvesting as "false egalitarianism," because the principle of shared economic benefits through a rational division of labor had been replaced with the principle of shared drudgery. "Furthermore," he said, "harvesting by households penalizes households containing only the weak and the old by forcing them to drag the heavy threshing machines through the fields by themselves."

In spite of these arguments, the people of Sandhill and Pondside preferred to harvest by household, and the rice fields of the teams were assigned by lot to the constituent households for harvesting. The misery of the rice harvest was being apportioned evenly among all team members. Households drew, if necessary, and if possible, on the aid of their close patrilineal relatives, in order to complete their own share of the harvesting.

County-level cadres who came on a visit of inspection felt that events were "moving too fast." They directed that production responsibility should no longer be delegated to smaller groups or households. Brigade cadres were told to use ideological education rather than material incentives to improve people's work. The Sandhill villagers who had finished their small group agricultural tasks perfunctorily, so as to seek private employment as construction workers in Chashan town, were singled out for criticism. They had threatened the existence of the collectives by negating the importance of the rights of the team over the labor of all team members. But the brigade- and commune-level cadres listened politely to the county-level cadres, assented to what they said, and ignored their directions. "We were reading the newspapers," one commune-level cadre said, "and we knew what was happening around the country. Some of the county cadres were too leftist. We did not listen to them."

The next important step in decollectivization took place in late 1980 and 1981. A new system, called, rather clumsily, the "specialized contract system for managing team property" (juanye chengbao), was implemented. Concessionary rights to manage all team property other than rice fields were sold at auction to households and groups of households. The concessions included the management of the teams' orchards, fishponds, rural industries (such as the brick and tile kilns), vegetable fields, and flocks of geese and ducks. Also auctioned-off were concessions for plowing the teams' rice fields by tractor and caring for the teams' water buffaloes.

People who had access to capital, such as those who could borrow from their Hong Kong relatives, were at an obvious advantage in the bidding. Powerful people, including cadres, also had advantages in acquiring the use of collective property for their private gain. As a result, team members did not, in fact, have equal opportunities to bid for the use of the collectively owned means of production.

Initially, Pondside's and Lu's Home teams restricted bidding rights. Only team members could bid for rights to team property, because it seemed unfair to give outsiders the privilege of profiting from property in which they had no ownership rights. From the very first, however, Sand-hill teams permitted anyone to bid, even people from other brigades or communes. The reasoning was that the threat of outside competition would force the bids up, maximizing the lease income of team members from their collective property; at the end of the year, the team would distribute this income to its constituent households. Also, open bidding might prevent one household or one group of households within a team from monopolizing rights to collective property unfairly. If one group was successful in bidding for a brick kiln, for example, the unsuccessful bidders would have to find other occupations, and there would be no one left within the team to give the successful bidders competition at the next bidding.

By the end of 1982, all Zengbu teams had instituted open bidding. The only stipulation was that outsiders must have a friend or relative in the village where the property was located, as an assurance that the contract would be fulfilled. However, most bidders were from within the team or village. Outsiders hesitated to bid for concessionary rights in villages other than their own. Outsiders were thought of as fair game, and their fish or produce might be stolen. In 1980, for example, several Zengbu villagers with expertise in the management of fishponds won concessions to manage fishponds in other brigades. However, the fish were stolen from the ponds and the managers could not afford to hire enough labor to guard the ponds continually. Prior to Liberation, farmers from one village were afraid to rent land in the territory of another village in case crops were stolen or irrigation ditches cut. Now this old village parochialism was reinvoked.

The winning bidders signed contracts with the team. An actual production contract for the management of a fishpond provides detailed examples of the considerations regarded as important.

*Sandhill Number 1 team fishpond contract*

1. The winning bidder rents this fishpond from the date of the auction [December 1982] until the end of March 1984 A.D. It is agreed that the contractor will take over the fishpond filled with existing fish and will return a dry pond with no fish.
2. The contractor is to sell to the state each year 800 *jin* of fish. One day before the New Year's Eve of each Spring Festival the contractor is to hand over to the production team 300 *jin* of silvercarp, gratis, each carp weighing from four to five *jin*. [The larger the carp, the more prized they are. The carp are to be distributed to team households for the New Year's Eve dinner.] If the 300 *jin* of free carp is not provided to the team by the contractor, the team will purchase the equivalent amount of fish at his expense.
3. The production team will have no responsibility for the capital costs of operating the fishpond and will not be responsible for the cost of electric pumping, or anything else.
4. The fish in the existing pond are agreed to be worth 5,000 *yuan*.
5. Each year the contractor is to pay the team 6,097 *yuan*. [This is the lease fee.]
6. The contractor is to hand in 30 percent of this 6,097 *yuan* by the end of June 1983, 30 percent before the Spring Festival of 1984, and 40 percent by the end of next March [1984]. In addition, the contractor must pay 50 percent of the 5,000 *yuan* value of the present fish in the pond, of 2,500 *yuan*, to the team before the Spring Festival of 1983, and another 50 percent before the end of March 1984. In case the money is not paid to the team by the stipulated times, the contractor will pay the team interest on the amount due, interest to be calculated by the floating interest rate of the state bank.
7. The team agrees to provide the contractor with a small boat worth 115 *yuan*.
8. Neither Party may break this contract.
9. Each Party retains one copy of this contract.

> Signature of the production team head, Liu Dengjia
> Signature of the contractor, Liu Bingdui

These contracts had historical precedent in the traditional techniques used for managing lineage estates. In Hong Kong's New Territories, for example, lineages auctioned-off the right to organize the village guard, and the right to sell crop and house protection "insurance," by competitive bidding. The contracts specified a sum of money to be paid to the central ancestral hall of the lineage, to be distributed as income to all members of the lineage at the end of the year, or used for collective purposes. In addition, the successful bidders were required to furnish a banquet for the elders of the lineage, with particular foods specified as to quality and amount. Traditionally the lineages of Guangdong were accustomed to auctioning-off collective property for private exploitation, in return for a fixed and carefully specified lease fee in cash or kind. The auctions of rights to collective property in Zengbu during the decollectivization of the early 1980s were following a traditional structural pattern, based upon an implied analogy between the lineage and its ancestral estates, on one hand, and the production team and its collective property, on the other.

In the initial bidding for concessionary rights, some villagers appeared to act in the belief that the teams had indeed mismanaged collective resources, and that private management would yield far greater profits. The bidding was extraordinarily high. The bidding for fishponds provides an interesting example. Some people overbid for ponds whose past production records they knew well. However, the following year fish production was, at best, only 10 percent greater than it had been under team management, and in many cases production had actually dropped. This was because there had proved to be a number of problems in the transition from team to private management. The fishpond entrepreneurs had not calculated their labor costs accurately enough, for example. As private managers, they had to pay labor instead of relying on team members, and in the developing post-Mao economy private wages had come into existence and were beginning to rise. The management groups sometimes found that members broke their agreements, and refused to do their share of the work. The managers of small fishponds did better initially than the managers of large fishponds. This was attributed to the fact that expenses were more easily calculated. The managers of large fishponds lost a sum estimated at 50,000 *yuan* in the first year, and this was attributed to the greater difficulty of calculating management expenses on a larger scale.

The teams initially bid out the right to manage team property for only one or two years. When these first contracts expired, in 1982, and the concessions were auctioned again, bids were much lower, only 40 to 50 percent of what had been bid the first time. The villagers had realized that the contract system was a two-edged sword. One might as easily lose as make money.

Rice land had continued to hold a special status, and was not available for bidding. The final step in Zengbu's decollectivization, the division of the rice land, occurred in two stages. In 1981, Zengbu peasants and cadres were told to adopt a production responsibility system for the production of rice, but they were allowed to choose the form that best suited their local conditions. Experimentation at the local level was encouraged. This precipitated heated debate in Zengbu brigade party committee meetings between cadres who continued to see value in collective forms of production and cadres who sought to decollectivize quickly and completely.

In 1981, both Pondside and Sandhill adopted the *bao chan dao hu* (fixing production to the group) form of household production responsibility. Under this system, collective rice fields were to be distributed by each team to its constituent households. In order to do this, the villagers had to decide on the criteria to be used in dividing the land. The process raised ideological issues. Should the land be divided to households on a per capita basis? This would be more egalitarian. It meant that households with more dependants would have more land. Or should the land be divided on the basis of how many laborers a household had? This would maximize productivity by putting land in the hands of households with the labor to work it effectively.

It was the form favored by the upper levels. Two valid principles were in conflict, and in typical Zengbu peasant fashion a compromise was made. Half the teams' rice land was distributed to households on the basis of the old team grain-rationing tables (see chapter 5), which took into account both the size and the labor power of a household, and half on a per capita basis, which took into account only the household's size. The compromise was in favor of egalitarianism and in opposition to the upper levels' stated preference. The peasants were anxious to ensure that every household had enough land to feed itself, since there would no longer be rice rations from the team. However, there were certain to be inherent inequalities in the distribution process. Some teams had more rice land per capita than others, as a result of the perpetuation of pre-Liberation village landholding patterns (see chapter 3) which meant that some villages had less land than others for purely historical reasons, and also because of population growth. Thus, families from some teams would receive more rice land per capita than families from others.

In distributing land to households, measurement was in terms of expected rice yield rather than in terms of area, just as it had been at the time of land reform. Households drew lots to see which particular fields they would get. Closely related households – the households of fathers, sons, brothers, and first patrilineal cousins – sent one representative to draw for the entire group, in an effort to ensure that their fields would be contiguous, for the sake of convenience. Cooperative labor arrangements between kin were now necessary, since the cooperation of team members was no longer an institutionalized resource. The peasants were reviving a family and kinship mode of production in response to the ending of the collective mode of production. And indeed, the old system was the only available structural alternative to the collectives.

The private plot system was continued unchanged. The same amount of land per person was allotted as before, and these private garden plots continued to be managed as they had been (see chapter 5).

A specific example of the team distribution of land to a particular household is provided by Secretary Liu of Pondside. His household of five persons received a total of 4·8 *mu* of land at the implementation of *bao chan dao hu*. (The average amount of land allotted in Pondside was 4·4 *mu* per household.) Secretary Liu's fields, like the fields of all households, were of different grades. His first grade land could produce peanuts and other crops in addition to rice; his second and third grade land was good for growing rice only. Since each household was allotted a combined package of first, second, and third grade fields, the land was scattered. Secretary Liu's household's land, for example, included four different fields or fractions of fields. The farthest of these fields was 1 kilometer, or 15 minutes' walk, from the field nearest the village. When a family's fields were widely separated, all their crops were less likely to be destroyed by natural disaster: if a flood were to inundate part of the village's fields, for example. But the disadvantages of small, widely separated holdings, outweighed this hypothetical advantage. The small fields were difficult to cultivate with tractors. Time was wasted going from field to field. These inconveniences had formed part of the rationale for collectivization in the first place. The advantages of rationalizing Zengbu's land holdings by creating large and uniform collective fields, more easily worked by tractors, were nullified by the new distribution. The pattern of village landholdings reverted to its traditional form, the dispersed family holdings of the pre-revolutionary era. Initially, the length of time for which a family was to hold the land was limited to three years. Policy might change, as it had in the past. The cadres of Pondside and Sandhill hesitated to encourage people to make expensive capital investments, such as interplanting fruit trees on their land, until the policy was firm. At the end of 1983, the policy appeared to be a lasting one, and household tenure of the land was confirmed for up to ten years. By 1985, the period of tenure was 15 years or more. However, there was a reluctance to assign team land to households for longer than 15 years, for reasons of fairness. The longer tenure permitted productive capital investment, but it also perpetuated the inequalities of the original land distribution lottery. Some households had received fields to which they objected, and which they did not wish to hold indefinitely.

Although the land was distributed to the households for long periods of time, it remained team property, and there were certain restrictions on its use. For example, the peasants were prohibited from digging fishponds or erecting buildings of any kind. Later, however, even these remainders of the team's formal control would weaken (see chapter 17).

Under the household responsibility system, the peasants assumed the responsibility for growing their own rice rations, and for paying their share of the team's tax grain and state-purchase grain quotas. The peasants were free to hire others to grow rice for them, or to buy rice on the open market, in order to meet these obligations.

The Lu's Home villagers adopted a different form of production responsibility system, *bao chan dao lao* (which meant "fixing production responsibility to the individual team worker"). At the time, party thinkers considered this form of responsibility system to be the most advanced and complex of the alternate systems. It was said to be especially suitable for villagers in comparatively rich areas with a diversified economy, like Zengbu, where the teams were characterized by a complex division of labor. Unlike the *bao chan dao hu* household responsibility system adopted by Pondside and Sandhill, which divided the land among team households for household cultivation, almost eliminating the team's role in accounting and management, the Lu's Home production responsibility system was designed to maintain the production teams as functioning concerns. The people of Lu's Home village had consistently been more collectivist-minded than the people of the other two villages. They did not wish to destroy the collectives entirely, but rather to implement a form of production responsibility system that would retain the integrity of the collective.

The Lu's Home system, assigning responsibility to the individual laborer, differed in several important ways from the household responsibility system adopted by the other two villages. Rice land was not distributed among the team's households for cultivation. Instead, the responsibility for the cultivation of rice fields was assigned on a yearly basis to individual team workers who specialized in rice production. This system maintained the integrity of the production team by avoiding the delegation of responsibility to households entirely, and delegating responsibility to individuals on a yearly basis only. The team's functions of collective planning, distribution, and accounting were maintained.

The process was as follows. The team committees met as they had always done, and decided how to utilize the team's land and other productive resources during the coming year: how much land to put into the profitable vegetable production that was now being encouraged, how much land to put into rice, and what rural industries the team would operate. When the plans had been made, each team committee accepted competitive bidding for rights to manage the team's resources for the team's agreed-upon purposes. The Lu's Home teams accepted bids only from team members, and restricted bidding in order to ensure a fairer distribution of resources. In the case of vegetable land, for example, plots were limited in size to 1 *mu* each. Only one person per household was permitted to hold a vegetable plot. The vegetable grower agreed to pay the team the amount of the successful bid (approximately 1,000 *yuan* in 1982) in cash. The grower's profit would be whatever was earned after paying the contracted amount to the team.

The brick kilns and other industrial enterprises were not available for bidding. Instead, the management of enterprises was contracted only to groups of team members who had previously worked there. These contracts were negotiated by the team and the group of workers, and the aim of the negotiation was to ensure that the contracting management group would get a fair return.

The management of rice fields was a residual category, allotted to those who had not been successful in bidding vegetable land, were not engaged in team enterprises, and who were unable to find employment, such as construction work or peddling, outside the framework of the team. The team assigned production quotas (based upon previous production of the land in question) and provided production costs. Plowing was done by the successful bidders to the team's tractors and buffaloes. Rice growers were required to deliver a quota of rice to the team. From this rice the team members' rations would be distributed as before, according to the rationing charts. Rice growers were also required to deliver tax grain and state purchase grain to the state grain purchasing station in Chashan on behalf of the team as a whole.

Under this form of production responsibility system, Lu's Home retained a modified workpoint system. For example, the team gave each vegetable grower 4,500 workpoints for the year's work, the average number of workpoints earned by a first-grade male worker under the former collective system. Rice growers, raisers of pond fish, orange growers, forestry team workers, tractor drivers, buffalo herders, and team committee members were assigned workpoints on an analogous basis. Workers who earned money privately, or in the brigade's factories, outside of the team framework, were required to turn a portion of their wages over to the team in exchange for workpoints.

At the end of the year's operation, each team distributed the team income from all sources to team households, on the basis of the workpoints earned by the households. Rice was distributed, as before, according to the basic grain rationing chart. Team members kept all over-quota earnings. The vegetable growers kept the profits after paying their contracted amount to the team; the rice growers kept the rice they produced over their assigned quotas; those employed outside the team, whether privately or by the brigade, kept whatever they made in excess of the amount they were required to turn over to the team in exchange for workpoints.

The Lu's Home production responsibility system preserved the integrity of the team as a unified body for ownership, overall management, and distribution. The rice land was not distributed to households in Lu's Home village, as it was in Sandhill and Pondside, so the key material and symbolic element of the collective ideology – the collective management of rice fields – was maintained. Furthermore, this complex system continued team responsibility for the social welfare of its members. Everyone in Lu's Home village was provided with employment by the production team, including the old and the disabled, who were able to earn workpoints cleaning the village roads. An old couple, or a widow, would not be required by the economic necessities of the household responsibility system to undertake the heavy work of rice cultivation or to depend on kinsmen to do it for them.

In 1981, under this complex system, the Lu's Home production teams enjoyed approximately the same economic success as the teams which had adopted the household responsibility system. However, internal conflict within the Lu's Home teams, together with the increased possibilities for employment and entrepreneurship outside the collective framework, brought this experiment with the assignment of production responsibility to an end.

Internal conflict, in the form of petty economic dissatisfactions, in the context of an extraordinarily, indeed almost grotesquely, complex framework for the calculation of reward, made the system unworkable. Among the most dissatisfied were the rice growers. They resented their restriction to the unshared drudgery of rice agriculture. They symbolized their dissatisfaction by delivering inferior rice to the team for distribution as rice rations; they kept the best rice for their families to eat, or for sale on the open market. Lest the team members who did not grow rice fail to take the point, small rocks were left in the team's ration rice.

Team members employed in factories were dissatisfied because of the cumbersome arrangements for the payment of wages. Part of their earnings were given directly to their team in return for workpoints and rice rations; the rest was paid in cash. The factory workers would have preferred to receive their wages directly in cash. The same was true of team members working privately outside the team.

There was also the issue of inequality of income. Collective team control over the labor of its members was vitiated. This was a crucial aspect of decollectivization, even more important than the distribution of land. Having regained control of their own labor, the peasants moved out into the newly emerging private economy; they took private jobs and set up their own small businesses. Disparity in peasant incomes quickly became apparent. A basic structural principle of the Maoist collectives had been the maintenance of economic equality among team households. The new economic environment made it impossible to maintain economic equality among team members. The resultant envies and jealousies made the continuance of the teams as collectives impossible.

At the beginning of 1983, the Lu's Home villagers gave up their attempt to retain collective forms of social organization and adopted the household responsibility system (*bao chan dao hu*) as Pondside and Sandhill had done. This was the final step in the decollectivization of Zengbu brigade. Half-measures of change had failed. The Maoist collectives could not exist in the altered political and economic environment. With hindsight, the adamant opposition of the Maoists to the introduction of capitalist practices was justified. There was now no choice but to push on inexorably toward complete decollectivization. Zengbu's rural economy and society had entered the post-Mao era.

# 9

# The cultural construction of emotion in rural Chinese social life

The human capacity to experience emotion can be made to serve a wide range of social purposes. Cultural definitions of the appropriate relationship between the emotions of the individual and the social order may vary greatly. The familiar cultural context that provides a frame of reference for anthropologists who are at home in the United States is unusual for its extreme level of emphasis on the importance of emotions as the legitimizing basis that establishes a relationship between a person and a social context. The significance of emotions in Zengbu village life is quite different. The villagers do not assume that the emotional life of individuals is utilized in the service of the social order. As a result, the meaning of the person, and the relationship between the person and society are thought of in different terms. In order to understand these terms without ethnocentrism, some familiar Western assumptions about the meaning of emotion, and the influence of these assumptions on anthropology, must be made explicit.

In the cultural context that is American anthropology's referential framework, it tends to be assumed that the form and meaning of social experience are directly derived from the emotions of a person having the experience; it is not assumed that emotions are a trivial concomitant of experience, of interest only to the person who feels them. Rather, personal emotion is a critical component of experience.

It is also assumed that social relationships are appropriately formed, perpetuated, or dissolved, on the basis of personal emotion. For example, the appropriate emotional prerequisite for marriage is love, and a marriage without love is regarded as an impoverished social form. When love no longer exists, it is legitimate to dissolve the marriage. So, emotional experience is taken as a legitimizing basis for social action. This is applied to birth-ascribed kin ties as well as to marriage. In parenthood, as in marriage, there is a sense that appropriate validating emotions should be provided. Although the relationship between parent and child continues to exist legally whether it is emotionally affirmed or not, a merely legal relationship seems incomplete and insufficient in the face of the cultural demand for the emotional affirmation of relationships. Similarly, appropriate patriotism goes beyond the fact of citizenship, and demands an appropriate experienced emotion, or it is felt to be invalid. In politics, an important factor is the ability of a candidate to arouse the warm emotional response that serves as the experiential referent for validating the legitimacy of leadership. And in a murder trial, the defendant's emotional state can be a decisive factor in the court's decision.

In purely commercial settings, as well, maintaining appropriate relationships between buyers and sellers is thought to require continuous validation provided by expressions of experienced emotion. Much advertising is based on this assumption. The capacity to care, or to experience other integrative emotions, is attributed to nonhuman entities, such as corporations, which are parties to relationships, although such entities are obviously incapable of feeling. Arlie Hochschild's *The Managed Heart* (1983) provides an extensive description of this phenomenon.

So, it is being assumed that social relationships are continuously created by individuals, and maintained by individual feeling and individual enactment. Relationships are derived from and affirmed by feeling, and feelings are direct expressions of the self. The expression of feeling is the medium of communication between the self and the social order. To root all meaningful social experience in the self is, from one point of view, an affirmation of the self, and of the importance of the individual. Yet from another point of view, it puts an intolerable burden on individual experience. If relationships are based on affirmation derived from the emotions of the individual, they can be destroyed, vitiated, or invalidated by the continuing presence of inimical, inappropriate, or ambivalent emotions, and the lack of capacity to feel attacks the legitimacy of one's relationships. If emotions must be expressed sincerely, and the lack of sincere feelings invalidates relationship, then the individual is required to produce a continuous stream of emotional expression that is simultaneously sincere and appropriate; if this does not occur, the social order is endangered. Important social relationships are made to depend on varieties of personal experience that are in many ways involuntary, or difficult to control.

Because emotions in this cultural framework have such great social importance, they are far too important to be experienced freely; ironically, the great importance attached to individual emotional experience, and its significant social consequences, has resulted in a system in which individuals must modify and distort their own experiences, if these experiences are not to endanger their social relationships in particular, or the social order in general. Trapped by the requirement to have an emotionally appropriate self, people must reformulate their own inner experiences by the use of psychologically forceful methods, such as defense mechanisms, directed against their own genuine or authentic responses to their own reality. If they do not do so, their continued relationship to the social order is put at risk. Maintaining an inner life that is consistent with the formal requirements of the social order is a formidable task. In comparison, the ability to weep real tears for ritual purposes, like the Andamanese who so impressed Radcliffe-Brown (1964, p. 117) seems a manipulation of the self of a far more superficial order.

The necessity to feel appropriately has important implications from the point of view of individual freedom, which is attacked from within the person; these implications have been eloquently discussed by, for example, R. D. Laing (1972, pp. 100–101). From the point of view of the nature of the social order as a whole, these cultural beliefs produce two kinds of highly significant patterns. First, there is a pattern of continuous and pervasive attention to psychological processes, which must be defined, explained, expressed, analyzed, understood, and utilized so as to facilitate social life without endangering it. Second, there is the enactment of a social world which is experienced as having no inherent integral basis for continuity, since the social order must be continuously reinvented and reaffirmed from within myriad individuals. As Shweder and Bourne put it, "Cut adrift from the larger whole, the self has become the measure of all things" (1984, p. 195).

In social theory, scholarly and analytical ideas emphasizing the relationship between the social order and the inner responses of individuals have had an important influence on anthropology since its inception. When Durkheim speaks of sentiments, when Radcliffe-Brown applies Durkheim's ideas, referring to "the individual sentiments on whose existence the social order itself depends" (1952, p. 146), when awe is associated with kingship, or a sense of solidarity with membership in a lineage, the importance of the connection between inner experience and the social order is being made the focus of analysis. More recently, there has been an increased emphasis on the nature and qualities of the experienced emotions as such. As Catherine Lutz puts it, "the concept of emotion, then, can provide a critical nexus for understanding the individual's creation of, and participation in, social institutions" (1983, p. 257). The empirical value of investigating the relationship between inner experience and social life, and of understanding the social meaning of emotion, has been demonstrated over and over again, and is beyond question. However, in such social contexts as Zengbu, the native theory of the relationship between the person, the emotions, and the social order is greatly at variance both with Western cultural assumptions and with accepted social theory, so that the latter can only provide a partial explanation for social action. How is emotion to be understood in relation to a social structure conceived of as a continuous entity, existing independently without reference to the self, and *not* as the product of continual creation, recreation, and affirmation from within the self, with the process being mediated by emotional experience?

The people of Zengbu believe that experienced emotion is irrelevant either to the creation or to the perpetuation of social institutions of any kind. They certainly recognize the existence of emotions, and are aware of them as aspects of experience, but emotions are not thought of as significant in social relationships. An emotion is never the legitimizing rationale for any social significant action, and there is no cultural theory that social structure rests on emotional ties. Thus, social relationships persist legitimately without an emotional basis, either real or fictive. This view might be tagged the "Image of Irrelevant Affect." Because they are assuming the existence of a continuous social order that requires no affirmation in inner emotional response, but only in behavior, there is no need for them to treat emotions as inherently important. Emotional experience has no formal social consequences. (It may, of course, have informal ones.) Nor do they feel that they are continually creating and affirming social relationships from within, using their own emotional experiences as the raw material for the process.

The villagers assume that a person's significant characteristics are products of the social context, rather than derived from within; they are, in a word, sociocentric. When the children of former landlords are stigmatized, because they partake of landlord characteristics, or when political loyalty is regarded as tainted because of the disloyal opinions of a relative connected through a single ancestor several generations back, the superior importance of the social, as opposed to the manifestations of the inner characteristics of the individual, is being affirmed. What is uniquely characteristic of the individual's private experience – in particular, the emotional – is socially irrelevant.

Thus, the important aspects of social continuity are external to the self. The social order exists independently of any emotion, and emotions are thought of as lacking the power to create, maintain, injure, or destroy social relationships. Society does not define the emotions as an aspect of identity with social significance. The villagers express this lack of significance in their conventional response to questions about emotional experience, "How I feel doesn't matter." By this they mean that their feelings are not important for the understanding of those aspects of experience that they themselves regard as worthy of being understood.

This attitude is based on early experiences such as the adult response to childhood tantrums described by Barbara Ward: "In the setting of the Hong Kong fishing village it was observed that, 'as a general rule, the child is left to cry himself out.' Adults neither comfort nor scold the raging youngster, with the result that after a number of ineffectual tries at influencing the offending elder, the child gives up the tactic as useless' (unpublished ms. cited in Solomon 1971, p. 62). In Hong Kong, there is a proverb used by the parents as they withhold response in such situations, "I have borrowed the ear of Deaf Chen." In using this proverb, parents tell the child that their lack of response is deliberate. However, they do not require that the child cease to express, or modify the expression, of emotion. The child's expression of feeling is socially ineffectual. But it is not treated as dangerous, or as an intolerable display that must be checked, but rather as an idiosyncrasy; people will not take it seriously, but they will put up with it until it is over. Active willingness to pay attention to emotional response, like active attempts to elicit it, are attitudes that strike the villagers as peculiar. When asked to discuss their lives in terms of a relevant series of emotional experiences, people are puzzled. They do not deny that such areas of experience coexist with areas of experience that are recognized as relevant, but the idea of deliberately trying to understand and explain the significant seems unprofitable to them.

Although villagers do not, generally speaking, discuss their emotions as such, they do not appear to feel constrained against letting many emotions be seen when they occur. In daily life they are most vividly expressive. Without apparent self-dramatization, they neither avoid the expression of most emotions, nor treat them as if they were intrinsically dangerous. Love, to be considered below, is the significant exception to this generalization.

What, then, are the kinds of emotions that are openly expressed in village daily life? A series of examples provide a sense of what is being expressed, and in what contexts. These examples deal with what is overt and manifest, concentrating on readily observed phenomena such as tears, shouted words with angry content, or the explicit comments of other villagers.

A dignified and respected village man, of senior status, wept openly as he described how, as a boy, he watched his mother lighting the lanterns for a humiliating ceremony his parents were being required to perform. A widow did not hide her tears as she told of being required by her stepmother to marry a repulsive man of twice her age. A man from a neighboring village appeared overwhelmingly sad as he described his brigade's perfectly ordinary production statistics. Later a woman from his village, who had married into Zengbu, commented, "He has never looked happy since the day his daughter drowned in the East River." A woman wept bitterly as she described her little daughter's accidental death: a group of children took a lantern into a house used for the storage of straw, so that they could play cards there. The lantern overturned, the straw caught fire, and the child was trapped. A man's wife said that he wept for several nights after agreeing to let his daughter marry into a village so far away as to be beyond a walk. A man wept as he told how his mother went to Singapore, in hopes of earning money to send back, but she fell ill and died there, and he never saw her again. A woman interrupted an elementary school class. In front of the teacher and all the children, she slapped a girl who had hit her son, and screamed angrily at her. A mother-in-law cursed her daughter-in-law openly in the village lane. Another mother-in-law said, in her daughter-in-law's presence, "This is my daughter-in-law. She is absolutely worthless. She is so stupid that she didn't even remember that today is an unlucky day to wash your hair, until I reminded her." A young man's face was wreathed in smiles as he was awarded a rare opportunity to better his status by joining the army. A man gave a loud repeated cry, something between a sob and a groan, when he was brought back to the brigade headquarters after an unsuccessful attempt to flee to Hong Kong. A woman spent the morning screaming angrily at brigade officials when they denied her a permit to travel to the border town of Shenzhen. A brigade leader responsible for the implementation of birth planning policy said that people scream at her, yell, and scold, when they dislike the policy.

The behavior of villagers who show these strong feelings is consistent with the idea that the expression of most feeling is not a significant act, in and of itself, rather than with the idea that affect is in some way intrinsically dangerous and to be concealed. The villagers would be perfectly capable of self-restraint, if they believed that open expressiveness were damaging either to their social position, or to the esteem in which they were held by others. The open expression of emotion, as illustrated by these examples, is regarded as perfectly normal, and other villagers do not appear shocked or surprised; there is no suggestion that the people showing emotion are abnormal or deranged. Both men and women are expressing emotion, and expressiveness does not seem to be thought of as more characteristic of women. The villagers do not expect emotional expressiveness to help in achieving an end. Expressiveness could not prevent a hateful marriage under the old regime. It cannot now make a permit available, or modify birth planning policy, any more than it can bring a dead child back to life. Just as the villagers assume that their expressiveness will not be efficacious, they also assume that it will not be dangerous, in the sense of producing social consequences that will rebound against themselves. This is particularly striking in the case of anger directed against authority figures. Leaders at the brigade level describe open expression of anger when policy is unpopular. Anger is not experienced as an attack on the legitimacy and continuity of relationships; anger at policy does not imply either that the government is losing control or that the policy will not be carried out. The free expression of emotion is not perceived as a threat to authority, and anger, per se, is not punished. What is perceived as a threat to authority is inappropriate judgment, rather than inappropriate emotion, and thus the government thinks it is important to correct what it perceives as misunderstanding, through formal re-education. Attention is directed away from the psychological processes of individuals, especially their feelings, and onto the appropriate expression of shared intersubjective agreement about moral values and the social world. Rather than trying to feel appropriately, people are supposed to bring their understanding into congruence with what is defined as valid. While the expression of heterodox opinion, particularly in writing, has formal consequences, the expression of emotion does not. By comparison, in the West, differences of opinion are supposed to be accommodated within the social order, but inappropriate feelings are interpreted as symptoms of a need for the re-education of emotional life.

To take one specific example, the woman who was angry because she was denied a travel permit did not appear to feel that her behavior was likely to be remembered and held against her. Brigade leaders told her that it would not do any good to be angry, and that she should go home, but they let her sit outside their office and scream. If her anger had been regarded as intrinsically dangerous, either because it implied a threat to their authority, or because it was embarrassing them, she could certainly have been quieted or removed. The inference is that they did not regard her open expression of anger as a serious matter. Had she violated propriety in some way that is taken seriously, she would have been stopped.

Anger expressed by authority figures often receives a similar detached response. Lower-level officials frequently comment that they ignored the expressed anger of the "upper levels" and made their own decisions. For example, one commune-leader said, "During the Cultural Revolution, rural enterprises were criticized as capitalist by the upper levels, but we just let them scold, and continued as we were." Similar responses in pre-revolutionary China are reported by a former Maryknoll missioner (Kathleen Bradley, private communication).

The expression of anger appears to have a connection with morality that helps to legitimize it. The historian Thomas Metzger provides an example of anger defined as legitimate in terms of traditional values, "the feelings of 'righteous anger' (kung-fen) aroused by authority figures perceived as morally deficient" (1981, p. 19). This sort of righteous anger has been utilized since 1949 as the basis for public meetings in which leaders are criticized, and feelings of bitterness expressed. It is quite possible that such meetings as this have provided a context of social legitimacy for the open expression of anger against authority, and that as a result there has been a real change in the range of emotional expressiveness regarded as permissible, where anger against authority is concerned. However, the range was probably never as narrow as Westerners have supposed. (For another example, see Chu 1985, p. 263.)

The expression of anger when the anger is not a moral statement is a slightly different question. Tu Wei-ming cites Confucius' effort to grapple with the social ramifications of this problem, and he provides an enlightening insight into traditional Chinese views of anger. "[I]n the Sayings of the Confucian School, Confucius instructs the filial son to endure only light physical punishment from an enraged father ... To run away from a severe beating, the argument goes, is not only to protect the body which has been entrusted to him by his parents but also to respect the fatherliness in his father that has been obscured by rage" (1985, p. 239). The importance of this formulation is in the distinction being drawn between the relevant social self of the father, his "fatherliness," and the expression of rage which is not

regarded as an integral aspect of the self, but rather as a separable phenomenon, which cannot legitimately be allowed to "obscure" the aspects of the
father that are significant. Because the rage is not a relevant aspect of the
father's social self, it does not require respect; the social role of the father is
emic (meaningful and significant), but the rage he expresses is etic (not to be
regarded as significant).

The open expression of sorrow is also unstigmatized. Witnesses of sorrow
are not expected to provide an emotional response that the sorrowing person
can recognize as a valuable token of relationship; the expression of sorrow
does not require a display of socially patterned sympathy. Since it is not
expected that any emotionally expressive response will be forthcoming, when
an expressive response is offered, it is passed over without comment by the
sorrowing person. Expectable behavior does not include a performance of
empathy, attempts to explore the feelings of another with questions or a
counterdisplay of one's own response. The exact parameters of appropriate
response to the emotional display of another are somewhat unclear, but
people act as if others will neither provide emotional affirmation nor attempt
to interfere with expressiveness.

The contrast between this and the expectable response when a taboo is
violated is so clear and dramatic that there can be no question of classifying
the display of feeling as tabooed or impermissible. There is, for example, a
taboo against shaking hands with a gravedigger. Open expressions of horror
followed the violation of this taboo.

The fact that expressiveness is not expected to elicit a valued response is
probably related to the lack of apparent calculated effort to induce an
emotional response from an audience. Nor is expressiveness utilized to
confirm relationship. The open expression of sorrow does not imply a sense
of intimacy in a favorable atmosphere for emotional expression.
Expressiveness is independent of, and implies nothing about, relationship.
The villagers are expressive entirely in their own terms, and do not share
Western conventions about the connections between the sharing of feelings
and intimacy.

The conception of emotion as mere idiosyncrasy, lacking in symbolic
significance for the creation and maintenance of social relationships, has
important (if by no means complete) explanatory value for many aspects of
Chinese social life that are otherwise baffling. Since emotional expressiveness
is not required to affirm an encounter, the villagers are not required by
convention to provide a continuing symbolic pattern of emotionally
expressive response; the absence of this pattern leaves those who expect it at a
loss, and is probably the basis for the old stereotype that the Chinese are
inscrutable. Since valid social action does not have to be consistent with inner
feeling, the Chinese definition of sincerity does not exist in reference to inner
feeling, but requires only the enactment of civility (Solomon 1971, p. 110). A

public confession that would be dismissed as invalid in Western terms, if there were doubt that it reflected the inner feelings of the person confessing, is fully acceptable, since what matters is the public affirmation, not the inner feeling.

This way of understanding emotion provides a particularly Chinese construct of what it is to be a person (cf. Geertz 1974). A Chinese person is a person whose emotions are understood as irrelevant idiosyncrasies, of no intrinsic importance to the social order. Such a person is significantly different from a person whose emotions are culturally defined as a fundamental aspect of the self, giving meaning to social experience, and providing a necessary validation of the connections between the individual and society. A person whose emotions have no significance for the social order experiences social reality differently. In many important contexts, such a person has no need to manipulate emotions in order to serve social ends, either within the self, or in terms of social expressiveness, since emotional experience is not thought to have a significant role in the symbolization of relationship. (The influence of such views on, for example, the Oedipus complex, has not been studied, but perhaps a conviction that one's emotions do not harm the fundamental continuity of relationships would tend to ease the level of guilt and anguish involved.) Francis L. K. Hsu, in his article "Suppression versus Repression" (1949) points out the lack of continuous reference to inner processes in Chinese social behavior. His focus of attention is the comparison between the importance of internal and external controls on behavior, rather than on emotions as such, but his views are consistent with the argument that a Western cultural rationale requires the individual to support the social order by reference to inner feelings, and a Chinese cultural rationale supposes the continuity of the social order to exist independently of inner feelings.

When the Chinese view that emotion is not a significant aspect of the self encounters the Western view that emotion is fundamental, the consequence is frequently to hammer the square peg of the Chinese assumption into the round hole of Western interpretation, and to conclude that the Chinese have important emotional reasons for their refusal to recognize emotions as important. Some authors have argued that in Chinese culture emotions are strongly disvalued, in and of themselves, and are, as a result, carefully concealed. For example, Arthur Kleinman, whose research is concerned with the study of depression in a clinical context, says, "During socialization, individuals ... learn that their own personal affects, particularly strong and negative ones, should not be openly expressed ... Revealing their own feelings might result in shame for themselves and their families" (1980, p. 133). He has also generalized that "dysphoria (depression, sadness, irritability [is] suppressed. Dysphoric emotion traditionally has been regarded as shameful to self and family; for that reason it was not to be revealed outside the family" (Kleinman and Good 1985, p. 438). Richard Solomon, whose research is aimed at understanding Chinese government and politics from a psychoanalytic perspective, also takes the position that emotion in general is strongly disvalued. He says, "Adults act as if emotions were dangerous" (1971, p. 63). He makes the argument that it is particularly necessary to conceal feelings of hostility, especially if they are directed against authority figures, referring to the "impermissibility of hostility" (p. 67). (He also points out, correctly, that feelings of love and affection cannot be freely expressed.)

The generalization that the Chinese think of emotion in general, and "dysphoric" emotion in particular as dangerous or shameful is not consistent with observed social reality, as it is enacted in the village context. The villagers do not act as if emotions were dangerous; they act as if contact with menstrual blood or gravediggers were dangerous. When they devalue the importance of emotions in social life, they are not describing an emotionally charged intrapsychic process, as a result of which the emotions are manipulated in order to render them socially acceptable. Instead, they are stating a shared cultural assumption, which provides the context for emotional life. If the process were intrapsychic, all emotional expressiveness would indeed be carefully guarded, for fear of its social consequences, but this is not the case. Furthermore, the emotions being expressed include open displays of sorrow, hostility, and anger: emotions which could certainly be subsumed under Kleinman's categories "dysphoric," "strong," and "negative," or Solomon's category "hostile." Judging by observed behavior, these categories reflect Western ideas about which emotions are dangerous or unwholesome, rather than the values of the villagers.

Chinese emotions, then, are natural phenomena without important symbolic significance for the maintenance and perpetuation of social relationships. They are understood at the level of the twitch, not at the level of the wink (Geertz 1973, p. 6–7). When the Chinese wish to affirm and symbolize relationships, they must utilize symbolic forms that do not draw on emotional expressiveness, but on other means of social action. The critical symbolic dimension for the affirmation of relationships is work, and the related and subordinate concept of suffering, which is thought of as an intrinsic aspect of work. Both work and suffering are understood, not in terms of inner experience, but in terms of outward results, especially measurable ones. By contrast, in Western terms, the critical symbolic dimension for the affirmation of relationships is love, thought of as a validating inner experience. Freud's famous dictum points out the supreme significance of the human capacities to love and to work. The West has used the capacity to love as the symbolic basis for social relationships; the Chinese have used the capacity to work as the symbolic basis of human relationships.

In order to understand this, it is useful to examine the meaning of love in the village context. The emotion certainly exists. But how is love experienced when it lacks social meaning as the legitimizer of relationships? And how are relationships affirmed without using emotion as a symbol? As an experienced emotion, love has the intrinsic capacity to lend importance to relationships, whether they have structural significance or not. Since the patterns of pre-existent structure have primary importance in Chinese social relations, love is the rival and the potential enemy of structure. Rather than affirming structure, love is understood to endanger it. Thus, it is the emotion that most threatens the social order. Even when love is apparently most congruent with the social structure, as in the case of love between a father and a son, the expression of love is understood as being inherently in opposition to valued structural continuity. Villagers believe that when a father is openly affectionate with a son, he is, in effect, inviting his son to flout the formal patterns of respect and obedience that ought to characterize their relationship; a display of affection is dangerous to appropriate behavior in the relationship, which is optimally maintained when there is due distance between the two. If love is openly expressed, the form and strength of the relationship between the father and the son are thought to be damaged. (For the distance between father and son, see for example Martin C. Yang [1945, pp. 57–58], Marion J. Levy [1963, pp. 172–73], Olga Lang [1946, pp. 246–247].)

Related to this belief is the view that distance, physical as well as social, is a favorable circumstance for the maintenance of appropriate relationship. What is well preserved by distance is a relational ideal, and an abstract idea of connectedness, which cannot be tarnished by the inevitable stresses of daily contact. What cannot happen at a distance is the continuous recreation and experience of relationship that are regarded as essential if the social order is understood as continuously regenerated from within the self, rather than as having an abstract, independent existence.

When relationships are being newly formed, as in the choosing of a marriage partner, love is also suspect as a basis for social action. Emotional response of the kind that is put to use in the tradition of romantic love has always been strongly stigmatized in conventional village terms. When village exogamy was required, as it formerly was, all potential marriage partners were from outside one's social world, and there was no opportunity for the kind of social contact that engenders emotional intimacy. It remains improper for an unmarried village women to claim acquaintance in an adjacent village where appropriate potential marriage partners might be supposed to dwell. Love between people who knew one another would be love between fellow villagers, and this was defined as incestuous; the woman in such a case was enclosed in a woven pig basket, and drowned in the village pond. Some informants continue to say that they would not wish to marry a fellow villager, because it muddles the appropriate forms of address (by confusing the terms for in-laws with the terms for fellow villagers) and leaves them without appropriate in-law relationships. In essence, they are saying that, from the traditionalist point of view, the integrity of the kinship system is better served by an exogamous choice. However, it is also recognized that, from the point of view of getting along together, there are advantages in knowing one's partner.

The reformed marriage laws of 1953 and 1981 have influenced the formation of marriages, and the definition of the relationship between feeling and marriage choice. Perhaps the most critical reform was to make it illegal to require a person to marry without his or her own consent. (Previously, young people had to marry as their parents directed.) In preventing the imposition of a personally repugnant marriage, however, the law did not substitute the necessity to form marriages on a basis of love; rather, the law takes it for granted that marriages will be formed in a moral Chinese way, in a Chinese cultural context, and this is not a context which defines romantic love as an important element in marriage choice. Presently, marriage choice is ideally based on what are called "good feelings," but the phrase is never used in the sense of a romantic or passionate emotional response. Rather, the idea of "good feelings," as advocated by such organizations as the Women's Federation, stands in opposition to purely mercenary and selfish considerations. It implies social responsibility and altruism. Thus, a person with "good feelings" would not insist on marrying into a well-off family, or reject a potential partner from a poor family for economic reasons. A person with "good feelings" would favor the principled refusal to exchange brideprice and dowry. There would be a focus on the good qualities of the potential partner, qualities such as industriousness, rather than on the material advantages of the match. A person with "good feelings" would be willing to work and sacrifice on behalf of the other. The Women's Federation provided an example of a marriage not based on "good feelings." A young village woman (from another part of the county) agreed to marry a man from Hong Kong some twenty years older than herself, although such age disparities are culturally regarded as disgusting. The man was very wealthy. When the Women's Federation remonstrated with the woman, she said she wanted to marry him because he would die soon, and she could have his money and marry again. Such purely mercenary motives as these are regarded as ignoble by comparison with less selfish "good feelings"; the latter are thought of as providing a better basis for a relationship.

A marriage based on "good feelings" was described by the husband, who had chosen a wife within the village. He said,

We were on the same team, and we met working together. In 1973, we began to have good feelings for one another. I helped her family, and she helped mine. I helped them to build a house, to weed their plots, and took them to the hospital when they were ill. When we were the right age, we registered the marriage. My wife's side did not ask for the little cakes the groom's family is supposed to contribute, but I gave them anyway.

It is reasonable to infer the existence of emotion in this relationship. But from the point of the view of the husband, the significant events leading up to his marriage were not emotional events. Rather, significance lies in the work done on one another's behalf, the help provided in illness (taking people to the hospital means transporting them on a bicycle-wheeled hand cart for half an hour's walk) and the willingness to provide the marriage cakes even when they were not required. The expressive forms that validate the relationship are not enacted in an idiom of love as an emotion, but in an idiom of work and mutual aid. Love itself remains infinitely private.

This view of love as so profoundly inward as to be, in effect, unshareable except through the expressive medium of work, shapes communication in all relationships, not only those which are being newly formed. The villagers have a proverb, "The son does not know the mother's heart; the mother does not know the son's heart." This proverb emphasizes the uncommunicated nature of feelings even when the people involved are certainly very close. A mother, speaking of her daughter's recent marriage, said, "My daughter didn't tell me how she felt, but I guessed that she liked the young man, because he was kind, and didn't scold. I asked if she agreed to the marriage, and she said she had no opinion on the subject [this is a polite way of saying that one does not raise any objections]. The boy came and helped us to build a house, collect straw, and harvest our sugarcane." Emotion was never mentioned, but the young man had shown "good feelings" in the idiom of work, and the marriage took place.

In marriages of long standing, whether successful or unsuccessful, work as a symbol of relationship is the most significant element in the villagers' evaluation of the quality of the union. One married woman said cheerfully, "It is quite all right between my husband and myself. We are both strong. And we get along well with my parents-in-law – we have just separated households." The phrase "quite all right" is a strongly positive response. (People who are not happy with their relationships generally describe them as "the usual sort of thing.") Her positive response is directly followed by the reference to strength. She means that they are both able to work effectively and well. (Physical strength is the most highly sought after quality in a marriage partner, since it implies the ability to work.) Having separated from the parents-in-law in due form shows that the relationship is presently harmonious and appropriate; no failure in human relations is implied by the separation. The villagers usually carry out a formal separation of households a year or two after the marriage of each son, so that each married couple has a household which is a separate accounting unit, with separate cooking and eating. When asked about the rationale for this formal separation, people respond that good relationships are better preserved in separate households.

Another village woman described her parents' unhappy marriage succinctly. She said, "In my own family, my father would scold and beat my mother for working too slowly, or not knowing the work." She added, "There is always a difference between the rich and the poor – with the poor, there is more beating." Here ill feeling is expressed as resentment against the partner's perceived inability to work; the ultimate cause is understood by this woman as being rooted in the unjust social order of her childhood. The conflict between the husband and the wife is not thought of in emotional terms but in terms of the symbolic significance of the capacity to work, and in relation to the economic and social contexts of the marriage.

The villagers described a wide variety of other relationships, and in every case the capacity to work rather than the capacity to feel was what was significant. Their descriptions of relationships that they themselves thought of as close and loving were expressed as if the emotional aspects of relationship were not the relevant ones. Rather, they would recast the discussion into a form which emphasized the willingness to work on the other's behalf. One woman, speaking of her parents, said, "I had to love my mother because she supported the family alone. I didn't care about my father – he didn't do anything to support the family." In speaking of child rearing, informants emphasized the importance, not of emotional ties, but of working to support their children and teaching them not to be lazy. Only by working for one another is the relationship between parents and children confirmed. As Chang Tsai, who lived between 1020 and 1077 put it, "If one does one's work with joy and without grudge, this exemplifies the purity of filial piety. To do the contrary is to deviate from one's moral virtue" (Unschuld 1985, p. 165).

These values produce an interesting result in the case of the relationship between parents and daughter, which is structurally liminal. The daughter is not as much a family member as the son, since she will marry into another family. The prodigious efforts to earn made by young unmarried women (in Zengbu they earn more than their brothers, in spite of a reward system that is biased against them) must be interpreted in the context of an effort to affirm the validity of their status as family members. (Young women's earnings were turned over to the head of household through 1979, and they continue to feel obligated to give a proportion of their income to their parents when they are not employed in household-run agriculture.) There is a lament, formerly sung by unmarried women in the houses where they live together (this traditional custom, described by Topley [1975], is still practiced), which poignantly expresses the young women's inability to affirm their relationship with their parents as completely as they would wish, however hard they work, since the structural context nullifies the symbolic medium available to them. The song goes as follows:

> Your enemy goes out from your dragon door
> You will feel lucky when I am away
> I have worn hollows in your stone steps going about my work
> But however many names are engraved on your ancestral tablets
> Mine will not be among them.

The reference to the woman's feet having worn hollows in the stone steps is a way of measuring the labor she has performed on her family's behalf. Yet in spite of this extraordinary amount of measurable labor, the woman remains an "enemy," and she has no way to affirm the legitimacy of her membership in the family into which she was born. The tragedy of the song arises from the contradiction between what is symbolically affirmed by the young woman, and what is predetermined by the social structure; it is comparable to the tragedy of a lover whose depth of feeling and intense emotion are rendered null and empty by enforced permanent separation from the beloved.

Outside the family, the expressive idiom remains the same. Asked what happens when there is a good relationship between neighbors, a man said, "We help one another with mutual aid." A team leader, asked whether team members felt close to one another, and whether there was any sense of team solidarity, answered, "It's hard to say if they feel close. Sometimes they do, when they work together. But other villagers, not on the team, will also help, if they see someone pushing a heavy load, or something like that." Conflict among team members was expressed in terms of the refusal of some people to work as hard as others. The underlying assumption is consistently that work shared means a close relationship.

In the wider society, the exemplars of appropriate behavior are people who work for others without stinting or selfishness. A model worker in a mattress factory in a nearby town was held up as an example because she "worked very hard without complaint"; she went to work early, returned late, and had never asked for leave since 1970, when she was urged to go to the hospital for the treatment of a serious illness. Other model workers are praised for their extraordinary output, for the intensity and tirelessness with which they work, and for their willingness to sacrifice personal comfort in order to labor well. The symbolic importance of these exemplary workers is very real. Their hard work means that they are valid and worthwhile as human beings, and have affirmed the importance of their relationships to the wider society, according to the measurable criteria that the Chinese prefer. No mere emotional state or response could provide the wealth of meaning that measurable labor provides. An articulate villager discussing this issue said, "We Chinese show our feelings for one another in our work, not with words." This is a clear and concise summary of a cultural characteristic with far-reaching significance and implications.

In speaking of work, the villagers are speaking about the symbolic affirmation of human relationships. The search for the best way to understand and enact the connection between the person's capacity to work, and the reward for work, is so pervasive and continuous because it is such a critical symbolic aspect of the social order as a whole. If the relationship between work, reward, and the social order can be correctly understood and practiced, then human relationships will be as they should be. These assumptions have been enacted in the context of capitalist entrepreneurship and in the context of communist theory, but in either case, the intense focus on the importance of work as the symbolic medium for the affirmation of human relationships remains the same. The world of people who speak of emotion in order to symbolize and affirm human relationships is an exotic, alien world to the villagers; it is a world founded on assumptions that they regard as trivial. From an outsider's point of view, the social world of the Chinese villager is characterized by an insistent emphasis on work, drudgery, and production. But work is the symbolic medium for the expression of social connection, and work affirms relationship in the most fundamental terms the villagers know.

# 10

# Marriage, household, and family form

Marriage, the household, and family organization are intimate and funda-mental structures of social life. Since 1949, there have been some dramatic efforts to alter the nature of these structures in rural China. Yet, at the same time, many aspects of these deeply familiar structures are taken for granted as natural, inevitable, and beyond question (however arbitrary they may appear to the outsider) for they are an integral part of Chinese culture, and one does not pause to reevaluate processes that are as familiar as breathing. Further-more, in the flux and shift of policy changes over the years, many choices have been made that tend to reinforce certain aspects of traditional patterns. Crane Brinton comments,

It is on the social arrangements that most intimately and immediately touch the average man [sic] that the actual changes effected by our revolutions seem slightest. The grand attempts at reform during the crisis period try to alter John Jones' relationship with his wife, his children, try to give him a new religion, new personal habits. The Thermidoreans [Brinton's term for those who direct a reaction against the "strain of prolonged effort to live in accordance with very high ideals" (1965, p. 203)] abandon most of this attempt, and in the end John Jones stands on certain matters about where he stood when the revolution began . . . in some very important ways the behavior of men changes with a slowness almost comparable to the kind of changes the geologist studies . . . (1965, pp. 243–244)

Alfred Kroeber, speaking of the nature of culture in more general terms, says,

The culture of today is always largely received from yesterday: that is what tradition or transmission means; it is a passing or sending along, a "handing-through" from one generation to another. Even in times of the most radical change and innovation there are probably several times as many items of culture being transmitted from the past as there are being newly devised . . . on the whole the passive or receptive faculties of culture tend to be considerably stronger than its active or innovative faculties . . . it is profitable for cultures to carry a considerable degree of ballast in the shape of consistency and continuity . . . to maintain a real continuity, a culture must put a

genuine value on what each generation hands to its children; it must, in short, be
receptive to its own past, or at least largely acquiescent to it ... (1948, pp. 256–257)

No culture has demonstrated greater continuity, or a higher value for
continuity than the Chinese. So the influence of revolution on the most
intimate and fundamental aspects of Chinese social life has not been simple;
some important changes have taken place, some social forms have persisted
unexamined, and in some cases the new contexts have had the effect of
reinforcing the old ways rather than doing away with them.

The formation of marriages is the critical stage in the regenerative process
which continues the family and the household. It is a process that has been the
focus of attempts at reform since the Marriage Law of 1950. Working on the
basis of a traditional social context that assumed that emotion was an invalid
basis for the formation of social relationships (see chapter 9), that young
people must obey their parents in the choice of a marriage partner, and that
economic motives held by the families of the bride or groom were legitimate
factors in the choice of a marriage partner, the Marriage Law of 1950
established the right of marriage partners to reject a marriage that they did not
themselves agree to, and disavowed the legitimacy of "commodity marriages," in which the economic benefit of the parties controlling the future of
the young people involved were the sole significant factor. The law did not
require that marriages be formed on a basis of love, or without the concerned
intervention and advice of senior relatives. However, it gave the potential
partners veto power over any arrangements made on their behalf, and
pledged the support of the state in upholding the veto. As a matter of
continuing policy, the role of economic exchange in marriage formation was
supposed to be minimized. The law also affirmed the legality of marriages
within the village, or between people with the same surname, formerly
regarded as incestuous; the new definition of incest was far narrower. (Selden
provides a translation of the text of this marriage law, 1979, p. 193.) So, the
new law made it possible to refuse to marry a particular partner, and to marry
endogamously; village exogamy was no longer necessary.

These important changes resulted in marriage formation patterns in which
the families continue to play an important role, but the power of the family
over the young people is now limited in certain important respects. Chinese
marriage reform was never intended to produce a process resembling
Western courtship, and the facile assumption that the marriage law has failed
as a reform because courtship patterns remain so unlike those of the West is
an ethnocentric fallacy. The normal pattern is that potential partners are
suggested by the mothers of marriageable sons and daughters, since finding a
marriage partner is women's business. The young people look one another
over in a brief meeting, exercise their veto if they wish, and marry if both
agree. A wedding is not supposed to be the culmination of a process of

developing emotional intimacy, but it is supposed to be a legitimate agreement, without coercion.

As well as enforcing the marriage laws, the state also regulates the legal age of marriage. The minimum legal marriage age enforced in Chashan commune in 1979 was 23 for women and 25 for men. However, during the five years from 1975 to 1979, the Zengbu household registers show that the actual average age of marriage for Zengbu men was 25·5, and the age for women was 24·5, indicating that families were delaying the marriages of their sons and daughters longer than they were required to do according to the regulations. The reason for delaying the marriage age was that daughters, who earned full workpoints in their teams and good salaries in rural industries, were valuable sources of income to their families. The reluctance of parents to lose their daughters as sources of income is reinforced by the reluctance of the young women themselves to marry: they do not wish to leave their homes for a new life in a strange place, where they will be required to work even harder, on behalf of their new families.

The later age of marriage during this period was a significant change in comparison with the pre-revolutionary custom. According to the findings of John L. Buck in 1929–31, women in this region of rural China married, on the average, four to five years earlier than the 1975–9 regulations required (1937, pp. 377–381). By the ages of 15 to 19, almost four out of five young women were already married, and beginning to bear children. By contrast, between 1975 and 1979 no woman in Zengbu married below the age of 21 or over the age of 30. Almost everyone married between the ages of 23 and 26. In 1981, the minimum ages for marrying were, in effect, lowered to 22 and 20, respectively, allowing couples to marry earlier. But there is still a clear rise in the age of marriage, which remains later than it would have been without the reforms. This change is important for family life and the nature of the household. Mature women with work experience and independent earning power, rather than more malleable and inexperienced teenagers (as would have been the case traditionally) are participating in the formation of their own marriages. Their assent is likely to be based on greater experience than formerly. And added maturity is likely to make these women slightly less vulnerable as daughters-in-law. They are less likely to remain subordinate to their mothers-in-law, and to consent to the handing over of their own and their husbands' earnings to their parents-in-law. The late age of marriage, and the comparative maturity of daughters-in-law, as well as sons, is probably related to the earlier division of the sons' households from the parents' households which has become common in Zengbu.

The person responsible for making sure that a marriage is legal, in terms of the marriage laws and in terms of the age regulations, is the commune (district) level cadre in charge of civil affairs. He checks the ages of the people who come to him for marriage certificates, and interviews them to make sure that the marriage is voluntary. He takes this responsibility seriously, and the interview is not purely pro forma. He invites the couple to sit, and asks them how they came to know one another, if they have an understanding together, and whether anyone is making them marry. He observes their behavior as they talk, and tries to form a judgment about their relationship. If their stories are not consistent, he talks to them separately, to make sure that they are not being coerced. He sees few attempts at forced marriages. However, in one case, he and the Women's Federation returned a panicky bride to the mountain commune from which she had come as the result of an arrangement over which she had no control.

The Women's Federation is another delegate of the central government which influences marriage formation. It has the job of making sure that propaganda about marriage policy reaches the local level, and actively supporting people who want to make marriages that are legitimate now, but violate pre-revolutionary custom. The Women's Federation is concerned to promote and validate marriages based on mutual choice, and to eliminate the importance of purely financial considerations which might be used to separate young people who want to marry.

The legal constraints on marriage, enforced at the civil affairs office, are paralleled by the traditional constraints enforced by custom. One of the most important constraints is the attitude that relationships between men and women ought to be regulated by the strictest sort of puritanical decency. Any overt indication of any possibly sexual relationship between a man and a woman, however minimal, is interpreted as an act of public impropriety. These fundamentally puritan attitudes are expressed in the separation of young people into separate sex groups at school and at play, and in the separate sleeping houses for adolescents, both male and female. These sleeping houses separate sexually mature young people from contact even with siblings of the opposite sex. Customary decency is maintained by the extreme shyness of the young people and their desire to avoid the merciless teasing of their peers, which is the inevitable result if a couple is seen together. This customary decency, and the avoidance patterns it creates between young people of opposite sexes, are important forces in village life. It is difficult to get to know a fellow villager of the opposite sex under these conditions, and quite impossible to seek an acquaintance with a potential marriage partner from another village.

Another important cultural factor is the shared view of marriage as a traumatic event for the woman and her family. It implies pain and loss and separation, as well as the end of all freedom and comfort for the woman. The reluctance of young women to marry is real. They do not look forward to marriage, do not enjoy being teased about it, and view it as an inevitable ordeal which is, unfortunately, a necessary part of a woman's life. This genuine aversion is difficult to encompass, because it is so unlike the conventional Western assumption that marriage is, or ought to be, what happens just before you live happily ever after. Older women, who were married without any say in the matter, still weep when they describe their experiences, and if asked to compare marriage in the old days with marriage now, they say it used to be worse, but it is still bad. The girl's family is often sad at losing her. In former times, it was possible for the women of this area to undertake to remain unmarried and to lead a life of chastity in association with other women who had made the same choice (cf. Topley, 1975). There is one woman in the brigade who did so, and she now runs one of the adolescent girls' sleeping houses on behalf of her team. At the present time, there is no alternative to marriage. In the old days, the women of Zengbu sang bitter songs about their pain at having to marry out. The songs are no longer sung, but the villagers of Zengbu still define marriage as a painful time of disturbing change and tension, particularly for the woman.

A third important cultural factor influencing the formation of marriages in Zengbu is the shared assumption that a person's feelings are not a legitimate basis for social action of any kind; thus, an emotional attraction is not in itself a legitimate basis for a marriage (see chapter 9).

As a result of these cultural constraints, it is not easy for young people to find their own marriage partners. However, it is probably legitimate to assume that young people have played an active role in finding their own marriage partners in marriages made within the village. The numbers of such marriages are on the increase. In 1964–8, in Zengbu, 10 percent of the total number of marriages in the brigade were endogamous, in the sense of being within the village of the couple. In 1979–81, 21 percent of the brigade's marriages were village endogamous. This is an important change. The magnitude of the change is even greater than it appears at first glance, because marriages within the single lineage villages of Zengbu are also marriages with people of the same surname, marriages that would have been considered incestuous before Liberation. Couples who have chosen their own mates from within the village have also had to overcome opposition to marrying within their own lineage, making the innovation more difficult.

Zengbu people tell a story to illustrate the difficulties of marrying a person of the same surname prior to 1949, even when the potential husband and wife were from different villages and lineages. A woman from Lu's Home village in Zengbu married a man, also surnamed Lu, from the neighboring village of Lubian. The people of Zengbu were so outraged by this marriage, which they considered a crime against public morality, that they never allowed the woman to return to Lu's Home to visit her natal family. The people of Lubian drove the couple from their village: they had to find somewhere else to live, not an easy matter when people were expected to live with their patrilineal kin. Even though the couple were of different lineages (and marriage within the lineage would have been even worse), their same-surname marriage was considered an outrage against propriety which is still remembered. This social climate provided a chilly welcome for the marriage reform laws which made such marriages legitimate.

The taboo against choosing one's spouse within one's own village was broken by a pioneering couple, aided by the Zengbu cadres, in 1957. The two had worked together as fellow members of the Lu's Home Number 3 production team; they decided that they wished to marry. However, they kept their relationship a secret, since they feared that they would be denounced by the entire village. The young man's parents felt that it was time for him to marry, and introduced him to several suitable young women, but he refused them all. His mother was baffled by her son's unwillingness to marry any of the women she suggested. The young couple were afraid to ask their parents for permission to marry, so the situation was at an impasse. Secretary Lu of the brigade's party committee heard of the case, and thought that it presented an opportunity to put the marriage reforms into practice. At his instigation, the brigade cadre in charge of matters concerning women approached both sets of parents, to seek their permission for the marriage. Both sets of parents were strongly opposed to the marriage, as were the vast majority of other villagers. They insisted that such a marriage as this was a crime; there was no precedent for it, and it was believed to result in childlessness or deformed offspring. However, Secretary Lu and the other cadres argued that these objections were superstitious and outmoded. With this support, the young couple persisted, and they were married in 1957. Contrary to expectations and predictions, they had a perfectly formed and healthy son the following year. This birth helped to demonstrate that the old taboos against marrying a person of the same village, lineage, and surname could be broken without incurring a disaster. A year later, another couple from Lu's Home village were married. They also had a healthy son, a year and a half after their marriage, and this gave further legitimacy to the innovation. The force of the taboo was weakened, and parents no longer felt that they could openly oppose such marriages on moral grounds, particularly since the young people would have the support of the cadres.

However, many Zengbu people of all generations retained some doubts about the new forms of marriage, and hoped that such a situation could be avoided in their own families. Parents applied informal pressure in the hope of forestalling endogamous marriages. Marrying within the village was referred to as "plowing one's private garden plots." The phrase suggests inappropriateness, since rice fields are worked with a plow, but private garden plots are not. There is also an implied sexual significance in plowing. But, on the other hand, people realized that fellow villagers were in the best position to make an informed choice. Women who married out were sometimes referred to as "the picked-over mandarin oranges in the bottom of the basket, after the best ones have been taken."

There are several reasons, aside from pure traditionalism, why marriages continue to be formed between young people who do not know one another well. Social and cultural logic sees no value in marrying for love. Instead of sharing the Western cultural postulate that love legitimizes marriage, the people of Zengbu think it an inadequate basis for contracting a relationship. For them, marriage means that two young people agree to help one another with their work, raise children, and care for the husband's parents in their old age. While it is preferable if affection develops between a husband and a wife after their marriage, this is serendipitous, rather than essential. Since the marriage bond is based on a social contract rather than an emotional one, the cessation of affection is not a justification for divorce. Given this attitude, it is not surprising that the people of Zengbu do not utilize forms of courtship aimed at the development of emotional attachment. When such attachments develop spontaneously, they do not fit naturally into the accepted forms, since there is a sense that choosing a marriage partner without consulting one's parents is an act of disrespect. People who choose their own marriage partners need someone to play the role of introducer, in order to avoid the appearance of disrespect. The introducer makes it possible to tell the parents about the hoped-for marriage without insulting them in the process, as direct communication by the child would do. (This graceful solution is also used on Taiwan, Diamond 1969, p. 55).

Using Chinese cultural logic, the mothers of Zengbu seek prospective mates for their children without considering the couple's compatibility as distinct personalities. They want good husbands for their daughters and good wives for their sons, but the wealth and social standing of the family, the presence of a sympathetic female relative of the bride in the groom's village, or the kinds of work available in the new village and the prosperity of that village are far more significant factors than the merely personal. From the point of view of personal attraction and emotional compatibility, every healthy young person of a suitable age and the appropriate sex is treated as interchangeable in forming a marriage. It is the other family, rather than the other person, that is important; young women often speak of marrying into a certain family rather than of marrying a particular man. As an experience, marriage does not imply the formation of a satisfying new relationship; rather, it means that the woman must leave her natal family, and the village where she has grown up, in order to go to a strange village, bear children to a man she does not really know, and come under the authority of a mother-in-law with whom it will not be easy to live in harmony.

The 79 percent of marriages currently being made between young people from different villages are almost certainly formed without the bride and groom being well acquainted. In these cases, someone is needed to play the role of introducer in a more practical sense. The introducer is a woman with ties to both families. She suggests possible marriage partners to one another, through their mothers. The young people are then given an opportunity to meet and see if they like one another. It is clearly understood that they have the right of refusal, and this is what makes the difference, in the villagers' minds, between the old system of "arranged marriage," and the new system under which marriage has been reformed. (Similar innovations are practiced on Taiwan as well, according to Croll 1981, p. 135.) The introducer generally receives a small gift at the wedding. Because introducers are also used by partners who chose one another independently, but wish to observe the forms of respect to their parents, the use of an introducer does not differentiate between a marriage suggested by others and a marriage initiated entirely by the young people concerned. From all points of view, the marriage is defined as legitimately noncoercive under the reformed marriage laws if the young people had the right to refuse one another. The right of refusal is regarded as a significant and highly valued change, and an important modification in custom. It is not a change that the villagers regard as insignificant or trivial by any means.

Once a potential partner has been suggested, arrangements are made for the two young people to meet at the market town tea shop or some other location, so that they can decide whether or not they wish to marry. Before the chaperoned meeting, the young people already know the family background, age, occupation, and village of origin of the other person, so they are aware of one another's external social characteristics. The meeting is to allow them to form some judgment about the personal qualities of the prospective spouse, and to decide whether or not they wish to veto the marriage. Plainly, everyone assumes the primacy of social rather than personal characteristics, since a great deal of evidence is available about the former, and one meeting provides very little evidence about the latter. It is clear, from examining a number of cases, that most young people do not make the decision to marry on the basis of any significant familiarity with the character or personality of the potential spouse. Rather, the choice is made on the basis of superficial impressions gained during a short, embarrassed, and formal interview which takes place in the presence of other people. After only a few minutes of stilted conversation, which usually consists of questions about production and earnings, or speculations about probable rice yields, the young people have to decide whether or not they want to spend the rest of their lives together.

Young people frequently reject the proposed match with any excuse that comes to mind. Many say that, after thinking the matter over, they have concluded that they are still too young to marry, and would prefer to wait longer before making a choice. One Zengbu man rejected a proposed wife because she did not know how to ride a bicycle. Some people reject match after match, angering their mothers and the introducers on account of the waste of their time and trouble. Others accept the first person who is offered.

Once both parties agree to marry, their engagement period – several months between the agreement and the wedding – begins. During this time, the young couple are allowed to meet in parks or tea shops, or the young man may visit the young woman in her home, so that they may become better acquainted before the wedding. This is an important innovation. Traditionally, there was no social contact between the bride and the groom until the wedding, when the groom raised the bride's red veil and the two looked upon one another for the first time. Such "blind marriages," as they were called, were what had happened to the parents of today's brides and grooms. However, the meeting of engaged couples at the present time are not comfortable. The conversation is stilted, and the young people do not become well acquainted. One young woman described her introduction and subsequent courtship. She said, "My mother's elder brother's daughter had married to Zengbu. She suggested my husband as a possible spouse for me, and my mother thought it would be a good thing if I married here. We met once, and had no criticisms of one another, so we were engaged. I never visited Zengbu before my marriage; I felt very shy. My husband visited from time to time. When he came, we had nothing to say." Nonetheless, the fact of being able to meet before the wedding is an important modification in local custom.

The young people of Zengbu, when asked about the best way to find marriage partners, frequently make rather traditional answers. Most of them say that they prefer to let their mothers make the initial suggestion "because it has always been done that way here." Some feel that the relationships between husbands and wives who have taken an active role in finding one another tend to be better than relationships where the partner was suggested by the mother, and they use this idea as the rationale for finding their own partners by themselves. Still others say that it makes no difference, and point to acrimonious marriages in which the partners found and chose one another independently, or to notably harmonious marriages formed at the suggestion of the parents. Some unmarried women say that they would prefer to marry out. Some of those who would prefer to marry out give the traditional taboo against same-surname marriages as the reason, while others say that they would rather marry out if they can better themselves economically by doing so. But most young women comment that it does not matter; they will have to do the same kind of work in the household and in the fields, whether they marry within the village or outside it.

The parents of sons generally prefer to find a daughter-in-law from another village, for a variety of reasons. They do not like to have relatives by marriage who are also fellow villagers. If a daughter-in-law lives some distance away from her natal family, the family she marries into has more control over her. She can more easily be prevented from taking money or food from her husband's family to her natal family, or from working on behalf of the latter; the husband's family wishes to control the labor of the daughter-in-law unambiguously. Villagers believe that when a marriage takes place within the village, quarrels between husband and wife can easily turn into quarrels between the two families, amplifying the adverse consequences of the quarrel. Also, marrying a daughter into another village tends to expand one's network of social ties; this is to the advantage of families who wish to develop such ties for purposes of mutual aid or labor exchange. With relatives by marriage (*qinqi*) who are real outsiders, with different surnames, and who reside in other villages, there is a different kind of relationship than there is with "one's own people" of the same village and lineage (*zijiren*). Zengbu villagers do not feel themselves in direct competition for status and wealth with relatives by marriage in other villages, and consequently the relationship can be relatively free of competitive tension. Such relatives can be called upon for help in building a house, or paying for a son's wedding, or coping with a serious illness. A man may be able to establish a business partnership with his brother-in-law, or secure a useful introduction from him. If one marries within the village, one has, in effect, no relatives by marriage, since the new relatives are already fellow villagers and members of the same lineage. Marriage within the village merges *qinqi* and *zijiren* relationships, and therefore removes one kind of relative. There are no useful social contacts to be gained from marrying within the village. Besides, people say that they enjoy visiting relatives in other villages, and exchanging gossip, news, and opinions with them. Zengbu men do not wish to lose the added security of having relatives by marriage, and women are doubtful about the structural conflicts which such marriages produce in the patterns for appropriate kinship and ritual behavior. Are same-village in-laws to be invited to weddings and expected to give the gifts given by in-laws, or are they to be classified as one's own people, from whom gifts are not expected? The mingling of lineage and affinal relationships produces a degree of confusion.

However, marriage within the village benefits the parents who have daughters, but who do not also have sons, by helping to ensure that they will not be left without care in their old age. Daughters living in the same village are in a position to provide needed care. This is likely to assume increasing importance now that the number of permissible attempts to give birth to a son is regulated.

When marriage partners are found with the help of the family, the family member most involved is clearly the mother rather than the father. Marriage formation is unambiguously defined as women's business, not men's business. This suggests that marriage is not being used as a means of developing or strengthening alliances between specific men or specific patrilineal kin groups; if ties between particular groups of men were important, the choice of partners could not be safely left in the hands of women.

Since marriage is patrilocal, the woman's family has the choice of a range of families in a range of locations, but the man's family is fixed as to location, and chooses a woman to bring in, rather than a complete social setting. The man's family seeks a girl who is hardworking, physically strong, and not quarrelsome. Young women say that it is important to be perceived as hardworking, because "no one will marry you if you are lazy." The young man hopes she will be good looking, and the older family members hope she will be kind. The woman's family seeks an economically comfortable situation for their daughter, and a young man of good character as her husband. It is better if the daughter marries to a village which is close enough to visit easily. It is also useful if the husband's family has relatives in Hong Kong who send back money and gifts. The woman's family considers the economic circumstances of the young man's family very carefully. Under the collective system, conditions in the team and brigade to which the young man's family belonged were an important factor, both in terms of the kinds of work done there, and in terms of the relative prosperity of the place as measured in the money value of a workpoint. One man commented that when Zengbu was building levees in 1960, women didn't like to marry in, because the work was so very heavy. Another man explained how he and his wife reasoned when their daughter married to adjacent Wentang brigade. He said, "In Wentang, production and living standards are high – they have more land than here. In my daughter's new team, the value of ten workpoints is 1·1 *yuan*. It is an advanced brigade." In Zengbu, at that time, the value of a workpoint was only 1 *yuan* per ten workpoints, or 10 percent less.

As well as these economic criteria, there is another important factor, the need to find one's daughter the best possible place in the network of relationships between women in the village to which she goes. Women seek marriages for their daughters which will reinforce existing ties between women, and provide the bride with as large and helpful a network of female allies as possible. Outmarrying women form a network across the countryside, tying their villages of birth to their villages of marriage. These social networks are maintained by the frequent visits women make back to the villages into which they were born. On all the major holidays of the year, women dress in their best clothes and prepare a chicken or some other gift of food for their parents. Leading their younger children by the hand, and carrying their gifts in ceremonial baskets hung from carrying poles, they retrace the lanes and paths back to their village of origin, where they visit with their parents, their brothers' families, and the sisters and aunts who have also returned. At these gatherings, information about young people who are ready to marry can be exchanged, and possible matches can be suggested. The network of ties between women is an effective one for making marriages.

The women who acted as introducers for the couples who married in Zengbu in 1979 had a range of important relationships with the families of the young people they introduced. Women who had married out introduced young people from their village of origin to their village of marriage, and vice versa. Women friends from the same team, women who were neighbors, and women who were the relatives of cadres, and thus met a wider range of people, suggested potential spouses. Female relatives of the groom who suggested marriages included the groom's sister, the groom's father's younger sister, the groom's father's older brother's wife, the groom's mother's older sister, and the groom's mother's older brother's wife. On the bride's side, the following relatives served as introducers: the bride's father's younger brother's wife, the bride's mother's older brother's wife, the bride's father's sister, the bride's sister, and the bride's father's brother's daughter. A series of examples can show how this works. One woman who had married into Zengbu suggested that her sister marry into the same village. Another woman suggested that her sister's daughter might marry her next door neighbor's son. A third woman, who had married within her own village, suggested that her brother marry a close female friend of hers from another village. (The two women were both politically active, and had become friends while attending meetings together at the commune town.) A fourth woman, who had married into Zengbu, suggested a Zengbu husband for her father's sister's daughter. This pattern of suggesting marriages which reinforce existing ties between women is an important one, and frequently it is a primary determinant of marriage choice.

There is no pattern of preferred marriages in which people from a particular village are especially sought after as marriage partners, nor is there a pattern of preferred marriages between cousins. However, according to the Dongguan County Women's Federation, such practices are not unknown in other parts of the county. There is one district in which marriage by exchange was formerly practiced: each family would give an adult daughter, and receive an adult daughter-in-law in return. This practice is illegal, and the Women's Federation is responsible for preventing such marriages. It has never been the custom in Zengbu. However, there is one village into which the people of Lu's Home village refuse to marry. This village, a little distance away to the southwest, quarreled with Lu's Home before Liberation, and the people of both villages vowed not to intermarry. The vow has been kept. This is not surprising; since the network of women with ties in both villages has been broken, it cannot easily be re-established. Sporadic low-level conflict, like episodes of thieving, still occurs between the two villages. Marriages based on the adoption of a child daughter-in-law never occur, and have never been known to occur in the past. Villagers could not believe that such a practice could possibly be Chinese. (It is reported in Taiwan and other parts of China, A. P. Wolf and Huang 1980.)

When the young couple have become engaged, the amounts of the brideprice and the dowry are negotiated; the ritual transactions of the wedding include both. The money given by the groom's family to the bride's family is called "ritual or gift money" (*lijin*). The usual translation for this is brideprice, but the money is a ritual and ceremonial gift, and is not thought of as a purchase price in a commercial transaction. The ritual money, and the gifts that are sent with it – cloth to make suits of clothes for the bride to bring with her, and meat and cakes for the bride's family to serve to their relatives – are a symbolic repayment to the family of the bride for the cost of rearing her. They are a symbolic recognition of her social status and worth. However, the bride's family must supplement the amount of the brideprice in order to provide their daughter with an appropriate dowry (*jiazhuang*) and to serve their own relatives an appropriate wedding feast. Because the bride's family is required to spend more than they receive from the groom's family, there is a traditional saying among Cantonese peasants, "Daughters are goods on which one loses." One man said, "I lost 500 *yuan* in marrying my three daughters." This means that his ritual responsibilities for the three weddings required to him spend 500 *yuan* more than he received from the families of the grooms.

In 1979, there were 29 weddings in Zengbu. The average brideprice for these weddings consisted of 115 *yuan* (U.S. $ 76) in cash, and 42 *yuan* worth of pork, 50 *yuan* worth of geese, 30 of fish, 75 of small cakes, and 110 *yuan* to be used for the purchase of cloth for the bride's clothes. Thus, the total monetary value of the average brideprice was 422 *yuan*. In addition, some grooms' families gave gold rings and earrings worth approximately 100 *yuan* to the bride. The brideprice and the ritual gifts of food are supposed to be used by the bride's family to help pay for the banquet they traditionally give for their close relatives the night before the bride goes to the groom's house. During the negotiations over the brideprice, the bride's family say how many tables of guests they are going to invite, and they ask for enough to cover the costs. It is customary for the bride's family to ask for more than they hope to get; the high amount is a measure of their sense of their daughter's worth. It is equally customary for the groom's family to give less. The bride's family must always supplement the amount they receive to pay for the banquet and must add money of their own to provide the bride with an appropriate dowry. They usually complain about the stinginess of the groom's family. In one typical transaction, the bride's family asked for 100 *yuan*, and were given 80. They requested 30 *jin* of pork, and received 15, 30 *jin* of fish, and received 20, 4 geese, and received 2, and sufficient cloth to make 10 suits of clothes for the bride, of which they received enough for 8.

In 1979, the wealthiest families tended to be those with relatives in Hong Kong. Such families could afford to give a higher brideprice. Some families of brides asked that wealthy families of grooms include sewing machines, electric fans, bicycles, and watches in the brideprice. These items would then return to the groom's family as part of the dowry. The value of the brideprice also varied in relation to the amount the girl's parents had received at the weddings of other daughters, or the amount paid at the wedding of other daughters-in-law. Disparities would tend to imply the lesser value of some in comparison to others.

Dowry was larger than brideprice. The dowry included all the items from the brideprice not specifically intended for use at the banquet, plus a supplement provided by the bride's family. In 1979, the portion of the dowry provided by the bride's family averaged 178 *yuan* in value. It included such items as chairs and a table, a suitcase of clothes, usually red, a trunk, an umbrella, and a wash basin. It included items purchased with the brideprice cash – 115 *yuan* worth of miscellaneous items, and 110 *yuan* worth of clothes for the bride. The dowry would be larger when the bride's family wished to make a more active effort to assert her social status. A typical bride's family invited 59 guests to their banquet in 1979, at a cost of 208 *yuan*, of which 90 *yuan* was a supplement by the bride's family to the foodstuffs sent by the groom's family.

To consider these transactions merely as financial exchanges obscures their social and cultural meaning. The most expensive element of a marriage, the house provided by the groom's family for the groom and the bride, does not appear as part of the exchanges at all, but it requires years of savings. The brideprice money amounts to an earnest of the willingness of the groom's family to support the bride, and it is spent by the bride's family in the manner that they think appropriate. Brideprice money not spent on the banquet is returned to the groom's family (where the bride will make use of it) with a supplement provided by the bride's family; at this point it is spoken of as the "dowry." The money contributed by the groom's family to the banquet given by the bride's side suggests that they are anticipating the bride's status in their family, and are assuming to some extent the role of hosts. In establishing the new couple, the groom's family bear the expense of the new house, and pay for a large proportion of the new clothes and furnishings, but these items remain in, or are returned to, their possession. The bride's family pay for the supplement to the brideprice money which they must make in sending the dowry, and for the supplementary food they must provide for their banquet; these items they are ritually required to give away. In the end, the groom's family have the house, the furnishings, the bride, the trousseau, and the sense of having confirmed the importance of a new affinal relationship by their contribution to the banquet of the bride's family. The bride's family have spent money to ensure that their own status, and that of their daughter, is appropriately recognized. They have contributed to the material comfort of the new family by their addition to the dowry, and they have formally become affines.

The amounts both of brideprice and of dowry given in 1979 varied according to the ideological level of the people concerned. There had been a consistent effort since 1949 to simplify the customs surrounding weddings, and to reduce the amount of money spent on wasteful social display, rooted in what were felt to be feudal attitudes. From the purely ceremonial point of view, the ritual elements in Zengbu weddings had been greatly simplified over this period of time, in comparison with traditional practices. The isolation of the bride, the use of the sedan chair, the bridal costume, the wedding songs, the wedding procession, and the ceremonies in the ancestral hall, had all passed out of usage. However, the ritual exchanges of money and gifts and the banquets given by both families were more complex matters to reform.

The goal of the reforms was to eliminate superstition and to save money for productive uses. After 1949, joint wedding receptions were held under the auspices of the cadres in the main hall of the brigade headquarters although by 1979 this practice was falling into disuse. Each couple paid only 2 *yuan*, and this covered the cost of the candy, cigarettes, preserved fruit, and tea served to guests at the reception. Brideprice was limited to 50 *yuan*, and dowry was supposed to be reduced in proportion. However, these reforms did not prove successful. When asked about the amount of the brideprice the bride and groom always said that it had been the approved 50 *yuan*. Their relatives gathered for the new ceremony at the brigade headquarters. But in private, the groom's family would add 100 *yuan* to the brideprice, to bring it up to a more customary figure, and after the simple ceremony at the brigade headquarters, people would hold private ceremonies with banquets along more traditional lines. Even the families of cadres insisted in the face of ideological arguments that the only appropriate way to marry was a wedding that included all the appropriate gifts and the banquets. Mass meetings were held by the cadres to criticise people who insisted on more traditional weddings, but people's thinking did not change. Ironically, the efforts to reform and simplify marriage customs had resulted in duplication of effort and added expense, rather than ensuring that money was spent productively. Weddings had been made less elaborate from the ceremonial point of view, but the exchanges of ritual money and the banqueting were still regarded as essential.

There were important reasons why this was the case. Women, in particular, were insistent that kinship ties could not be maintained without the banquet and ritual money. These ties had a real importance because they provided a source of help when a family was in difficulties. People felt that, although the collectives furnished some security, they were not entirely stable and reliable: there had been, for example, the disaster of 1958, the initial year of the Great Leap Forward. Villagers still had to depend on kin, friends, and relatives when building a house, in times of serious illness, or at funerals. They said, "We must invite these people to banquets when our children marry. If we do not, they will not be there to help us in times of need." So the banquets and exchanges persisted, in a ritually simplified form, not out of cultural inertia, but because they were, and were perceived as, functioning parts of a kinship system on which the peasants still depended.

The actual wedding ceremonies begin with the banquet given by the women's side for their relatives, both agnatic and affinal. Female friends of the bride, such as those who have shared the same sleeping-house, or co-workers, are also invited. Guests at this banquet customarily bring a length of cloth sufficient to make one suit of clothes as a gift to the bride's mother, who may or may not give it to the bride, as she wishes. These guests receive as gifts the small wedding cakes which are traditional. Forty cakes per family is the usual quantity.

A detailed description of a Zengbu wedding in 1979 provides a sense of the ceremonial process. At this time, Zengbu weddings were celebrated in the middle of the night. The bride and her family were sound asleep when the old ladies who were acting as the ritual assistants woke them by knocking on the door. Having entered the house, one of the ritual assistants told the bride to bathe before putting on her new clothes, and she retreated to the back bedroom to do so. Meanwhile the bride's mother took a bowl of water and a pair of chopsticks, and dripped purifying water on the new suit of black clothes, and the new black umbrella, which had been set out on a large tray of woven bamboo. The tray of purified clothes was carried into the back room, so that the bride could put them on. The bride's sister was sent to the girls' house where the bride had formerly slept, to fetch the bride's "house sisters." Meanwhile, the old ladies packed the dowry. They tore red paper off a big wooden chest, and brought out a suitcase, two woven carrier baskets, and two large round baskets. These were packed with the dowry goods, and made up into balanced loads for carrying. They were taken to the groom's house (nor far away in the same village) by one of the old ladies.

The bride's friends from the sleeping-house came in, and the bride's father and brothers joined the group. They were the only men present. The bride's mother lit two red candles, and a wick floating in oil in a tiny saucer, and the bride came out of the back room dressed in her new suit of black clothes. In the dim light, one of the girls combed the bride's hair, dressed it, and tied it into place with red plastic string. By now the bride was crying, and she left the house supported by one of the old ladies, who held the new black umbrella (with its handle of clear lucite, in which a red rose was embedded) carefully over her head. The bride's mother was left sitting alone in the empty room, weeping at the loss of her daughter. The remaining old ladies and the bride's friends followed the bride through the village; they had firecrackers (and sticks of incense with which to light them) which they exploded in the narrow dark alleyways. Dogs barked, and sleepy exclamations were audible behind barred wooden doors. The weeping bride walked at the head of the procession, her head and face hidden by the umbrella, black upon black. The old lady carrying the umbrella murmured words of encouragement to her. Beside the village pond, where the road from the bride's house met the road to the groom's house, the procession stopped and waited in the chilly darkness.

Traditionally, these rites would have been carried out in the daytime. The bride would have been dressed in a brightly colored gown. A lucky married woman, with a good husband still living, and many children, would have combed the bride's hair and put it up, and as she did so, she would have spoken magical incantations wishing the bride a prosperous future and many children. Then, amidst the sound of whining oboes, gongs, and firecrackers, the woman would have been carried from her father's house through a shower of thrown rice, and placed in a sedan chair. The bride's father would have wrapped the sedan chair with a broad red cloth, and the procession would have set off for the village of the groom.

In 1979, there was a somewhat uneasy wait at the crossroads. The old lady supporting the bride suggested that the girls set off more fireworks, so the groom would know that they were there, but the fireworks had been used up. Finally the groom came along, accompanied by two male friends. He took the umbrella from the old lady, and escorted the bride the rest of the way to his house. His two friends walked behind, throwing firecrackers of their own. At the front door of the groom's house, a fire of straw and paper had been built on the ground. The bride was led over the fire, and through the door. In this case, her umbrella was too wide for the doorway, so a flat woven basket was held over her head as she went through. The dowry, which had been set down outside, was brought into the groom's house, and the bride was led into the back room, which had been screened from the main room by a new door cloth.

Traditionally, the bride would have arrived at her husband's door in the sedan chair. The groom would have greeted her arrival by coming out and kicking the door of the sedan chair. Then a lucky woman would have carried the bride on her back (as a baby is carried) over the fire on the groom's doorstep. The fire was believed to purify the bride, so that she would not bring anything unlucky or impure with her into her husband's house. They would have stepped over a steaming tub of water in which pomelo leaves had been steeped, and in which a hot plowshare had been plunged. An umbrella would have been held over the two women all the while.

At the 1979 wedding, there was a new bamboo sieve, intended for the straining of rice flour, suspended by red string from the inner doorway through which the bride was led. The sieve has a magical significance which no one could explain. On either side of the doorway, and over the top of the doorway, strips of red paper with felicitous black character inscriptions had been pasted. The inscriptions wished the couple fertility, wealth, and happiness. Within, the bride sat on the bed, looking rather dazed. On a shelf opposite the bed were two yellow candles, a lighted wick in a small saucer of oil, and a shallow bowl containing a pyramid of small fruits and leaves. An old lady from the groom's side brought in a folded blanket cover and two embroidered pillows from the dowry, and placed them on the bed. Then she set out a woman's blouse and a pair of man's trousers, arranging them on the bed as if an invisible androgynous wearer were lying down. Over the hip region of the trousers, she placed a red paper, and on the red paper she placed leaves, fruit and some peanuts, the shells of which had been dyed red. Then she began to sing. The song wished the couple happiness, prosperity, health, and children. At the end of the first verse, she interrupted herself to call for a little pitcher of water with a long curved spout. Then she sang again. When the song concluded with the wish that a little son "would be making water here by this time next year," she poured water from the pitcher onto the floor, directing the stream in a line parallel with the bed.

According to custom, the groom's family sit up all night, and entertain their kinsmen, relatives, and friends all the following day. The bride and groom do not rest, but sit up all night also.

When dawn breaks, the groom's kin from the village come to help in the preparation of the wedding feast. These closest agnatic kin come as a matter of course, without formal invitation. Two meals are served, one in the late morning and one in the evening. Geese and fish are cleaned and dressed, vegetables are chopped, tables and chairs are set in place, and everything is made ready. Sometimes a skilled cook is hired to oversee the preparation of food. Meanwhile, the bride ritually serves tea to the close senior kin of her husband – his parents, his agnatic uncles, and their wives. These closest relatives do not bring gifts, since they are so close as to be virtually co-hosts.

The groom's female relatives come from many villages bearing the traditional carrying pole loaded with gifts (called *yidan*, a "poleful"). The poleful includes two packs of lucky money wrapped in red paper, in the amount of at least 2 to 10 *yuan* per pack. (Traditionally, one packet of lucky money was to be used to buy shoes for the groom, and the other was to buy land.) A poleful also includes a chicken, 2 *jin* of pork, two bottles of rice wine, four bottles of soft drinks, and 7 *chi* of cloth for the groom's father. Usually, the father gives his son an amount of cloth sufficient for three suits of clothes from these gifts of cloth, and keeps the rest for himself. These lengths of cloth are the traditional gifts of affines, and symbolically express concern for health and well-being.

Guests who are less closely related bring money (at least 10 *yuan* from each family) wrapped in red paper, to give to the bride and groom at the banquet. They may also bring other gifts, such as blankets and bed sheets, mirrors with congratulatory messages written on them in red characters, thermos bottles, or a table clock. These gifts are all displayed in the groom's house.

In 1979, an average of one hundred people were invited by the families of grooms to attend their wedding banquets. The average cost of each banquet was 216 *yuan*, with the range extending from 100 to 480 *yuan*. However, the expenses of the banquet were largely covered by the gifts of food and money brought by the guests. The parents of some grooms were even reported to have made a profit on their wedding banquets.

The wedding festivities at the groom's house do not conclude with the second banquet. In the late evening there is another ritual meal. In Lu's Home village, the guests are a small group of male friends and kinsmen of the groom. In Sandhill and Pondside, female friends of the couple may also be invited. (This illustrates the astonishing diversity of custom from village to village; it is odd in its context, since Lu's Home is normally less traditionally minded than the other two villages, and the all-male group is more traditional.) The guests drink tea, smoke, eat candy, and tease the newly married couple, especially the bride. In fact, the name for this meal is "playing with the bride" (*wan xinbao*). The bride serves the guests, and they make teasing remarks to her. For example, a young man might ask the bride to light a cigarette for Uncle, using the kinship term that will be used by her children in the future. Traditionally, the bride and groom are made to play games together that have sexual overtones. They may be asked to transfer objects from mouth to mouth, keeping their hands behind their backs. The groom may be forced to nibble at pieces of candy suspended from a string that is placed around the bride's neck like a necklace, so that the candy is close to her breasts. The couple may be given insolvable puzzles to solve. Sometimes the bride may burst into tears at this hazing, which comes at the end of over twenty-four hours of celebration, and just before she and her husband are to go to their wedding bed for the first time. In Zengbu, the hazing is not as severe as it was in former times; traditionally, such severe hazing sometimes occurred that a lasting enmity might be created between the groom and one of his more brutal kinsmen. When the "playing with the bride" is over, the guests show the bride and groom to their bedroom, and the ceremonies are over. (In former times, the young men might have thrown a final firecracker into the bedroom before they left, and this evening supper, with its drinking and games, might have been repeated for several nights more.)

With the recent changes in economic and social policy, wedding customs have changed dramatically, becoming strikingly more expensive and elaborate. Not only do families have more money to spend, but the structural basis of their economic activities is household and kin relationships, rather than the suprafamilial team relationships that had been important before. The government no longer takes the position that peasant ceremonies and rituals have an ideological significance requiring the active intervention of cadres. Kinship has a greatly increased importance, and people have the financial resources to symbolize this in more elaborate wedding ceremonies. The changes were dramatic between 1979 and 1981 alone. Brideprice rose from the average 1979 figure of 422 *yuan* to a new average of 754 *yuan*. The brideprice included greater amounts of meat, more small cakes, more cash, and more of the formerly rare items such as sewing machines, watches, fans, and jewelry. Dowries increased in value from the 178 *yuan* of 1979 to a remarkable average of 1,000 *yuan* (in a wide range of 200 *yuan* to 3,000 *yuan*).

The average number of guests at the bride's banquet rose from 59, with 208 *yuan* spent to feed them, to an average of 175 guests in 1981, with 753 *yuan* spent to feed them. The average number of guests at the groom's banquet rose from 100, with 216 *yuan* spent to feed them, to 222 with 1,138 *yuan* spent to feed them. By 1985, the cost had risen again, although not so dramatically, to a typical figure of 1,500 *yuan* for the groom's banquet. Other customs have been modified: weddings take place in the daytime, not at night, and a truck is used for transportation, rather than having people walk or go by bicycle. (The use of the truck resembles similar innovations in Hong Kong's New Territories, where it was introduced during the fifties and sixties as a substitute for the traditional sedan chair.) The elaborate new marriage ceremonies symbolically reflect the increased importance of family wealth and family ties, and provide occasions for competitive display. Wedding banquets, and the accompanying gift exchanges affirm the social status of families, and present opportunities to solidify and reconfirm ties with patrilineal kin and with affines.

This is not a mere survival of old customs, or a meaningless recrudescence of what had been suppressed before. Eric Wolf has said, "To say that a population is 'traditional' or that a population is bound by tradition, does not explain why tradition persists, nor why people cleave to it. Persistence, like change, is not a cause – it is an effect" (1966, p.vii). In Zengbu, new conditions have provided new reasons for practicing the old customs. The production responsibility system has produced a greatly increased emphasis on the practical importance of kin ties. Since the disintegration of the collectives, kinship is the most important basis for business relationships, for borrowing money, and for help and support in time of need. With the increase in the importance of kin ties, the rituals which reaffirm them have become more important as well.

A marriage initiates the formation of a new household. The concept of the household, and the rather dissimilar concept of the family, are highly significant aspects of social structure in Zengbu. The government has formally defined the basic social unit of the Chinese countryside as the *hu*, or household. Zengbu's five thousand-odd people reside in 1,100 households. The crucial characteristic of a household is the fact that it shares a common budget, and the members cook and eat together. Married sons who live in a separate dwelling, but share a common budget with their parents, and eat with them, are spoken of as members of the same household. Conversely, one might share a dwelling, but keep separate accounts and eat separately; in this case, one would be a member of a different household. Thus a common dwelling is not the structural differentiator. Neither is kinship, for married brothers with separate accounts are not household members with their parents, while other brothers who share a common budget and eat with their parents remain members of the same household. This can be interpreted as a symbolic statement about the importance of a shared economic life in Chinese human relationships. The concept of the family, as opposed to the household – the patrilineal extended family, the patrilineal stem family, or the nuclear family, all of which can be observed in Zengbu households – is less often expressed in customary local usage. This implies that it is not regarded as relevant as the concept of the household. The villagers of Zengbu customarily use the term *nguk khei* (Mandarin *wuqi*) to refer, rather ambiguously, both to their houses and to their household group. Thus, people say that they are returning to their *nguk khei*, meaning that they are going home. One can ask how many persons there are in a *nguk khei*, and be given the size of the household. If, for example, an old couple lives in the same household with one of their married sons, they refer to this unit as the *nguk khei*. Their other married sons, who have already formally separated their account-keeping, are equally close, in kinship terms. However, they are not members of the household.

Thus, the household group has a common budget and divides the labor of living. It is different from the family conceived of as a unit connected on a basis of kinship. Membership in a particular household does not imply that social obligations are limited to members of the household, or that the household is socially isolated. The Chinese household, like the Chinese nuclear family, and even the Chinese person (see chapter 9) exists in a web of social obligations and mutual responsibilities, rather than with the clear boundaries that Western experience leads one to expect. Kinship obligations, such as supporting aged parents, or cooperating with brothers, remain equally important whether these kin happen to be co-resident in the same household or not. Sons take up independent residence as close to their parents as possible. The grandmother continues to take care of her sons' children, so that her daughters-in-law can work, whether they are members of the same household or not. The children of brothers are likely to grow up in neighboring households, may be cared for together, and frequently play with one another. Married older brothers who have formed separate households assume responsibility for helping to build houses for their younger brothers who have not yet married; they may agree to contribute a fixed sum every month to their father's household for this purpose. In one case, the father was dead and a group of brothers agreed that it was their joint responsibility to see that every brother had a house. So, the obligations of kinship are not restricted or delimited by household membership, but exist independently.

The household group is under the authority of a household head (*hu zhu*), who collects and administers their earnings. The following set of rules for the selection of household heads may be inferred from current practice in Zengbu. If the household includes one married couple and their children, the household head is always the husband/father. If the husband is absent (in the army, or employed outside the village for example) the wife serves as head while he is away. In 1979, 19 percent of household heads were women. If the household is extended over two or three generations, including an older couple with one of their married sons and family, the older man is almost invariably the head of household. In these stem-family households, in two out of three cases, the son became household head upon the death of the father, superseding the widowed mother. This means that in the majority of cases, sex outweighs seniority. When the widowed mother assumes the position of household head, she retains it until loss of alertness and physical strength make it necessary for the son to assume headship.

In the village, the name of the household head is formally entered in the record books, and he or she is empowered to represent the family to team, village, and brigade cadres. (In urban China, status as household head is sometimes a pro forma affair, and teenaged children may be listed as household heads because it is more convenient for them to collect the family rations.) Each household has a separate page in the household register of the brigade (the *hukou pu*), and the name and social characteristics of every household member are listed. The name of the head of household appears first, then the names of the other household members. Beside each name is listed the county and date of birth, sex, relationship to head of household, class status designation (from the time of land reform), occupation, education, and marital status. When households separate, a new page is created for the new household, and the names of those who are no longer members of the old household are crossed off on the old page. If a household member dies, the name is crossed off the page, and a note is made of the date of death. When a daughter marries out, this is entered in the book, with a note of her new place of residence. When a daughter-in-law marries in, her name is added at the appropriate page, with a note of her former place of residence, and the date at which she became a resident of Zengbu.

Throughout the collective period, when the teams made up their accounts at the end of the year, the total amount owed to each household was calculated, and it was turned over to the head of household, rather than to the separate earners. The workpoints earned by household members were listed separately, so that it was plain how much each person had contributed, but nonetheless, the total was collected by the head of household. Since the implementation of the production responsibility system, most income is not received from the collective. However the small distribution of collective profit that still takes place continues to be turned over to the head of household.

The majority of households in Zengbu, 60 percent, consist of simple nuclear families (a married couple and their unmarried children). The next largest category, 25 percent, consists of patrilineal stem families (a married couple, one married son and his children, and the unmarried children of the senior couple.) The remaining 15 percent of Zengbu households consist of broken households, mainly one-person households. Most of these people are widows living apart from their sons.

Polygynous households, in which one man lived with two or more wives and their children, would formerly have been a significant category. No polygynous marriages have taken place since the marriage reforms made them illegal. When the law was put into effect, existing polygynous unions were not broken up, because of the extreme hardship this would have worked on the cast-off wife. There were two polygynous households in Zengbu in 1979; during that year one of these households changed form at the death of the husband, leaving only one.

The joint family, consisting of parents and two or more married sons with their wives and children, is a social form that does not occur in Zengbu. It has been extensively discussed in the literature on the Chinese family, and the reasons for its absence in Zengbu require examination. The joint family was a social form highly valued by the gentry prior to 1949. It was closely correlated with wealth and high status, and the argument has been made (see Croll *et al*, 1985, p. 14) that it is, in itself, a structural form that is conducive to these ends. The argument has also been made that under conditions of prosperity and wealth, the Chinese family becomes larger and larger and more complex, so that there are more likely to be joint families (C.K. Yang 1959, p. 9). In analyzing the joint family form, it has been usual to seek an explanation of the relationship between joint family form and economic circumstances. There is no evidence that the joint family form was ever actually practiced in Zengbu, under any economic circumstances. It might be supposed (if one ignores the fact that social and economic relationships do not depend on common residence in the same household) that when private landed property provided a basis for economic life, married sons were motivated to remain in the same household in order to facilitate their use of the family resources, and await their inheritance. When families engaged in business enterprises, it might be supposed to be to their advantage to concentrate capital and labor. However, these ends could certainly be achieved without the co-residence in the same household implied by the term joint family, since kin relationships and obligations remain significant however the household may be constituted. It is apparent that under collectivization, there was no economic reason for brothers to remain in their father's household after they were married. Under collectivization, privately owned land, or concentration of labor or capital in families, were not important factors in economic life. The team and the brigade controlled the land, the capital, and the labor of family members, and rendered family cooperation on a large scale less important. Considered as a residence pattern, joint family households would make little difference one way or another in economic terms.

With decollectivization, theory would suggest that there would be increasing numbers of joint families, if increased economic resources did indeed produce increasing expansion and complexity in Chinese family form. With decollectivization, resources devolved upon families, and families could band together to cooperate in agriculture, pool capital, and provide mutual support in times of crisis if they wished to do so. However, the supposition that these economic changes would be correlated with an increase in the number of joint families has not proved to be the case in Zengbu. Whatever economic arrangements family members may be making with one another (and there are many such arrangements), they have retained the same patterns of household membership that were customary under the collective system. The households of 1985 follow the same patterns as the households of 1979. There are no joint households (containing more than one married brother), and stem households (including parents and one married son) are normally temporary, with each son moving out as the next marries. (In the end, the youngest son generally assumes responsibility for the parents in their old age.) When the villagers themselves were asked about the relationship between increasing prosperity, family form, and household size, they took the position that the new economic policies make it *less* likely that married sons will remain in their parents' household for a longer period of time, or that joint families will be formed. They said that, since conflict between a married couple and the husband's parents was inevitable as long as they remained in the same household, early separation was desirable, and increasing economic prosperity made it possible to form a separate household sooner. They are certain that there are no economic advantages to themselves in the joint family form. The people of Zengbu are acutely aware of the economic implications of social structure, and fascinated by the idea that modifying social structure can improve economic circumstances. If the joint family form could have real economic advantages for them, they would be alive to the importance of adopting it. M. L. Cohen (1976) and the Gallins (1982) have shown that married brothers on Taiwan remain together in undivided households when it is to their economic advantage, either in agriculture or in operating small businesses. The villagers of Zengbu are convinced, and say explicitly, that the joint family household offers them no economic advantage. The Zengbu data indicate that even if the joint family form was historically correlated with prosperity, it is not regarded as instrumental in producing it. Perhaps the joint family was used by the traditional gentry not as a way of earning wealth, but as a way of displaying it.

Even as a form of status display, the joint family is not utilized by the villagers of Zengbu. The villagers' way of displaying status is building a superb new house for a newly married son to live in. Years of labor, savings, and effort go into housebuilding. In Zengbu, joint family residence would imply that the family was too poor to afford a new house for each married son. This would tend to reduce rather than to enhance their status. So, at present, in Zengbu, the joint family form offers neither economic utility nor status enhancement, and it is not the valued social form it has been thought to have been.

Data from Hong Kong reveal a smiliar pattern. In Ping Shan, a lineage village in Hong Kong's New Territories studied by Jack M. Potter in 1961–3, only 1 household out of the 143 in the village had adopted a joint family form. Since this is a wealthy village in a capitalist setting, there were no constraints on the establishment of joint families either from the economic or from the ideological point of view. This shows that Cantonese peasants have no particular wish to form joint families whether they are living in capitalist Hong Kong, in Maoist collectives, or in the decollectivized settings of present policy. The idea that Cantonese peasants in general strive to achieve the joint family ideal is inconsistent with the data, and must be dismissed as untenable.

People become members of Zengbu households either by birth or by marriage. Adoptions are rare. (One childless village family adopted a boy who was a refugee from Vietnam.) There are no adoptions of girls with the intention of raising them to be daughters-in-law. Household membership does not have the same meaning for boys that it has for girls. The son is a permanent member of the family in a sense that the daughter is not. Since marriage is patrilocal, the girl will marry, leave the household in which she has grown up, and become a member of another household. This is deeply felt, and the son's presence has a legitimacy and an importance that the daughter's presence does not.

In 1979–80, the average Zengbu household contained 4.5 persons. This average is the same as the average figure for household size in Dongguan county, which has 200,000 rural households. So, from the point of view of household size, Zengbu is, in general terms, typical. However, when Zengbu is compared with other brigades in the same commune, a wide range of variation in patterns of household size at this comparatively local level emerges. Within Chashan, the brigade with the smallest average household size has 4.3 persons per household, and the brigade with the largest average household size has 5.7. There is no simple explanation for this range of variation; household size is not correlated with the relative dependence of a given brigade on local-level industry rather than agriculture, nor is it correlated with the relative wealth of each brigade.

The dynamics of family and household life in Zengbu must be understood in the context of the domestic group cycle, through which the family and household must move in the course of their existence (Goody 1958). An ideal-type structural model of the Zengbu domestic cycle is shown in figure 15. The cycle begins with the marriage of a young couple and the subsequent birth of their children, forming a nuclear family. (See phase I.) As the children grow up, the daughters marry out of the household, and go to live in the households of their husbands, into which they are incorporated. Sons marry in sequence of age. Each son and his wife live as members of his parents' household for a period of time which varies from a few months to several years. When the son's wife gives birth to children, and a new nuclear family is attached to the one which initiated the cycle, the structure of the household as a whole is modified, and becomes a multigenerational patrilineal stem family composed of parents, unmarried sons and daughters, and the married son and his wife and children. (See phase II.)

If there is only one son in the family, he and his wife and children remain as part of the same household with his parents; ultimately, the son will assume

I

New nuclear family:
parents and unmarried
children

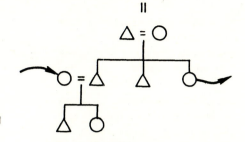

II

New patrilineal extended stem family:
daughter marries out; first son takes
a wife and has children

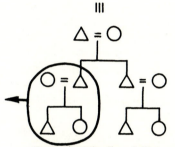

III

Dependent family of first son
separates from parents and
moves into separate house.
New extended stem family
created by marriage of
second son.

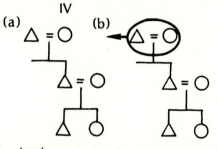

IV
(a) (b)

Aged parents remain
in household, with
youngest son,
supported by sons
jointly

Aged parents live
alone, supported
by sons jointly

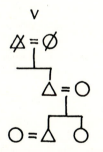

V

Parents die; cycle begins
again

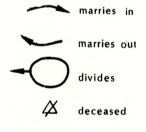

marries in

marries out

divides

deceased

Figure 15. Phases in the family and household cycle

the status of head of household from the father. If there is more than one son
in the family, the first son separates his household from the household of his
parents before the marriage of the second son. The second son and his wife
become members of the parents' household.

Phase III of the domestic group cycle is represented in figure 15 as the point at which all the daughters have married and gone to live with their husbands. The oldest son and his wife and children form an independent household. A second son has married and lives with his wife and children in the same household as his parents.

Phase IV of the domestic cycle is the point at which the youngest married son assumes the position of head of household. This implies the weakness or death of the father and mother. At this point, there are two alternative household forms used by the villagers. The preferred form is for the aged parents, or more frequently, the widowed mother, to remain as members of the youngest son's household. The alternative form is for the old parents or the widowed mother to separate and maintain a separate household. The cultural rationale for this choice is normally expressed in terms of food and eating (e.g. that the elderly need softer food, and cannot share the meals enjoyed by the younger people.) If this household form is chosen, the son receives the house that was formerly the parents', and a smaller separate dwelling is provided for them.

In a 25 percent random sample of brigade households drawn from the household registers, there were 130 widows or widowers over 46 years of age with married sons alive. These people had chosen between living as a member of the son's household or living as a separate household. Out of these 130 people, 87 had chosen to live as members of the son's household; this is about 67 percent. The remaining 43 (about 33 percent) lived as separate one-person households. Considering the oldest people in this group, those aged from 66 to 95, 39 out of 74 (52 percent) lived in separate households, and 35 (48 percent) lived as members of their son's household. So these more elderly parents were *less* likely to live in a son's household than was the group of widowed parents as a whole; as time passed, more households must have been divided. In practice, there does not appear to be a strong effort made to keep the aged parent in the same household. This does not imply that the obligation to care for the parent is at all diminished; however, it does imply that co-membership in the same household is felt to have been inconvenient or disharmonious.

The cycle ends when both parents of the original nuclear family have died, and the independent households of their sons are progressing through the stages of the cycle in their turn.

In discussing the household, the house itself is of critical symbolic and cultural importance. For this reason, it is important to consider the house and its social implications. Houses were the only important form of private property remaining to the villagers under collectivization, and they have come to serve as the major expression of economic status. Houses have remained inheritable property, both under the collective system and at the present time. As was traditional with land inheritance prior to 1949, sons inherit, and daughters, who marry into another family, do not. If a couple has no son to inherit, the close patrilineal relatives who have cared for them in their old age will receive the house. If a couple without a son is supported by the charity of the team, the team inherits the house. The traditional moral obligation of parents to pass on land and a house to each of their sons now centers on the house alone. The house is the son's most significant inherit- ance. If the son has no house, he will not be able to find a wife.

Consequently, the economic lives of Zengbu parents center around planning houses for their sons, receiving a house site (these are provided from publicly owned land, a practice which requires local-level government to diminish its own land resources in order to subsidize families and support population increase), saving money, and accumulating building materials, which are frequently expensive and in short supply. Every *yuan* in excess of what is needed for the basic daily necessities is set aside to be used for house building. Parents apply the earnings of all household members – of unmarried daughters, of newly married sons and of daughters-in-law – to this family enterprise. The wish to control their own earnings, at least to the extent of deciding how much is to be spent on house building and how much is not, underlies many decisions to form separate households. In 1979, when the total income of an average village household was 1,348 *yuan* (U.S.$ 898), houses cost between 3,000 *yuan* ($ 2,000) and 4,000 *yuan* ($ 2,666). The value of the house was in the range of 2.6 times the household's annual income. In 1985, the average total income of a village household was estimated (by Secretary Cai of the Chashan district) at 3,000 to 4,000 *yuan*. A good brick house of several stories was costing approximately 20,000 *yuan* ($ 7,407). The value of the house was in the range of 5·7 times the household's annual income. It required years of saving to build one house, let alone several. Public land resources were as badly strained as private financial resources. By December, 1981, building sites in the established villages had all been used, and satellite villages were being established. Village quarrels arose over the allocation of building sites, and a special committee of cadres was established to adjudicate these disputes.

The ritual focus of the house was traditionally the family ancestral altar. This was located at the rear of the large central ground floor room in each house, on a shelf reached by a wooden ladder. Twice daily, according to the old custom, incense was burned by the women before the wooden ancestral tablets, or before the ancestors' names written in black characters on orange paper pasted to the altar. Frequently the altar also held portraits of the deceased. On the first and the fifteenth of each month, and on festival days, food offerings were placed on these altars. During the Cultural Revolution, efforts were made to stamp out these practices, and Red Guards destroyed all the ritual paraphernalia they could find. Some families hid what they had in order to avoid criticism. The ancestral altars were removed. In their places, portraits of Chairman Mao were displayed; he had, in effect, assumed the status of a state-level deity. From a symbolic point of view, this suggested that it was now the state that was the most potent source of support and aid. In addition to political portraits, some houses in 1979 had a statue of Guanyin, the Buddhist goddess of mercy, enshrined in a glass-fronted cupboard.

Incense was burned before this statue on ritual occasions. (Such statues were mass-produced locally by a porcelain factory in adjacent Wentang.)

Since 1981, no efforts have been made to restrict the practice of the family-level ancestral cults. The family ancestral spirits are enshrined as before on the traditional altars at the rear of the main hall of each house. Incense is burned, and food offerings are made as they used to be. The revived household ancestral cult is a symbolic statement of the renewed economic and social importance of the household. The replacement of the state-level deity by the family-level deity is a ritual recognition that peasants must now look to their own households rather than to the state for the basic securities of life.

7. Modern, post-Maoist altar, with ancestral names written on orange paper at the upper left altar shelf

# 11

# Chinese birth planning: a cultural account

Birth is universal. However, the meaning of giving birth is not universal, but culturally specific. Preventing the process of giving birth is also inevitably replete with cultural significance. To these social actions, the villagers bring an immensely complicated set of assumptions. They are unexamined assumptions, existing as a basis for thought rather than as a conscious plan of action.

In order to understand the cultural significance of birth planning, it is necessary to discuss these culturally specific assumptions. Children are understood as the solution to adult problems that the villagers take very seriously indeed. They can share the work, with all that this implies; if male, they can dignify existence by providing a sense that the family line is being carried on; most importantly, they provide a solution to the burning psychological question, "Who will ever take care of me?" Being a legitimate recipient of care is deferred until old age, in this cultural setting: no care before that time has the legitimacy of the care provided by the young for the old. The dependency needs of the young must wait, since elders have prior claims. By old age, the wish to be taken care of is an unfulfilled desire of long standing. Yet a lifetime of feeling the obligation to care for others, and deferring the wish to be cared for one's self, has provided an experience which makes people doubt that they will ever be cared for, or if it is possible for them to receive enough care. In having children, the villagers see a solution to their wish for care, rather than thinking of themselves as assuming responsibility to care for another. The child is to care for the parent in the future. Having been brought up to this purpose, the child is left with a residue of longing for care which ensures the perpetuation of the system. (Richard H. Solomon, 1971, makes a related argument from a rather different perspective, which the interested reader may find useful.) These attitudes have their effect on the social significance of giving birth. They also influence other issues such as the social definition of what it means to be a person, and the nature of the appropriate relationships between individuals, families, and the power of the state. Because birth planning evokes these highly significant issues, the process of implementing birth planning policy emerges as a drama in which the most deeply held values are socially enacted.

Social values find their expression in public morality. Villagers in Zengbu believe strongly that they are moral people, acting in a moral society. They believe that the social changes they have witnessed are evolving changes, taking them in the direction of greater social morality, and that the claims of Chinese society in general to be an exemplar of social morality are higher than the claims of any other society. They believe that those who act in opposition to public morality are not acting rightly. They are not open to the potential value of systems and forms of behavior unlike their own; they are not relativists, and they dislike social deviance. When they explain social action, they do it in terms of shared values and social morality. There are two levels of social structure which organize morally valid social action in their eyes, the government and the family, and these structures take on an intrinsic moral significance. In practical terms, people know that both the family and the government may do harm as well as good, and both may be resented, but in terms of ideals and morality, respect for these institutions is a fundamental quality of the social order. The government is expected to demonstrate moral legitimacy, and public policy is always presented and explained in moral terms. When policies are changed, or even reversed, the moral justifications for them are modified, and different principles may have the primary emphasis, but a moral justification is always made. The family, being the other important repository of social morality, has associated with it a whole complex of social and behavioral forms that are regarded as appropriate ways to demonstrate moral worth in action. Since the issue of birth planning is so important to the national government and so important to the family, the differing interests of the two levels of structure produce contradictions between two highly valued sets of moral principles.

The central government takes the position that birth planning is not only a practical but also a moral necessity, given China's inordinate population size (over a thousand million in 1982), the impossibility of meeting the needs of such a population with the resources available, and the human suffering that will inevitably ensue if effective action is not taken at once. This position is explained and supported with statistical evidence so overwhelming that no dissenting interpretation could rationally be brought forward. (For recent studies of China's population as a whole, in demographic terms, see among others Tien, 1983, and Keyfitz, 1984). The central government has been at pains to emphasize the extreme importance of birth planning by labelling it a matter of "strategic significance." This is a culturally encoded political phrase meaning that birth planning is critically important to the safety and continuity of China as a whole, and that it is, in effect, a national security issue. The government's long-term commitment to the implementation of birth planning has also been emphasized, by describing it with the phrase "basic state policy." This phrase sets birth planning in a special category, above the shift and flux of interpretation and implementation that frequently characterize Chinese policy in matters regarded as less fundamental. The phrase defines birth planning as a continuing policy to be enforced over time, rather than a transitory measure. The Chinese government has chosen its strongest expressive language to convey the acuteness of the problem, its devastating implications, and the long-range importance of finding an effective solution.

Chinese familism approaches the question of birth planning from a different angle. From the point of view of the family, children are the means of its highly valued continuity, the basis of its prosperity, and the only valid source of interpersonal help and care. The patrilineal Chinese family claims the right to require, with all of the mighty moral force at its command, that young women who marry in produce sons on its behalf. There must be sons, not only daughters, since daughters do not carry lineal continuity, their labor is not defined as equally valuable – in spite of the fact that they can be demonstrated to earn and produce more, in Zengbu, at least – and they marry out, to live and work in another family. There must be a large enough number of children to make it seem reasonable that they will be able to care for their parents and grandparents in their old age.

The problem of caring for the aged has two aspects, the aspect of the economic realities, and the aspect of the cultural realities, and the problem cannot be understood without considering both. From a purely economic point of view, Chinese peasants (unlike urban dwellers) have no retirement pensions. It is written into the Marriage Law of 1983 that all children and grandchildren are responsible for the support of their aging parents and grandparents, both patrilateral and matrilateral. So, both in practice and in law, old peasants depend on their children and grandchildren for support, with no source of support from outside the family.

If there are no children, old peasants may receive the state's "five guarantee" support. In 1979–80, old people in Zengbu on "five guarantee" support lived in pitiable circumstances, in decrepit dwellings, with barely enough to eat, a tiny allowance of a few *yuan* a month from their teams, and tattered and inadequate bedding. They were dependent on the goodwill of their neighbors for water from the well and fuel to burn. The introduction of the production responsibility system could only reduce this already exiguous support system. The inadequacy of the "five guarantee" system is officially recognized, and a provincial-level official commented, "We want to intensify our work on this problem." But in any case, the recipients of "five guarantee" support feel humiliated in accepting it, and ashamed of the inability to work which forces them to do so, because being unable to work suggests that one has no right to receive. One old lady said, "I do not like to accept this; I have my conscience, and other people are working hard." It is felt that the only right and appropriate way for the aged to receive care is in their own homes, from their own sons. When Happy Homes for the Aged were tried in Chashan commune during the Great Leap Forward, they were a failure, and the reason was that the old people were miserable in the role of the recipients of care given by outsiders.

This idea of the appropriate care of the elderly is a cultural construct of the most complex kind: that it *should* happen is taken for granted; when it fails to happen, it is a matter of great sorrow; and the meaning of it, when it does happen, is replete with the expectations of happiness, the burden of obligation, and feelings of ambivalence and despair. The needs of aging parents are great. Indeed, they are conceived of as virtually insatiable. This sense of the insatiability of a parent's needs is traditional, and can be confirmed in the *Book of Filial Duty* (trans. Chen, 1920) for example. In this text, a series of sons make superhuman efforts to meet parental needs which have no limits and no end: sometimes they are unable to meet these needs without supernatural aid. Furthermore, the moral force of a parent's needs supersedes all other considerations, however urgent. It is felt that the satisfaction of parents' needs would be impossible without extraordinary human resources. This is why no finite number of sons seems like enough, and the village proverb says, "The more sons, the more happiness." The happiness implied by many sons is a particular kind of happiness, a happiness based on knowing that appropriate care will be provided in one's old age; this is a happiness which signifies an economically secure, culturally approved state of recipient dependence. Children, especially sons, are the means to this most desired end.

The idea of limiting the number of one's children, or contenting one's self with daughters rather than sons, raises the possibility that in purely practical terms, the aged will not receive their basic needs. At the same time, it raises the possibility of moral failure, a moral failure that would be deeply felt. In cultural terms, when a family has many children, security and happiness are possible for them, because the manpower and the resources to care for the aged will not fail. But a family with a limited number of children is more unlikely to find the kind of happiness they seek. If they fail in practical terms, they fail in cultural terms as well, and their sense of security cannot be solidly grounded.

The villagers make the assumption that it is the old, rather than the young, whose need to be cared for is most legitimate, and that the young are the ones who bear the obligation to care for the old. The Western assumption that parents bear an important moral obligation to be a source of security for their children is reversed, and children are thought of as the source of future security for their parents. When one looks at human dependency as dispassionately as possible, it seems clear that care is legitimately needed in childhood *and* in old age, but in the West, the moral emphasis is on the importance of caring for children, and in China, the moral emphasis is on the importance of caring for the old. Child care is a means to an end, a form of long-range self-interest. The contrast between Western and Chinese values can be brought out clearly using literary sources, in the comparison between the *Book of Filial Piety* and the Gilbert and Sullivan opera, the *Pirates of Penzance*. In the *Pirates of Penzance*, even people so lost to conventional morality as pirates nevertheless sympathize with the plight of an orphan, deprived of care by the untimely death of both parents. In the *Book of Filial Piety*, there is an analogous story about a group of bandits. Even these bandits display some remnants of moral decency, however, because they are moved by the plight of a poor old lady who will be left helpless in the world if they kill her only son. In these two stories, the weight of sympathy is distributed analogously, but in opposite directions. To have children is to be protected from the pitiable situation, analogous to being orphaned, of being left without care in one's old age. When villagers speak of having children so that old people may be taken care of, they are invoking a whole complex of cultural ideas embodying a definition of happiness resting on dependent security. This cultural complex is inseparable from the family system itself. In examining this complex, the relationship between family structure and cultural assumption, as they work in an integrated way to become social organization in process, is easily seen.

When an idea exists at the level of a cultural assumption, it exists pervasively, and appears at every level of society. The people who are the central government policy-makers are cultural beings and family members, as well as administrators with a clear interest in seeing the importance of national issues, and the interests of the nation as a whole. It is inevitable that central policy will draw on cultural assumptions, and it does so, producing a confusion of direction that tends to affirm the importance of the family point of view, and to weaken, however unintentionally, the stated position of the state. One very clear example of the primacy of culture over political theory is to be seen in the system of production responsibility by households. This system is plainly based on the traditional cultural assumption that the peasant family, with all its members working together, is a wholesome economic unit likely to produce prosperity. (Chinese history provides considerable evidence that this is not necessarily the case.) Although, in formal terms, the policy comes from the central government, actually, it draws on the assumptions of familism, and is congruent with the belief that more children provide more labor, and thus contribute directly to prosperity. The household responsibility system is a policy that makes population increase appear to be the social solution it traditionally was, rather than the social problem it now is. It has been implemented at a time when the central government is most acutely aware that in the wider context, and from any point of view larger than that of the family, more children, and the cumulative population increase that they imply, nullify hard won economic gains and make prosperity impossible in the long run. So, the central government's overt message stands in opposition to the covert message implied by an economic policy based on the cultural assumptions of traditional familism. The policy-makers are the bearers of their own culture, and cannot stand aside from it, in spite of the unambiguous logic of their own analysis of the significance of China's rising population.

Peasants also perceive both points of view simultaneously. However narrowly familistic they may feel inclined to be, they have seen the private plots becoming smaller over the years, as Zengbu's limited land supply is distributed among increasing numbers of villagers. Some villagers have concluded that they should have more children, so that their families can control a larger number of the tiny plots, an involutional solution that intensifies the problem it recognizes and tries to solve. The villagers have seen available house land built over, so that new houses must be built in undesirable outlying locations; the deliberations of the committee that assigns house-building land are tense. Everyone can clearly see the intrinsic opposition between the interests of the villagers considered as a whole, the limited resources available, and the legitimate needs of the family as the family understands them. It is plain that these urgently felt needs and interests are incompatible.

In this social context, where the claims of the family and the government are so pervasive, the private interests of the husband or wife, or of the couple together, have never been regarded as important; indeed, they are scarcely relevant. An emotional rationale for marrying or having children would strike the villagers as flimsy and insubstantial at best, indecent at worst. Rather than emphasizing the relationship between husband and wife, people think of marriage as the taking of a daughter-in-law to help continue the family line, and the husband's parents, rather than the bride and groom, are congratulated at the wedding. Marriage is to create family continuity, and the explicit purpose of marriage is to have children: this is the pattern of human existence. When a child is born, its importance lies in its social relationships. It exists in relation to the family, as one who is carrying on the line, if male, or as one who will help to carry on the line of another family, if female. The child also exists in relationship to society at large, and so the government's interest in births, which is based on the aim of administering morally so as to produce prosperity, is understood as a direct and legitimate concern. But a child is not thought of as having validity or importance in isolation from its social context. Social experience is valid experience; isolated experience is insignificant experience. The social aspects of the person are relevant; the separate aspects of the person are not relevant. Valuing a child as a "human life," in isolation from its significance to the family and to society, is a senseless abstraction when considered in terms of Chinese ideas about what it means to be a person.

For these reasons, it is clear that the Chinese do *not* have a concept of birth as legitimately the personal decision of a woman about her body. They are not "pro-choice," rather, the importance of a birth to levels of society greater than the individual legitimizes the intervention of these levels in the process. It is interesting to make the comparison between Chinese assumptions and the U.S. Supreme Court decisions in Roe v. Wade, January 22, 1973. According to the decision,

We recognize the right of the individual, married or single, to be free from unwarranted governmental intrusion into matters so fundamentally affecting a person as the decision whether to bear or beget a child. That right necessarily includes the right of a woman to decide whether or not to terminate a pregnancy.

In Chinese thinking, primacy is given to the fact that the birth fundamentally affects the family and the state, and whether it fundamentally affects the person is a less important consideration. By contrast, the U.S. Supreme Court regards the fact that birth fundamentally affects the person as the validation for superseding the claims of the state, and by implication, in the phrase "married or single," of the family as well. Yet, the fact that the Chinese are not "pro-choice" does not at all imply that they are "pro-life." Both the family and the state understand a birth in purely instrumental terms, as it affects the welfare of the family unit or of the polity. The idea of valuing an unborn life in and of itself, without regard for its social significance, is alien and irrelevant in Chinese social thinking. So, the paired opposition, "pro-choice" versus "pro-life," reflects specifically American cultural concerns. Attempting to impose these categories on Chinese birth planning leads only to misunderstanding.

The people of Zengbu, living a social life based on these assumptions, inhabit a social world in which no normal adult remains unmarried, for the social meaninglessness of a single life is unthinkable, and no married couple remains childless by choice, for a childless marriage is a tragic inability to fulfill cultural expectations, rather than a personal sorrow or a private decision.

In 1979, these cultural assumptions existed in conjunction with the general principles on birth planning formulated by the upper levels, and with specific regulations implemented by the brigade. At this time, birth planning was not yet a matter of strategic significance or a basic state policy, but it had been explained by Chairman Mao, and was clearly understood as a goal of appropriate social change. As Women's Federation leaders from the county level said,

We are instructed by Chairman Mao himself that birth planning is closely connected with the national economy, the Four Modernizations, health, the development of science and culture, and prosperity. It protects women's health, and liberates them from the burden of having too many children. It also protects children's health and education, and helps to nurture them well.

In this formulation, the emphasis is primarily in terms of the nation, and secondarily in terms of the people whose exploitation is legitimized by the traditional family system – the women, urged to produce child after child in order to fulfill the wishes of their husbands' parents, and the children, brought into the world as means to the end of the future comfort and satisfaction of others, rather than as beings with important claims or interests of their own. Mao's formulation links the interests of the government with the interests of those exploited by the traditional family.

More specifically, policy was, as it had been for several years, to encourage one birth, strictly control second births, and resolutely prevent third births. But this gnomic formula was variously interpreted and implemented by the different levels of government. Furthermore, its significance and implications were quite different in rural and urban areas (see chapter 15). In urban areas, the policy was implemented as the "one-child family." There is not, and has never been, a one-child policy implemented in Zengbu. It is solely for urban residents. In rural areas, like Zengbu, policy is filtered through a complex bureaucratic process which has produced entirely different regulations. Tracing the different interpretations of policy from level to level demonstrates the kinds of modifications that are made as the policy moves farther from theory and closer to implementation; it also illustrates the extent to which each level is free to act independently. Any preconception of Chinese society as a series of subordinate levels carrying out with unthinking obedience the fiats they receive from above is a considerable distortion of Chinese political process.

There were several important regulations bearing on birth planning being implemented in Zengbu in 1979. The first of these concerned the required late age of marriage. Peasant men were not permitted to marry until they reached the age of 25, and peasant women until they reached the age of 23, unless hardship could be demonstrated. A legitimate hardship would exist, for example, if the parents of an only son were extremely old and infirm, and could be better cared for with the help of a daughter-in-law. In no case could a marriage take place if the man was younger than 20, or the woman younger than 18. This regulation was not the administrative responsibility of the brigade, but of the civil affairs office at the commune headquarters, one level up, which issues marriage licenses. According to their figures, 93 percent of all marriages in the commune were between men over the age of 25 and women over the age of 23. The relationship between this regulation and birth planning is that it tended, in the long run, to reduce population by lengthening the time between generations. It was an acceptable regulation, rather than a hateful one, because it involved no direct intervention, and imposed a wait to bear children, rather than a prohibition. It was consistent with the interests of the families of adult daughters, who are prodigious earners, and whose earnings are paid to the head of household. The young women themselves preferred to marry late because the life of a daughter-in-law is indubitably harder and less pleasant than that of an adult daughter.

The brigade level was responsible for enforcing the other regulations affecting birth planning. They received general principles from higher levels, rewrote them into specific regulations taking "local conditions" into account, and transmitted them to the villagers. "Local conditions" can be decoded as the power of traditional familism, exerting pressure for many births and valuing sons rather than daughters, and the degree to which this exerts its influence on the brigade's capacity to implement and enforce. The regulations bearing on birth planning in 1979 stated that each married couple in Zengbu Brigade was allowed four births in the attempt to have at least one son, without paying any penalty at all. Each child would receive a ration of grain at the artificially low state supported price of 9.8 *yuan* per 100 *catties* (about 12 U.S. cents per kilogram), rather than having to pay the normal off-ration price of 25 *yuan* per 100 *catties* (about 32 U.S. cents per kilogram). So the rule was actually providing a lifelong food subsidy to up to four daughters per couple. This rule is in dramatic contrast to the ideals of the "one-child policy" applied in urban areas; when it is remembered that 80 percent of the Chinese are classified as peasants, the impact of such rules as this is enormous. (It is interesting, also, to compare this rule with the position of the Catholic church in favor of births: the Catholic church makes a moral case for having children, but it also provides alternatives to marriage, and it does not provide lifelong food subsidies for up to four children of parishioners under parallel conditions.) Such subsidies as this importantly modify the relationship between a family's economic circumstances and a decision to have more children. They reduce the economic deterrents to having children by having society, rather than the family, shoulder the cumulative financial burden, which in capitalist systems, remains the family's own.

This rule seemed surprising, but the women's leader of the brigade, who is the person responsible for birth planning work, said that "local conditions" were an important factor. She added, "If people here were not allowed to try for a son, there would be trouble." If a couple had children after the fourth daughter, or had more than two children including at least one son, these children would not be subsidized, but rice would have to be purchased from them at the unsupported price. Versions of this rule have been misunderstood by the Western press in China, because lack of access to a ration of subsidized grain has been interpreted to mean that excess children would receive no grain at all, rather than that they would have access to unsubsidized grain instead. In any case, from the local point of view, the rise in the price of rice for

8. The brigade birth control team, 1985

children over the subsidized number was not a deterrent. The women's leader said, "Most families think it is worth it."

Another rule regulated the spacing of births. The first child could follow immediately upon marriage, and almost invariably did. Subsequent children were supposed to be born at intervals greater than four years. If the interval between children was less, grain for the child was to be purchased half at the subsidized price, and half at the unsubsidized price. When a situation has two significant aspects (that the child was within the permitted number, but violated the permitted spacing), it is common to deal with it using a regulation with two aspects (grain shall be half subsidized and half not subsidized); the calculations of payment for work, for example, or the formulae for selling pigs fatter than the required quota to the state follow this pattern (chapter 5). Such rules were also used historically in the distribution of lineage resources. From the point of view of the villagers, these rules are a fair way of dealing with factors that are present simultaneously and have conflicting implications.

In order to make it possible to observe these regulations, it was expected that all couples of childbearing age should practice some form of birth control. The women's leader was responsible for providing birth control supplies to all the married women in the brigade. She knew which methods were used by each of the 701 couples still in their childbearing years in the

Table 12. *Methods of birth control used in Zengbu, 1979*

| Method | Women | Men | Couples |
|---|---|---|---|
| Pills | 101 | | 101 |
| Sterilization | 19 | 2 | 21 |
| Ring-shaped loops | 424 | | 424 |
| Injections | 3 | | 3 |
| "Own methods" | | | 69 |
| Legitimate non-users: | | | |
|   a. Recently married | 57 | | 57 |
|   b. Recently gave birth | 26 | | 26 |
| | | | 701 |

brigade. The methods were as shown in table 12. When asked what "their own methods" would mean in practice, the women's leader replied austerely, "I never asked them." It is more likely that this category includes the methods for which the husband is directly responsible, condoms and withdrawal, about which a woman could not appropriately ask; in Zengbu, these matters cannot be discussed between people of opposite sexes.

Abortion was used as a backup method of birth control if other methods failed, and there were modest incentives – 15 days' rest, 30 *yuan* (U.S.$ 20), and continued workpoints while resting – to encourage the use of abortion to end an unplanned pregnancy, rather than letting the child be born by default. If these incentives did not appear sufficiently attractive, the pregnancy could continue, and the penalty would be in the price of rice.

So, birth control methods were a subject of public record. This may be resented as an intrusion inimical to the family's interests, but it is not thought of using the Western category, "invasion of privacy." It is felt to follow logically from the legitimacy of the state's interest in births. In similar fashion, the husband's parents are felt to be legitimately concerned in a couple's decisions about birth control. For example, one commune-level women's leader commented, "If there are only two daughters, the husband's mother will not agree to birth control for the daughter-in-law." This shows clearly how decision-making, if it is not in the hands of the state, is in the hands of the family, and not in the hands of the individual. Because the individual interests of the husband and wife are not defined as socially significant in Zengbu, the concept of privacy, which validates these interests in the West, does not exist to be invoked. Indeed the concept of privacy is difficult to translate without conveying connotations of crass lack of respect for the needs of others and the claims of society as a whole. Attempts to act on a concept of personal privacy would appear antisocial in a Chinese cultural setting. Since the concept does not exist, it is not present in people's thinking, and when birth planning policy is resented, the resentment is conceptualized in other terms.

As well as being the person to implement policy into practice, the women's leader also had the job of educating people about the importance of birth planning from a more general perspective. She tried to make people see the importance of population control in principle, and urged the villagers to limit themselves to two children. (She herself had had two children, a son and a daughter, and had then undergone a tubal ligation.) Her message was generally received as an irksome and uncongenial matter of little practical importance, since it was not enforced; people did not like hearing the subject discussed. They tended to think of her as the personal agent of policy, so she was the recipient of considerable criticism, some silent, and some overt. Since she is herself a villager, concerned with behaving appropriately, and finely attuned to the social pressure applied by her fellow villagers, bearing the criticism was a form of labor that was part of the job. It was an added source of difficulty to have one's mother-in-law as one of the silent critics. The women's leader indicated that, should her mother-in-law become a vocal critic, it would be impossible to continue doing the job and also maintain a sense of being a culturally appropriate daughter-in-law. The more vocal critics in 1979 would say things like, "If you want to have just two children yourself, that's fine, but why don't you let other people be, so they can do what they want?" But she defended herself on ethical grounds, affirming that, in her opinion, population control was of importance to the country as a whole. In her social role as the structural mediator between levels, she was criticized by familistic fellow villagers, and defended her position by citing the importance of the needs of the country. In dealing with the upper levels, she was called upon to put the other point of view, and to explain that "local conditions" made it impossible to enforce regulations more stringent than the ones in place. She was unable to satisfy either side with these explanations. She carried out an extraordinarily demanding social role, and in 1979, she carried it out alone. In terms of practical support, and in terms of political emphasis, other issues were regarded as primary.

This could be gauged by the attention devoted to birth planning at the three-level party cadre meeting, the political ritual of affirmation and reintegration which is held twice a year in the commune. The three-level meeting is the time for introducing and explaining new policy measures. At the three-level meeting in Fall, 1979, birth planning received a single mention in passing on the third and final day; it was referred to as a state goal which would, it was hoped, be achieved successfully in the indeterminate future. In spite of the theoretical importance of birth planning, in a political context it was not, in 1979, the central focus of attention it was shortly to become, and no particular resources beyond the personal dedication of women's leaders were allocated to the process of implementation. There was a clear disparity between the formal importance of birth planning, and the actual degree of attention given to it at the local level. It was an issue that local-level leaders preferred to handle as little as possible, unless they were required to intervene. In 1979, with "local conditions" being given the greatest consideration, and with the subsidization of four daughters per couple, it was clear that birth planning policy was dramatically pronatal in practice, and that the forces of traditional familism were well in the ascendant.

By June 1980, however, concern with birth planning had intensified, and the brigade put out a new set of regulations. As before, these regulations were formulated in specific terms at the brigade level, on the basis of general principles handed down from above. The regulations were based on economic incentives and penalties which were intended to be more significant than the previous penalties related to the price of rice. The incentives were stated first. Couples who agreed to limit themselves to one child would receive an incentive of 100 *yuan* (U.S.\$ 67) annually. No couple in the brigade regarded this as a rational choice. The brigade was unable to offer the further incentives that are offered to one-child couples in urban areas, such as special high-quality schooling, free child care, and access to better jobs, because these benefits do not exist in the countryside, and are not available to peasants. Another urban incentive, more living space, was meaningless in the countryside, because of the fact that peasant houses are privately owned and built. The negative economic sanctions were to fine couples who had a third child 250 *yuan* (U.S.\$ 166) annually; there was a retroactive fine of 150 *yuan* (U.S.\$ 100) for couples who had already had a third child. Generally speaking, village families could afford these fines. The brigade also stated that no private plots, litchi trees, or collective income were to be distributed to children born in excess of the rules. Under the collective economic system in use in 1980, this would be a serious loss of future income, and it would require the family rather than the collective to absorb the economic disadvantages of population increase. Furthermore, no house-building plots would be provided to the parents of supernumerary male children on their behalf. (House-building plots are not provided for female children in any case.) This too was a serious sanction, since so much of a family's economic efforts are bent to accumulating the money necessary to build a house for each son on a building plot distributed by the collective.

The brigade also ruled that people who did not observe the required interval of four years between births would be fined 10 *yuan* (U.S.\$ 7) per month until the interval was up. These fines, and all other fines, were to be paid to the teams. The "combined teams," the new administrative unit equivalent to the natural village, would adjudicate violations. Finally, the concluding rule stated, "Everyone is equal under these regulations." This rule reflected the villagers' concern that if good was to be limited, as George Foster (1965) would put it, no one should receive an unfair advantage. This is a crucial element of the villagers' definition of justice. They will accept an unpopular policy if the hardship appears to be equally shared. However, if they think that some people are receiving privileges denied to others, they will resent it so much as to threaten the possibility of enforcing the policy.

Early in 1981 a series of important changes took place which altered the institutional constraints on birth planning, and introduced new elements. First, and most importantly, the new system of production responsibility by households was brought into use. The distribution of economic resources under this system made the brigade's economic sanctions of the previous June meaningless, since families now had a lasting claim on resources, rather than receiving distributions that were re-evaluated from year to year. The economic power of the brigade was vitiated, and its political power as well. The production responsibility system provided apparent advantages to households with large numbers of laborers, and this increased peasant motivation to have more children.

At the same time, the national marriage law was changed. Although the language of the law was to raise the minimum age for marriage, it imposed no legal delay on marrying, and at the local level, late marriage policy was no longer enforced. As a result, the effect of the change was to *lower* the permissible age of marriage for peasants to 22 for men, and 20 for women. Everyone who became eligible to marry under the new law married as soon as possible. In the long run, this would have the effect of increasing population by shortening the length of time between the generations. Coming into effect when it did, it enlarged the category of young people eligible to marry just as an unusually large demographic cohort was entering that category in any case (see figure 16). As a result, the number of births that were culturally imperative because they followed new marriages also increased. The brigade, in a renewed effort to find an effective economic sanction, announced that it was planning to raise the penalty for having a third child to 400 *yuan* (U.S.$ 266) annually. In the light of this, some peasant families concluded that they should try to have another child immediately, rather than waiting for the approved interval only to pay a higher fine.

At this time, early in 1981, a new birth planning policy was introduced by the upper levels. It was based on using abortion as a means for preventing excess births, rather than continuing to rely on the economic sanctions that were ineffectual in practice. Under the terms of this policy, as it was implemented at the brigade level, couples who already had two children including one son were called upon to have an abortion if the wife became pregnant again. If both children were daughters, the abortion was not urged. In order to understand this policy, it is important to understand the cultural meaning of abortion in China, and in order to do this, it is necessary to stand

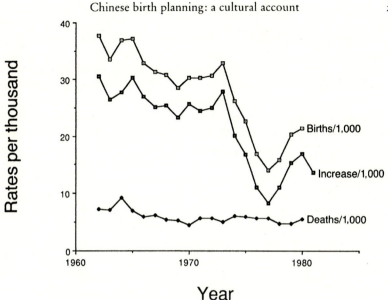

Figure 16. Chashan commune's birth, death, and increase rates, 1962–81

aside from the emotionally powerful connotations that abortion has in American society, particularly at the present time. The American association of abortion with sex, guilt, violence, and the question of the relationship between being female and the necessity to assume the social role of motherhood are profoundly beside the point to the Chinese. Devereux has pointed out in his book, *A Study of Abortion in Primitive Societies* (1979) that "we are culturally conditioned to assume that an abortion is an extralegal act, whose purpose is to conceal the dereliction of a woman" (p. 133). He adds that "we may hope to overcome our ethnocentric bias ... most effectively by examining in detail those instances of abortion which are imposed upon the women ... in a more or less *public* and *legal* manner." Chinese policy is certainly such a case. The use of abortion has a long history in China. According to Alan F. Guttmacher (1973, p. 164), "The earliest medical manuscript extant, a Chinese herbal 5,000 years old, recommends mercury as an abortifacient." It is reasonable, then, to assume that abortion is indigenous and traditional. The current cultural view of abortion was put as follows by a county-level leader. She said, "In our opinion, abortion is not cruel. It would be much more cruel to let the population continue to grow, and to let the future generations suffer. If we don't stop the population from growing, there will be what we call a human explosion calamity. People will be reduced to eating people. There will be no land and no houses." She is thinking of abortion in pragmatic and instrumental terms. It is seen as a trivial evil compared with the horrors of mass starvation. And starvation is not an abstract concept in this

context; every villager in Zengbu over the age of 40 has actually seen people
starve, and younger people have known shared hunger.

The second point that needs to be understood is what it means to be
"called on" to have an abortion. In this non-relativist system, people either
share the system's values or are defined as incorrect, and the solution is to
persuade them to change their minds by the use of example, explanation, and
discussion. This is a traditional solution, rather than an innovation since 1949
(Cohen 1968, p.98). Persuasion of this kind is considered an appropriate and
legitimate way of dealing with an erroneous outlook. Family visits are made
by local-level leaders to carry out persuasion; if repeated visits fail to change a
person's mind, leaders of higher and higher rank are brought in. This
simultaneously respects the importance of the dissenter, and makes the social
system one in which dissent is more and more difficult to sustain as the
process continues. At the same time, fellow villagers begin to fear that the
dissenter will succeed in avoiding the sacrifice that they themselves have
already been required to make. They apply social pressure by indicating the
resentment they will feel if the sacrifices are not clearly equal. The cumulative
social pressure is so stong as to be virtually irresistible. However, a
distinction is made between social pressure and physical force, the use of
which would be wrong. Indeed, the Chinese Communist Party Central
Committee sent out a letter, dated September 25, 1980, reminding local-level
leaders engaged in birth planning to work to "avoid any forceful methods." A
county-level leader explained the position by saying, "A good leader won't
force an abortion. They rely on education. An effective leader would
repeatedly educate a person who was in violation of the rules. Leaders at the
brigade, commune, and team levels would come again and again to the
person's house, and yell at her constantly. If they discovered a person trying
to escape, they would mobilize all of her relatives [to help persuade her], and
check out all her sisters. Usually nothing can be done if the woman absolutely
refuses. They just fine her." This shows the intensity of persuasion permitted,
as long as it remains verbal, and the way in which the person's relatives are
drawn into the persuasive process, rather than being defined as separate and
uninvolved. The reason for investigating the woman's sisters is that, in this
strongly patrilineal society, they will have married out, and be difficult to
trace, so it is easier to conceal one's self among them or other matrilateral
relatives. These remarks also indicate that the failure to persuade, or the use of
physical force, imply failure of leadership.

In implementing birth planning policy then, local-level leaders were
permittted to apply persuasive social pressure and forbidden to apply direct
force. Fellow villagers would apply social pressure as well, as long as the
policy was seen to be fairly applied and effectively carried out, but if the
policy was perceived as variably enforced, the villagers would cease to
pressure for universal compliance, and start to pressure for the opportunity

to be one of the exceptions. This gave the villagers who refused to comply a tremendous political significance, and presented local-level leaders with almost insoluble problems.

In Zengbu, the brigade women's leader was now being helped in her task by the other ten brigade-level leaders, rather than working alone as before. This was a clear indication that the importance of birth planning was much greater than it had been. From the point of view of the women's leader, the problem lay in implementing an unpopular policy in a way that would be perceived as perfectly fair. She emphasized to the villagers that there were to be no exceptions whatsoever, "even cadres." At first, villagers were not sure if the policy was really firm. Some families resisted the pressure to have an abortion in the hope that they might outwait the leadership. The political significance of these families was great. If villagers were told that they were being called upon to have abortions, and yet saw that others, who refused to comply, were allowed to bring their pregnancies to term, the policy ceased to have any meaning. The women's leader said, "With these pregnancies, neighbors pressured the couple, and watched them, and gossiped. The gossipers said, 'If the cadres allow this birth, why can't *we* have more children?' We decided that either we had a policy, or we didn't."

One woman who was pregnant at this time described the effect of policy on her as follows:

I preferred to have two sons and one daughter, and I was trying for a second son. Well, actually, I was using an I.U.D., but it failed. I chose to be fined and have the third child. But then the campaign started at the upper levels, and the local-level cadres had to follow. The women's leader said, 'Now the campaign has come. You have one son and one daughter, you must go get an abortion.' At first, I refused her request. Later, the head of the Women's Federation at the commune level came to see me. She told me not to give birth. She said it was unfair of me to try to have more children than other people. She said 'You must carry out the abortion. If you refuse to do so, and try to give birth, cadres of higher and higher levels will come to educate you, and you will be fined.' I didn't want to be fined 400 *yuan* for the third child, so I got an abortion.

In Zengbu brigade, there were two crucial test cases in which the pregnant women and their husbands' families did not concede to mounting social pressure. One case involved a couple from the village of Sandhill, who had one son and one daughter when the wife became pregnant again. Cadres tried to persuade this couple to have an abortion, but they refused. They left the village and concealed themselves among the wife's matrilateral relatives. The Zengbu cadres sealed up their empty house and went to look for them, but could not find them. The woman gave birth to a daughter away from the village. When she returned, the brigade cadres imposed a fine of 1,000 *yuan* (U.S.$ 667) and 400 *yuan* (U.S.$ 267) annually for life. This was reduced to 200 *yuan* (U.S.$ 134) annually when she agreed to have a tubal ligation. The women's leader commented that the initial 1,000 *yuan* did not even cover the cost to the brigade of the unsuccessful search. Public reaction to this case was to call the woman twice a fool: first to give birth to a daughter rather than a son, which is culturally defined as being her own fault, and second, to give birth at all when the penalty was to pay such an exorbitant fine. Yet this case also raised the possibility that people who could hide successfully would not be bound by the same rules as the others.

The second test case involved a woman from Lu's Home village. She and her husband had two daughters and one son already. She would not agree to have the abortion, in spite of efforts to convince her to do so by the brigade women's leader and other leaders from levels as high as the county. Ten days before the baby was due, the couple left the village in hopes of giving birth elsewhere. The brigade cadres closed up their house and nailed a sign to their door. They urged the husband's brothers to get the couple back. They said that in three days the husband's brothers' houses would be sealed as well. This reflects the cultural assumption that the acts of family members can be thought of as linked and inseparable, and that it is reasonable for a man's brothers to share in his punishment. The brigade cadres met with the wife's mother and the wife's mother's brother. (The latter was the traditional mediator in cases involving conflict between the lineage and a woman who married in.) In meeting with these relatives, the cadres made the cultural assumption that the couple were likely to have turned to the wife's matrilateral relatives. In this meeting, the brigade cadres told the wife's relatives that the land which had been distributed to the couple would be taken back, both private plots and production responsibility land. This would leave the couple with no share of the village resources with which to make a living. At 8 p.m. on the second day, in time to avoid having the husband's brothers' houses sealed, the couple returned. The abortion took place on the following day, using the injection method. The brigade women's leader explained that the injection method would not necessarily kill the baby at once. She said that if the child was born alive, it would not live for more than two or three hours. In this case, no attention was paid to the child, nor were any measures taken to save it; the child died as a result of deliberate inattention to its perinatal distress, which was presumably the result of the method of abortion. The women's leader could not tell this story without evident distress of her own, even after an interval of two years. She repeated the justifications for the brigade's actions: "Everyone in the village was watching this case. The cadres felt that if she had her baby, the whole policy would become unenforceable. If we had let her go freely, it would have had a very bad effect on everyone else." In spite of the validity of these justifications in her mind, her distress indicated the presence of another point of view, the family's point of view, existing simultaneously, and recognized as valuable.

Several years earlier, in explaining her reasons for becoming politically active, the women's leader had described the extreme poverty of her bleak childhood, and the abusiveness within her family that was the direct result, in her opinion, of the economic circumstances of the surrounding society. Her idea of socialism was that it would provide prosperity and economic justice, and that as a direct result, there would be social justice and harmonious family life as well. Socialism was the natural, complete, and far-reaching solution to the problems of family life, and the exploitation, particularly of women, inherent in the family structure. Her political goals included the presupposition that it was important to make family life less sordid by making it closer to cherished ideals. What was socialist and what was most valuably and validly Chinese were linked in her way of thinking. Her own social idealism, and her ways of being kind and considerate to others, were expressed using the formulae of socialist theory. Now, by carrying her principles through to their logical conclusion, she served her goals in the long run, but in the short run, she injured the family interests of some fellow villagers. Respect for the principles of the state conflicted with respect for the principles of the family, with the essentually tragic result that people on either side of the question could no longer define themselves as good, because they were inevitably in conflict, if not with one, then with the other aspect of their own valued principles.

This second test case demonstrates that letting the neonate die is regarded as socially legitimate when the reasons are compelling. In this case, the compelling reasons were those of the state. But the question can also be raised, under what circumstances might it seem legitimate to the family to let the neonate die? Clearly, given the importance of a male rather than a female child, families would be more motivated to let a female neonate die. Female infanticide existed in traditional China. It has been reported and deplored in the national press as an immoral act; the state takes the position that all children appropriately and legitimately conceived should be protected. It is only if they violate the legal restriction on giving birth that they can be allowed to die.

According to the brigade women's leader, there has been no infanticide of female babies in Zengbu, in spite of the clearly displayed assumption that males are more important and more fully human than females. Since all pregnancies are monitored and their results known, the statement of the women's leader is to be accepted. Families, although wishing strongly for sons, are not experiencing sufficient desperation to make female infanticide seem legitimate. Women's leaders at the commune level say that there has been no female infanticide in Chashan commune, although they have heard that it does sometimes happen in "remote areas." The phrase suggests that it is more characteristic of people in less civilized areas, and, by implication, that it is not really a civilized thing to do. At the county level, birth planning leaders report one case of attempted infanticide in their experience. (The population of the county is more than one million.) In this case, a young woman tried to abandon her female baby "on the hillside" but her fellow villagers found it and brought it back. At the provincial level, a birth planning leader reported that infanticide exists in certain remote islands along the coast that are difficult to control. Presumably, limitations on pregnancy are also difficult to implement in such areas, so stringent policy enforcement and female infanticide are not logically linked. The leader affirmed the official position that once appropriately born, the child must be protected. She said that in her opinion, the amount of infanticide in Guangdong province must be negligible, since the sex ratio for newborns is well within the bounds of the normal. According to Li Chengrui, the Director of the State Statistics Bureau, a normal sex ratio for newborns is defined as "about 100:105, with a margin of 103 to 108" for males outnumbering females (Anon. 1983, p. 11). Li gives Anhui province as an example of a locale with an abnormal sex ratio; there, the sex ratio is 100 girls to 111·12 boys. It is interesting to compare these modern figures with historical ones. For example, under the old regime, in the village near Shanghai studied by Fei Xiaotong, the sex ratio was 100 girls to 135 boys (1939, p. 34). So it would not be reasonable to suggest that the state birth planning policy had precipitated female infanticide by families in Guangdong province, and probably elsewhere as well.

The villagers did not like the policy using abortion as the focus of birth planning implementation, and by comparison with it, the former policy, which had been disliked in its day, appeared preferable. One male villager, asked what people thought about being called on to have abortions, said, "The attitude of the villagers is that cadres should fine people, rather than requiring them to have abortions." However, if the policy were to exist at all, public opinion supported universal enforcement. In the second test case, for example, they supported the leadership's actions on the grounds that it would have been unfair to permit the couple to have their baby when other people were not permitted to do so.

The women's leader, asked about the feelings of the women who had the abortions, said that if the child would have been a son, the women were really upset, but not if it would have been a daughter. This exchange reflects, in the question, the Western assumption that an experience takes its meaning in an important way from the emotions of the person having the experience. In the answer, it reflects the Chinese assumption that a person's response to an experience will reflect its social implications – in this case, the importantly differing significance of having a son rather than a daughter.

The policy based on abortion can be understood more clearly if it is looked at in perspective, and in the light of some comparative figures. In evaluating the degree of completeness with which the policy was implemented, it is worth noting that according to the provincial level, in 1982, in the province as a whole, 19 percent of all births were third or higher order births. This bespeaks a very considerable gap between policy and implementation, suggesting that many areas had leaders whose efforts were weak or ineffectual in comparison with Zengbu's leaders, and that many supernumerary pregnancies were brought to term. Rather than suggesting a high degree of successfully enforced compliance, the figure, on the contrary, indicates that in the province as a whole, policy was implemented with a wide disparity between theory and practice. This does not surprise the leadership, since they think of policy as a goal, an ideal to be approached, rather than a law. As Vivienne Shue put it, in discussing the land reform period, "they were prepared for only partial fulfilment of goals ... they did not expect or insist on perfect compliance" (1980, p. 5). This distinction between policy and law is critical and complex, and produces a socially specific and distinctive attitude to social control.

In considering the qualities of the policy in comparative perspective, it has been easy for the uninformed to assume that such a policy would produce a number of abortions that could be considered excessive or shocking in international terms. A comparison with abortion figures for the United States is surprising and instructive. Using the format of the *Statistical Abstracts of the United States* produced by the U.S. Census Bureau (1984), abortion figures are quoted in terms of the numbers of abortions per 1,000 live births. In the U.S. as a whole, in 1980 (the most recent figures available), there were 428 abortions per 1,000 live births, in a range between Utah's 97 and the District of Columbia's 1,569. In New York, the figure was 780, and in California it was 598. In Guangdong province, in 1982, using figures provided by provincial officials, there were 523 abortions per thousand births. (The officials provided the most recent complete figures for an interview in August, 1983, and did not rehearse the data for earlier years.) In Dongguan county, in 1982, there were 816 abortions per 1,000 births. In Chashan commune, in 1981, there was a ratio of 727 abortions per 1,000 live births, based on actual figures of 656 births and 477 abortions. In 1982, 605 births and 370 abortions yielded a ratio of 612 to 1,000. In 1983, for the first six months of the year, there were 213 births and 96 abortions, yielding a ratio of 450 abortions per 1,000. The average for the entire two-and-a-half-year period is 640 per 1,000. In Zengbu brigade, where the women's leader provided figures showing 150 abortions and 257 births in the two-and-a-half-year period, the ratio is 584 per 1,000. These figures indicate clearly that at the height of the policy emphasizing abortion as a method of population control, the figures remained well within a range currently found in the United States. And this policy created an extreme number of abortions for a Chinese social setting.

The policy relying on abortion only yielded temporary results, since a woman who had an abortion under the policy might soon become pregnant again. Its cost was high: financially, in terms of funding many abortions, in stress, because it forced people between the jaws of two conflicting sets of principles and then required them to act, and in administrative difficulty. Under this policy, only the people whose refusal to respond to the claims of the wider society was most adamant, determined, and wily, would be rewarded with a supernumerary child. The policy-makers raised the issue that repeated abortions were harmful to the health of women, signaling a change in the official attitude and the policy was discontinued. It was necessary to construct a new policy that would be exquisitely fair in equalizing the sacrifices, that would be effective in reducing population growth, and that would be within the capacity of local-level cadres to enforce.

In 1983, the state formulated a new policy for peasants, requiring those who had given birth to two children and were demonstrably at risk for having a third, to undergo sterilization. This policy was intended only for the rural areas, not for the cities, where the "one-child policy" was the rule. As one provincial-level leader explained, "There is no sterilization policy in the city, where people have only one child. We will never ask couples with one child to undergo sterilization, because that would prevent them from having another if their child died." The sterilization policy for peasants with two children was a state policy, and provinces were encouraged to adopt it, but it was not mandatory. Rather, provinces which adopted the policy would sum up their experiences and a mandatory policy would be formulated later. Guangdong province and four other densely populated provinces – Sichuan, Hebei, Shandong, and Henan – adopted the policy. Guangdong provincial leaders spelled out the meaning of the policy from their point of view in great detail. Peasant families could give birth to a second child if and only if the first was a girl, which would, it was felt, constitute a hardship in household based agriculture. But one son, or two children if the first was a girl, was, from the province's point of view, to be the limit. Exceptions were carefully described. A deformity or defect complete enough to make the child incapable of working in later life would permit the birth of another child to compensate for the incapacity. Families in debilitating occupations, such as mining or fishing, could have extra children. So could people in remote mountain areas or small islands, and minority peoples. A remarriage renewed the right to have children; a provincial leader said, "We must remember that the purpose of marriage is to have children." Children born in multiple births resulting from approved pregnancies were unquestionably legitimate exceptions to the ordinary limitations.

In effect, the policy rationed the right to have children. Because of this, it became important to prevent people from exceeding their ration. Sterilization was to be the means whereby this was to be ensured, and it was to be used in cases where the risk that a couple would exceed the ration was apparent. Thus, if a couple had two children already, and the wife became pregnant again, she was to have an abortion, and one member of the couple was to be sterilized. (If the wife was over 40, however, sterilization was not required, on the grounds that her fertility was almost over in any case.) If the couple had two children and were not using any contraceptive method, one of the couple was to be sterilized. If the couple had violated the four-year spacing rule by having two children since 1979, one of the couple was to be sterilized. Finally, if the couple used contraception, but the wife had had an abortion since 1979, indicating contraceptive failure, one of the couple was to be sterilized.

The decision to turn to sterilization as a method was the result of a long-term experience of repeated contraceptive failures. A provincial-level leader said, "In the countryside we've had a lesson. Contraception is not effective. The peasants are not used to condoms, the side effects of contraceptive drugs are strong, the rings and other I.U.D.s have many failures, and repeated abortions harm the health of women." In conjunction with the sterilization policy, there was a new propaganda emphasis on raising a "healthy superior child." This new emphasis marks an attempt to make an important shift in underlying attitudes: the shift from the expectation of large numbers of children, with the failure to thrive of one or another of them a matter to be endured, to the expectation of fewer children, each more important, and each to be nurtured with resources formerly spread thin.

The sterilization policy differed from previous policies in that it required a permanent rather than a temporary measure to be taken. It also differed from previous policies by requiring a measure that has extremely serious cultural implications. Traditional values attribute far more horrifying significance to sterilization than to abortion. (By comparison, in the United States at the present time, there is significant religious feeling that abortion is a wicked and immoral procedure, yet there is no comparable outcry urging the prevention of sterilization procedures on moral grounds.) According to these traditional values, the social worth of a person depends on the ability to work and the ability to carry on the family line. These abilities are believed to be linked, and men are believed to possess them to a higher degree than women. The assumption is made that people who are sterilized have their capacity to work permanently damaged, and this, as well as the loss of the capacity to reproduce, damages the meaning of their relationship to the family. Because work, reproduction, and the family are as one and inseparable, sterilization is understood as damaging all three. Sterilization is regarded as even more damaging to men's "greater" capacities than to women's "lesser" ones, and many people regard the idea of a vasectomy with horror. Tubal ligation for women is thought of as the less damaging alternative, so, faced with the choice, many women accept sterilization themselves, rather than letting their husbands be sterilized. It is a reasonable inference that this policy would not have been implemented, or even formulated, if the provincial leadership did not think of it as the only remaining possibility in a situation where the consequences of failing to act were worse than the consequences of acting.

The county level modified this policy in such a way as to permit more children. A county-level leader said, "Central policy is that, if you have a son first, you have to stop, but our county lets the peasants have a second child, even if the first child is a son." This decision freed 100 percent of peasant couples to have two children, instead of limiting 50 percent of them to one child; in so heavily populated a county the practical implications of this decision are great, and produce a much higher birth rate than if provincial-level policy were followed as formulated. But, a county-level cadre said, "While the upper levels were scolding us, we agreed to what they said, but when they had gone, we did what we thought was right." Nonetheless, the county level's liberalized policy was still painfully restrictive by peasant standards.

At the commune level, at a three-level meeting devoted to the topic, in May, 1983, the local cadres heard the policy explained, and found themselves confronted with the problem of implementing the sterilization of everybody who fell into the categories called the "four yardsticks." The four yardsticks measured couples who already had two children and defined which of them must now be sterilized. As at the provincial level, the commune required sterilization if the wife was pregnant again, if the couple was not using any form of contraception, if the second child had been born after an interval of less than four years, or if the wife had had an abortion since 1979. Couples who had used contraception effectively would not have to be sterilized, a powerful implicit incentive for future contraceptive use. In implementing this policy, the commune emphasized that the force of example was even more important than persuasion, and the local cadres were told that, if they fell into the categories, they had to be sterilized first. The women's leader of the brigade said, "When the cadres heard this, they couldn't understand it in their minds. They looked around at one another. They were told, 'If you don't take the lead in this drive, how can you get the peasants to follow you?'" Both of the brigade-level cadres from Zengbu who fell into the categories, underwent vasectomies. In its social context, this was undoubtedly impressive. Only when the vasectomies had taken place did the brigade present its own modified version of policy to the villagers.

Brigade policy respected the urgency of the cultural preference for a son by saying that couples with two daughters, who would otherwise have fallen into the four categories, were not required to be sterilized. This modification reduced by 25 percent the number of couples who would otherwise have fallen into the commune's category for required sterilization. There was a clear implication that later on, these couples could have a third child in trying for a son, and pay a fine. Brigade cadres felt that their ability to implement the policy at all hinged on this crucial provision, and that without it, they could not succeed in getting the villagers to comply. The brigade also announced that, since the four-year spacing rule had not previously been enforced, they would not sterilize couples who had violated it. Brigade cadres felt that the sterilization of couples who violated the four-year spacing rule would leave those couples unable to replace children who might not be viable; children born since 1979 were still too young to make it reasonable to assume that they would survive, it was argued. The argument shows that at the brigade level, people still lived in the expectation of high infant mortality. However, the brigade announced that it would enforce the four-year spacing rule in the future.

The villagers' reaction to the policy was predictably strong. One man commented, "We preferred abortion to sterilization, because then, if a child died, it could be replaced." Another man said, "I oppose it! You *must* have a son to carry on the family name. If you don't have a son, you won't have anyone to worship the dead parents' souls. [This in spite of the fact that ancestor worship was forbidden from 1949 to 1981.] It will cut the generations, there will be no ancestors. You raise sons, sons support you in your old age. It is impossible for daughters to take care of the aged, because they marry out. The men believe that the strength of the man is in his sperm. They fear the weakening of the body through sterilization. The men must go out to work. If the man dies, the family will be destroyed." A male cadre, speaking of his daughter-in-law's sterilization, said sadly, "It is easy to agree to the necessity for sterilization in an open meeting, but it becomes very hard when it is a member of your own family."

In order to make the situation as acceptable as possible, commune-level leaders hired more highly qualified doctors from the medical school in Guangzhou, so as to allay fears that the operations would not be competently performed. The brigade offered financial incentives to those who had the operations immediately. The incentive was 200 *yuan* ($71). There were 216 couples in the brigade who fell into the brigade's sterilization categories. In the two weeks following the announcement of the policy, 187 sterilizations, including 8 vasectomies, were performed. This took place in the second two weeks of May, 1983. The rest were to be sterilized in June, or, if they were ill, in September. In August, 1983, the brigade women's leader said, "At first they didn't understand. But no one refused the operation, and no one ran away. Their thinking changed. In the beginning, they shouted at us. Everyone was watching the main trend. They saw the others were doing it, so they got caught up." By using the force of example, explanations, incentives, the hiring of special doctors, and the momentum of social pressure, the leaders succeeded in implementing their version of the policy.

Over the short span of the four years between 1979 and 1983, Zengbu brigade had seen four birth planning policies: first, the refusal to subsidize supernumerary children, second, the imposition of fines, third, the policy relying on abortion, and fourth, the policy relying on sterilization. These policies have evolved from partial subsidization of traditional values toward a comparatively active and painful rejection of these values. Yet by December, 1984, there were signs that policy was retrenching. Provincial-level officials had been told that there should be more emphasis on research, and less on the practicalities of implementation and enforcement. Some leaders had lost their jobs in the wake of the 1983 campaign.

As of June, 1985, brigade policy was as follows. There was a four-year birth spacing rule, and a pregnancy which violated this rule would be ended by abortion. Couples were permitted to have two children, including at least one son. If a couple with two children, at least one of which was a son, used birth control successfully, sterilization was not required. If the wife became pregnant again, however, the pregnancy would be ended, and either the husband or the wife would have to be sterilized. Any sterilized person would receive a 300 *yuan* ($111) bonus from the brigade. Couples with two daughters could try again for a son if they were willing to pay a 150 *yuan* ($55) fine. If the third child was also a daughter, the couple could try once more, on the payment of another 150 *yuan*, but the husband had to agree to have a vasectomy before the fourth child was born.

This is a system which respects the urgency of China's population crisis by rationing the right to have children. The rationing is enforced by requiring abortion or sterilization when the rationing regulations are violated. It is a system which respects the urgency of the peasant family's preference for sons to a remarkable degree – a frightening degree, in fact, when the dangers posed by population growth are considered. It does not respect the essentially un-Chinese idea that the individual has exclusive rights over his or her reproductive capacity. Instead it is a system in which a birth is seen as appropriately the concern of the state and the concern of the family; because a birth is important to these levels, its importance to the individual is superseded. It is a culturally specific Chinese way of understanding the meaning of birth, and birth prevention, and in order to be understood at all, it must be understood in its own terms.

The conflict continues between the values of familism and necessities of a nation burdened with the most overwhelming population on the face of the earth. There is a recognition that the cherished values embodied in familism are agents of destruction to China as a whole. Yet it is overwhelmingly difficult to reject cherished beliefs, even in the certain knowledge that such a rejection is the only possible alternative. If the extraordinary pronatalism of traditional culture is overcome, then what it means to have a child in China, and to be a child in China, will change, yielding dramatic new cultural and social forms. There will be the resources to provide decently for those who are born, and to care for them so that they can indeed be healthy and superior. If the extraordinary Chinese pronatalism is not modified, future generations of Chinese children will suffer increasingly until they are destroyed by the weight of their own numbers.

# 12

# Lineage and collective: structure and praxis

The controversy between the relative explanatory merits of structuralism and Marxism is one of the most important theoretical controversies in anthropology. Are human affairs more importantly determined by productive action, and its relationship to an economic matrix, as the Marxists would have it, or are human affairs more importantly determined by the structures of the symbolic organization of experience, as the structuralists believe? Does the way people think determine what they do, or does what they do determine how they think? In his book *Culture and Practical Reason*, Marshall Sahlins argues that structuralism is superior to Marxism for the understanding of history. "What structuralism seems to offer," he writes, is "a conception of the continuity in history," and an explanation for the "seeming resistance of [cultures] to experience in the world." He writes of the "immunity of the existing order to historical contingency" and the "domination of practical action by cultural conception" (1976, pp. 3–4, 18).

This debate provides a particularly apt setting for the analysis of the continuity in basic kinship structures which is apparent in the social lives of the peasants of Zengbu over the past three revolutionary decades. For the facts of the matter are that 35 years of living and working in socialist collectives have failed to change the deep kinship structures of the villagers. Is this continuity explainable simply by the enormous strength and absorptive power of the fundamental ideas of Chinese civilization, demonstrated repeatedly over the centuries – as the structuralists would have it? Or can this continuity be explained by the use of Marxist arguments: that the persistence has a material basis, and is the result of a failure to change the basic economic structures and relationships of production which produce and sustain the social order?

This small cluster of villages in the southeastern Chinese countryside is an ideal setting for the testing of this important theoretical question, because the protagonists – the deep structure of Chinese civilization on the one hand, and the material constraints of Chinese peasant social life on the other – are so evenly matched. On the one hand, the kinship institutions of the southeastern Chinese peasants (Baker 1968, Freedman 1958, J. M. Potter 1968, 1970, J. L. Watson 1975, R. S. Watson 1985) are among the strongest, most resilient, and longest-lived structures in the history of human society. On the other hand, the revolutionary plan to change the peasantry through praxis, by setting them to live and work in socialist collectives under the leadership of party cadres, represents one of the most conscious and sustained efforts to change a social formation by changing the material basis of social life that has ever been made.

The basic kinship structure in the old society was the localized corporate landowning patrilineage (see chapter 1). As Freedman (1958, p. 127) and J. M. Potter (1970, pp. 129–138) have pointed out, corporate landed property was the essence of the Chinese lineage. As a collectivity, the lineage had as a primary goal the effective management of its common property. To this end, it regulated its own internal affairs, made decisions for the group as a whole, maintained its own internal law and order, and defended its interests against hostile lineages, by military means if necessary. The lineage did not, however, serve an organizational function in directing the social relationships of production. The peasant household, rather than the lineage acting as a whole, was the basic unit for the social organization of production. Traditionally then, Cantonese peasants did not have a "lineage mode of production," of the type formulated by Claude Meillassoux (1964) and discussed by other French anthropologists (see Terray 1972, pp. 95ff.). Rather, the lineage was a *rentier* group which leased out its land and other productive resources to the highest bidders, whether they were lineage members or not.

Beneath the surface manifestations of the southern Chinese lineage lies a pattern of general and abstract structural principles that form the ideational basis for this traditional kinship order. This traditional deep structure is formed by two sets of dualities acting upon one another, in a configuration that is Levi-Straussian in its form and symmetry. Indeed, the first duality is composed of the opposition between the male and the female. Historically, the opposition between male and female was symbolically reflected in every facet of Chinese culture – kinship, economics, politics, religion, and even in the differing definitions of self of men and women. The human significance of a man was profound and fundamental. The human significance of a woman was different; never truly a lineage member or entirely an outsider, a woman was liminal, dangerous, and necessary, since relationships between men and groups of men were only possible through the symbolic mediation of women. It was as if men were more truly human, and women were less so, being merely mediators between the real human beings.

The second duality is the opposition between hierarchical order and competitive struggle in social organization (Freedman 1958, p. 77; R. S. Watson 1985). The lineage was a structure of inherent order based on age and seniority. This order was supported by an ideology which stressed the value of lineage solidarity, rather than continuing competition between equals. However, competition between equals was as powerful a nexus of social action in the lineage as hierarchical structure; it was a critical and pervasive dimension of social life. Not only did men compete constantly with their lineage brothers, lineage branches competed with other lineage branches. It was assumed that every lineage member would use and exploit others for his own advantage. It was assumed, and borne out by experience, that powerful lineage members would do their best to use the collectively-owned ancestral property for their own personal benefit. Interpersonal relations were marked by wariness, suspicion, and guardedness. Successful lineage members flaunted their wealth and status in an effort to shame other lineage members by comparison. Yet the successful were envied and resented by the less successful on moral grounds, since success was believed to be due, not only to the appropriation of more than one's rightful share of the limited good available to lineage members, but also to the exploitation of other members of the same group.

The opposition between formal hierarchy and competitive struggle was reflected on a duplicated pattern of leadership within the lineage (Freedman 1958, p.67). On one hand were the village elders, leaders who had been chosen on the basis of formal kinship criteria such as age and seniority. These were often poor and inconsequential men. On the other were the effective leaders, who had achieved their positions by competitive success.

The allocation of rights to collective property reflected the same opposition. The ancestral estates were divided into two kinds of property. Some ancestral property was owned by lineage branches, and rights to it were allocated on a *per stirpes* basis reflecting the inherent hierarchical order. Other ancestral property was owned by all male members equally, on a per capita basis (see J.M. Potter 1968, pp.108–117). This opposition was elaborated in the arrangements made for using and profiting from such collective property as was owned by the lineage as a whole, or by a lineage subbranch. There was a strongly held idea that a lineage member should not be able to use collective property for individual profit, or to enhance his private competitive advantage. The lineage was most reluctant to permit strong members to consolidate their competitive advantages by the use of collectively owned property. As a result, when lineages leased collective property to the highest bidder, they did not restrict bidding to their own members, but leased to the highest bidder, regardless of lineage membership. The implication is that it would be preferable to see an outsider profit from the use of lineage resources, rather than to provoke envy within the lineage by letting one member profit from the private use of common resources while other lineage members could not.

Thus, the hierarchical solidarity of the lineage, and the competitive struggle within the lineage stood in opposition to one another as poles of a cultural dialectic; with dialectical logic, the expression of these conflicting values was tolerated within a single institution. The process was sustained partly by the situational application of the different principles: lineage solidarity had its place when there were outside threats to the group as a whole. In the absence of an outside threat internal competition thrived and flourished, producing segmentation.

The structural oppositions of the lineage, and their practical consequences, were mediated both symbolically and in social interaction by women. Women sustained the illusion that competitive brothers were actually solidary by serving as the social scapegoats for conflict: when brothers fell out, the disharmony was attributed to their quarrelsome wives. Women, not men, mediated between the generations at the family ancestral altar. Wedding arrangements were always the province of women. It was women who represented their families by attending such ceremonies as weddings and funerals, the socially accepted occasions at which kinship ties were validated and strengthened.

Marriage was the symbolic vehicle of expression for the social meaning of women. Marrying a "lineage sister" was incest, a danger from within the lineage. Marrying out preserved the intrinsic hierarchic structural logic of the lineage, as opposed to affirming its internal competitiveness. Wives had to be obtained from competing lineages. Thus, they represented a danger from outside; many aspects of the marriage ceremony reflect this belief. Women, by marrying from one lineage into another, mediated between these opposing male-centered groups. Intermarriage established a network of affinal ties that could help to link families from lineages that were in all other respects competitors and rivals. The importance of the mediating role of women was made apparent in instances where hostilities broke out between lineages. In such circumstances, the lineages ceased to intermarry, thus making any kind of social intercourse between them impossible. In the absence of inter-marriage, hostilities or avoidance were the only choices (see chapter 10).

It is paradoxical that affinal kinship ties through women, although not recognized or valued in the formal lineage ideology of the society, were among the most valuable ties that a family could have. When in need of capital to start a business, a loan to help build a house, or financial help in order to survive an illness, a family would often turn to its affinal relatives. Lineage brothers, competitively minded, would often be less willing to help than relatives by marriage, who, being members of other lineages, were theoreti-cally more hostile. Through the mediation of women, members of hostile lineages were turned into allies; the relationships involved were not subject to continual competitive challenge but transcended the internal competitive struggles within the lineage. In traditional conflict resolution, the mother's brother, as a representative of the mother's lineage, was seen as the appropriate mediator between competitive brothers. (Cf. however, R.S. Watson's somewhat different interpretation, 1985, pp. 117–136.)

Since women simultaneously mediated between groups of men and embodied threats to their existence, their structural ambivalence was symbolically represented in the belief that they were ritually dangerous to men. Menstruation was one symbolic focus of this fear. Sexual intercourse was another. It was traditionally believed that the vital *yang* essence, the source of a man's virility and strength, was concentrated in the sperm, and drained away and absorbed by the female during intercourse. Men were advised to avoid the emission of semen in order to conserve their strength. Thus women were believed to weaken men in the very process of serving the continuity of the male line.

Starting with Liberation, the traditional lineage structure was systematically attacked. Lineages were defined as feudal relics: the lineages were criticized for being intrinsically exploitative because of their control of property, the harm done by their traditional hierarchy, their subjugation of women and of the slave caste, and the misery caused by the economic results of competition within the lineage structure, where the rich and powerful dominated the weak and helpless. The Revolution located harmfulness both in the traditional hierarchical structure and in the competitive struggles which took place within the structure, and the lineage itself was seen as the source of these evils. New structures were to replace the old: collectives were to replace the lineage. Collective ownership was to ensure economic and social equality, and to eliminate the exploitative class nature of the lineage. Equality was to be established between men and women. Loyalty to the collective and to the state were to replace former kinship and lineage loyalties. Competition was to be replaced by cooperation, and labor was to be fairly rewarded. It is plain that the new structures were an attempt to create a purer social order, which would more fittingly embody deeply held values.

During the 30 years between Liberation and the end of the Maoist era, the cadres understood their political work as the substitution of a new social, economic and kinship order, for the old lineages. The process of living and working in socialist collectives was to modify the peasants' most deeply held values and ideas, and the very structure of their thinking would be revised and re-established on a new basis. What, then, were the results of these three decades of conscious efforts at change? To what extent did revolutionary collectivist praxis eliminate the old lineage structures?

In discussing lineage continuity and change in Zengbu (and in the rest of southeastern China) it is important to distinguish the surface features of the old kinship institutions from the more fundamental deep structures we have been discussing. Many of the surface features of the old lineage system *were* changed by three decades of revolutionary praxis. Traditional marriage practices, with their attendant social abuses, were prohibited by law. The position of women was strengthened, and the status of women improved, by the public recognition of their labor and its reward in workpoints, and by the Women's Federation, which acted as their organizational advocate. Women could participate in political life at least to a small extent, as cadres. The traditional economic base of the old lineage and lineage subbranches was destroyed at the time of land reform, with the confiscation of the ancestral estates. Lineage branches were much reduced in importance when close relatives were distributed into different production teams (see chapter 5). The new teams were not the same as the old lineage segments. The landowning elite, which had dominated the old lineages, was replaced by new party cadres. The old ethic of lineage solidarity was replaced by the new ethic that cadres must work for the state and for the common good of the group as a whole; cadres who favored their own families were criticized without mercy. (Many cadres describe testing times when they were required to demonstrate publicly that they would support the public good in direct opposition to, for example, the interests of a brother.) The rituals that affirmed the lineages were no longer carried out. The ancestral ceremonies were proscribed, and the ancestral halls turned into private dwellings, schools, or warehouses. The stone and concrete faces of the graves were removed.

Substantive changes were made in the organizational form of the economy. The substitution of the collective organization of production for the old household mode was essentially new. By the mid-fifties each lineage village of Zengbu had been redefined as a noncompetitive community, and a nonhierarchical one as well, since the hierarchy of the old lineages had been replaced by the purified social order of the new leadership. On the surface, the face of collectivist, universalistic, and egalitarian rural China was qualitatively different from the old lineage and class-based society that had existed before Liberation.

Despite these surface changes ("shallow structures"), however, a closer inspection reveals remarkable continuity in the deep structures of the old society.

In fact, the lineage had survived the radical revolutionary changes of land reform and collectivization with its core structure – a group of co-resident, property-owning kinsmen, related through the male line – intact. The basis of each of Zengbu's higher-level socialist cooperatives, as created in the mid-fifties, was a single lineage village. Of the 45 natural villages in Chashan commune, almost all were single lineage villages or segments of single multi-village lineages; there were very few mixed surname villages in the commune. During the three-level (team, brigade, and commune) system, which superseded the cooperatives and lasted from 1961 to 1981, the outlines of the newly established brigades tended to replicate the outlines of former traditional lineages. Whether the lineage had been limited to one village or spread over several, the brigade was cut to the same pattern (see chapter 6).

Lineage villages still retained separate identity, even when merged into a single brigade with other lineage villages, as in Zengbu. Villages had their own cadres, and controlled some collective property over the 20 years from 1962 to 1980, in spite of the fact that the village was at that time a structural "null level" (see chapter 8), rather than being of administrative significance. During this period the villages fluctuated in importance as structures, in relationship to the brigade. In 1979, Secretary Lu used the phrase "the three divisions and the four amalgamations," to describe the history of the comparative importance of the village level in relation to the brigade level in Zengbu. In the mid-seventies, village property was formally placed under the control of the brigade, but even then each village retained its own cadre representatives. This comparatively complete subordination of the village level to the brigade level in Zengbu lasted only five years, from 1975 to 1980.

Then, the administrative reforms of 1983 and 1984 re-emphasized the importance of the natural village as a unit in China's rural administrative structure. As a result, in 1984, the fourth amalgamation in Zengbu was ended by the fourth division, as the villages became structurally significant, and the brigade a "null level." Each village presently has an elected citizens' committee. Villages hold a small amount of property derived from the teams, which yields a modest income used by village officials to build and maintain roads and to manage irrigation water. Day-to-day affairs are administered by the village, and not by the *xiang* (as the brigade is now called) or team levels, as was formerly the case. Most of the local enterprises (including two of the Hong Kong processing factories) are owned and managed collectively by individual villages. Land, orchards, and fishponds are still owned by the teams, but this property is managed for the teams by village officials. Each village has a village accountant and a village cashier who handle the financial affairs of the production teams within the village. (Formerly these were team or brigade matters.) Village accountants lease the collective property of each team to the highest bidder, collect the income, pay team expenses, and distribute the remainder of each team's income (a few hundred *yuan* a year per household usually) to the separate households of each team. Village cashiers are in charge of the funds of all the teams in their village, but they make up the accounts of each team's finances separately.

So, the village level of organization is clearly re-emerging in Zengbu as the most significant local social unit. Since the natural villages in this part of China consist either of a single lineage or a localized segment of a multivillage lineage, the new administrative arrangements, by reinforcing the village, have reinforced the traditional lineage structure as well. The old lineage village community now has an economic base (comparable to the property of the old central ancestral halls) and an administrative apparatus (comparable to the old elders and managers) and is once again becoming a key unit in local society. Thus, both lineages and important village-level lineage branches are now strengthened.

The restored social and economic importance of the lineage village is being

9. Rebuilt Sandhill ancestral tomb, 1985

expressed in the revived interest in lineage ancestral cults (worship at the ancestral halls and tombs) and in the dragon-boat races – the forms of traditional cultural symbolism associated with the lineage. In 1984, each of the three lineage villages of Zengbu rebuilt the ancestral tombs of their founding ancestors. Men of each lineage now carry out yearly ceremonies of ancestor worship at the tombs.

The activities in Pondside village provide a specific example of the new practices. Pondside village men, under the direction of their village's citizens' committee, are refurbishing the central ancestral hall of the Pondside Liu lineage. For three decades, this ancestral hall had been used both as a warehouse for storing agricultural implements and as the site of the village's collectively-owned sugarcane-crushing mill and sugar-making operations. The rear of the hall had been torn down in the mid-seventies to obtain bricks for building the brigade headquarters, and it is now being rebuilt. The Lius of Pondside have either "found" their old lineage genealogy, or have reconstructed it. They are planning to make new ancestral tablets for the main altar of the hall, in order to replace those which were burned by the Red Guards during the Cultural Revolution.

The renewed importance and significance of the lineage is also displayed in the dragon-boat racing. Before Liberation, competitive dragon-boat racing between the men of local lineages was an important symbolic form that

10. Zengbu lineage dragon boat, 1985, showing the levee built along the river just after the Great Leap forward

expressed inter-lineage hostility and competitiveness using ritual means. The racing of dragon boats began again in Chashan in the summer of 1984. Every sizable lineage village in the adjacent Dongguan countryside, including Pondside's Liu lineage, Sandhill's Liu lineage, and Lu's Home's Lu lineage, launched a dragon boat. The long slender dragon boats are constructed from wooden planks lashed together with bamboo strips and thongs. In addition to the oarsmen, each boat carries a coxswain, a gong-beater, and a drum-beater, who beat time vigorously for the rowers while jumping rhythmically up and down on wooden platforms placed at the front and middle of the boat.

Each dragon boat has a colorfully-painted carved dragon head, with wisps of grass sticking out of its mouth ("because dragons eat grass") as its prow. The dragon boats are traditionally buried in mud near each village temple to protect them against termites. Each year, before the dragon-boat festival, the boats are exhumed and an old Taoist priest is hired to recall the soul of the dragon and animate the boat once again for the races. In 1984 and 1985, the Zengbu lineages, which lacked their own boats, had to rent or buy boats from villages near Dongguan which had kept the craft alive.

Spirit tablets, representing the altar deities of the newly constructed Chashan village temples, are placed on the dragon boats. The spirit tablets are proxies for the village deities, and represent the lineage village as a whole. The oars of the boats have black and white *yin* and *yang* symbols painted on them to increase their magical power. The crew members of each dragon boat are attired in colorful matching costumes. A brightly colored pennant, with the name of the lineage village inscribed on it, is flown from each boat. During the race, men from each boat throw white paper money into the water as offerings to the spirits. Spectators fire off long strings of noisy firecrackers, frightening away marauding ghosts and creating a heightened and dramatic atmosphere.

The dragon boats are explicitly said to represent the strength, potency, and power of the men of each lineage (the phallic symbolism of the long, narrow dragon boat is obvious), and the competitions are serious. In Geertz's terms (1973, p. 412), the races are, like the Balinese cockfights, "deep" cultural play. A winning boat means that the men of a lineage can take pride in the open display of their strength and discipline; a losing boat embarrasses and shames them. The humiliated men of a boat that performs slowly and badly (such as the boat of Lu's Home village in 1985) are greeted at the finish with laughter, derision, and the loudly-whispered suggestion that it would not be worth a woman's while to marry into so weakly a lineage.

The dragon boats are exclusively a male preserve. Women are not allowed on the dragon boats, because it is believed that a woman's menstrual blood would pollute the boat and rob the men of the strength to move it; the notion that the ritual impurity of females can pollute male spheres of activity has retained its significance. The return of the old male-centered lineage rituals are a revived symbolic expression both of the importance of the men and of the inferiority and separateness of the women of Zengbu. As obverse sides of the same symbolic coin, both of these beliefs are returning simultaneously.

The intensity that indicates the "deep play" of dragon-boat racing is expressed in the level of conflict and controversy aroused by the contest. The first dragon-boat races in Chashan district since Liberation were held in 1984 on the Hanxi river between Zengbu and Chashan. The Sandhill village boat won the competition, narrowly defeating the boat from Xiagang village. But, as was frequently the case in the old days, the race ended in controversy. Xiagang claimed that Sandhill had committed a foul: the paddles of the Sandhill boat had passed outside the ropes marking the boundaries of the course. Xiagang demanded that the Sandhill boat be disqualified and that the Xiagang boat should be declared the winner. On a technicality, the party cadre judges ruled in Sandhill's favor. They said that the Sandhill boat's *paddles* had indeed passed outside the boundary, but that Sandhill was still the winner because the *bodies* of the Sandhill rowers had not passed outside the boundary. The members of Xiagang's losing crew, and spectators from that lineage (who had lost a great deal of money gambling on the race) were furious at this decision. Xiagang villagers began to fight with Sandhill villagers. A pitched battle between the men of the two lineages was averted only because the district cadres were there to break it up. The next day, however, a brawl broke out between women of the two villages who encountered each other in the Chashan market. District security personnel arrested the women and brought them to the district headquarters, where the party secretary managed to calm them down. So concerned were the district government and district party officials at the reappearance of these violent lineage rivalries, that they banned dragon-boat competition in Chashan in the summer of 1985, substituting an exhibition race instead. The exhibition went smoothly, but the spectators were bored because there was no competition and no betting; in their eyes, the play was too "shallow" to be of interest.

However, competitive dragon-boat races were held that year at higher levels. The boats of 200 lineage villages competed in two days of elimination heats that led up to a final race on the river outside of Shilong on July 6, 1985. Cash prizes, roast pigs (called "golden pigs"), and commemorative banners (like the banners awarded to Zengbu brigade by the state for their heroic accomplishments in building levees in the early sixties), were awarded to the winning boats. The winners took their pigs and banners back as offerings to their ancestors and to their village deities, as they had done in the pre-Liberation lineage competitions.

A fascinating twist to the revival of the dragon-boat competition is that the local cadres are the ones who take the lead in financing, organizing, and racing the boats, and they are the coxswains. In taking control of these ceremonies and symbolic activities, rather than leaving them to ceremonial leaders, the cadres are asserting the party's control over the re-emergent traditional cultural ritual forms. Both the Communist party and traditional cultural forms have symbolic import, and the assumption is that both should be affirmed in the dragon-boat races.

The continuance of the lineage village signifies the persistence of a fundamental structural idea about the relationship between people and property: that collective property should be owned by groups of patrilineally related men residing in the same community. Traditional kinship was, in important respects, an expression of this idea of property. As Edmund Leach wrote of Ceylon, "Kinship is not 'a thing in itself.' The concepts of descent and affinity are expressions of property relations which endure through time ... A particular descent system simply reflects the total process of property succession as effected by the total pattern of inheritance and marriage" (1961, p.9). The descent system may reflect other things as well, but the relationship between descent group and property is a critical one.

So the basic structural idea that property should be owned corporately by groups of co-resident, patrilineally related men, has persisted unchallenged, and has been the basis for all the collectives implemented in China since Liberation. Whatever the form of the collective – whether team, brigade, higher-level cooperative, commune, or, now, lineage village – at its core was a group of patrilineally related men owning and managing property. The lowest administrative and accounting economic units continued to merge with traditional patrilineal kin groups (the lineages or lineage branches). The collectives continued to be structured on the implicit model of traditional kinship groups. Thus, the deep structure of the old lineages was perpetuated. It could even be argued that the solidarity of the traditional lineage village was actually reinforced during the Maoist collectivist period. With the elimination of private property, all property was owned collectively by the group, whereas before Liberation, most property was in the hands of lineage subbranches or families. Furthermore, under Maoism, methods of work assignment and reward for labor tended to reduce the possibilities for competition within the collective unit, in the traditional style, virtually to nil. This strengthened the group as a whole, at the expense of separate segments; it reinforced the ethic of solidarity at the expense of the ethic of competitiveness. Small, weak, tenant lineages, like Zengbu's Upper Stream village, had formerly been lineages in name only, since they lacked a property base of ancestral estates. Such villages were strengthened when they gained a collective property base under the rubric of being redefined as a production team. Such villages, after reform, were more like the old rich lineages than they had been before.

The rules of patrilineal inheritance and patrilocal residence were unconsciously transferred from traditional kinship group to new collective. When these rules are challenged, the response tends to be in terms of the moral rightness and economic advantage of traditional practices – an equally unthought-through reaction in support of structural form. Decisions to maintain patrilocal residence and patrilineal inheritance of the rights to collective property are still being made. For example, the Women's Federation of Dongguan county, in 1979, with the backing of the state, was attempting to promote the idea that a newly married man could go to live with his wife, in her collective. This would break down the patrilineal patterns of residence and inheritance that, as the Women's Federation realized, were the foundation of the old lineage order. (Such reforms are more easily implemented in urban areas, where residence is subject to other factors – the work unit of the couple, or the availability of housing – rather than being solely controlled by the concept of patrilocal marriage in the context of a lineage village.) Secretary Lu and the male party committee members of Zengbu objected to the introduction of matrilocal residence patterns on the ground that they did not want to share their limited property with in-marrying men. On the contrary, they stipulated that all women had to leave the collective within three months of their marriage, after which time their rice rations would be discontinued. The property interests of the collective, as understood by the core group of village men, thus acted to prevent the reform of the old residence and property rules. Membership in the collective and rights to collective property continued to be passed down from males through males, just as they were in the old lineages. Women were not considered to be full members of their collective of birth and had no rights to its property. They married out and became members of their husbands' collective units. The retention of the old structural idea that all property should be in the hands of co-residential groups of patrilineally related males, whose wives were to marry in, fostered structural conservatism: the residential solidarity of male lineage members was preserved, and so were their property interests. This reinforced the old structure.

The maintenance of male property rights also prevented women from exercising their legally guaranteed right of divorce. In the new society as in the old society, women fell between two stools, structurally speaking. They literally had nowhere to go after a divorce. Before Liberation a divorced woman (in the few cases when divorce occurred) could not remain in her husband's lineage, nor could she return to her father's lineage; her tablets could not be placed upon her father's ancestral altar. After collectivization, a divorced woman was not allowed to stay in her estranged husband's collective. The men of her father's collective (her natal collective) did not want an unattached woman back, because she would be a drain on their resources and a burden to support in her old age. The right to divorce, if it could have been fully exercised, would have given women a far greater degree of independence and freedom of action. But in spite of the fact that the right existed in theory, the social structure made it a practical impossibility.

Another striking continuity in form between the old lineage and the new collective was to be seen in the relationship between the old lineage genealogies and the new household registers. The household registers of the brigade, like the old lineage genealogies, were legal documents that legitimized the membership and property rights of the men entered into them. Only those who were bona fide members of a lineage by birth or adoption had rights to the collective property. As in the clan registers of the old lineages, the names of males who left the group were crossed out of the brigade's household registers; and women's names were also crossed out upon marriage and re-entered in the books of their husbands' units.

Another element of continuity was the persistence of the male-headed household, and not the individual, as the basic social unit. This was a continuation of the traditional Chinese practice. Land was distributed on a per capita basis during land reform, but in Zengbu it was put in the hands of male heads of household who proceeded to treat it as family property, to be inherited, in the old way, by males only. Thus the social position of women was never strengthened or reinforced by the separate ownership of property. The structural assumptions embodied in the male-controlled household – which persisted as the basic unit in all the later collectives – continued to slow efforts to improve the position of women. Although workpoints were earned by women in their own right, and the workpoint earnings of every individual were publicly posted on the walls of the production team headquarters, the actual earnings of all family members at the end of the year were given to the heads of household, almost invariably men. This practice prevented women and young people from gaining the economic independence that would have come from controlling their own earnings. The male household-head's social position, status, and authority was maintained under the collective system by preserving his power over the earnings of his family members. Although, during the collective period, the family no longer served its former functions as a property-owning unit (except where the ownership of houses was concerned) or as a unit for the social organization of production, it remained an integral economic unit under the financial control of a male head, and economic power reinforced the social authority of the male head of household.

The inferior economic and social position of women was also sustained by the cultural presuppositions underlying the systems of labor reward used by the collectives. No matter what the mode of payment – women's work was usually classified as less difficult and less important than men's, and women were usually paid less, no matter what the intrinsic nature of the work they performed. The leading cadres of the Woman's Federation of Dongguan county were well aware of this form of discrimination. They told a story of a man who objected publicly to granting women so many workpoints for carrying mud out of an excavation for a fishpond. The women challenged him to prove his point by showing that he could do it faster and better. Picking up his carrying pole, he set to, only to fall exhausted a short time later. He agreed that the women deserved the number of workpoints awarded them. Unfortunately, such discriminatory assumptions were so much a part of the familiar furniture of the male cadres' minds that they were not often challenged, and still less often came to such a satisfactory conclusion for the women. And women themselves tended to acquiesce in the idea that men's work was in reality harder and more valuable than women's work. The brigade cadre in charge of matters concerning women, whose concern for affirming the value of women was central to her life, told us that it was only right that men be paid more for such man's work as plowing, since it was actually and intrinsically harder and more valuable than any work women could do. Women would not be offered the opportunity to plow.

Another important factor impinging on women's ability to earn was that their families retained the right to requisition them for child care and other household tasks. But in spite of these limitations on their earning power imposed by the social structure, the workpoint data for Zengbu show that under the collectives women were actually earning at an extraordinary level (see chapter 5). The average Zengbu woman, at the age of 35, earned almost 5,000 workpoints, more than the highest average earnings of men at any age. Unfortunately, the higher earning power of women lasted only two or three years, at which point child care obligations became overwhelming and women's earnings began to decline. The traditional symbolic structures, which embodied ideas about the proper relation between men and women continued to resist economic praxis as a force for change.

It is clear, then, that during the collectivist period, roughly from the mid-1950s to 1981, the deep core structure of the lineage institutions of Zengbu remained unchanged, because of the persistence of the ownership of collective property by co-resident men. This form of property ownership negated concentrated attempts to change rural society through socialist praxis; socialist praxis had not acted to alter property relations fundamentally enough. The deep structure of the lineage continued, not simply because of a persistence of structural ideas in people's minds but because these ideas corresponded to the materialist interests of the dominant men who designed and ran the collectives.

During the post-Mao period there has been so clear a return to traditional kinship structures that the significance of these structures is affirmed, and it is apparent that socialist praxis, although based on reform, was not based on reform sufficiently fundamental to produce the significant changes that were its goal. The post-Mao period is characterized by a shift to forms of peasant social and economic structure which resemble the traditional Chinese peasant lineage structures at a clear and overt level, as well as at a more profound one.

The basic post-Mao change is to the new production responsibility system and away from the collective mode of production. Under the collectives, the team members worked their fields as individuals under the supervision of team cadres. The household responsibility system is a household mode of production, in which households work their own allotted share of land. The obligation to labor is derived from family membership rather than team membership, and the organizational decisions belong to the head of house-hold rather than to the team leader. The peasants have been allowed to retain their household land allotments for a period of 15 years. Although the ultimate ownership of land will remain collective (see chapter 17), rights to the use of land allotments are now being inherited by sons, following the old patrilineal inheritance rules.

These revived elements of the household mode of production reinforce traditional family roles. The old status distinction between men's work outside the home and the less highly regarded women's work within the home and in the family's fields has been reaffirmed. The inevitable result of this change in the method of allocating work is to lower the status of women remaining at home. The gains made when women's work and earnings were publicly recognized under the collective system are vitiated. However, there are new opportunities to work outside the home that were not available under the collective system, and women who work outside the home are in a somewhat stronger position than women whose labor is controlled by the head of household. Many young women are employed in the rural industrial factories now operating by the hundreds in Zengbu and the coastal regions of China proper. Since they receive their payment in cash and in person, rather than in workpoints paid out to the head of household, they have more financial autonomy now than they had during the Maoist period, and are able to retain part of their earnings (see chapter 16).

Social ties formally based on membership in the collective had never superseded ties of affinal and consanguineal kinship. Collective forms were changed frequently and the forms taken by the various collectives were not stable throughout the Maoist period. The membership of a collective fluctuated as it shifted in form. The relative stability of team membership from the mid-1960s to 1980 did lead to an increased social importance of the team in some respects: for example, when team leaders presented wreaths on behalf of the team at the funeral of a team member. However, ties with fellow team members, although not insignificant, never became as crucial to the peasants as ties with close kinsmen and relatives.

With the return to the household mode of production has come a dramatic re-emergence and increase in the importance of patrilineal and affinal kinship ties. Closely related families of brothers and first cousins (the core group of old agnatic kinsmen) make a point of drawing their allotments of production responsibility land jointly from their teams. This is so that these families may conveniently assist one another in field agriculture, especially at transplanting and harvesting. Members of such groups also share out the use of this land among themselves, rather than adhering rigidly to the formal distribution. The core group of close patrilineal kinsmen has now replaced the collective as the major group larger than the household in the organization of agricultural production.

Affinal ties are also being strengthened. As new opportunities to go into business have arisen in the economy, there has been an increased demand for capital to exploit these opportunities. Many families are drawing upon their relatives by marriage, in the countryside and abroad, for capital loans. The recent elaboration of wedding banquets represents a new effort to strengthen these wide-ranging kinship ties by ritual means.

The implementation of the production responsibility system, with its collective ownership and private management of the means of production, is a move towards an arrangement which resembles the handling of property and production under the pre-revolutionary lineages. Having allotted their land and other productive resources to individual households, the collectives now remain as *rentier* units. They lease out their remaining collective property – fishponds, orchards, and small rural industries – to the highest bidder, whether the bidder is a member of the cooperative or an outsider. The rental income is divided among the member households at the end of the year. This is exactly how collective property was managed under the old lineage. Also, as before, villages blessed with valuable property will probably remain strong and stable cooperatives. However, poorer lineages, such as those in mountainous areas, which have little common property remaining to be leased out after the agricultural land has been allotted to the households, will be weaker, with less solidarity. Corporate property reinforces lineage solidarity, just as it did before Liberation.

The previous restrictions on economic activity outside the framework of the collective no longer apply, and recent changes allow the peasants to pursue their own economic interests separately, as they did before Liberation. The emerging entrepreneurial economy has already made it possible for some peasant households to become wealthy. Yet the vast majority, albeit better off than they were during the Maoist period, are poor in comparison with the newly wealthy. This is producing structural differentiation within the lineage, and with it a return to the inequalities and associated social tensions that characterized the old socially differentiated lineages, with their continual competitive struggles. The desire to advance in wealth and social status, traditionally the driving force for a highly competitive rural society, is once more being allowed expression after three decades of suppression. The dialectical tensions between ideas of valid pre-existent ordered relationships and the hierarchical differentiation of families have reappeared.

So, although there have been changes in the surface features of the kinship institutions of rural southeastern China over the past 35 years, the deep structural patterns have exhibited amazing persistence, a persistence which was never fundamentally attacked, and which is likely to be further reinforced by present policy. It remains to assess these data, and to understand their significance for clarifying the theoretical dispute between structuralism and Marxism. From the structuralist point of view, the data demonstrate the power of structure – in this case Chinese kinship structure – to resist the sustained attacks of revolutionary praxis. In spite of land reform, collectivization, the Great Leap Forward, the communes, and the Cultural Revolution, the old structures persisted. Plainly, cultural ideas about the proper structuring of social life are amazingly tenacious in the face of countervailing historical events. The tremendous "cunning of structure" (to modify a phrase from Hegel) in preserving its own patterns, is most impressive. Revolutionary praxis was never able to confront structure in rural China in a pure and undistorted form. Instead, the new socialist collective forms were subtly remolded in a Chinese way by Chinese minds which were saturated with the deep structural ideas of their own culture. So pervasive were these old ideas about the proper relation between men and women, people and property, and between patterns of residence, kinship, and inheritance, that by the time the collectives were implemented they had already been infused with traditional elements and meanings that made them intelligible to the Chinese but which also, and at the same time, blunted their revolutionary potential. The Chinese case shows that the analytical goal of testing the relative strength of structure as opposed to praxis cannot be carried out, because the separation between structure and praxis is an artificial one: in reality structure and practice are effectively inseparable. There is no such thing as pure ahistorical praxis, totally unmediated by human symbolic structures.

This structural analysis supports Sahlins' contention that structuralism has important contributions to make in the analysis of culture history. Yet this analysis also shows – and equally powerfully – that structuralism alone is not sufficient to understand the preservation of the deep structures of Chinese kinship through the revolutionary period. Praxis itself had an important part to play in preserving and maintaining structure.

A structural theory such as Sahlins' has a quality of mystical idealism, in that it conceives of unchanging ideas, persisting through time and space in a Platonic manner. But structures are not metaphysical ideas floating freely; they are ideas in the minds of real flesh-and-blood people who live within history. The data from post-revolutionary China cannot be understood without reference to Marx's view that ideas alone, unreinforced by material interests, are never determinants of social history. Specifically, basic change in a society can never take place without a fundamental revolution in its economic base – especially in the forces of production. Using a Marxist analysis, it is clear that the persistence of Chinese rural kinship structure over the past 30 years demonstrates only that the changes in the mode of production were never sufficiently fundamental to bring about changes in the social and cultural superstructure.

Structural tenacity is a fact, but a materialist analysis is necessary to explain the transition from one kind of social formation to another, or the failure of such a transition. Fortunately, we do not have to choose between structuralism and Marxism. Marx was not so unimaginative as to fail to recognize the importance of ideas in history, and structuralism is not foreign to Marxist analysis, as Sahlins himself has noted. (Sahlins has gone so far as to say that Marx was the first structuralist [Sahlins 1976, p.47].) Marx recognized the conservative power of structure in history, as witness his famous statement in *The Eighteenth Brumaire* (1973) that "Men make their own history, but ... under circumstances ... given and transmitted from the past. The tradition of all the dead generations weighs like a nightmare on the brain of the living." So Marx did not doubt either the importance of structure or the difficulty of changing it. Rather, from a Marxist point of view, structural change requires material constraints of enormous power, applied continuously over a long period of time, if the "tradition of all the dead generations" in a society like rural China's is to be changed fundamentally. Only changes on the order of the industrial revolution that has taken place in the West and in Japan, with all the massive geographical and social mobility that this implies, could succeed in breaking up the residential kin groups of patrilineally-related and property-owning men that form the core of rural southeastern Chinese kinship structure.

Furthermore, the fact of industrialization alone will not accomplish this task if the restrictions of the household registration system continue to prevent social and geographical mobility for peasants. This system has required that peasants remain in their native lineage communities, preserving the old structure (see chapter 15). A structure and an economic base so tightly intertwined as to be inseparable have produced a fundamental continuity too powerful to be altered by efforts to induce change that have merely scratched the surface of social life. Until there is a revolution in the economic base of the rural society which recognizes and alters the fundamental structural base of rural society as well, the traditional structures must persist. The fact that greater changes have been made in cities (see Whyte and Parish 1984), where the people are not restricted to a social and economic life in the context of a lineage village or a structural simulacrum of one, indicates that change is not impossible. But praxis, however intrinsically powerful, cannot prevail when it is established on a working foundation of equally powerful and entirely unexamined structural assumptions. Effective revolutionary theory cannot be based on praxis alone. Structuralism is an essential component of revolutionary action: without it, a revolution cannot be carried through to completion.

# 13

# Party organization

The Communist party of China is the architect of modern Chinese society. Its record is one of enormous revolutionary accomplishment. From a small ragged band of marginal outlawed intellectuals in 1921, the party has become the largest political organization in world history and now decides the destinies of one-fifth of humankind. By successfully mobilizing the Chinese people to resist the Japanese during World War II the party rose to power. Then, organizing the poor and landless peasant masses of China, it decisively defeated the Guomindang in civil war. After Liberation, the party established China's full independence from foreign imperialism, broke the power of the landlords and capitalists – the old ruling elites – and, over the past three-and-one-half decades, has revolutionized the structure of the largest society on earth. Mistakes have been made – and they have cost dearly – but the party has succeeded in providing order, food, clothing, shelter, education, pride, and hope for a society that lacked even these bare human essentials prior to Liberation, in 1949. In the thirty-five years following Liberation, the party directed the industrialization and economic development of China. World Bank figures show that China's growth rates were among the highest in the world between 1950 and 1975 (see Rawski 1980, table 30). Unfortunately population increase has absorbed most of China's economic growth, stifling the country's development and preventing the people from prospering as much as they otherwise would have done. Since 1979, demonstrating continuing flexibility, the party has audaciously changed China's economic and foreign policies. The record since then has been one of increasing prosperity of a remarkable kind. China is now attempting, albeit without complete success, to bring its explosive population under control, something that no other underdeveloped country with population problems of a similar magnitude has been able to do.

The Communist party has proved to be an effective instrument for governing an enormous country that includes over 200 million urban residents and over 800 million peasants. Its record is remarkable. The

11. Chashan Commune Communist Party headquarters, 1979

organizational ability of the Chinese Communist party, in fact, makes the rural administration of other large peasant-based societies with similar problems, like India, seem ineffectual by comparison.

What, then, is the structure and process of party organization that makes such achievements possible? Party committees are the organs of power at all levels. Party members hold almost all important leadership and management positions, in all fields, from the pinnacles of bureaucratic power in Beijing, down to the grassroots-level units, like Zengbu. All general policies of import to the countryside are made by members of higher party levels, at the center, and then transmitted to the lower levels of the society, to be implemented by the rural cadres.

Although the Chinese party-controlled state is often depicted as a monolithic and totalitarian system of bureaucratic domination, this is not exactly so. From within, it is best understood as a system in which party committees at different administrative levels – province, prefecture, county, district, and township – negotiate with the higher levels over the degree of implementation of central policy. This system, best described by the term "policy bargaining," means that the Chinese peasants have some representation of their views, reactions, and interests, as their reaction to policy is transmitted up through the bureaucratic hierarchy to the higher levels. It means that the party Central Committee does not have complete and absolute control.

However, the party Central Committee may state its policy in a more extreme form, so as to allow for modifications by lower levels, as one does in bargaining. Lower-level party committees may modify higher-level policies to some extent to suit local conditions or to take account of resistance by the populace so strong that implementation would be inordinately difficult. The variable implementation of birth planning in recent years (see chapter 11) is one good example of this process.

Nevertheless, the party is in many respects an authoritarian, centralized, and hierarchical Leninist structure of governance.

The level that most directly affects the peasants of Zengbu is the Chashan district (formerly commune) party organization. The Chashan Party Committee has its headquarters in an office and dormitory complex, with its own kitchen, cooks, and dining hall where the cadres eat. It owns its own fleet of trucks and vans. As the Chinese say, "The unit may be only as small as a sparrow, but it contains inside it all the necessary organs." This means that party units, like other work units in China, try to be as self-sufficient and self-contained as possible, organizing their own essential services, rather than depending upon separate functionally specialized outside units to provide such services to them.

As of 1979, only a small proportion of people in Chashan commune, about 2·5 percent of the population, were party members: 869 out of a population of approximately 35,000. Of these, 106 were women and 763 were men. Twenty-five percent of the commune's party members were townspeople, although the town contained only 11 per cent of the commune's total population. Party members were required to demonstrate their commitment in actual practice, through dedicated and effective work. They were not supposed to be passive, or to limit their commitment to the realm of ideas. Following both the communist and Confucian traditions, the ideal was active public service as an official.

Chashan commune was run by the Chashan commune Party Branch Standing Committee. This committee had four primary members: a party secretary, who had authority over all aspects of commune life, and three functionally-specialized deputy secretaries, who supervised production, security and party discipline, and the Youth League and Women's Federation. There were eight other members of the Commune Party Branch Standing Committee, each of whom directly administered a specialized area of commune life: party recruitment, organization, and the Youth League; the commune militia; finance and economics; commune industry; propaganda, culture, and education; irrigation, electricity, and capital construction; fisheries and animal husbandry; and the party committee.

The party secretary and deputy secretary of Chashan commune were designated by the county-level cadres, so that the county had direct control over the Chashan committee. The other members of the Chashan Party

Branch Standing Committee were elected by the Chashan Party Representative Assembly, a group of delegates selected by the members of the town and brigade party branches. (These delegates numbered about 10 percent of all the party members of the commune.) The delegates to the party assembly worked from a list of eligible candidates provided by the Dongguan county party authorities. Although the assembly had, in theory, the right to add names to the list given to them by the county party authorities, they usually accepted it as given. After the Chashan committee members were elected by the assembly, they apportioned committee positions among themselves under the guidance of the party secretary, following an old Chinese procedure (see chapter 5 for similar procedures in team elections; see also Willmott 1960, p. 145).

The positions of cadres at the commune or district level, and their future advancement in the party hierarchy, are controlled by the party committee at the county level. Similarly, county-level party cadres are in the same position *vis-à-vis* their superiors at the prefectural and provincial levels. This tends to promote the compliance of cadres to the policies of the upper levels. If a Chashan cadre openly opposed the orders of the county committee, his career would be endangered, to say the least. For this reason, commune-level cadres are less responsive to the direct pressure of constituents, in comparison with brigade cadres.

In 1979, a staff of 25 commune cadres, all party members, assisted the Party Branch Standing Committee in administering the commune. Eighteen were state cadres, paid by the state; seven were commune cadres, hired and paid by the commune itself, out of its own resources. The state budget did not allow sufficient administrative staff, according to the commune leaders, so the commune had to hire additional staff out of its own funds. The seven cadres paid by the commune were cadres who "eat the rice of the commune," as opposed to the state cadres, who "eat the state's rice," and as opposed to brigade peasant cadres who "eat their own rice." There was a caste-like status distinction between the two categories of commune-level cadres (see chapter 15). The regular commune cadres were state cadres and, thus, legal urban residents; the seven cadres eating the rice of the commune were members of the peasant caste, who were temporarily allowed to reside in town.

Those seven cadres who eat the rice of the commune were recruited locally. They constituted a liminal category of officials – warrant officers of the party bureaucracy – who were higher in status and power than brigade-level peasant cadres, but who did not have the power or prestige or the salary and benefits of the regular state cadres. Lacking urban resident status, they had no opportunity to rise higher in the party bureaucracy. This liminal intermediate category of party cadres, however, provided at least a limited measure of higher status to distinguished, able, and locally powerful peasant cadres from the villages. The cooperation of such powerful local leaders was essential, in order for the state cadres to govern effectively. The commune cadre status was a way of motivating and rewarding such cooperation. It meant little in the grand scheme of Chinese society, but it was an important step for peasant cadres, and it was as high as they could usually advance.

The Chashan commune cadres who ate the state's rice, and had the status of urban residents tended to be from Dongguan county, but not from Chashan. Two-thirds of the commune cadres in the 29 communes of Dongguan county were native to the county, but served in communes other than the ones in which they had been born. This makes them less subject to local pressures by kin and fellow lineage members. Only about one-third of the commune party secretaries in Dongguan county were natives of the communes they administered. Prior to 1983, no secretary of Chashan commune had been native to the commune. A local man became secretary of the commune in 1983, and was still serving in 1985, however.

Commune-level cadres represented the state rather than the local populace, both because of their relationship to the upper bureaucratic levels, and because generally they were not local. In addition, they served short terms of office, averaging only two or three years. The party took the position that officials in the countryside should not serve so long in one commune that they became partial to entrenched local interests and "were thus unable to make rational decisions." When party and local interests were in conflict, the party tried to ensure that local officials would act in the party's interests. Other reasons for the short terms of office were to provide mid-level cadres with broad institutional and geographical experience, and to preserve bureaucratic mobility, rather than stabilizing people in fixed positions. The ideal was to produce bureaucratic generalists. Cadres were expected to be able to handle any job given to them by the county committee.

Governance by officials with broad rather than specialized training, who were not native to the locality, and served short terms of office, is familiar to students of traditional Chinese society. The county magistrates of the old imperial government were humanistically educated generalists who did not consider themselves technicians or specialists; they were supposed to be virtuous amateurs, educated in Confucian doctrine, and able to handle any situation. They, too, were assigned to areas other than their native villages and towns, in an attempt to keep them from favoring their own family and lineage members. They too were transferred frequently, to prevent the development of political ties with powerful families and lineages in their area of administration. The emperor attempted to ensure that the bureaucracy upheld the state's interest instead of local interests; so does the party.

Brigade party branches were under the formal control of the commune's party committee, which had to approve all the brigade branch committee's important actions. In addition to this, the commune assigned its cadres to

12. Secretary Lu, of Lu's Home village, head of the Zengbu Brigade Communist Party Branch, outside brigade headquarters, 1979

supervise, inspect and control the brigades, each cadre being assigned supervisory responsibility for one particular brigade.

Zengbu's party branch provides an example of the working of brigade party organization. In 1979, there were 110 party members in Zengbu; 15 percent were women, which is slightly higher than the average for female party membership among the Chashan peasantry. In Zengbu, as elsewhere, the party branch was overwhelmingly a male-dominated organization. (But prior to Liberation, women did not participate in public life at all.) Zengbu brigade's Party Branch Committee (*Zengbu dadui zhibu weiyuanhui*) was a structural analog to the commune committee. Brigade administration was indistinguishable from party organization. The Zengbu branch was under the overall authority of the Zengbu party branch secretary. He was assisted by four deputy party secretaries and ten members of the Party Branch Standing Committee. (Smaller brigades had fewer standing committee members.) The deputy secretaries were in charge of agricultural production, finance and economy, security, and industry and sidelines, respectively. The first four of the ten brigade standing committee members supervised women's work, the Zengbu branch of the youth league, party recruitment and organization, and the brigade's militia. Three other committee members were each in charge of one of Zengbu's three major villages; the eighth was the brigade accountant;

13. Brigade cadres in headquarters' courtyard, 1983

ind the final two brigade cadres were in charge of production in the brigade's
ndustries and enterprises.

The brigade's party committee was elected by the party members of the
Zengbu party branch.

The Zengbu Party Branch Committee, like the commune party committee
above it, assigned cadres to inspect and oversee the separate Zengbu villages.
However, at this level it was not possible for the party to isolate its
representatives from their own family, kin, and village; the villages would not
tolerate direct intervention by an outsider, particularly a cadre from a
neighboring rival lineage village. As one villager put it, "Brigade cadres
represent their own villages because it would be impossible for cadres from
one village to give orders to people from a neighboring village." In addition,
each brigade cadre was assigned one production team to inspect and oversee.
This cadre would attend team meetings, and supervise team elections. Thus,
each team was led by its own elected leaders, most of whom were party
members; each was supervised as a team by a brigade cadre, in a formal
administrative capacity; and, in addition, each was supervised as part of a
village by another brigade cadre from the same village. Just as the commune
party committee enmeshed its constituent brigades in multistranded and
overlapping webs of control, so the brigade controlled its constituent villages
and teams. Through these overlapping administrative techniques, the party
organization, in Trotsky's words, "penetrates the very pores of the society."

The brigade standing committee cadres were required to be party members, but this requirement did not extend down to the team level. However, 66 percent of the team leaders in Chashan commune were party members. The practice was to recruit those who served effectively as team leaders into party membership. In Zengbu, 14 of the 17 team leaders were party members. For two-thirds of the people in Chashan commune, and most of the people in Zengbu, then, party supervision extended down to the level of the team leader. Even team leaders who were not party members were under the direct supervision of the brigade party cadres in all important matters. Yet being directly elected by their fellow team members, the team leaders saw themselves more as peasant representatives than representatives of the state.

At the peasant level, the brigade cadres were the agents for the transmission of upper-level party policies to the peasants. They used prosaic, down-to-earth language that the peasants could understand. They appealed to the peasants on the basis of the practical effect of policy on the latter's lives and economic well-being, rather than on the basis of arguments based upon general ideals or abstract principles. From the point of view of the Zengbu brigade cadres, the commune cadres represented the state first of all, while they represented the party and the peasants as well. They transmitted peasant reaction to party policies back to the party hierarchy. Brigade cadres were thus Janus-faced intermediaries, who represented the party-state policies to the peasants, and the peasants to the party-state. The brigade cadres had to maneuver carefully to avoid the danger of being crushed between party and peasantry – the two major tectonic plates of Chinese society.

The Zengbu brigade cadres fell into three cohorts: older, middle, and young. The older cadres were the early activists. This cohort had been responsible for land reform and collectivization in Zengbu; they were seasoned and experienced men, and they were survivors. The second cohort were too young to become cadres during the initial years of the Revolution. They managed to obtain a primary or lower-middle school education and, after demonstrating political reliability and skill as leaders, they had been selected by the older cadres to fill leadership posts in the party. This cohort was better educated than the older generation; and several of them had served in the army and gained some knowledge of Mandarin Chinese and a more cosmopolitan view of China. The youngest cohort entered the party at the time of the Cultural Revolution, and managed to survive the end of that period to become regular career cadres.

As representatives of the party which rules China, the cadres of Zengbu commanded overwhelming legitimate authority over the persons, the labor, the livelihood, and the thinking of the peasants. They implemented policies from above which directly and intimately affected the lives of all the people under their charge. At perhaps no other time and place in history has a rural elite commanded such political, economic, and ideological power over a peasantry.

The party cadres' hegemony over Zengbu and the rest of rural China was greatly changed by the process of decollectivization. The cadres' roles as managers and directors of the rural agricultural economy had been eliminated by 1984. The party's decision to de-emphasize politics and class struggle, and no longer to interfere in the peasants' religious practices and social ceremonies, ended the cadres' roles as reformers of feudal practices.

The administrative reorganization of the countryside also diminished the power and authority of the party cadres. In 1983, plans were being circulated that would eliminate the communes, production brigades, and production teams. The rationale for the reorganization was to separate party organization from government administration and economic management at the new district (the old commune), *xiang* (the old production brigade), and village levels. The party now believed that the merging of politics, economics, and government administration during the Great Leap Forward had been a mistake, and that the party bureaucracy had exerted unnecessary administrative domination over the peasants' lives, choking economic development. The new plan was "to free the initiative of the peasants" from the control of the party. The economy was to be taken out of the hands of the cadres and placed under the management of private households, private entrepreneurs, or skilled economic specialists and managers. The party discussed plans to recruit new local cadres with technical and managerial expertise into the party, to replace some of the old politically-oriented cadres, who would be retired. Party committees at all levels were to restrict their activities to seeing that general party policies were followed; they were not to interfere in the day-to-day management of economic enterprises or routine government administration. This implied a significant loss of power, prestige, and jobs for the Zengbu cadre corps.

Many cadre positions were eliminated. The new village citizens' committees were to take over the management of the affairs of all village teams; instead of each team having an accountant, now one village accountant would do all the work. The production teams no longer needed full-time leaders, so team leaders were put on half-time, at half their former salaries. Rural industries and enterprises were no longer operated by the brigade, but (with the important exception of the new Hong Kong processing factories) had already been returned to the individual villages or bid out for private management. It was no longer necessary to deal with so many state quotas, or to deliver such voluminous state statistics as had been the case in the past. The militia, the Youth League, and the Women's Federation, once important areas of cadre activity, had been allowed to lapse.

In 1983, the Zengbu cadres were suffering an ideological crisis. The changes in economic policy which emphasized seeking profit in a market economy, and the new policy of cooperating with Hong Kong capitalists, violated all the ideals that the cadres had espoused since Liberation. They found themselves being asked to implement social and economic policies that they had spoken against for almost three decades. This represented such an abrupt ideological shift that some of the Zengbu cadres were confused, and appeared to be losing their ideological moorings. Articles against "conservative" cadres were appearing in the national newspapers of the time, exerting pressure on them to change and change quickly. Their world had been turned topsy-turvy; what had formerly been denounced as capitalism was now being praised as enlightened socialist policy; and what was formerly revered as socialism was being denounced as false socialism. And no convincing new ideological synthesis was provided to make sense of this changing world.

There was a crisis of confidence in the rural party branch of Zengbu. The cadres were demoralized, their key roles in Maoist society were threatened with elimination, their jobs were in danger, their retirement was no longer secure, their thinking was confused, their incomes were falling farther and farther behind that of the ordinary peasants, and many were ignoring their reduced official duties and were trying to make money on the side, in the private sector. The organizational apparatus that had been so carefully developed over the decades following the Revolution appeared to be falling apart; the basic-level party structure semed to be in danger of losing its *esprit de corps*.

Party cadres at higher levels, however, said flatly and unequivocally that this was not a significant matter, but part of the process of transition: that the party still wielded all political authority in China, over all areas of China's social life, including the economy, and that it would continue to do so.

In fact, this view proved accurate. The party members and the cadres of Zengbu passed through the administrative shake-up of 1983–4, and re-established their preeminent position in rural society, on a modified basis. Formal separation of the party from local government and economic management took place in late 1983 and 1984. At the Chashan district level (the old commune level), party and government were divided into three separate administrative branches: the Chashan District Party Committee, the Chashan District Government, and the Chashan District Agricultural and Commercial Enterprise Company, a public corporation created to handle the economic functions previously handled by the commune.

Since the reform, the leading cadres of the District Party Committee are not supposed to intervene directly in the operation of the district's economic corporation, or in routine district governmental administrative affairs. As long as they follow general party policy, the district head and the manager of the district economic corporation are supposed to operate separately and autonomously.

Similar reforms took place in Zengbu at the brigade level, now called *xiang*, rather than brigade. There is a new Zengbu Party Committee, elected, as in the past, by all party members. There is a new Zengbu government, formally separate from the party committee, and elected by all the people of Zengbu; however, the candidates had to be chosen from a slate approved by the party, in the sense that the names of candidates unacceptable to the party would not appear on the ballot. The *xiang*-level government consists of a *xiang* head (*xiang zhang*) and two deputy *xiang* heads (*fu xiang zhang*). These three officials each represent one of the three Zengbu villages in the *xiang* administration. They deal with the routine administration that was formerly the work of brigade cadres.

There are three new village citizens' committees (*cun weiyuanhui*). These are elected by the people of each village from a party-approved slate, and consist of a village head (*cun zhang*), all the production team heads of that village, a member for women's affairs, one for security, and an accountant and a cashier responsible for the financial affairs of the village committee and all the village's teams.

The village committees are theoretically separate from the Zengbu *xiang* government and the Zengbu *xiang* party committee. They make up their own budgets, drawing income from small amounts of village property placed under their control and from their collective factories, and have some autonomy in managing their village's affairs. But village citizens' committees are informal people's organizations, on the analogy of the urban street committees, rather than formal governmental levels. They are still under the authority of the Zengbu *xiang* Party Committee and the *xiang* government, which ensure that they follow general party policy.

The new district, *xiang*, and village organizational reforms may, in the future, further the goal of separating the party from government administration and economic management, but this has not yet been achieved. The realities of the situation are that the party is still in firm control. For example, at the district level, formerly the commune level, the heads of the new Chashan District Government and the Chashan District Agricultural, Industrial, and Commercial Enterprise Company are concurrently vice-secretaries of the Chashan District Party Committee, and under the direct authority of the district party secretary.

The same administrative overlapping has occurred in Zengbu *xiang*. The men elected to the new positions of *xiang* head (*xiang zhang*) and deputy *xiang* heads, are men who served as brigade cadres prior to the reforms; they are all members of the Zengbu *xiang* Party Standing Committee and, as party members, are all under the control of the party secretary.

Similarly, the heads (*cun zhang*) of Zengbu's village citizens' representative committees are former brigade cadres and current members of the Zengbu *xiang* Party Standing Committee. For example, one village head is also a member of the *xiang* party committee and a deputy *xiang* head.

The team leaders have continued in their old positions, and receive small part-time salaries of 50 *yuan* a month. As a result of the reorganization, they have been made official representatives of their teams on the citizens' committees of their villages.

One of the reasons why party cadres remain in so strong a position is that they have consolidated their opportunities, through managing factories and doing business, to make a great deal of money. The Zengbu party cadres control the Hong Kong processing factories – a most important sector of the local economy. These factories, from their beginnings in 1979, were managed by brigade cadres as part of their official duties. Now, under the production responsibility system, their management is contracted by the Zengbu *xiang* government (which the party controls) to the *xiang* party cadres. Each of the most powerful members of the Zengbu *xiang* party committee, including the local party secretary, is at the same time a contracting manager of one of Zengbu's Hong Kong processing factories. The cadres' official salaries now come from the management profits and bonuses they receive from their jobs as factory managers; the *xiang* supplements the cadres' salaries only if they fall below the minimum set by the state. The *xiang* party cadres now spend only part of their time as party cadres and *xiang* government officials; most of their time is devoted to managing factories, in cooperation with Hong Kong investors. In their roles as factory managers, they control employment and wage levels, giving them continuing power over the economic lives of Zengbu families. In the initial period following the implementation of the production responsibility system, the cadres' economic position appeared to have deteriorated; now the material base of their positions has been re-established on a new basis. The administrative changes of 1983 and 1984 were form rather than substance; the party's hegemony over all important aspects of rural Chinese society is unchanged. In the blunt and salty language of the peasants, as one local wag remarked in the aftermath of the reforms, "They are holding up a sheep's head, but they are selling the same old dog meat."

Convincing evidence that the party is still firmly in control of rural society is provided by the sterilization program carried out by the local cadres in 1983 (see chapter 11). In India, in 1977, public resentment of a sterilization program was a significant factor in the government's loss of power; in China, the party cadres carried out this most difficult task successfully and in a disciplined manner, even in the face both of cadre doubts about the policy and firm peasant opposition. If the Chinese rural party apparatus can do this, it is still strikingly strong and effective.

Even after the reforms, then, the party cadres still retain control of the economy and the local government administration at all levels of rural society – district, *xiang*, and village. This was by no means predetermined. Yet the party managed to control and guide the reorganization, so that the party cadres retained the key positions of local society, as well as their incomes, their power, and their prestige. As one party cadre said, "The party may be separated clearly from the economy and from government administration somewhere at the upper levels, but not here."

# 14

## The party ethic: a devotion born of distress and enthusiasm

Every complex civilization includes several social strata, each with its own material interests, its own kind of power, its own world view, and its own concept of status honor (see Weber 1951, 1952, 1958). And there tends to be one dominant stratum – the brahmins of India, the aristocracy of Medieval Europe, the business class of the United States – whose cultural influence is so great as to shape the character of its civilization. These dominant strata enact and exemplify not merely material interests but also ideal interests, embodied in the great world religions, of which they are the most powerful exponents (see Bendix 1962, pp. 257–281).

In the great peasant-based societies, local rural representatives of these dominant strata govern the peasant masses on behalf of the elite. The local brahmins and other upper castes who dominate village India, the clergy and minor nobility of Medieval Europe, and the traditional Chinese gentry are examples of such groups. These local elites are, in Eric Wolf's (1956) terms, "cultural brokers," hinge groups forming the connection between the peasant masses on the one hand, and the urban elites and the state on the other. They transmit elements of their civilization's literate Great Tradition (Redfield 1967, p. 26) from the urban elites to the peasants, and they are political brokers, who transmit and interpret state policy to the peasants. They are Janus-faced, in the sense of "looking both toward the requirements imposed by the larger political and economic order and toward the custom- ary expectations of the peasant community" (Diaz and Potter 1967, p. 164). The members of these rural elites are intermediaries. They seek both to control the minds and actions of the peasants on behalf of the elite and to represent the interests of the peasants to the state, all the while maintaining their own ideal and material interests as a separate stratum. They are inferior to the urban elite, but superior to the peasants.

In contemporary China the basic-level rural cadres of the Chinese Communist party are just such a hinge group in the revolutionary context. They share material interests, and they are the local-level exponents of a set of

14. Brigade party cadres listen to eulogy at the funeral of their fallen comrade, *1979*

shared ideal values. Their values and their view of the world have shaped and molded post-revolutionary rural China. To understand the new rural China it is necessary to understand the way they think. And their thinking has been based on their membership in a party which is, in essence, a religion, and a religion which exhibits the processual qualities of a revitalization movement.

The religion of which the party is the organizational expression is non-supernaturalistic and non-anthropomorphic, but a religion nevertheless. Religion may be defined, following Durkheim (1965, p.62), as "a unified system of beliefs and practices relative to sacred things ... which unite into one single moral community called a Church, all those who adhere to them." As a functioning religious system in a practical sense, the party displays a number of religious trappings. It has its prophets – Marx, Engels, Lenin, and Chairman Mao – and its sacred canon of writings. These doctrines furnish a consistent system of moral values and an ethical orientation to life and work. The party has its sacred symbols. These are displayed in the meeting halls of rural party-headquarters, which are more than merely the meeting places of a bureaucratically organized and instrumentally oriented political organization. The local party secretaries are priests of the faith and keepers of the ideology, as well as administrators of the party organization. Party assemblies and small-group discussion meetings are inspirational in aim and tone. There is an atmosphere of affirmation and faith. The cadres' belief in the central values and goals of the party is confirmed in these assemblies, and their personal resolve strengthened.

The religious aspect of Chinese communism has been noted in passing by a number of scholars. Franz Schurmann has commented briefly (in a public lecture, late 1950s) on the similarities between Chinese communism and Protestant Christianity. Schwartz has noted that "Maoist virtue, one might say, was to play the role of a kind of Protestant ethic" (1970, p. 165). Urban remarks that "Maoism is a serious call to a socially responsible moral conduct which has a great deal in common with Christian rectitude, especially in its Protestant and Victorian embodiment" (1971, p. xii). Mazlish (1976, pp. 157–158) sees Mao as one example of a "revolutionary ascetic," and quotes similar observations by James Reston and Maurice Meisner.

The religious character of communist movements has been commented upon by Anthony Wallace, who says:

[T]he Russian communist movement and its derivatives have been officially atheistic, but the quality of doctrine and of leader-follower relationships is so similar … to the religious doctrine and human-supernatural relations, that one wonders whether it is not a distinction without a difference. (1956, p. 277)

The party's ideological doctrine is a reformulation and recombination of sets of cultural elements from two civilizations which met and merged in early twentieth-century China. From the West came Judaeo-Christian eschatological beliefs, the humanism of the Renaissance, and the rationalism of the Enlightenment, which had diffused into China as an integral part of Marxism-Leninism. (It must be remembered that Marxism is as much a part of the Western tradition as Liberalism [see Mills 1962, p. 13].) From indigenous sources came elements of Confucianism, the religion and status ethic of the scholar-bureaucrat class which dominated traditional Chinese government and society. The symbolic order of Chinese communism was formulated by the party's founders from the raw materials provided by these two disparate sources. In this the communist innovators resembled those innovators who first introduced Buddhism into China from India, around the time of Christ (Wright 1959, pp. 21–41). The Buddhist innovators expedited their task by translating key Buddhist concepts like *dharma*, "the teaching," and *bodhi*, "enlightenment," in a way that would make them acceptable to the Chinese. They also used a method of matching concepts, equating *nirvana* with the Chinese philosophical term *"wu-wei,"* meaning "non-action" and *sila*, or "morality," with *xiaoxun*, "filial submission and obedience"; and so on. Mao and Liu did something essentially similar. By equating the moral behavior expected of a party cadre with Confucian ideas about the proper behavior of an ethical official, the role of party cadre was rendered more intelligible and acceptable to the Chinese. In the process of adapting communism to Chinese culture, communist ideas were clothed in a familiar and valued Chinese garb. From the point of view of content and purpose, Confucianism and communism are utterly different: Confucianism seeks to adapt harmoniously to the world, while communism seeks to transform it through iconoclastic struggle. But ideas derived from Confucianism, defining the proper behavior of an official and the proper modes of governing, have been retained in the new society, and merged with the Marxist-Leninist methods and ethics borrowed from the Soviet Union. The world view and ethic of rural party cadres has its basis in this qualitatively new religious and ideological configuration.

As might be expected, the ideological doctrine of Chinese communism is complex, combining Marxist social theory on the nature of human societies and their history, an apocalyptic message of future salvation for humankind in a this-worldly communist utopia, the designation of the party as the agent which is to bring about this utopian consummation of human history, and a set of moral and ethical beliefs and principles. These beliefs and principles – the "Communist ethic" – form the basis for cadre self-cultivation and serve as a guide to revolutionary praxis. The doctrine also provides the symbolic coin for denouncing evil (for example as feudalism, capitalism, social chauvinism, or ultra-leftism). The doctrine justifies and legitimizes the cadres' authority as leaders of China.

In *How To Be a Good Communist*, a set of lectures which Liu Shaoqi gave in 1939 (later published as a pamphlet in 1964), he set out the basic ideology of the party in the form of a sort of catechism:

What is our most fundamental duty as party members? It is to achieve communism ... The whole world will be transformed step by step into a communist world. Will the communist world be good? We all know it will be. In that world there will be no exploiters and no oppressors, no landlords and capitalists, no imperialists and fascists, nor will there be any oppressed and exploited people, or any of the darkness, ignorance, and backwardness resulting from the system of exploitation. In such a society the production of both material and moral values will develop and flourish mightily and will meet the varied needs of all its members. By then all humanity will consist of unselfish, intelligent, highly cultured and skilled communist workers; mutual assistance and affection will prevail among men and there will be no such irrationalities as mutual suspicion and deception, mutual injury, mutual slaughter and war. It will of course be the best, the most beautiful and the most advanced society in human history. (1964, p. 35–36)

Party doctrine is accorded the same kind of reverence that was regarded as the appropriate response to traditional Confucian ideology: it has a symbolic significance that is almost magical. According to Confucian belief, all social behavior is to be guided by one true authoritarian ideology, which forms the basis for social order. Furthermore, as a major task of government, officials should educate the people in this ideology. Hsiao Kung-chuan (1960, p. 191) describes the reading-out of the Sacred Edicts (which pithily summarized the moral code of imperial Confucianism) to the peasantry by distinguished and respected scholars. He says: "To make all subjects obedient ... the Ch'ing government sought to indoctrinate them thoroughly with the basic precepts of imperial Confucianism." According to Confucian doctrine, the use of force is inappropriate in the dissemination of ideology: rather, people should be educated and persuaded. Cadres act on the same principles in relationship to party doctrine. They must present and explain communist theory to the masses, in order to make appropriate governmental order possible. Although governmental force was and is available if needed, education and persuasion are the methods of choice. Weber's (1951, p. 153) summary of the Chinese attitude applies equally to old and new: he says simply, "Everything was an educational problem."

The Confucian idea of the official as exemplary prophet, influencing the people by the example of his personal conduct and virtue, also persists. As was the case in traditional China, "Everything depended upon the behavior of the officials and these men were responsible for the leadership of a society" (Weber 1951, p. 153). Weber (1951, pp. 109 and 128) compared the characteristics of officials to those of ordained priests. If the ruler and his officials embodied virtue in their own conduct and set a proper example, the people would follow their lead and the society would be orderly and prosperous; if they lacked virtue in their own conduct and set a bad example for the people, society would fall into disorder and people would suffer. The essence of this idea is found in Confucius' famous saying that "The people are like grass, the ruler like the wind." This means that the ruler and his officials (by virtue of the charismatic power which was the result of their mastery of Confucian doctrine and the embodiment of it in their own conduct) had the capacity in effect, to charm the people into harmony, influencing them by the invisible force of example, just as the wind blows the grass. Because of this belief, the ruler and the officials were held personally responsible for the state of the society and polity. In the *Analects*, Confucius wrote that "When a prince's personal conduct is correct, his government is effective without the issuing of orders; if his personal conduct is not correct, he may issue orders but they will not be followed."

This cultural definition of officials as exemplary prophets, carried over from Chinese Confucian tradition, leads contemporary Chinese to make moral and ethical explanations of rural policy successes and failures. Cadres both in Zengbu and at higher administrative levels explained the differential success of production teams, brigades, and communes by the quality of their cadre leaders; if the cadres were morally and ethically cultivated in party ideology, and set a good example, the masses would follow them, and the unit would be successful. If the cadres did not set a good example, people would not listen to or obey them; units would be unsuccessful and party policies would not be effectively implemented.

These Confucian elements in the ideal model of cadre behavior do not, however, suggest that Chinese communism, as a total configuration, is merely Confucianism in a new guise. Revolutionary Marxism is not Confucian conservatism and party cadres are not Confucian mandarins. In borrowing from the Confucian past, selected elements were merged with elements from the Marxist-Leninist party tradition, creating a qualitatively different configuration. Levenson is correct in objecting to those who stress only the continuities between traditional and revolutionary China. He comments,

Some compulsion seems to exist in many quarters to see Chinese communism not, indeed, as a foreign creed tamed down to traditional Chinese specifications ... but as Confucianism with another name and another skin but the same perennial spirit. Canonical texts and canonical texts, bureaucratic intellectual elite and bureaucratic intellectual elite – nothing has changed, allegedly – except, possibly, everything ... The categories of Chinese communist thought are not traditional. This is the salient fact. And it is belied neither by some communist taste for traditional achievement ... nor by some communist casting in traditional roles ... (1964, pp. 210–211)

Chinese communism is a new configuration. It resembles and differs from both Confucianism and Marxism-Leninism.

As well as being a religion, Chinese communism is also, intermittently, a revitalization movement as well. These movements, common in situations of social stress, when the existence of a society is threatened, were named by Wallace (1956). Wallace was drawing upon Weber's sociology of charismatic authority (see Gerth and Mills 1958, pp. 245–264). He defines revitalization movements as "deliberate, organized, conscious effort[s] by members of a society to construct a more satisfying culture (1956, p. 265)." These movements commonly arise in a context involving foreign domination; a prophet or other charismatic leader emerges, reformulating existing and borrowed cultural elements into a new configuration that is believed to be wonderfully powerful.

Examples of such movements include the early Christian movement, the rise of Islam, the Ghost Dance of the American Indians (Mooney 1965), the Anabaptist movement in Munster (Cohn 1970, pp. 252–280), the Taiping movement in nineteenth-century China (Michael 1966), and the rural guerilla and social bandit millennial movements in north and south China described by Friedman (1974, chapters 7 to 9).

The authority of charismatic leaders is, as Weber points out, the characteristic form of authority in periods of psychic, physical, economic, ethical, religious, and political distress (Gerth and Mills 1958, pp. 245–264). The leaders who arise in such periods – like Mao – are not leaders produced in the normal processes of conventional social organization. They validate the legitimacy of their authority by the virtue of their mission. As Weber puts it so succinctly:

Pure charisma is contrary to all patriarchal domination (in the sense of the term used here). It is the opposite of all ordered economy. It is the force that disregards economy ... Charisma can do this because by its very nature it is not an "institutional" and permanent structure, but rather ... the very opposite of the institutionally permanent.

[The charismatic leader's] power rests upon [the recognition by his subjects] of the personal mission of the charismatic master ... It is devotion to the extraordinary and unheard-of, to what is strange to all rule and tradition and which therefore is viewed as divine. It is a devotion born of distress and enthusiasm. (Weber, in Gerth and Mills 1958, pp. 245–249)

In order to be legitimate exponents of this revitalizing religion, moral followers of the charismatic order, party members must strive to attain a certain ethical stance in their personal lives. They are supposed to remold themselves, to subordinate themselves to the interests of the party – even to the point of self-immolation. Chairman Mao sketched the personal ethical characteristics of a good party cadre:

At no time and in no circumstances should a Communist place his personal interests first; he should subordinate them to the interests of the nation and of the masses of people. Hence, selfishness, slacking, corruption, striving for the limelight, etc. ... are most contemptible (quoted in Liu 1964, p. 46).

There is an emphasis on work as the symbolic expression of commitment that is as significant in this context as in other Chinese social contexts (see chapter 9). As Chairman Mao said, "Working with all one's energy, wholehearted devotion to public duty, and quiet hard work are the qualities that command respect" (Liu, 1964, p. 46).

There is a similar emphasis on the importance of the willingness to suffer and to sacrifice. Cadres are supposed to be so committed to the party as to be willing to give their very lives in its cause. Liu says:

[A good party member] is "the first to worry and the last to enjoy himself" [a quote from classical Chinese scholarship]. Whether in the party or among the people, he is the first to suffer hardship and the last to enjoy comfort; he compares himself with others not with respect to material enjoyment but to the amount of work done for the revolution and the spirit of hard endurance in struggle. He has such revolutionary firmness and integrity that "neither riches nor honor can corrupt him, neither poverty nor lowly condition can make him swerve from principle, neither threats nor force can bend him" [a quote from Mencius]. (1964, p. 48)

Party members who follow these strict ascetic prescriptions gain a form of inner enlightenment and strength that enables them to withstand all trials and struggles: they achieve, in effect, a state of grace. When this happens, as Liu continues:

[The party member] has nothing to fear ... Because he has the courage of righteous conviction, he never fears the truth, [he] courageously upholds it, spreads it and fights for it. Even if ... in upholding the truth, he suffers blows of all kinds, is opposed or censured by most other people and so finds himself in temporary (and honourable) isolation, even to the point where he may have to give up his life, he will still breast the waves to uphold the truth and will never drift with the tide. (1964, pp. 48–49)

At the same time, the party member "is the most sincere, most candid, and happiest of men ... [He] has no problems of personal gain or loss ... Even when he is working on his own without supervision and is therefore in a position to do something bad, he is just as 'watchful over himself when he is alone' [a quote from Confucius] and does not do anything harmful" (1964, pp. 49–50).

There are important analogies between these doctrines and the Protestant ethic. A "state of grace" is the goal of appropriate ethical individual behavior in both systems. The communist methods for proving one's self worthy, and affirming the "state of grace" through selfless and exemplary labor, are precisely analogous to Protestant attempts to make salvation demonstrable through dedicated, systematic labor in one's calling.

The issue of the individual's relationship to uncertainty is also a parallel factor shared by the two religious ethics. In Calvinist doctrine, the source of personal religious uncertainty and tension is the will of a transcendent and unknowable God. In China, personal religious uncertainty is produced in a parallel manner by the will of a distant, secretive, and unknowable party Central Committee. The specific embodiment in policy of the abstract doctrine of the Chinese Communist party historically has been susceptible to many abrupt changes, and as a result China's party cadres are under as much psychological stress as early European Calvinists. Policy changes are often sudden, radical, and contradictory. Party members must simultaneously adapt to changes and maintain an unswerving commitment and loyalty to the party. The orthodoxy of one period becomes the heterodoxy of another, often swiftly and with little warning. Like the will of God, the policies of the party upper levels are changeable and unfathomable, and they must be obeyed on the basis of faith.

There are other significant social parallels in the experiences of cadres and Calvinists. The early Calvinists were taught to be suspicious and aloof, even from family and friends, because it was not possible to distinguish the saved from the damned, and association with the damned would threaten one's own salvation. Similarly, party cadres must maintain social distance even from colleagues. In the shifting sands which are the arena of inner-party struggle, a fellow party member might come to be denounced as anti-party (the equivalent, in this context, of being damned). Association with such a person would be contaminating. Or, one might be denounced by a colleague from whom one had failed to maintain distance. (In Chinese thinking, social distance is the ally of social harmony, and closeness threatens harmony.) And, like the Calvinists, cadres were supposed to remain aloof from the profane demands of family, kin, and friends. The ritual holders of charisma, and this includes the disciples and followers as well as the master, must stand outside the routine obligations of family life in order to do justice to their mission (Gerth and Mills 1958, pp. 245–249).

Those who wish to become members of the cadre stratum must show that they are capable of enacting the party's precepts in an appropriate way. They must demonstrate willingness to undertake unselfish labor. They must be seen to work hard, to take the lead, and to assume the most difficult tasks, whatever the personal sacrifice. They must also be ideologically flexible, and capable of adapting constructively to changes in policy. The demonstrations of dedication and sacrifice that the party demands tend to discourage those who wish to use the party as a means of personal advancement, without having real political convictions.

One becomes eligible to join the party at the age of 18; by this age, most Zengbu candidates for party membership have already spent three years in the Young Communist League, the party's youth organization. Candidates must display an extensive history of appropriate revolutionary activity, using the expressive medium of observable and measurable work. As one cadre said, applicants for the party had to be people "who took an active role in their work. If the cadres tell people to plant seedlings on one *mu* of land, according to a certain standard, an activist will plant more than one *mu*, and do it at a level far above the accepted standard." Without having publicly demonstrated this willingness to work, a person cannot become a party member. In 1979, to demonstrate their worth, young candidates for the party volunteered to write party-propaganda messages on Zengbu's open-air blackboards, or carried water for poor and childless old people who were supported by collective charity. They familiarized themselves with the party's policies, and, as one aspirant to the Zengbu branch of the party put it, "We study the situation to try to distinguish between genuine and false Marxism."

The importance of the process of recruitment, both to the party and to the candidates, makes it a source of anxiety. Secretary Lu of Zengbu brigade compared the process of joining the party with the process of courtship. He said:

Most people are shy about saying that they want to join. They are afraid that they will be laughed at. In the countryside, most people wait to be asked, rather than applying on their own initiative. They would be embarrassed to put themselves forward in this way. So, when the party recruits, we don't start off by saying, "Will you join?" We talk about work, the future of socialism, or the greatness of the party. If the person being recruited says, "Oh, I am not up to the party's high standard," it is like a young couple talking love and saying, "Oh, I am not good enough for you." So we take this response as an oral application for membership.

One Zengbu party member described his recruitment into the party, which took place in 1959, while he was serving in the People's Liberation Army:

In the army I saw that the party members were tougher in mind and body than ordinary people; they always volunteered for the most difficult and dangerous tasks. I wondered what gave them such strength and courage, and I wanted to become like them. I wanted to become better educated in the party's policies; I did not simply wish to follow the policies blindly. I tried to modify my behavior so that I could come up to the party's high standards. I performed the hardest work – I did things that ordinary soldiers were not willing to do; and I took the lead in everything, to set an example for other members of my unit.

The ethic requiring party members to dedicate their lives to the organization, to take the lead in all things, no matter how difficult the task, and to set an example for others, is a demanding ethic, and requires many sacrifices in the performance. As one young candidate for party membership put it, "You gain as a party member, and especially as a cadre; you get a good salary, and you gain the respect of the villagers, who look up to the cadres; but you also lose because it is very hard work."

The high ideals of party membership are not easy to carry out in practice, and many local party members do not succeed in living up to them. Local cadres accept this realistically. Secretary Lu commented that people who join the party do so from diverse motives. Although, in his opinion, most applicants genuinely believe in the party, and wish to devote their lives to building a modern and prosperous socialist rural China, others have mixed motives, or less idealistic motives. Some people who are poor and have no social standing join the party to become officials, and enjoy the concomitant social status and authority. "This kind of person," said Secretary Lu, "joins the party in order to scold the peasants and lord it over his fellow villagers." Others were opportunists, seeking party membership only to further their own careers: "These people think that they could rise to the top of the party's ranks like helicopters, as the saying goes. Many of them have not been successful because they are not able to bear the sacrifices or do the work required by the party. Needless to say, we try to weed out the insincere and accept only genuinely dedicated and able people." The party also rejects people who are considered too rigid and fanatical. A practical ability to work effectively and constructively with others is an important quality in a party member.

The history of the party as a religious revitalization movement is also the history of a series of attempts to conclude the revolutionary process with what Weber has called the routinization of charisma. At some times in its history, the party has functioned very intensely as a revitalization movement. At others, there has been an effort to routinize the charismatic meaning of authority, and a corresponding de-emphasis on revitalization. In the initial stages of the Great Leap Forward, for example, the party functioned at the peak of its intensity as a religious revitalization movement. But charismatic enthusiasm is vulnerable to events. As Weber (Gerth and Mills 1958, p. 249) points out, charismatic leaders maintain legitimate authority only so long as they succeed; if they fail, then their legitimizing charisma has failed as well. The failure of the Great Leap Forward disillusioned peasants and cadres alike (see chapter 3). It suggested that the charisma of the revolutionary leaders could not be relied upon. Religious belief in the magical power of the party, which had been strengthened by the successes of the Revolution itself, waned in the face of this disaster.

In the aftermath of the Great Leap Forward, many members of the party, under the leadership of Liu Shaoqi, reinterpreted their position, and came to feel that the charismatic period of great deeds by revolutionary heroes should come to an end; it was undisciplined. Order should be restored by the creation of a rationalized bureaucratic regime which would be capable of developing China's economy on a more realistic basis. This group succeeded in modifying Maoist policies in favor of what they considered more rational means of development. Material incentives were to replace ideological inspiration. This was the first attempt of the Chinese Communist party to initiate the end of the revitalization movement and the transformation to the routinization of charisma. However, the forces of routinization were not strong enough to take control of the party or of China. Instead, there seemed to be a countervailing wish to rekindle the charismatic process and experience, rather than to proceed with a transition to routinization. The Cultural Revolution can be understood as an effort to produce such a result. It was a revitalization movement within a revitalization movement, an attempt to keep the charismatic fires burning in order to complete the work of the Revolution. And the reaction against the Cultural Revolution following the death of Mao has taken the form of yet another attempt to shift the emphasis from religious revolutionary activity to economic development, drawing more upon material interests than ideological commitment.

Routinization has, sooner or later, been the fate of all charismatic movements. Weber wrote that "It is the fate of charisma, whenever it comes into the permanent institutions of a community, to give way to powers of tradition or of rational socialization" (Gerth and Mills 1958, p. 253). There is no doubt that a revulsion against reliance on charismatic process has taken place. But the question remains, to what extent do the post-Mao policies actually represent an end to the party as a revitalization movement and the beginning of the permanent routinization of the party's charisma?

Formerly, the common material interests of local-level cadres were a logical consequence, rather than a prior condition, of their shared ideological commitment. But with the introduction of the new economic policy, the party provided no new ideological synthesis, apart from a crude anachronistic Benthamite utilitarianism, which claimed that people who were getting rich deserved to, because they were performing useful services for society. Initially, this produced what the Chinese regard as a dangerous situation, the state of disorder and anomie in which the world is out of joint with the belief system, and the ideological center on which the social order is based does not hold. The response of local-level cadres, after an initial period of confusion (see chapter 13), was to reassert themselves on a material rather than ideological basis. They transformed themselves into a group whose shared material interests had a primacy over principle, ideology, and revolutionary action.

This was a new phenomenon in the Chinese countryside. Formerly, shared material interests had been subordinated to religious and ideological considerations as a matter of principle; maintaining this stance was a focus of ethical action. When ethical affirmation for the importance of subordinating material interests was withdrawn, shared material interests became the basis for action; economics became more important than politics. At this point in the history of the Revolution, it can be said that charisma was routinized. The ideological confusion of the local-level cadres, followed by their redefinition of the nature of appropriate social action, was a specific manifestation of the general process postulated by Weber's theory.

However, there are important reasons for believing that contemporary policies are not the end of Chinese communism as a religious revitalization movement, and these reasons cannot be ignored. The Chinese economy and society remain complex, shifting, and unstable, and so do the attitudes of China's villagers. As social inequalities based upon differential wealth, and incompatibilities between the capitalist and socialist economic systems emerge (see chapter 17), the explosive resentment of differential access to wealth and power that helped fuel the Revolution in the first place is recreated. The party's traditional strict moral and ethical code is the frame of reference for the expression of resentment against the new social differentiation.

Furthermore, state cadres at the commune level and above are in a different position with relation to the new policies. They are the real elite, rather than the dominant stratum at the local level which governs on behalf of the elite. They control China's destiny. In a context of potential peasant revulsion at the social inequalities produced by the differentiation between successful and unsuccessful peasant capitalists, state cadres may reassert a moral dedication to public welfare which would be likely to have considerable appeal. The intrinsic revolutionary charisma of the party, and its capacity for revolutionary reform, remain highly valued. The economic and social difficulties that China still faces make it inevitable that there will be many more social struggles and crises to come, and that the wish for a revitalization movement to transform China will be re-expressed through the party as it has been before. The power of the party is still very much alive. When new crises occur, the party is likely to rise to the occasion by mobilizing itself once again. The charismatic potency of the party's most intensely revolutionary times will be reinvoked, in the service of China's continuing need for revitalization.

# 15

# A caste-like system of social stratification: the position of peasants in modern China's social order

The distinction between rural and urban dwellers in the People's Republic of China has been made the basis for classification into two caste-like civil status groups, a higher status group called "urban personnel," and a lower status group called "rural personnel." Membership in either group is inherited from the mother, assigned at birth, and cannot be changed except under the most extraordinary circumstances. The result is a system of birth-ascribed stratification which, considered as a whole, displays caste-like features.

The system is simultaneously a product of Chinese cultural assumptions and of a characteristically Chinese interpretation of Marxist ideas. The idea that membership in a class status category is inherited is present at the level of an assumption in Chinese society. As Hinton says, discussing the matter in *Fanshen* (1966),

Was one to consider the present status of the family, the status several years back, or the status in the light of several generations? When left to themselves, the peasants of Long Bow tended to go back two and even three generations. This was in accord with habits deeply ingrained in the Chinese people, habits which had much precedent in the culture of the past. Under the old imperial examination system, for example, candidates had to prove not only that they themselves were not representatives of some barred category (boatman, actor, prostitute, or other "wandering" type) but also that their parents and grandparents were free of any such taint. Settlers in Shantung whose parents or grandparents had migrated from Hopei still regarded themselves as Hopei people. (p. 287)

Hinton calls this assumption a "concept of hereditary social status" (*ibid*).

The assumption that status is inherited has continued to be made in a post-revolutionary context. The analytic categories describing class distinctions in Marxist terms have been reified and perpetuated by inheritance, rather than being regarded as descriptive of social relationships in a particular time and place. Membership in the class background categories which were assigned between 1950 and 1953 at the time of land reform, for example, has been treated as inheritable, although the class backgrounds themselves were being deliberately obliterated. (Membership in class background categories was inherited from the father, rather than from the mother, however.) Like good class background, political reliability has also been treated as inheritable. In the early years of the Cultural Revolution this was called the "theory of bloodlines." (See Bernstein 1977, p. 19, and Rosen, 1981, p. 26.)

Inherited status categories have not been regarded as perpetual, however. Class background categories are no longer officially regarded as important, and the "theory of bloodlines" is no longer invoked. There is a general expectation that inherited classification into the categories of rural and urban personnel will no longer be necessary when China has achieved the transition from socialism to communism, so that the birth-ascribed status system produced by the distinction is a long-term but ultimately temporary expedient. In the meantime, it remains the most important social distinction in modern China.

China's system of stratification into urban and rural personnel is not a peculiarity of Zengbu, or Guangdong province. It is a universal feature of Chinese society. Hinton, in his book *Shenfan*, reports that in north China "far-reaching measures permanently divided the people into two groups – an urban group with guaranteed employment and guaranteed subsistence – and a rural group in direct confrontation with nature, fending for itself to the best of its ability and unable to leave the land except by invitation" (Hinton 1983, pp. 106–109). Whyte and Parish describe a "rigid urban hierarchy of limited access that still persists. At the bottom are peasants ... who are generally unable to move into urban places to establish residence – even into nearby commune towns" (1984, pp. 18–19).

The historical context for dividing the population into urban personnel and rural personnel was the effort in the late 1950s to avert the threat of a national emergency posed by a massive exodus from the countryside to the cities, which could not provide a living for so major an influx of rural population. In discussing this period, Selden refers to:

the rush of the peasants to the cities in search of jobs, higher incomes, and the promise of urban life ... Despite government restrictions, the urban population swelled from 57 million in 1949 to 89 million in 1957. Rural migrants accounted for two-thirds of the increase, more than 20 million people. The capital intensive strategy of the first five-year plan, however, produced only one million new nonagricultural jobs a year, while agricultural employment increased only slightly ... at this time the total labor force grew at a rate of 8 million per year. Official estimates placed urban unemployment at 3 million in 1952 prior to the plan, but by 1957 unemployment was approaching crisis proportions. And it was compounded by the increasing difficulty of obtaining sufficient marketable grain to feed the cities. The problem of the flight to the cities and massive urban unemployment is one that has plagued every developing country. (1979, p. 55)

The administrative solution to these grave problems was to formalize the distinction between the people who lived in the cities and were responsible for nonagricultural production, and the people who lived in the countryside and were primarily responsible for producing the vital food supply; the latter were forbidden to leave the land. This formalized distinction became law throughout China. It was closely tied to the household registration system, which is the bureaucratic basis for finding employment and being provided with rations, and thus was most effectively enforced. The significance of the formalized distinction between urban personnel and rural personnel tends to have gone unnoticed outside of China, and it has been little discussed in print by the Chinese themselves, yet it is an essential element in modern Chinese social structure.

The rural personnel of Zengbu think of themselves as peasants (*nongmin*), and refer to urban personnel under the broad classifying term, workers (*gongren*). From the peasants' point of view, workers are classed together in structural opposition to themselves. The category is inclusive and undifferentiated. Urbanites are acutely aware of status gradations within the worker category; factory workers, high-ranking cadres, and intellectuals hold clearly distinguishable statuses. But these distinctions are less important to peasants than the peasant–worker distinction.

The peasants of Zengbu express the distinction between peasants and workers in terms of the source of a person's rice. A person who eats rice supplied by the state is, in these terms, a worker, and a person who eats rice supplied by the household or the team is a peasant. One would not ask, "Is so-and-so classified as rural or urban personnel?" but rather, "Does so-and-so eat the state's rice?" This way of expressing the question dramatizes the structural distinction between peasants and workers. Peasants have a particular relationship to the state, a relationship in which the rice they eat is not provided for them under the terms of their employment. And this specifically peasant type of relationship to the state is maintained in practice by specifically peasant forms of bureaucracy and social organization which are not used by workers, who have differing specific forms of their own. These peasant forms of social organization reflect the assumption that the relationship between peasants and the means of production is different from the relationship between workers and the means of production; the difference may be seen in the way peasants are paid, and in the economic risks they are required to assume.

Peasant forms of social organization in China are in a remarkable state of flux, but two underlying principles persist: that the peasants are rewarded in direct proportion to the success of the lowest relevant social unit, and that peasants bear the losses if the social unit fails, whether as a result of incompetence or of natural disaster. In 1979–80, the lowest relevant social unit, the primary level of specifically peasant social organization, was the production team. By 1985, most of the economic functions of the production team had been taken over by households as delegates of the team. The two principles continued to operate, however, with the household replacing the team as the lowest relevant social unit.

Membership in the household is inherited, and so is membership in a team, village, or brigade. As a result, kinship and governmental organization are not discontinuous. A peasant's relationship to these levels of organization from birth thus comes to imply directly a relationship of obligation to deliver grain on behalf of the nation. The peasant and the land are structurally bound together.

The economic rewards of peasants are linked to the success or failure of the household or the team. They do not receive salaries, like urban personnel. Pay is in proportion to the success of the social unit carrying out production. This method of rewarding peasants for their labor makes them responsible for the inherent risks of agricultural production, many of which are beyond their control. The organizational structure of workers' units provides a clear contrast to peasant households, teams, villages, or brigades. Workers do not use the household as a level of production responsibility. They are not assigned to their units at birth, but when they finish school. Workers know in advance what they will be paid for their services. They do not have their salaries figured as proportions of the actual profits of their units. They can count on their earnings, and they are cushioned from the economic vicissitudes their units may encounter. Since workers are not producers of grain, they receive a grain ration from the state as a condition of employment. It is this which has been taken as the key indicator of the distinction between peasants and workers by the peasants themselves.

Peasant forms of social organization and peasant forms of reward for labor are based on arbitrary social and cultural definitions, rather than on rational economic considerations. There is no reason to suppose that peasant forms of organization and payment have any particular superiority over urban forms of organization and payment in facilitating agricultural production. In any case, approximately two-thirds of the income of Zengbu brigade is from local-level industrial enterprises, and only one-third from agriculture. Although the work done by peasants in these rural enterprises is similar in all essentials to the work done in urban factories by people classified as workers, the people working in such enterprises retain their social classification as peasants. And these rural industrial enterprises run effectively using peasant forms of social organization; there is no evidence that the organizational conventions of Chinese urban industry would be functionally superior for the purpose.

Historically, social attitudes and values have imposed a stigma on peasants. It is not unfair to say that a negative attitude toward peasants has been deeply embedded in Chinese thinking for more than 2,000 years, legitimized by Confucius, who apparently felt that it was morally preferable for officials to regard the concerns of peasants as beneath their notice. (For example, there is the story in the *Analects* about the student Fan Chi, who offended Confucius by expressing an interest in studying agriculture.) Socialism also provided a theoretical understanding of peasants which was not entirely friendly to them. Socialist theory questioned whether peasants could unite sufficiently to make them useful in creating a revolution. For example, according to Engels,

the agricultural population, in consequence of its dispersion over a great space, and of the difficulty of bringing about an agreement among any considerable portion of it, can never attempt a successful independent movement; they require the initiatory impulse of the more concentrated, more enlightened, more easily moved people of the towns. (1973, p. 307)

Socialist theory also expected that peasants as a class would disappear, to be replaced by a rural proletariat of farm laborers, in the natural course of events leading to socialist revolution and industrial modernization. Yet in China, following a revolution in which peasants had played an important part, a socialist state was established in which the peasantry as a class had by no means disappeared. Mao took the position that the only peasants who could really be relied on were the poor peasants. He commented, "There is a serious tendency to capitalism among the well-to-do peasants" (1966, p. 33). He felt that peasants were less likely than workers to understand their own class interests, or to act upon them in a genuinely revolutionary way (see Mao, 1966, pp. 31–33, and Mao, 1969, p. 247).

A more specific political statement on the peasantry was formulated by Zhuang Qidong and Ye Fang in an article entitled "On Reducing and Eliminating the Essential Differences Between City and Country, Worker and Peasant, and Mental and Manual Labor" (1959). They traced the distinctions between city and country to historical roots in the division of labor and the emergence of classes, and quoted Engels:

Engels said, "The first major division of labor, i.e., the separation of city from country, enabled the rural population to remain in a foolish state for thousands of years. Meanwhile, the urban residents were enslaved by individual expertise. This separation damaged the basis for the spiritual development of rural residents as well as for the physical development of urban residents." Besides, this new social division led to the emergence of social classes and private ownership, which in turn aggravated the contradiction between city and country, worker and peasant, and mental and manual labor. (Zhuang and Ye 1959, p. 177)

Zhuang and Ye classified the differences between workers and peasants into three categories. First, the state owned the means of production used by the workers, whereas the local collective owned the means of production used by the peasants. Second, there were differences in the development of productive power, modernization, and technology. Third, there were differences in cultural and material life. Zhuang and Ye emphasized the length of time it would take for China to become so highly developed that the peasants' means of production could be owned by the state rather than the collective. Implicit in this long-range view was the idea that China was not rich enough to provide a truly communist economic base for peasants as well as for workers, since state ownership implies responsibilites as well as rights. In more practical terms, the distinction between peasants and workers was set forth in a State Council document, entitled, "Regulations on the Criteria for Defining Urban and Rural Areas," dated November 1955, and published in 1956 in the *Collection of Legislative Documents of the People's Republic of China*. This document, which carried the proviso that it was intended to define an administrative distinction, not an ideological one, said, "Because there is a difference in the economic conditions and way of life between rural and urban people, the work of the government should be carried out in accordance with the distinction" (p. 411). The government intended to treat peasants and workers differently. However, it was not until 1958 that the regulations implementing the distinction between peasants and workers were put into effect, with a revised version of the "Regulations for Household Registration of the People's Republic of China," signed by Mao to indicate his approval, and published in 1959, in the *Collection of Legislative Documents* for that year. Briefly put, the household registration system acted as a means of identifying every citizen, registering all changes in status, controlling all changes of residence, whether temporary or permanent, and providing the basis for the distribution of rationed food and goods. Without valid registration documents, rations were unobtainable, nor could an unregistered person find regular employment. Changes from urban to rural residence status required elaborate documentation. Urban and rural residents followed somewhat different registration rules. (For example, "In the city, each household should be given a [registration] booklet. In rural areas, the booklet is given to a collective unit" [1959, p. 20].) In Zengbu, the household registration records were maintained by the brigade, and are now maintained by the *xiang*. They are careful, accurate, and complete. The system as a whole is a formidable instrument of social control.

The household registration regulations did not include an explicit statement that they were drawn up at least partly to keep rural residents out of urban areas. But a document called "Explanatory Notes on the Regulations for Household Registration of the People's Republic of China," which was published in the same volume as the regulations themselves, over the signature of the Minister of Public Security, Luo Ruiqing, devoted explicit attention to the importance of forbidding immigration to the cities. Luo's explanation is so relevant that it is worth quoting at length:

Citizens who move from the countryside to the city should have a certificate of employment from a city unit, a certificate of school enrollment, or a certificate of permission to change household registration to the city. Why do we have these regulations? Because in the past few years there has been a serious tendency for the rural population to move into the city. Some offices, businesses, and factories have not earnestly carried out the policy of limiting and reducing urban population, and have gone so far as to employ people from the countryside, and even to send to the countryside on their own initiative for the certificates of rural residence of these people, which they caused to be changed. Some units, instead of cooperating with the government in returning them to the countryside, permit this unplanned influx of rural population to become permanent urban residents, and this has aggravated the present unstable conditions, resulting in difficulties with the urban construction plan, the stability of urban life, and social order. As a result, problems have occurred in city transportation, housing, market supply, employment, and educational opportunity. Meanwhile, because of the outflow in large numbers of rural labor power, agricultural production has been affected. This is not favorable for the development of agricultural production and socialist reconstruction as a whole ...

We must allow neither an unplanned increase in urban labor power nor an unplanned outflow of rural labor power. Furthermore, our country at present already has an excess of urban labor power, but there is a great potentiality for rural production which can contain large numbers of labor power ... From this point of view, it is not difficult to understand why we should stem the unplanned outflow of rural population.

In addition, the unplanned rural population in the city, because of unemployment, is confronted with difficulty in making a living, and some people are likely to find themselves wandering in the street. A small proportion even go so far as to become hand-in-glove with some bad elements and engage in criminal acts like theft, robbery, and swindling, and thus produce a threat to urban security. (1959, p. 212)

According to this document, the 1959 regulations superseded a previous certification program which was not effectively enforced, but which classified people as rural or urban. In explaining the new regulations, the importance of keeping peasants out of the cities was central to Luo's argument; he justified the regulations because they would help to achieve that aim. He pointed to the dangerous social results when peasants come to the city seeking employment. His point of view was urban-centred, and the focus of his concern was urban unemployment and the potential for urban unrest. He spoke in general terms of "the great potentiality for rural production," but did not raise the issue of the actual conditions peasants faced in the countryside as long as the potentiality for rural production remained unrealized. The regulations were justified on the grounds that they would help to keep the cities safe and well supplied, and would relieve pressure on the availability of urban jobs.

During the Cultural Revolution, the official attitude toward peasants underwent a change of emphasis, and it became part of the current political morality to emphasize the ideological importance of learning from poor and lower-middle peasants. This was to be accomplished by going down to the countryside to live and work among them. However, being sent down to the countryside had devastating social consequences, of which participation in agricultural labor was among the least; more important were loss of status, loss of economic security, loss of access to urban life, separation from family, and the knowledge that the painful new status would be inherited by one's children. Bernstein, describing this period in *Up to the Mountains and Down to the Villages* (1977), quotes an example in which young people in a town were, in effect, being asked to leave their high-status classification and join the lower-status classification, and the only volunteer was already a member of the lower-status category:

Some time ago my classmates wrote criticism articles in which they expressed a determination to go to the countryside after graduation in order to repudiate with concrete deeds Confucius' fallacy " only inferior men do farming." The teacher in charge said to us at a class meeting: "All of you have said that you are going to the countryside after graduation. Now, has anyone made a firm promise to do so? If, so stand up and let us see." I felt this was a challenge to the younger generation and stood up to announce resolutely: "I promise that I will go to the countryside after graduation." He said, "Yours is not a good case. Your home is in the suburbs. You are on grain ration in the countryside. You simply have to go back even though you are not willing." I asked him: "Are you citing such a case to prove that nobody is taking the brilliant road indicated by Chairman Mao?" He said flamboyantly: "Such is the case – we cannot but admit it." Not only did he in theory oppose educated youths going to the countryside, but he even warmly encouraged those students who wanted to leave school to look for jobs [in town]." (p. 99)

Urbanites experienced going down to the countryside as a humiliating penance of indefinite, perhaps permanent duration: to live like a peasant was a punishment. This attitude in itself very clearly illustrates the status gulf between peasants and workers. From the viewpoint of the peasants, the influx of untrained and resentful young people, who had to be supported by taking shares of the teams' profits when they were not fully capable of pulling their weight, created reciprocal resentment and strain, and mutual resentment reinforced mutual prejudices. Rather than closing the gap between peasants and workers, the program opened it wider. And the mechanism for enforcing the structural distinction between the two, the household registration system, remained in effect, nor was it suggested that it be changed.

The household registration regulations provide some of the elements that are symbolically significant in marking the status distinction between peasants and workers. The possession of the identification card of an urban resident is an important mark of status. In Zengbu, visiting workers display their identification cards with pride, and peasants speak of them with envy. The identification card of an urban resident validates a person's right to be present in a city. Peasants have no such right. In 1979, a peasant who left the brigade had to have a letter of introduction from brigade officials to produce

on demand, stating the justification for the trip. This regulation was seen as a
public symbolization of lower status, and hence humiliating.

Another status marker related to the household registration regulations
has to do with the rationing system. Foods which peasants are not permitted
to buy are available to urban residents; the food available to peasants is not so
wide in variety or so high in quality. Peasants resent this; urbanites comment
disparagingly on peasant fare. The food on one's plate is likely to be a subtle
and accurate status indicator throughout China.

Other culturally-understood status markers include the wearing of city
clothes, which identify the wearer as a worker rather than a peasant, and the
ability to speak Mandarin. Peasants in Zengbu are pointedly and effectively
excluded from participation when higher-ranking urban cadres choose to
switch from Cantonese to Mandarin in front of them. But the problem
extends beyond the symbolization of status difference. Peasants are remote
from the urban centers, where the apparatus of power and government are
located, where there are movies, music, opera, and other performances, and
where the best schools are found. Urban centers have a wider range of
manufactured goods available, as well a greater variety of food items. This
lack of access is partially shared by workers who live in small commune
towns which are comparatively remote, and yet peasants are remoter still.
Compared with an urban worker in a large town, peasants have much less
access to a wide range of benefits. When the comparison is between a worker
from Beijing and a peasant from Zengbu, the difference is very great indeed.

The specific regulations which deal with the legal meaning of being a
peasant with regard to such matters as residence, marriage, and inheritance,
are administered at the district headquarters by the Office of Civil Affairs. (In
the cities this office also administers the analogous regulations governing the
lives of workers.) The Chashan district cadre in charge of civil affairs
administers a set of regulations implementing the peasant–worker distinction
which have been in effect since 1964. The regulations state that a child takes
his or her mother's status; if the mother is a peasant, the child will be, too.
The purpose of this departure from customary assumptions about the
inheritance of status (traditionally, a child belongs to the father and his
family, and shares their status) may be to restrict mobility as effectively as
possible. Since men are much more likely to shift status than women, having
the child take the mother's status means that far fewer children will shift
status.

The regulations also restrict the transfer of residence from one community
to another. The communities of China are ranked in order, along a scale with
Beijing at the top and peasant villages at the bottom. Thus, every household is
registered in a community with a rank. People are allowed to transfer their
registration only to a community of the same rank as their original one, or to a
community of a lower rank. A person registered in a rural, grain-producing

village can transfer only to another, as a peasant woman does when she marries, or as a man does in the exceptional cases when he marries into his wife's family and takes up residence with them. A worker, registered in a commune town such as Chashan, could transfer to another commune town but not to a town of higher rank, like the county town of Dongguan. People of Dongguan could transfer to another town of similar importance, like Taiping or Shilong, but not to a major city like Guangzhou. Since Beijing has the highest ranking, a worker from Beijing could move to Guangzhou, but not vice versa. Even permitted moves are rare and difficult to achieve. Most often, the application to move is rejected outright. But in any case, the ramifications of town ranking do not matter to a peasant, whose only choice is remaining in a peasant community.

The household registration regulations have important implications for the formation of marriages. For example, if a man who is a worker marries a woman who is a peasant, she will not be permitted to change her household registration to go and live with him. She could, in theory, stay with him temporarily in the urban area, but without a job or food rations. She could, in theory, stay in her own village, and live apart from her husband. However, male villagers tend to express resentment at the idea of a married woman's continuing to be the responsibility of the household, team, or village into which she was born. If the man was a worker who had only recently become so for special reasons, and had peasant parents, the woman could live with the man's parents in his native village. (This is the solution most commonly adopted in Zengbu.) According to the Chashan-level cadre in charge of civil affairs, a man who was born a worker was most unlikely to marry a peasant woman; it had happened no more than once or twice in his experience. He suggested that it would only happen if there was no other possible marriage partner for the man, or if there were exceptionally good feelings between the two. This second possibility is unlikely to arise because young peasants have few opportunities of meeting young workers, and when young people do meet, their behavior is regulated by very strong customary patterns of modesty, shyness, and puritanical decency. In cases where the women is a worker and the man a peasant, the woman would be faced with the prospect of shifting her household registration out of a workers' community and into a peasant community if she were ever to live with her husband. So, marriages between peasants and workers are made virtually impossible by the practical consequences of the regulations.

This means that the regulations have had the unintended effect of creating two endogamous groups crosscutting all of Chinese society. The marriage reform laws provide legal freedom of marriage in the People's Republic of China, so that peasants could marry workers if they wished; the commune cadre in charge of civil affairs drew attention to this. Yet the regulations have had the effect of restricting choice in marriage formation.

According to another regulation administered at the district level, a male worker married to a female peasant may transfer his job and status to one of his children, if he is willing to return to the countryside and be reclassified as a peasant himself. The child who inherits worker status may be of either sex, but, as the cadre in charge of civil affairs commented, in the countryside people generally choose a son. The only restriction on the inheritance of worker status is that the child must be under the age of 35. If a man of peasant origin who inherits a worker's job marries a woman who is also a worker, their household is registered as a worker's household, and their children are workers.

There are some regulations governing changes from peasant status to worker status which are administered by a branch of the Central Military Ministry because they involve veterans. Until 1981, veterans had priority when workers were recruited from the countryside, and this veterans' preference was one of the most important avenues along which male peasants became workers. When a man left the armed services, he was returned to his place of origin. If a worker's job became available for him he was given worker status and permitted to move to take the job, but his wife and children were required to remain behind. These regulations of the employment of demobilized soldiers were superseded in 1981, however, by the "Ministry of Civil Affairs Report on the Reassignment for Work of Retired Officers and Demobilized Soldiers as Authorized by the State Council for Promulgation." The report says that "the aim of the regulations is to avoid a concentration in the big cities, medium-sized cities, and places with better conditions, so that these places will not be overburdened" (p. 12). It continues, "There should be restrictions against assignment to the three major cities, Beijing, Shanghai, and Tianjin. We should encourage those soldiers who are willing to go back to the countryside. The assignment of work must definitely be governed by the principle of returning to the place of origin. The emphasis should be on the countryside" (p. 13). This is likely to mean that almost all peasant veterans will remain in the countryside, although rare exceptions might not be impossible. The document also states that "when urban workers are recruited from the countryside, other things being equal, demobilized soldiers should be recruited first" (p. 14). But the document is written from a perspective of urban employment pressure which makes the possibility of workers being recruited from the countryside appear unlikely. When soldiers originally recruited from the city are demobilized, "every unit, factory, and city should regard it as a political task to receive these demobilized urban soldiers, and cannot refuse the assignment" (p. 14). The phraseology suggests that the task of finding urban employment even for veterans who are urban residents will not necessarily be easy.

The limited possibilities for social mobility within this rigid system are of immense concern to peasants. An analysis of peasant efforts to become workers illustrates the nature and boundaries of the system. The most important ways for peasants to become workers, assuming there is no chance of inheriting a worker's job, are serving in the armed forces, rising within the organization of the Communist party, or making great scholastic achievements. For women, there is also the indirect and partial option of marrying a man who holds worker status, and thus gaining the limited and secondary benefits available to the wife of a worker, even if she herself is still classified as a peasant and must continue to live in the countryside. All of these methods have been used in Zengbu.

Under the regulations in force prior to 1981, serving in the armed forces was the single most important route to status change. Not only did veterans receive priority when workers were recruited from the countryside, but the experience of being in the army was highly valued in itself. The army taught useful skills. Its business was conducted in Mandarin, so recruits often become fairly fluent Mandarin speakers. Soldiers had certain physical comforts, including plentiful quantities of food and clothing. (The enthusiasm which the villagers expressed for the physical comforts of army life illustrates by implication the amount of privation the people of Zengbu have endured in relatively recent times.) Soldiers had the opportunity to visit other parts of China. They were paid in salaries, not in the form of workpoints. Zengbu families felt the loss of the earning power of a young man in the prime of life, but they received a small subsidy from the brigade as partial compensation. Families acquired prestige and benefited from their son's advancement. As the recruiting posters said, "If one person joins the army, a whole family is glorious!"

The opportunity of serving in the army was available only to a very few, and these few were overwhelmingly men, not women. (In 1979–80, there was only one woman soldier from Chashan commune currently serving.) The army set a quota of the number of men it needed. Each year the cadres were informed how many candidates (usually two or three a year) Zengbu might send. The choice of army candidates was in the hands of the cadres; it was one of the few benefits of the state which they were in a position to control. Zengbu sent extra candidates to take the physical examination, so that if some failed, others could take their places, and no opportunities would be lost. The candidates had to be unmarried, between the ages of 18 and 20, educated through lower-middle school, in good health, and with a record of hard work on the team. Sometimes there were also special political qualifications, particularly for the navy. For example, the navy once required a man with no relatives in Hong Kong for three generations back, and a "good class background," i.e. his family had to have been classified as poor peasants or lower at the time of land reform. Two of the three brigade villages could find no one at all who met these requirements, but the third was able to produce a suitable candidate. In 1979–80, two out of five recruits were members of the Youth League.

When the new recruits had been chosen and their letters of induction sent to the brigade, a ceremony was held, consisting of a parade through the village led by a brigade cadre beating an enormous drum. Schoolchildren followed, carrying red flags. The parade wound through the village to the house of each new recruit. Each recruit came forward, dressed in his best clothes, and accepted his letter, beaming with pride and pleasure, as his smiling parents, also dressed in their best, stood beside him. This was the only public ceremony conducted by the brigade for any purpose in 1979–80. Its effect, in a social context deliberately denuded of ceremonial forms, was to mark the importance of the occasion with a particular and vivid emphasis.

When a man's army service was finished, it was by no means certain that he would be recruited as a worker. The figures from the brigade's household registers show that over the fourteen-year period from 1964 to 1978, 67 people returned from the army. Of these, 12 were subsequently offered positions as workers, and left the brigade to take them. In one case, a man served five years in the navy. He returned to the village in March, 1977. The county-level government sent out a list of workers' jobs for which it was recruiting, and this list was passed on to the commune level and the brigade level. The brigade cadres chose among the returned volunteers, and offered a job as a bus conductor at the Dongguan bus station to this man in October, 1977.

Another man, recruited in 1960, served in the army for 15 years. Then he returned to the village and worked for his team. He had married while in the army, and his wife was a worker, employed in a commune hospital not far from Shilong. After a year, he was offered his present job in the department store in Shilong.

Another way for a peasant to become a worker is through the Communist party. However, social mobility is a rare by-product of usefulness to the party, not a direct reward for achievement or an explicit goal of membership. On the contrary, the party emphasizes that joining in order to advance oneself is a wrong thing to do, and violates the high standards expected of party members (see chapter 14).

Like all of Chinese society, the party itself is divided into two strata: peasant members and worker members. Most peasant party members who become leaders at the brigade level or lower do not make the transition to worker. In Zengbu, Secretary Lu, although still classified as a peasant, has eaten the state's grain on a temporary basis. He is the only brigade cadre to have done so. After a term of service as brigade secretary, he was given a worker's job as director of the commune-level office of communications and transportation.

There is only one recent example of a Zengbu villager making a permanent transition from peasant to worker as the result of valuable political work. The case is remarkable, not only because it involves reassignment as a worker but also because the person is a young woman. (There are over eight male party members for every female party member in Chashan commune, and most politically active people are male (see chapter 13).) This young woman was educated in the village, and then went to work for her team in the brick and tile kiln. At the age of 18 she joined the Communist Youth League. Then, three years later, in 1975, she was selected as brigade cadre in charge of Youth League work. (At that time the brigade committee included some young people, because of the policies of the Cultural Revolution.) She was responsible for doing political and ideological work among the young people, and for preparing them to join the Youth League. She was very successful. (People still reminisce with pleasure about the activities she organized, including tug-of-war and sampan races. Dragon boats [see chapter 12] were forbidden at that time as politically incorrect, but participants in the sampan races felt that their athletic prowess brought honor to the brigade.) In 1978, in response to a directive from the upper levels saying that there should be a young person as deputy secretary of the brigade, she was appointed to that post. (She was also offered the opportunity to become a soldier in the army, but her mother would not agree to this because she was an only child.) Then she was made a commune-level cadre, eating the state's grain, and was assigned to oversee the adjacent brigade of Lubian as resident commune cadre. In this capacity she supervised production and did some agricultural labor "so as not to lose touch with the peasants." She is presently a Chashan district-level cadre.

A third possible avenue of social mobility for Zengbu peasants is education. The only such case in Zengbu has the quality of folklore, invoking the traditional tales of studious boys who rose into the ranks of the scholar gentry on the basis of scholastic ability alone. The individual in question is the son of the man who ran the brigade's grain mill. He had always studied very hard; it is said that even in primary school, he studied every night until midnight. He graduated from the village school and passed the examination to go to Shilong middle school. The family's financial situation made it difficult to send him there – indeed, his parents began to fear that they would have to remove him – but the teachers said that they wished to train him, and that his parents need not pay. The year he finished school, only three students in the county (population 1,000,000) passed the university entrance examination, and he was one of them. University students in China are assigned where they are needed, rather than being asked where they would prefer to go. His assignment was to the Dalien Merchant Marine Institute in northeast China. He became a navigator. While he was at the university, he also became a party member because, as his father put it, "he loved Chairman Mao with a firm standpoint." Then he completed his course and passed the examination, which involved taking a ship from Dalien to Shanghai. He received the identification card of a graduate, and was assigned to Huangpu harbor, near

Guangzhou. When he arrived there, however, they did not ask him to work as a navigator. Instead, he was trained as a cadre because of his family history and personal experience. For four years he was secretary of the Huangpu harbor party committee. In 1976, he was reassigned to a new harbor near Huangpu as chairman of administration. He is married to a woman whom he met when they were both students at Shilong middle school. She is a worker, and teaches in Chashan primary school. The couple has two children. The family has no connections or influence that might have helped to bring about this man's success. He must be brilliantly intelligent, hardworking, dedicated, professionally competent, a good administrator, and politically committed and idealistic as well, a rare individual in every sense.

It is clear that opportunities for social mobility are far more limited for women than they are for men. Women join the army only under the most exceptional circumstances; normally the few positions available are for men. Women are also much less likely to be political leaders. (See chapters 5, 6, and 7.) No women in the brigade have succeeded in making the extraordinary academic achievements which might have led to their advancement. Women are left with the possibility of trying to better themselves by marrying a man who is a worker or is likely to become one. This is a factor in marriage formation.

In one case, a young woman deliberately sought out a young man in the army, on the assumption that he would be made a worker after his discharge. She made friends with his mother, wrote letters to the young man himself, and bought a watch which she gave to him as a present. When the young man left the army, they were married.

Since the wife had seemed so interested in marrying the husband, there was general surprise when she left him some months after the marriage. She was persuaded to return, and became pregnant, but left again and went back to her parents' home. The reason she gave for leaving was that she had expected her husband to be offered a job as a worker shortly after his return from the army, but this had not happened. The man and his family did not know that she had married with this idea in mind. Ironically, he had enlisted for a special short term of service, knowing that he could not expect to be offered a worker's job after his discharge.

Some indications of the rarity of the transition from peasant to worker are provided by the brigade's own figures for the years 1964–78. The population of the brigade is over 5,000. During these fourteen years, 22 men left the brigade to join the armed services. Twelve returned veterans out of a possible 67 (the brigade must have included veterans from an earlier period as well as 1964–78 in this figure) were offered jobs as workers, and left to take them up. Nine students transferred out of the brigade to continue their schooling; this figure probably does not imply a permanent change of status. Four people, all of them men, inherited workers' jobs from their fathers. Two women were made commune-level cadres eating the state's rice. This makes a total of 18 people who have permanently changed status; it means that over the whole fourteen-year period, people were able to change status at the rate of 3.6 per thousand, or 0.257 per thousand per year. Considered by sex, men have had 0.228 chances per thousand per year of making the transition, and women have had 0.028 chances per thousand per year. Now that the army has changed its policy for veterans, the possibilities are even further reduced. It is clear that during this period of time the boundaries between peasants and workers were, with numerically trivial exceptions, impermeable.

The economic policies introduced in Zengbu and the rest of China between 1979 and 1985 allow the peasants more opportunities to travel to the town and city, to trade and to find temporary work. Thousands have done so. However, temporary migrants do not achieve the status of workers, and their household registration still classifies them as peasants.

Following decollectivization, the boundaries of the caste-like status system were modified in certain limited ways for a brief experimental period. A group of 220 peasants, mainly women and children, dependents of men who were already classified as workers, were allowed to move into Chashan permanently. They were called "town citizens responsible for their own rice" (*zi li kou liang jiumin*). As the name indicates, they were required to furnish their own food rather than drawing rice rations from the state or the district government. They were also required to find their own living accommodation in town; the district government would not provide them with living-space. This status was to be transmitted through the mother, like peasant status. Holders of this status could, in theory, move to another town of the same rank as Chashan and continue to hold the same status. It is a liminal status, and those who hold it are not urban residents in the full sense; they are merely permitted to dwell in an urban area.

In 1984, yet another intermediate category was created: "staff and workers in district-run collective enterprises" (*qu ban qiye zhigong*). Membership in this urban status category was sold by the Chashan district government to 900 wealthy peasants from villages in the district for 4,000 *yuan* each. Peasants who purchased this status are entitled to eat the rice supplied by the district, but are not entitled to eat the rice of the state. Their position resembles that of commune-level cadres who ate the rice of the collective (see chapter 13). This status can only be claimed in Chashan town; if its holders move elsewhere, they will be considered peasants. The children of the members of this status group may inherit the status from their mothers, but not from their fathers. Thus, women must purchase this status in their own right if they wish to transmit it to their children.

The district government had planned to sell the "staff and workers in district-run collective enterprises" status to 1,000 peasants. The rationale for this was that it would raise capital to build more factory buildings, while securing more permanent factory workers for growing town industry. However, district government officials discontinued the experiment after selling the status to 900 peasants. They decided that it was cheaper to use temporary peasant labor in the factories than to shoulder the responsiblity for housing, feeding, and educating increased numbers of townspeople. This short-lived experiment was never general policy throughout Guangdong; it was tried experimentally in a mere handful of districts. By 1985, the purchase of this form of town-resident status was no longer possible.

The town's extraordinarily complex status system now includes a bewildering series of minute gradations of privilege: state cadres, state workers, collective cadres, collective workers, town citizens responsible for their own rice, staff and workers in district-run collective enterprises, and temporary peasant workers. Except for the temporary workers, however, all are higher in status than the peasants in the surrounding villages.

This system is an extraordinary one, and full of paradoxes. It is a deliberately created system of birth-ascribed status, in the context of a modern socialist state, enforced by bureaucratic methods rather than by custom. It is a system which, in spite of being based on birth ascription, is intended to be temporary rather than perpetual. It is a system in which status is inherited from the mother, in the context of a social order that has always been characterized by strongly patrilineal institutions. Considered separately, each of these features is striking enough, and taken together they form a remarkable complex. This system shapes the lives not only of the peasants of Zengbu but of the 800 million members of the largest meaningful category in the study of social structure – the peasants of China.

# 16

## The Chinese peasants and the world capitalist system

The question of the effects of the world capitalist system on the economic life of rural China has been an important subject of investigation and analysis for some fifty years. Although such topics are newly important in anthropology, where they are considered under the headings of world systems theory and dependency theory, they have a long history in research on China, and are familiar furniture of the mind, in Dewey's phrase, in the study of Chinese social life. The fundamental questions were originally formulated from within China, by such anthropological pioneers as Fei Hsiao-tung and Chang Chih-i, whose studies were made in the thirties and forties. Fei and Chang, like many other Chinese intellectuals of the time (*cf.* Meisner 1982, p. 84) took the position that economic contact with the West, as mediated by the treaty ports, was deleterious to the economic life of the surrounding countryside. This position was consistent both with Chinese culture, which is inclined to assert the intrinsic superiority of what is most purely Chinese and to ascribe responsibility for problems to outside influences, and with Marxist theory, which holds that capitalist intrusion would tend to destroy peasant economic systems.

It was Fei, in *Peasant Life in China* (1939) and in *Earthbound China* (with Chang Chih-i, 1945), who was the most influential anthropological proponent of this thesis. Fei and Chang argued that China had long relied heavily upon industrial employment. However, China's industry, unlike that of more modernized societies, was technologically backward, and scattered throughout the countryside. Fei held that the influx of Western manufactured goods destroyed the rural handicraft industries, on which the poorest peasants depended to supplement their inadequate income from agriculture. As a result, peasants were bankrupted and forced to sell their land to landlords and merchant-moneylenders, who had accumulated capital through Western trade. This led to the bipolarization of the rural class structure. A small number of rich peasants and landlords took their places at the top of the structure and increasing numbers of poor landless peasants sank to the bottom, dispossessed and rootless.

The Chinese Communist party took a similar position. It blamed foreign capitalist countries for turning pre-Liberation China into a semicolonial society with a semifeudal economy (see J.M. Potter 1968, p. 176). This Marxist–Leninist interpretation of the results of rural China's contact with the world economy was shared as well by many non-Marxist Chinese and foreign observers (see Tawney, 1966). It became a widely accepted scholastic orthodoxy, and was a popular explanation for the crucial role played by poor peasants in the Communist Revolution of 1949. Jack M. Potter has challenged this interpretation in his *Capitalism and the Chinese Peasant* (1968), arguing that the orthodox view was oversimplified: that Western commerce had stimulated as well as harmed China's rural economy, and that particularly in southern China, in the hinterland of Hong Kong, contact with the world capitalist economy benefited the peasants economically, however odious Western imperialism may have been on other grounds. This interpretation has remained controversial. With the recent reopening of rural China to participation in the world capitalist economy, the problem may be re-examined in fuller perspective, and in an intellectual context enriched by the scholarship on world systems theory that has developed since then.

In the context of recent scholarly interest in world systems theory and dependency theory, the effect of the world capitalist economy upon the peasants of Third World countries has become a major concern of anthropologists. Drawing upon the insights of Marx and Engels (in their "Communist Manifesto" [1962]), Marx (in *Capital* [1967], and his newspaper writings with Engels on colonialism [1972]), Amin (1974), Baran (1957), de Janvry (1981), Frank (1979), Hobson (1972), Lenin (1973), Luxemburg (1972), Mintz (1985), Stavrianos (1981), Wallerstein (1974), and E. Wolf (1982), all of whom have elucidated the effects of Western capitalism on the peoples of the world, anthropologists now take it as a starting-point that the lives of Third World peasants cannot be understood without considering the influence of the world economy on the societies in which they live.

The accepted view is that unequal dependent participation in a world capitalist economy dominated by the rich capitalist countries of Europe, the United States, and Japan, has produced and maintained underdevelopment in the countries being exploited. The capitalist countries extract raw materials, surplus value, and interest from these countries, making them poor and indebted, and keeping them underdeveloped. Only in rare cases, such as Taiwan and South Korea, which enjoyed special relationships with the United States for political reasons, have underdeveloped countries managed to industrialize and develop within the world capitalist system.

This implies that the way for the overwhelming majority of Third World countries to modernize would be for them to free themselves from participation in the world capitalist system, and to attempt to develop independently. Unfortunately, this is not easily done. Samir Amin (1981) has argued, in fact, that China is the only important recent example of an underdeveloped country that has been able to develop on its own, free from involvement with world capitalism. Amin believed that Maoist independent development was demonstrably a more successful strategy for the people of underdeveloped countries than the alternative strategy of trying to develop while participating from a dependent position in the world capitalist economy.

Amin's book reflects the intense interest of Third World peoples in China's efforts to modernize. From 1949 to 1977, the perceived development success of Maoist China (see Barnett 1981, pp. 16–27, and the literature cited there) seemed to hold out hope to many of the world's impoverished peoples (see Gurley, 1976). Finding themselves not only unable to develop but also suffering from actual regression because of the constraints of the world capitalist economic system, Third World countries looked to China as an example of an independent socialist path to development.

However, the Chinese themselves did not perceive their record during the Maoist period as successful. In the late 1970s, China regarded itself as a poor and underdeveloped country. As a consequence, in 1978, the Chinese leadership, under the Four Modernizations policy, decided to reopen China to the world economy for the first time in thirty-five years. Special economic zones for foreign investment were established in Zhuhai (near Macao), in Shenzhen, (just south of Zengbu on the Hong Kong border), in Xiamen, (in Fujian province), and in other cities of coastal China. The closed-door policy of the previous three decades is now seen as having hampered the country's modernization efforts. The question is, will the new policy of collaborating with world capitalism benefit the Chinese more than their previous iso-lationist Maoist policies? The results of this experiment will be profoundly important, not only for China, but for other developing countries. If China is successful in participating in a controlled manner in the world capitalist economy, deriving benefits, and avoiding ill effects, then other countries may well relinquish the idea of independent socialist development, and choose instead to enter into relations with world capitalism.

Within China, Zengbu provides a useful specific case for examining the initial consequences of the country's new policy on the lives of the peasants. Since Zengbu is adjacent to Hong Kong and the Shenzhen special economic zone, the first effects of contact with the world economy have quickly become apparent. Has world capitalism damaged or destroyed Zengbu's rural industries, bankrupting the peasants, bipolarizing the rural class struc-ture, and increasing the dependency of China on the capitalist countries? Or has participation in the world economy, as controlled by a strong and unified Chinese government, brought prosperity to the peasants and helped China to modernize? These questions may be answered by examining the effects of the world economy on Zengbu's rural industry and economic life. (For the effects on Zengbu's social life, see chapter 17.)

15. Hong Kong-Zengbu brigade factory, 1985

In 1979, the Chinese government made it possible for Hong Kong businessmen to invest directly in rural China, initially in partnership with communes and brigades, and later in partnership with other levels of government and with individuals. Hong Kong capitalists promptly explored the possibilities for setting up factories within China, where space was plentiful, and the underemployed peasants were an excellent source of very cheap labor.

The Zengbu brigade cadres were strongly interested in attracting Hong Kong investment. The benefits of such arrangements had already been demonstrated to them: two joint venture textile factories established in the town of Chashan in 1979 had given work to more than a hundred women, at wages that were excellent by local standards.

Throughout the fall and winter of 1979, the brigade cadres conducted a search for Hong Kong investors to establish factories in Zengbu in partnership with the brigade. They made use of established kinship networks. The people of Zengbu were requested to make contact with their Hong Kong relatives who were in business, and to publicize the brigade's interest in joint ventures.

The kinship net cast by the brigade brought forth a goodly number of potential investors in late 1979. Most were business people from Hong Kong. They were invited to the brigade for business discussions. Secretary Lu refurnished the brigade's reception room for receiving these visitors, commenting, "If we look and act like a bunch of penniless peasants, then these Hong Kong capitalists will treat us as such." The visitors were entertained at banquets. These meetings between the cadres, dressed in their blue Mao suits, and the Hong Kong capitalists, in their nattily-tailored Western garb, were confrontations between two culturally antithetical worlds. But they had a common goal, the establishment of capitalist processing factories which would provide jobs in a socialist system, and produce goods to be sold for profit on the world capitalist market.

Both sides were wary, and a series of visitors were unsuccessful in concluding an agreement. Then a businesswoman, made known to the brigade through the Hong Kong relative of a Zengbu villager, arrived to discuss the establishment of a knitwear factory. Early in 1980, the cadres made an agreement with her for the establishment of a spinning and knitting factory in Zengbu. The commune and the county administration, showing their willingness to foster the new economic policies, quickly approved the agreement. Such agreements were a new phenomenon, but a widespread one. Between 1979 and 1982 alone, according to provincial-level cadres, 182 million *yuan* (U.S.$ 113,500,000) of foreign capital, mainly from Hong Kong, was invested in equipment for such small rural factories in Guangdong province.

The brigade used savings from the profits of its enterprises, a loan from the state bank, and the labor of the brigade's construction team, to put up a large brick factory building in the Zengbu industrial quarter. Reconditioned commercial sewing machines were provided by the Hong Kong investor. (Initially, women who had worked in the factories established by Hong Kong entrepreneurs in Chashan had had to provide their own sewing machines as a condition of employment.) Raw materials were shipped from Hong Kong to Shenzhen. Brigade representatives transported them to Zengbu in brigade trucks. Brigade factory workers turned the raw materials into finished items of apparel, which were packed and trucked back to the border. The products of this factory were sold on the world market, usually to Europe or to the United States.

Both sides benefited from this arrangement. The Hong Kong capitalist received the free use of the factory building, free electricity, free transportation, and a labor force willing to work for by far the lowest wages available to Hong Kong entrepreneurs. (In Hong Kong, labor was expensive and in short supply, and work space for factories commanded astronomical sums per square meter.) The Chinese government did not collect income tax from the foreign investor for three years; after that there was to be a 20 percent tax.

The brigade obtained jobs for over one hundred of its underemployed young people. The families of those employed in the new factory enjoyed a substantial and immediate increase in income: one daughter could earn almost as much per month as an entire household had earned in 1978. A straight piecework processing fee was paid for finishing the goods, and the brigade received part of the processing fee as collective income. The Chinese government received taxes and earned foreign exchange. (Between 1979 and 1982, the province earned 11,000,000 *yuan* in foreign exchange from these factories.)

For ideological purists on either side, these economic partnerships presented nightmarish features. Capitalists entered partnerships with collectives led by party members who were supposed to be dedicated to the destruction of capitalism; communist cadres provided physical plant and workers for partners who they had been taught were the embodiment of evil. Both sides, however, had large stakes in seeing that the partnerships worked, and they did. More factories were established on the same model: in June, 1980 a factory for the printing and dyeing of cloth, in April, 1981 a factory for making plastic toys, and in July, 1981 another underwear factory, built in town, with the commune furnishing 60 percent of the workers and the brigade 40 percent. The brigade's peasant workers commuted to town daily. By December 1981, these four processing factories employed 187 workers. By mid-1983, they employed 330 workers, 70 unmarried men and 260 unmarried women.

Work in the factory was certainly less demanding, physically, than transplanting rice or making bricks in the kilns; and the conditions of work were considered better. The factories were sheltered from the elements and the work was clean. One cadre said:

Everyone wants to work in the factories. They don't have to farm, which is much harder work. If they work in the factory, they get to wear shoes and socks; they don't have to work out in the hot sun or the cold, wet rain. They don't even have to eat so much, because factory work requires less strength, which saves their families rice. They can learn new skills as well.

In 1980, when the factories were first being established, the work was not continual, and there were temporary lay-offs. By 1981, however, the factories were operating more regularly. Sometimes the factories worked overtime to meet production deadlines, and there were what the villagers called "added shifts." Workers who returned to work from 7 p.m. to 10 p.m. were given a bonus of 0·30 *yuan* (18 U.S. cents) per night. The entrepreneur provided 0·20 *yuan* of this, and the brigade 0·10 *yuan*. When necessary, the factory continued to process all night until the shipment was finished. For work after midnight, the piece-rate was doubled.

Zengbu, like the overpopulated Chinese countryside in general, provided the Hong Kong capitalists with ideal conditions for extracting surplus value. The labor force was eager to work and responsive to the needs of the

16. Young Zengbu women make British dolls for export, 1985

enterprise. Wages were held stable and the work force was disciplined by the party cadres. The workers were perfectly flexible: if there was work for them, they worked; if not, they returned home to weave shrimp traps or farm until the factory reopened. And they were paid from U.S.$ 1.90 to U.S.$ 2.50 per eight-hour day, or from 24 cents to 32 cents per hour (1981 rates). To the people of Zengbu, these wages did not seem low; they were double what people had been able to earn in previous years.

Over 70 percent of the new factory work force consisted of unmarried women in their teens and early twenties. Most of the young workers were between the ages of 18 and 20, but since the minimum age was set at 15, some parents took their daughters out of school at the age of 15 and 16 so that they could work in the factory. One brigade cadre explained:

Unmarried girls are young and strong and have the excellent eyesight and manual dexterity needed for minute and detailed work on the machines. Young women are better suited by nature for this deadening, repetitive work than men. We hire the young men, not for machine piecework, but for packing and loading the materials and transporting them to Hong Kong. Our young men would not put up with having to work at the machines all day. They are more unruly and more difficult to handle and would surely rebel and cause trouble.

He was stating the cultural rationale which made the young women ideally exploitable, both under socialism and under capitalism.

Young women who married lost their jobs in the factory if they left the brigade. If they married within the brigade (and this became a more popular choice after the factories were established) they were allowed to continue working until they became pregnant; after that they were not allowed to work in the factories again. The cadres said that married women would always be asking for leave to care for a sick child, or to fulfill some other family responsibility. Furthermore, following the introduction of the household responsibility system, married women were expected to do the major part of the agricultural work of the household, so that the men could be employed outside of agriculture. "Besides," said one cadre, "we Chinese have always considered a married woman's place to be in the home – taking care of the children, cooking, farming, and doing the housework."

Factory work was more intensive and more confining than work in the fields had been, and there was an eight-hour work day, rather than the six-hour work day of the team. The workers had minimal space, and the machinery constantly droned in their ears. The work was monotonous and repetitive. Working by the piece, the workers repeated the same quasi-mechanical motions over and over during the course of a day. They became, in truth, little more than appendages of their machines. From a classical Marxist point of view, their work was alienating; the substance of their lives was being expropriated in the form of surplus value.

However, factory work was not understood in this way by the villagers. The Marxist humanistic concept of alienation is not readily accessible in a Chinese cultural context. In Marx's "Economic and Philosophical Manuscripts" (1975), labor is a medium through which one expresses one's self creatively, but the Chinese do not understand labor in these terms. The Chinese affirm the social aspects of the self by measurable labor, which implies suffering to them. They do not affirm the inner aspects of the individual by seeking personally satisfying forms of labor (see chapter 9). The villagers think that they are supposed to work as hard as they can for as long as they can, on behalf of the group, whether the family, the team, or the nation. The idea of choosing work that is personally fulfilling and satisfying would seem impractical, selfish, and immoral.

However, as time went on, attitudes to working in the new factories began to change and develop. The disadvantages of the factory's routine became more apparent. Villagers began to comment that the factory owners were becoming wealthy by the exploitation of village labor, since the wages being paid by the joint venture factories were absurdly low by world standards. The vocabulary and theoretical structure for stating such inferences existed as a legacy of the political instruction of the Maoist era. However, when challenged, the Hong Kong investors simply threatened to take their factories and jobs to some more cooperative brigade. One cadre commented:

We cannot threaten the factory owners because we must have work for our people. The owners can easily move elsewhere; they retain ownership over their machines, and they can simply dismantle them and assemble them in another brigade or another commune. The bosses have competition abroad, and we have competition from other communes who would be pleased to take our factories.

When other well-paying work was available, factory work was regarded as less attractive. The young women of Pondside, for example, preferred to make bamboo sticks used in the manufacture of fireworks, at home. Pondside's cadres had made a lucrative agreement with a Dongguan fireworks factory for the production of these sticks. Someone in Pondside had invented a small hand-operated machine for the purpose. Using the machine at home, the young women of Pondside were able to earn more money making sticks for fireworks than they could working in the joint enterprise factories. Zengbu mothers began to encourage their daughters to marry into Pondside village because this industry provided such excellent opportunities. The young people of Pondside compared working at home to working in the factories, to the detriment of the latter. One said, in 1983, that "We like the freedom of working at home at our own speed; if we work for ourselves we don't have to add shifts or work all night."

The young women of Sandhill and Lu's Home did not have such profitable alternatives. In Lu's Home, women who did not work in the factories had the alternative of growing vegetables. The young women of Sandhill who did not work in factories peddled produce in small markets across the countryside. These specialities represent a return to the pre-revolutionary economic specializations of Sandhill and Lu's Home. However, neither of these alternatives paid as well as factory work, so the young women of these two villages preferred the factories.

Meanwhile, other brigades in Dongguan county were industrializing in the same sort of way, although perhaps not as rapidly as Zengbu. Some figures can illustrate the influx of joint venture factories at the brigade level. There were 520 brigades in the county. Between 1979 and 1983, the total number of enterprises operated by these 520 brigades grew from 3,500 to 3,938, that is, at a rate of almost one new factory per brigade. Formerly, brigades in Dongguan county had had an average of 6·73 factories each; now they had an average of 7·57. Most of these 438 new factories were processing Hong Kong goods for export. With its four new joint venture factories at the brigade level, Zengbu was attracting more investment than the average brigade in the county.

At the commune level, the number of joint venture factories in the town of Chashan increased from 31 in 1979 to 43 in 1983, a 38 percent increase. All of the new industries were engaged in processing for Hong Kong. By 1983, 1,500 of the 2,300 workers employed by the commune were employed in joint venture processing factories, and the Hong Kong factory owners were paying the commune 6 million *yuan* (over 2 million U.S. dollars) per year in processing fees. This represented a massive increase in family income and spending power. Wages in commune factories rose from an average of 35 *yuan* per month in 1979 to 110 *yuan* per month in 1983, an increase of 75 *yuan* (and still further by 1985, see chapter 17). Even allowing for inflation, the amount of the increase more than doubled real wages in four years.

These new employment opportunities produced a labor shortage in the town of Chashan from which peasants in the surrounding brigades also benefited. In 1981, the commune-level cadres hired 350 peasants from the brigades to staff their processing factories. In 1983 they hired 900 peasants, mostly from the four brigades that still had no processing factories of their own (see chapter 17).

As Zengbu became more and more prosperous and labor more scarce, wages in the brigade factories rose from the average of 65 *yuan* a month (U.S.$ 38) in 1980–81, to 87 *yuan* a month (U.S.$ 48; 21 cents an hour) in 1982, 100 *yuan* per month (U.S.$51; 23 cents an hour) in 1983, and higher in 1985 (see chapter 17). With the labor shortage, and the end of team control over labor, being bound to an assigned job for life was a thing of the past.

At the same time, both brigades and villages (villages were becoming the new basic collective management unit in the countryside) were hiring workers from outside the county. By mid-1983, over 300 people from the mountainous countries of Shantou and Chaozhou in northeastern Guangdong province, were working in Chashan commune – some as agricultural laborers, but most as factory workers. These people were required to have work permits, renewable every three months, from their native brigades. They were employed in the less desirable enterprises, like the kilns, in which local people were no longer willing to work.

The influence of the new prosperity spread from central Guangdong into the more remote areas, becoming increasingly dilute in the process. Peasants from less prosperous regions could earn higher wages in Zengbu than they could in their home villages, although they earned less than the people of Zengbu themselves, at more unpleasant work. The unprecedented mobility of labor also produced an outflow of labor from more prosperous areas, as people left Dongguan county for even better opportunities. At this time, 60,000 people from Dongguan county were working outside the county – some in Guangzhou, and some in the Shenzhen special economic district. During the Maoist period, there had been some labor migration, when teams sent gangs of men to work on government projects. There had also been a few peasants working illegally in the cities. Now, however, the movement of labor was on a much larger scale than before.

Underemployment of the rural labor force, contained within the egalitarian collective structure, had been one of the most pressing problems of the

Maoist period. The economic stimulus of contact with the world economy was providing a solution to this problem in Zengbu, Chashan, and most of central Guangdong province by 1983, and diluted economic opportunities were spreading outward to the poorer mountain districts.

The hiring of outside labor, both by private entrepreneurs and by collectives became an important factor in the economic life of Zengbu. For example, the villagers of Pondside decided, in 1983, to build a branch factory for the manufacture of fireworks, on concession from the parent factory in the city of Dongguan. (This is an example of a joint venture with an economic partner from within China.) There was not enough labor in Pondside to staff the factory, since most young women were already employed making the bamboo sticks that were one component of the fireworks, or working in the brigade's processing plants. Furthermore, the villagers were unwilling to undertake the risky labor themselves. The gunpowder used in the manufacture of the fireworks was unstable, and sometimes exploded. (Because of this, the size of the factory's work rooms had to be very small, to restrict the explosion in the case of an accident.) The village of Pondside contracted with a man from Chaozhou, in northern Guangdong (whom they knew because they had hired him in 1979 as a "veteran peasant" consultant on the planting of orange orchards), to bring 50 unmarried Chaozhou women to staff the new factory. In 1983 these young women, accompanied by a chaperone, were residing in the Pondside village center, which had been transformed into a dormitory for them. None of them spoke either Cantonese or Mandarin.

Private entrepreneurs also hired outside labor. For example, the Sandhill tile kiln was under private management. The new manager employed his own large family and some fellow villagers. In addition, he hired 40 laborers from poorer areas, people who were willing to accept lower wages than the prevailing rate in Zengbu to do this miserable labor. The kiln operator's household earned over 20,000 *yuan* (U.S.$ 10,000) from this business in 1982.

What was the effect of this on indigenous industry? Fei's theory suggests that such industry would be damaged and then destroyed. The actual situation was more complex. At the brigade level, the prime handicraft, shrimp-trap weaving, remained in existence. Children too young to work in the factories, older women who had retired from active work, and other villagers with spare time, continued to weave the traditional shrimp traps. The industry providing bamboo sticks for fireworks in Pondside village was prospering. Bamboo baskets also remained profitable. These traditional rural handicraft industries had not been destroyed by the renewed contact with the world economy; in fact they were not really much affected by it.

One handicraft industry that did close was Zengbu brigade's palm-leaf fan and mat factory. The brigade had operated the palm-leaf factory as an enterprise providing employment for older women in 1979. It was turned over to the village of Sandhill which operated it unsuccessfully on a collective basis during 1981 and 1982. In 1983, the right to manage the factory was auctioned-off to the highest bidder, a man from Sandhill. He signed a contract with a Hong Kong businessman to use the building for the manufacture of cardboard boxes. (This is an example of a joint venture formed between a Hong Kong investor and an individual, rather than a governmental level such as the brigade, village, or commune.) The factory employed 50 young men from Sandhill, and was profitable. The older women who were displaced occupied themselves with weaving shrimp traps. Perhaps the less profitable palm-leaf mat and fan industry was taken up by villagers in poorer mountainous communes.

The brigade's farm tool repair shop closed in 1980; people preferred to patronize private repair shops in town. The jute-processing factory was closed in 1980, because the state's mandatory jute quota was removed, so jute was no longer grown in Zengbu.

At the commune level, the industries which grew rapidly after 1979 were those directly stimulated by contact with the world economy. Shenzhen's construction boom supplied a ready market for the cement and building materials produced by preexisting commune factories; it also gave work to the commune's private construction companies. Some of the native industries of Chashan commune did decrease production or fail after 1979. The commune's chemical factory, which manufactured tar paper, closed down in 1980, because its former customers in northern China established their own tar-paper factories. The primitive steel-elongating factory operated by the commune in 1979 went out of business. This factory had served an ideological function under Maoism, demonstrating that China was producing steel at every level. Cheaper reinforcing steel was available from state factories. Both the tar-paper factory and the steel-elongating factory had been unprofitable in 1979, but had remained in business because they supplied jobs for the underemployed town labor force. The wheat flour mill ceased operation. This was because the state no longer required the teams to plant a crop of winter wheat after 1980, so there was no wheat to be milled. The commune's rice noodle plant closed because the state opened noodle shops of its own, and refused to allow the commune to share in this profitable business. Production in the commune's bamboo ware factory declined slightly from 1979 to 1983, for reasons that are not clear, particularly since this factory was producing the baskets in which vegetables were packed for export, and the export of vegetables continued to increase. The total sales of this unit fell from 79,482 *yuan* in 1979 to 70,186 *yuan* in 1981; and the number of its workers decreased from 37 to 32 during this period. Wages in the factory grew from 48 *yuan* to 56 *yuan* per month but, with inflation, this represented a decline in real value. Perhaps the mountain communes, where the bamboo raw material was grown, could produce bamboo containers more cheaply.

On the whole, most rural industries and enterprises were stimulated by the new prosperity. Some marginal uneconomic enterprises were put out of business, but most of the traditional handicrafts were still being practiced. Contact with the world economic system did not destroy indigenous rural industry and bankrupt the peasantry. The positive economic effects on rural brigade and commune industry outweighed the negative ones.

This was due in part to the state policy that the products of the processing factories must be exported, and could not be sold within China. This protected the internal market for Chinese industry. In the late nineteenth and early twentieth centuries, when China was in a weakened and vulnerable condition, and unable to protect its own interests effectively, this would not have been an alternative. In 1985 the state placed strict controls over imports, both to conserve China's foreign exchange and to prevent foreign competition with internal factories. The importation of foreign goods, unless absolutely necessary for development, was strictly limited. The state was attempting to use world capitalism for its own purposes while seeking to avoid detriment to the internal Chinese economy. These efforts to confine the effects of world capitalism have not been entirely successful (see chapter 17).

According to Fei's theory, the renewed contact with the world capitalist system, together with the operation of the new internal market economy, should lead to renewed economic differentiation and a bifurcation of Zengbu society into rich and poor. The Zengbu data corroborate this aspect of Fei's original thesis, but not, of course, his explanation for it in terms of the destruction of handicraft industry (see chapter 17).

Renewed participation in the world economy also makes the Zengbu peasants increasingly vulnerable to the fluctuation and cycles of world capitalism. The peasants of Zengbu are now so dependent upon the export industries and the import quotas of Europe and the United States that they are, as Tawney once remarked in another context, like people "standing permanently up to the neck in water, so that even a ripple is sufficient to drown [them]" (1966, p. 77).

The Chinese experience with economic development since Liberation warrants some tentative conclusions about the advantages and disadvantages to Third World countries of participating in the world capitalist economy. The Chinese attempt from 1949 to 1979 to develop independently of the world capitalist economy, although by no means a complete failure, was not successful enough to transform China from a backward agrarian-based society into a modern industrial society. During this period, China was isolated, not only from world capitalism, but also from modern technology and science and the knowledge to employ them. This hampered the country's development severely. And if a country is to benefit from modern science and technology, it has to pay for them, which means that it has to sell something. This implies participation in the world capitalist economy.

Third World countries may have to participate in the world capitalist economy in order to modernize, but this does not imply that their participation will be necessarily or entirely beneficial. China's initial success with joint ventures in areas like Guangdong drew upon the personal connections, business skills, capital, experience on the world market, and motivation to establish business ties within China, of Hong Kong investors. (Hong Kong reverts to Chinese control in 1997.) Furthermore, the Chinese government is strong enough to regulate participation in the world economy, with the aim of avoiding world capitalism's destructive effects, while taking advantage of the positive opportunities it presents. Most Third World countries cannot avail themselves either of such peculiarly favorable conditions for foreign investment or of a central government strong enough to regulate foreign investors. Countries without these advantages have little hope of developing unscathed by the world capitalist economy. Even in China, the *long-term* economic, ideological, and political effect of contact between the world capitalist economy and Chinese socialist society remains to be seen.

# 17

# The crystallization of post-Mao society: Zengbu in 1985

By 1985, six years of accumulated changes under the post-Mao policies had transformed Zengbu. There was a new and complex economic base containing multiple and mixed modes of production. There were capitalist joint venture processing factories. There were socialist economic enterprises at every level. There were new household-based modes of production, both in agriculture and in petty commerce. The countryside has experienced a dramatic increase in economic prosperity. Considered separately, each of the modes of production has had social consequences which require analysis, and considered in relationship to one another, the modes of production have produced new coherences and new conflicts which are the basis for a new kind of social order.

The increase in prosperity and the economic growth of the Chashan countryside between 1979 and 1985 have been remarkable. The peasants' new prosperity is demonstrated by statistics on the ownership of consumer goods compiled by the cadres as their measure of progress. In 1979, only 305 of Chashan district's households had television sets; by 1985, 1,832 households, or one-fourth of those in the district, owned a set. In 1979, there were only 8 refrigerators in the commune, all collectively-owned; by 1985, there were 485. In 1979, there were no electric washing-machines in the commune; by 1985, 5 percent of the households owned washers. The number of cars, trucks, and motorcycles had grown from 32, in 1979, to 156, in 1985.

In 1984, 585 households, about 7.5 percent of all households in the Chashan district, built new houses, averaging 162 square meters of floor space each. In Zengbu, the most obvious measure of prosperity has always been housebuilding. New three and four story brick houses costing 20,000 *yuan* (U.S. $ 7,353) were being built, and even ostentatious houses costing 40,000 *yuan* (U.S. $ 14,706) as well.

Wages continued to rise. The average earnings of factory workers (both in town factories and in Zengbu) increased by 290 percent, from 42·40 *yuan* per worker per month, in 1979, to 121·80 *yuan* per month in 1984, and were projected to reach 134 *yuan* per month in 1985. Inflation was an increasing problem and rising prices cut into the buying power of the increased earnings. (The rate of inflation between 1980 and 1983 was estimated by a county-level cadre at between 10 and 15 percent a year, slowing after 1983.) Nevertheless, the average per capita income of the peasants of Chashan district grew by 300 percent, from 245 *yuan* per capita per year, in 1979 to 732 *yuan* per capita per year, in 1984. The per capita savings of the people of Chashan district increased from 83 *yuan*, in 1979, to 958 *yuan*, in 1985.

Prosperity is also reflected in the use of money for public purposes. The provincial, district, and county levels are using their increased incomes to improve the infrastructure necessary for further economic development. Transportation and communication have been significant problems in this part of China. Roads were poorly paved and narrow, and the multiple branches of the East River had to be crossed by ferry. The provincial government has built a modern two-lane paved highway running from Guangzhou, through Dongguan county, and on to Shenzhen on the Hong Kong border, to carry the increased truck traffic with Hong Kong. There are plans to build a new four-lane toll highway that will run from Hong Kong and Shenzhen, along the east coast of the Pearl River delta, to Guangzhou. New rail and automobile bridges have been built across the East River.

At the district level, the streets of Chashan have been widened to handle vehicular traffic. New roads have been built by the district government to connect Chashan with the city of Dongguan, and with the towns of Shilong and Shenzhen. The district government has constructed a new spur track off the main Kowloon-Canton railroad line, which runs close to the town. The spur track connects the main line with the district's new warehouse complex, under construction nearby. The plan is to make Chashan a major warehousing center, an entrepôt (as it formerly was) between the railhead at Chashan and the city of Dongguan, which is not served by the railroad. New factory buildings have been constructed in the town's industrial park in order to attract even more processing factories to the district.

The existing antiquated telephone system, limited to hand-cranked phones owned by collective units, was inhibiting the development of the Hong Kong processing industries. It was sometimes impossible for local factory managers to get through to their Hong Kong joint venture associates without delays of several hours; and even then the shouted conversations were frequently unintelligible. The district government has installed a modern telephone exchange designed to make it possible for residents of Chashan district to communicate easily by telephone to Hong Kong.

A chemically-purified running water system was constructed in 1983, and now treated water is being pumped into the town from the East River. Over half of the district's households received running water in 1985. The water system is to be extended to the more distant villages, like Zengbu: the pipes have already been purchased and are lying in place awaiting installation.

The new prosperity rests on the new modes of production. As the French Marxist Althusser (Althusser and Balibar, 1968, and Althusser, 1977) has shown, drawing upon insights implicit in Marx's analysis of the gestation of capitalist society within the womb of European feudalism, it is sometimes theoretically useful to distinguish more than one mode of production in the economic base of a society – particularly in a changing underdeveloped society being affected by the world capitalist system. Different modes of production generate divergent and antagonistic economic and political interests in the people associated with them. The contradictions between these systems often precipitate radical change in the economy and society. E.P. Thompson (1978) has criticized Althusser's theoretical model, because in Althusser's usage, modes of production and social structures tend to be treated as reified machines, gears grinding against gears, with no attention paid to the role played by the conscious actions of flesh-and-blood human beings. Althusser's tendency to reify must be rejected, but his model of multiple modes of production can be usefully employed in analyzing contemporary Zengbu.

In 1985 the Zengbu economic system included three modes of production: a modern capitalist export industry jointly owned and operated by Hong Kong capitalists and local collective units; a socialist sector, consisting of state-owned industries and marketing units, together with collectively-owned and operated socialist enterprises producing for profit in the internal market; and a small-commodity peasant household mode of production in agriculture and rural commerce, connected to a privately owned and managed small-business sector.

Within the capitalist mode of production, class divisions between capitalist investors and peasant workers are becoming apparent, with the cadres in a meditating role. The capitalist joint venture investors have emerged as powerful figures, in a position to control the economic lives not only of villages but of regions. They place Zengbu in direct competition with other localities for their investments, and manipulate the situation so as to keep wages as low as possible. In doing this effectively, they appropriate a large share of the surplus value of the workers' labor and retain a competitive price advantage. They are currently making enormous profits.

The peasants employed by the joint venture factories have an economic interest in maintaining their jobs and their wage levels, in the face of inflation. They are aware that the capitalist factory investors are making fortunes from their labor, and they resent it, but given the potential competition from thousands of their unemployed countrymen in other less prosperous parts of Guangdong province, who would be eager to work at even half their current wages, there is little they can do about it. Protest movements or open class conflict are unlikely, because the peasants are provided with something to lose by the factories, and they cannot afford to lose it. Also, the local party cadre factory managers exert discipline and control over the factory employees. Since most factory employees are unmarried women in weak social positions, the capitalists' and the party cadres' job is easier.

The cadre managers are potentially torn between their material interests and their ideal interests. As party cadres they should be acutely aware of the interests of labor, yet as factory managers who are rewarded for increased profitability, their own material interests are those of the joint venture factories. At present, party policy encourages cadres to cooperate with capitalists, in order to foster the growth of the export industry. If cadres negotiate for wages so high as to discourage investment they will not be supporting the policy.

Allied with the investors and the cadre managers of the Hong Kong processing factories are the new peasant entrepreneurs who operate their own shops and businesses. This rural petty bourgeoisie is in direct competition with socialist economic enterprise, just as the capitalist processing factories are. Thus the interests of the rural petty bourgeoisie and of the joint venture factories are allied. These interests require the maintenance of the external and internal capitalist modes of production, and the continuation of the freer market conditions of recent years.

The people involved in the socialist sector of the economy have different interests. People who make their living in the socialist sector and people who make their living in the capitalist sector are in direct competition; the contradiction between capitalism and socialism is more than a mere opposition between two reified modes of production. Collective and state enterprises in Chashan town – stores, factories, and repair shops, for example – are presently in danger of being put out of business by private enterprises with which they are unable to compete in terms of variety, price, or quality. If the state does not regulate or limit the capitalist enterprise, the socialist enterprises are likely to be damaged by the expanding private sector of the economy.

It is a mistake, however, to underestimate the importance of the socialist elements in the overall economy. In 1985, urban heavy industry continued to be state-owned and this socialist sector still dominates the national economy. Wholesale trade is still in the hands of the state, although the private sector has begun to encroach. Socialist collectives either owned and managed (or, in the case of the jointly owned and managed Hong Kong processing industries, shared ownership and management of) all the important factories and commercial establishments in Chashan district. The work force was still supervised and controlled by party cadres. The agricultural land and rural means of production, although privately managed, remained collectively owned, at least formally. The economy retained significant socialist characteristics.

The peasant household mode of agricultural and petty commodity production, the third mode, supports and reinforces export capitalism. Each peasant household has production responsibility fields, for growing grain, and garden plots for growing vegetables, so the peasants are almost self-supporting in foodstuffs. Their cost of living is low. Factory owners do not have to pay sufficient wages to compensate for the total cost of reproducing the peasant labor force, since this is borne partly by the peasants themselves, using resources provided by the collective. The resources of the collective have thus been used indirectly in such a manner as to provide capitalist investors with advantageously low labor costs. And indeed, wages are very low. The articulation between the peasant household and the capitalist modes of production in Zengbu resembles plantation and hacienda economies where the workers are given land to grow their own food and then paid very little for their labor (see Taussig 1980, p. 83).

The peasant mode of agricultural and petty commodity production absorbs the unemployment produced by fluctuations in factory production. When there is a lull in factory production, unemployed factory workers find temporary employment in agriculture, peddling, or handicrafts, until factory work recommences. This also supports the low wage rates, since the factory workers can survive while unemployed. The peasant mode of production provides a cheap and flexible labor force of peasant workers.

Historically, the urban Chinese factories of the socialist sector have had a similar relationship with the peasant collectives. These factories have customarily contracted with peasant collectives for processing at piecework rates. The peasants did not have to be provided with housing, since they lived in their own villages, or rations, since they produced their own food; they enjoyed no pension or welfare rights and had no job security. Furthermore, they were unable to leave in search of better conditions. The advantages of these circumstances from the point of view of management are obvious. The Hong Kong processing system does not depart from established practice for the exploitation of peasant labor.

Goods produced by the export processing factories are not allowed to be sold within China, so the Hong Kong processing industry remains isolated from the Chinese domestic market. This limits potential competition, conflict, and contradictions between the capitalist export sector and the internal state and collective sector. China's vulnerable internal socialist industries are being protected from foreign capitalist competition, while at the same time China's government is accumulating foreign exchange, fostering internal economic growth, and creating full employment and higher levels of living for the Zengbu peasants. It is, in effect, trying to use and exploit world capitalism while at the same time preserving and maintaining China's overall socialist economy. Whether this can be done effectively is questionable, since the process creates dependency on the fluctuations of the world capitalist system and may have serious internal political consequences.

Agricultural production in general must now be considered as an aspect of the household-based peasant mode of production. Considered in general terms, agriculture, like industry, has become vastly more profitable since 1979. The value of Chashan district's agricultural production has increased from 5,531,000 *yuan*, in 1979, to 13,410,000 *yuan* in 1985. Even allowing for 50 percent inflation between 1979 and 1985, the increase was 71 percent. This rise in the value of agricultural production was partly the result of a onetime increase in the state purchase prices for agricultural crops; in 1979 state purchase prices were raised by approximately 25 percent. Mostly, however, it has been due to changes in state quota requirements. Formerly there was an emphasis on the production of rice, which had to be delivered in kind, and fixed quotas of other low-profit crops had to be produced, but under present policy, the emphasis is on raising commercial crops for profitable sale.

In 1979, Chashan commune planted 30,000 *mu* of land in double-cropped rice; by July of 1985, the area planted in rice had been reduced by 13 percent, to 26,000 *mu*. A new rule allowed the peasants to pay their rice-delivery quotas to the state in cash, rather than in rice: there is still a rice quota, as before, and the actual amount of the rice quota is the same as it was, but it may be delivered in the form of cash, rather than in the form of rice. If the shift from rice-growing to more profitable commercial agriculture becomes general, rice will have to be imported. This would have been ideologically unthinkable under Maoism, which stressed the importance of self-sufficiency for China. Under the present prosperous economic circumstances, the importation of rice is perfectly feasible. However, it does create a dependency.

During the same period, sugarcane acreage in Chashan district decreased from 3,000 *mu* to 2,400 *mu*, cassava from over 1,500 *mu* to less than 100 *mu*, and jute from 880 *mu* to none. The land thus freed was converted to fishponds, truck gardens, and orchards, all of which were more profitable. The area planted in fruit trees (bananas, litchis, and oranges) increased from 5,200 *mu*, in 1979, to 11,000 *mu*, in 1985, and the area planted in vegetables from 1,000 to 4,000 *mu*. The area in fishponds increased from 3,400 *mu* to 4,500 *mu* over the same period.

Agriculture is no longer determined by subsistence needs and the fulfilling of state purchase quotas, but emphasizes instead diversification and profit. This change from subsistence rice agriculture to a diversified commercial truck gardening (market gardening) resembles the commercialization of agriculture in the villages of Hong Kong's New Territories during the years after World War II (see J. M. Potter 1968, pp. 57–94). By the early 1960s, rice production in the New Territories had practically disappeared in favor of growing the vegetables, fruit, and fish that were more profitable.

The social significance of land use under the new system has important ramifications. Formal ownership of the land and the other means of production is still in the hands of the team. The team, however, is presently a null structural level. Formerly it was responsible for the social organization of agricultural production; now it has been greatly reduced in function. The teams have distributed all agricultural land to the households, and have leased out most other means of production to private entrepreneurs (see chapter 8). Some team resources have been placed in the hands of the individual villages, to support the new village citizens' committees. However, the team retains a perceived importance as an intermediary level between the village and the peasant household. Following the introduction of the production responsibility system, in 1983, the provincial and county governments suggested that the teams be eliminated, but this plan met with strong opposition in Zengbu. The villagers insisted upon retaining the team; the intermediary functions it provides are essential.

As of 1985, production responsibility land and litchi trees are distributed by the teams to the households for a period of 15 years. This represents a change from the two-to-five year tenure period of the early 1980s. Some teams are waiting for the short tenure periods to expire before adopting the new 15–year tenure rule. Long-term household control of land allotments from the team makes capital improvements on the land economically rational. Now the peasants are planting long-maturing cash crops, such as litchi and oranges.

The private garden plot system was clearly the initial model for the production responsibility system. Production responsibility fields resemble the private garden plots in being distributed to the households on a per capita basis, and in remaining collective property in formal terms, even though use rights are controlled by the households. However, with 15-year use rights in effect, production responsibility fields are not being reallotted to take account of changes in household membership, as private plots formerly were. At first, changes in household size were reflected by adjustments in the size of the household's rice production quota. Households which lost members, but retained resources of production, were required to deliver rice to compensate for disproportion. Then, as of 1985, changes in household size were reflected in cash payments. Households which lost members, but retained the use of the team's production responsibility land, were to pay cash to households which gained members while receiving no additional land. The team leader was the intermediary for this process. The production responsibility fields are conceived of as a substitute for the grain rations once supplied to the household by the team; therefore, it was considered fair compensation if a household which lost members gave money for the purchase of rice to a household which gained members, as a substitute for land on which rice might have been raised.

The importance of the rice quota, or the cash payment which substitutes for it, lies in the fact that the right to use the land rests on the obligation to deliver grain or a cash equivalent to the state. This is as it was when the use rights belonged to the collectives. The actual rice quotas remain unchanged. However, since most peasants will pay their rice quota requirement in cash, while using their land to grow fruit and vegetables, it is clear that the state will not be stockpiling the rice with which to supply shortfalls in rations, as it formerly did. Under present policy, the state claims reduced responsibility for supplying rice. This is not likely to be of much consequence in richer areas like Zengbu, but in poorer regions, where the peasants have little subsistence margin, household independence in production, in conjunction with reduced state responsibility for peasant welfare, may not necessarily be beneficial to the peasants.

The conditions of land tenure under present policy represent a return to pre-Liberation conceptions of property right. Traditionally, right to the "subsurface of the land" (ownership rights) remained in the hands of the lineage or the private landlord, while rights to rent and use the land (the "surface rights") were controlled by the tenant. Surface rights could be pawned or sublet to other tenants. They could be, and frequently were, inherited by tenant sons from tenant fathers. Presently, it is as if the subsurface of the land was considered to be owned by the team, with the state reserving the subsurface right to receive taxes and quota grain or the monetary equivalent. The surface rights are held by households. Rights to production responsibility land are being thought of as inheritable by sons along traditional lines.

Thus, production responsibility land is being assimilated into the institutional patterns of land tenure and inheritance which once defined the use of private property. It is increasingly a formality to claim that the land is collective property and will remain so, or that such collective ownership will serve as an effective basis for sustaining socialism in the Chinese countryside. When 15 years have elapsed, differential capital improvements will have been made on production responsibility land by the controlling households. Reallotment is likely to be tortuously complex, even by village standards. In the meantime, families with only one son will be able to pass on the rights to their production responsibility land intact, but families with two or more sons will have to divide their use rights, creating a new group of peasant households with fractional access to production responsibility land in the next generation. In succeeding generations the complications will increase, and inequality on the basis of differential land ownership will be firmly established. Land use is likely to become extraordinarily fragmented.

Before Liberation, surface rights to the land could be pawned, rented, or sold to others, under complex agreements. Even rights to receive inherited shares of the rental income of an ancestral estate could be mortgaged (see J.

M. Potter 1968, pp. 95–122). In 1985, Zengbu families who gained most of their income from factory work, construction, or commerce, and who did not work their production responsibility land themselves, were "loaning" their rights to relatives, since rental was not permitted. Pressure to permit rights to production responsibility land to be rented, to allow the use of such land rights as security on loans, or to permit the sale of such rights, will increase. The traditional complexities of Chinese peasant land tenure, eliminated by collectivization, are re-emerging.

In 1985, each Zengu household farmed an average of 3.8 *mu* (0.2 hectare) production responsibility land. (Considered village by village, the average was 3.10 *mu* per household in Sandhill village, 3.9 *mu* in Lu's Home, and 4.4 in Pondside.) In 1985, the Zengbu peasants were planting most of their irrigated responsibility fields in rice. Much of the land is so wet that it is difficult to grow crops other than rice. But peasants still chose to grow rice when unconstrained by the particular qualities of their fields. Perhaps they were hesitating to take full advantage of the new situation; perhaps they did not wish to become completely dependent upon the market for their rice. The cadres took the position that rice should continue to be grown, but they could not require it.

Theoretically, the villagers could plant their land in those crops which brought the highest market price, pay their state grain delivery obligations in cash, and buy all their rice and food on the open market. Many specialized households, fully employed in nonagricultural occupations, were doing this. In the summer of 1985, some fields were unplanted, and some were neglected and full of weeds. A few households were hiring labor to cultivate their fields; others were "loaning" their rights to relatives. Land was clearly of less economic importance than factory work or commerce to peasant households. A Zengbu cadre estimated that in 1985 only about 10 percent of the incomes of Zengbu households came from agriculture. (In 1979, 34 percent of team income was derived from field crop agriculture, see chapter 5.) A male household head, describing his division of responsibility land to his sons, commented that the young men did not really want the land and that many now consider the working of land to be a burden. Zengbu's agriculture is carried out within a marginal peasant mode of production. Since most income is derived from industry and commerce, rather than from the land, the agriculturalists of Zengbu are now best described as a marginal rural peasant-proletariat.

One unexpected consequence of the production responsibility system is a technological regression in agriculture. Plowing is less mechanized than before. The small and medium-sized tractors used by the teams are too expensive for a household to use on the small area of its production responsibility fields. Similarly, maintaining a water buffalo is too expensive for one household. The tractors have been sold. The teams retain formal ownership of the buffaloes, but allocate each buffalo to a group of house-holds. One family is paid to care for the group's buffalo throughout the year, and at plowing time the households take turns using the animal to plow. (This is reminiscent of the mutual aid teams of the early 1950s.) Threshing is also less mechanized. The motorized threshers used by the collectives in 1979 are too expensive for a single household or a small group of households. Peasants are threshing the grain by hand, beating sheaves of rice into a wooden tub, as they did before Liberation. The household is so small a production unit that only simple technology can be economically employed. The amount of human labor required for agriculture is greater than it was before. Such economies of scale as were characteristic of the Maoist collectives have been lost.

On the other hand, the villagers of Zengbu have recreated the small-scale commercial peasant economy which was eliminated when commerce, indus-try, and agriculture were collectivized in the early 1950s. This economy is characterized by what Sol Tax once called "penny capitalism" (1953), and what Marxist writers often call "small-commodity production." Peasant entrepreneurs can take advantage of opportunities for profit too marginal to justify the expenditure of collective effort. This is a way of putting smaller scale to use.

Social structure has been modified by the recent changes, which have strengthened the family, kinship ties, the lineage, and the village – the most important structures in pre-Liberation society. The household responsibility system makes each peasant household into an economic enterprise directed by the male head of the family. The male heads of household have, as they put it, "freedom" (ziyou). Freedom is a word with a special culturally-restricted meaning in this context. It is essentially a male-centred notion, signifying the men's right, reclaimed from team leaders following decollectivization, to direct the economic activities of the women and children of their households. Zengbu women do not have "freedom"; their former subordination to the team leaders who once directed their labor has merely been exchanged for subordination to their husbands. At present, the male-headed peasant household controls the use of the land and the other means of agricultural production, and organizes its own labor force of family members. The households of the village compete with one another for wealth and prestige as they did before, rather than being required to cooperate.

Simultaneously, and logically, the symbolic structures which express the old social order have re-emerged. Traditional peasant religion and magic were intimately connected with the traditional peasant household mode of pro-duction. The purpose of religious ritual was to ensure the health of family members and to further the household's economic success. There is still significant feeling in the village, particularly among cadres and the young, that traditional religious and magical practices are superstitions. However, the return of a household mode of production in material life has been accompanied by the resurgence of the corresponding ritual life. Religious and magical beliefs and practices, temple cults, the household ancestral cult and rituals at ancestral halls and tombs, are examples of such ritual forms. The return to pre-Liberation expressive culture is not simply a matter of the persistence or "survival" of tradition. Traditional culture is reappearing because the economic base and the social structures that were expressed by these symbolic forms are once again important. Relationships with relatives are increasing in importance in the absence of collective support, and these relationships are also symbolically affirmed by ceremonial means. The villagers give sumptuous wedding banquets and exchange luxurious dowries and brideprices when their children marry.

Since the village has become important once more, its symbolizing structures have been revived, as well. In 1984, Sandhill's village temple, which had been dismantled by the Red Guards during the Cultural Revolution, was rebuilt by the village citizens' committee, and decorated with gilt, red paint, new images, and altars. Dragon-boat racing (see chapter 12) is another symbolic affirmation of village solidarity, and competitive strength.

The new competitive economic world includes both the possibility of becoming wealthy and the possibility of being overwhelmed by poverty. Under Maoism, peasants looked to the collective social forms, the party, and the charismatic figure of Mao himself, as the powerful forces which might protect them against the economic disasters they feared. There was a logic, under Maoism, in forbidding household religious expression, and encouraging a quasi-religious response to state and ideological symbols. However, the structural pattern has changed, and the symbolic pattern with it. The collectives no longer provide employment, supply rice rations, offer support for old people without sons, or make medical insurance available. They no longer command a ritual reverence. This, like the means of production, has been reallocated to the households.

Clearly one significant negative consequence of the new economic policies is the re-emergence of economic classes and class antagonisms within the villages. Several estimates confirm the impression that economic class differentiation has proceeded rapidly. In 1984, district cadres said that an upper stratum of 15 to 20 percent of Chashan district's households was earning over 10,000 *yuan* per year, as compared to an average household's income of from 3,000 to 4,000 *yuan* a year; they based these figures on their own systematic surveys. Within Zengbu, one cadre estimated that in 1985, income levels were distributed as shown in table 13.

According to this estimate, 40 percent of Zengbu households make less than 3,000 *yuan* per year. They are, as they themselves say, "a little better off than they were during the Maoist period." Their incomes have increased, but inflation has reduced their buying power. These poorer people are already

Table 13. *Differentiation of household incomes in Zengbu, 1985*

| Percentage of households | Income per year |
|---|---|
| 2% | 20,000 *yuan* and above |
| 8% | 10,000–19,999 *yuan* |
| 50% | 5,000–9,999 *yuan* |
| 30% | 3,000–4,999 *yuan* |
| 10% | 2,999 *yuan* or less |

beginning to express envy of the richer villagers and anger at the factory owners and managers. Differentiation of the villagers into rich and poor is an inevitable consequence of policies which encourage the private control and exploitation of the means of production, and the use of these means of production by capitalist entrepreneurs to accumulate wealth by extracting surplus value from the labor of their fellow villagers. The breakup of the egalitarian collectives has produced a group of peasant entrepreneurs, and a supply of peasant workers who have to sell their labor power in order to live; their production responsibility land is not sufficient to furnish them with a living. As before Liberation, the strong and the rich are beginning to exploit the weak and the poor. Left unresolved is the question of who will take care of the welfare needs of the poor, and of families who suffer catastrophic illnesses or the premature deaths of major wage-earners. The re-creation of economic classes is a price the party is apparently willing to pay to foster economic growth. The price is a high one.

Zengbu peasants have consistently displayed two complementary orientations towards their own economic relationships. One orientation is an essentially competitive desire to become superior in wealth; it is based on covetousness. The other orientation is an obsession with preventing others from achieving distinction through wealth; it is based on envy. This orientation engenders a sort of negative egalitarianism. Instead of seeking economic success, one seeks to ensure that others cannot be more successful than one is oneself. The first orientation is freely expressed under present policy, when peasants recognize and hope to profit by new opportunities to become rich. It is easily transmuted into the second orientation, however, as differential wealth is recognized and resented, and the resentment is socially defined as having moral legitimacy. The two orientations are alternative forms of expression of a single underlying attitude to economic life and the social order. The social order is transformed each time the dominant orientation shifts. Leach's description of shifts between alternative social patterns in highland Burma (1954) presents interesting analogies.

The negative egalitarianism of the peasants of Zengbu provides a counter-argument to James C. Scott's contention (1976) that peasant villages are characterized by a sense of moral economy and seek to maintain a subsistence-oriented social order as an end in itself. In Zengbu, peasants understand egalitarianism as a means for preventing others from asserting superiority. Resentment at the success of others is morally legitimate. This is not a moral economy in Scott's sense. (It is more like Foster's Image of Limited Good [1965].) Scott also argues that peasants are inherently unwilling to take competitive economic risks, and this is equally untrue in Zengbu, where, in striving for economic success, peasants have been willing to take extraordinary entrepreneurial risks. They rejected the assured subsistence of the Maoist order – which certainly kept the market at arm's length – in favor of a post-Maoist order which promised an opportunity to gain wealth and social position through entrepreneurial activity.

The present policies have resulted in tremendous prosperity. However, contradictions exist, stratification is being created, and concern with social welfare has become secondary. Since the Revolution, the villagers of Zengbu have been engaged in the enactment of an economic dialectic, in which a synthesis between the dual goals of prosperity and social justice has not yet been achieved. The dialectic continues.

# References

"The Agrarian Reform Law of the People's Republic of China." 1950. In *The Agrarian Reform Law and Other Documents*. Beijing: Foreign Language Press

Althusser, Louis. 1977. *For Marx*. London: Verso

Althusser, Louis and Etienne Balibar. 1968. *Reading Capital*. London: N.L.B.

Amin, Samir. 1974. *Accumulation on a World Scale*. New York: Monthly Review Press

1981. *The Future of Maoism*. New York: Monthly Review Press

Anderson, Eugene N., Jr. and Marja L. Anderson. 1977. "Modern China: South." In *Food in Chinese Culture*, ed. K.C. Chang. New Haven: Yale University Press

Anon. 1983. "Sex Ratios of China's Newborns and Infants." *Women of China*, August: 11

Baker, Hugh D. R. 1968. *A Chinese Lineage Village: Sheung Shui*. Stanford: Stanford University Press

Baran, Paul A. 1957. *The Political Economy of Growth*. New York: Monthly Review Press

Barnett, A. Doak. 1981. *China's Economy in Global Perspective*. Washington, D.C.: The Brookings Institute

Barnet, K. M. A. (Census Commissioner). 1961. *Hong Kong: Report on the 1961 Census*. Hong Kong: Government Press

Bendix, Reinhard. 1962. *Max Weber: An Intellectual Portrait*. New York: Anchor

Bernstein, Thomas P. 1977. *Up to the Mountains and Down to the Villages*. New Haven: Yale University Press

Brinton, Crane. 1965. *The Anatomy of Revolution*. New York: Vintage Books. (First published in 1938)

Buck, John L. 1937. *Land Utilization in China*. Nanking: University of Nanking

Chan, Anita, Richard Madsen, and Jonathan Unger. 1984. *Chen Village: The Recent History of a Peasant Community in Mao's China*. Berkeley: University of California Press

Chao Kuo-chun. 1957. *Agrarian Policies of Mainland China: A Documentary Study (1949–1956)*. Cambridge, Mass.: Harvard University Press

Chen, Ivan, trans. 1920. *The Book of Filial Duty*. London: John Murray

Chen, Jack. 1975. *A Year in Upper Felicity: Life in a Chinese Village During the Cultural Revolution*. New York: Macmillan

Chu, Godwin C. 1985. "The Changing Concept of Self in Contemporary China." In *Culture and Self: Asian and Western Perspectives*, ed. A.J. Marsella, G.DeVos, and F.L.K. Hsu. New York: Tavistock

Cohen, Jerome Alan. 1968. *The Criminal Process in the People's Republic of China 1949–1963: An Introduction*. Cambridge, Mass.: Harvard University Press

Cohen, Myron L. 1976. *House United, House Divided: The Chinese Family in Taiwan*. New York: Columbia University Press

Cohn, Norman. 1970. *The Pursuit of the Millennium: Revolutionary Millenarians and Mystical Anarchists of the Middle Ages*. New York: Oxford University Press

Croll, Elizabeth. 1981. *The Politics of Marriage in Contemporary China*. Cambridge, England: Cambridge University Press

Croll, Elizabeth, Delia Davin, and Penny Kane, eds. 1985. *China's One-Child Family Policy*. New York: St Martin's Press

de Janvry, Alain. 1981. *The Agrarian Question and Reformism in Latin America*. Baltimore: Johns Hopkins University Press

Devereux, George. 1979. *A Study of Abortion in Primitive Societies*. New York: International Universities Press

Diamond, Norma. 1969. *K'un Shen: A Taiwan Village*. New York: Holt, Rinehart, and Winston

Diaz, May N. and Jack M. Potter. 1967. "Introduction: The Social Life of Peasants." In *Peasant Society: A Reader*, ed. Jack M. Potter, May N. Diaz and George M. Foster. Boston: Little, Brown

Durkheim, Emile. 1965. *The Elementary Forms of the Religious Life*. New York: The Free Press

Engels, Frederick. 1973. "Revolution and Counterrevolution in Germany." In *Karl Marx and Frederick Engels, Selected Works*. Vol. 1. Moscow: Progress Publishers

Fairbank, John K. 1979. *The United States and China: Fourth Edition*. Cambridge, Mass.: Harvard University Press

Fei Xiaotong (Hsiao-tung). 1939. *Peasant Life in China*. London: Kegan Paul, Trench, Trubner and Co.

   1953. *China's Gentry: Essays in Rural-Urban Relations*. Chicago: University of Chicago Press

Fei Hsiao-tung and Chang Chih-i. 1945. *Earthbound China: A Study of Rural Economy in Yunnan*. Chicago: University of Chicago Press

Foster, George M. 1965. "Peasant Society and the Image of Limited Good." *American Anthropologist* 67: 293–315

Frank, Andre Gunder. 1979. *Dependent Accumulation and Underdevelopment*. New York: Monthly Review Press

Freedman, Maurice. 1958. *Lineage Organization in Southeastern China*. London: Athlone

   1966. *Chinese Lineage and Society: Fukien and Kwangtung*. London: Athlone

Friedman, Edward. 1974. *Backward Toward Revolution: The Chinese Revolutionary Party*. Berkeley: University of California Press

Gallin, Bernard and Ritas S. 1982. "The Chinese Joint Family in Changing Rural Taiwan." In *Social Interaction in Chinese Society*, ed. Sidney Greenblatt, Richard W. Wilson, and Amy Auerbacher Wilson. New York: Praeger

Geertz, Clifford. 1963. *Agricultural Involution: The Processes of Ecological Change in Indonesia*. Berkeley, Los Angeles, and London: University of California Press.
1973. *The Interpretation of Cultures*. New York: Basic Books
1975. "On the Nature of Anthropological Understanding." *American Scientist*, January–February: 38–47

Gerth, H. H. and C. Wright Mills. 1958. *From Max Weber: Essays in Sociology*. New York: Oxford University Press

Goody, Jack, ed. 1958. *The Developmental Cycle in Domestic Groups*. Cambridge, England: Cambridge University Press

Gurley, John G. 1976. *China's Economy and the Maoist Strategy*. New York: Monthly Review Press

Guttmacher, Alan F. 1973. *Pregnancy, Birth, and Family Planning*. New York: Signet

Hinton, William. 1966. *Fanshen: A Documentary of Revolution in a Chinese Village*. New York: Vintage
1983. *Shenfan*. New York: Random House

Hobson, J. A. 1972. *Imperialism: A Study*. Ann Arbor: University of Michigan Press

Hochschild, Arlie. 1983. *The Managed Heart: Commercialization of Human Feeling*. Berkeley: University of California Press

Hsiao Kung-chuan. 1960. *Rural China: Imperial Control in the Nineteenth Century*. Seattle: University of Washington Press

Hsu, Francis L. K. 1949. "Suppression Versus Repression: A Limited Psychological Interpretation of Four Cultures." *Psychiatry* 12:223–242

Huang, Philip C. C. 1985. *The Peasant Economy and Social Change in North China*. Stanford: Stanford University Press

Keyfitz, Nathan. 1984. "The Population of China." *Scientific American* 250(2): 38–47

Kleinman, Arthur. 1980. *Patients and Healers in the Context of Culture*. Berkeley: University of California Press

Kleinman, Arthur and Byron Good. 1985. *Culture and Depression: Studies in the Anthropology and Cross-Cultural Psychiatry of Affect and Disorder*. Berkeley: University of California Press

Kroeber, Alfred. 1948. *Anthropology*. New York: Harcourt, Brace
1963. *Anthropology: Culture Patterns and Processes*. New York: Harcourt, Brace, and World

Laing, R. D. 1972. *The Politics of the Family and Other Essays*. New York: Vintage

Lang, Olga. 1946. *Chinese Family and Society*. New Haven: Yale University Press

Leach, Edmund R. 1954. *Political Systems of Highland Burma*. London: G. Bell and Sons
1961. *Pul Eliya, a village in Ceylon*. Cambridge, England: Cambridge University Press

Leeming, Frank. 1985. *Rural China Today*. New York: Longman

Lenin, V. I. 1973. *Imperialism: The Highest Stage of Capitalism*. Beijing: Foreign Languages Press

Levenson, Joseph R. 1964. *Modern China and its Confucian Past*. Garden City, New York: Anchor

Levy, Marion J., Jr. 1963. *The Family Revolution in Modern China*. New York: Octagon

Liu Shaoqi. 1964. *How To Be A Good Communist*. Beijing: Foreign Languages

Luo Ruiqing. 1959. "Guanyu zhonghua renmin gongheguo hukou dengji tiaoli caoan de shuoming" ("Explanatory Notes on the Regulations for Household Registration of the People's Republic of China"). In *Zhonghua renmin gongheguo fagui huibian (Collection of Legislative Documents of the People's Republic of China)*. Beijing: Falu chubanshe

Lutz, Catherine. 1983. "Parental Goals, Ethnopsychology, and the Development of Emotional Memory." *Ethos* 11: 246–262

Luxemburg, Rosa. 1972. *The Accumulation of Capital: An Anti-Critique*. New York: Monthly Review Press

Madsen, Richard. 1984. *Morality and Power in a Chinese Village*. Berkeley: University of California Press

Mao Tse-tung. 1966. *Quotations from Chairman Mao Tse-tung*. Beijing: Foreign Language Press

    1969. "Zai diyici Zhengzhou huiyishang de jianghua" ("Speech at the First Zhengzhou Conference"). *Mao Zedong Sixiang Wansui (Long Live Mao Zedong Thought)*. n.p.

Marx, Karl. 1967. *Capital: A Critique of Political Economy*. Vol. 1. New York: International Publishers

    1973. "The Eighteenth Brumaire of Louis Bonaparte." In *Karl Marx and Frederick Engels, Selected Works*. Vol. 1. Moscow: Progress Publishers

    1975. "Economic and Philosophic Manuscripts of 1844." in *Karl Marx and Frederick Engels, Collected Works*. Vol. III. New York: International Publishers

Marx, Karl and Frederick Engels. 1962. "The Communist Manifesto." In *Karl Marx and Frederick Engels: Selected Works in One Volume*. Moscow: Progress Publishers

    1972. *On Colonialism*. New York: International Publishers

Mazlish, Bruce. 1976. *The Revolutionary Ascetic,*. New York: McGraw-Hill

Meillassoux, Claude. 1964. *L'Anthropologie Economique des Gouro de Côte d'Ivoire*. Paris: Mouton

Meisner, Maurice. 1982. *Li Ta-Chao and the Origins of Chinese Marxism*. New York: Atheneum

Metzger, Thomas. 1981. "Selfhood and Authority in Chinese Political Culture." In *Normal and Abnormal Behavior in Chinese Culture*, ed. A. Kleinman and T. Y. Lin. Dordrecht: D. Reidel

Michael, Franz (in collaboration with Chung-li Chang). 1966. *The Taiping Rebellion*. Vol. 1. Seattle: University of Washington Press

Mills, C. Wright. 1962. *The Marxists*. New York: Dell

"Ministry of Civil Affairs Report on the Reassignment for Work for Retired Officers and Demobilized Soldiers as Authorized by the State Council for Promulgation." 1981. In *Bulletin of the State Council of the People's Republic of China*. Beijing: Zhonghua renmin gongheguo guowuyuan bangongting

Mintz, Sidney W. 1985. *Sweetness and Power: The Place of Sugar in Modern History*. New York: Penguin

Mooney, James. 1965. *The Ghost-Dance Religion and the Sioux Outbreak of 1890*. Chicago: University of Chicago Press

Myrdal, Jan. 1965. *Report From A Chinese Village*. New York: Random House

Myrdal, Jan and Gun Kessle. 1970. *China: The Revolution Continued: The Cultural Revolution at the Village Level*. New York: Random House

Peck, Graham. 1950. *Two Kinds of Time*. Boston: Houghton Mifflin

Potter, Jack M. 1968. *Capitalism and the Chinese Peasant*. Berkeley: University of California Press

1970. "Land and Lineage in Traditional China." In *Family and Kinship in Chinese Society*, ed. Maurice Freeedman. Stanford: Stanford University Press

1970a. "Wind, Water, Bones, and Souls: The Religious World of the Cantonese Peasant." *Journal of Oriental Studies* 71: 139–153

Potter, Jack M., May N. Diaz, and George M. Foster, eds. 1967. *Peasant Society: A Reader*. Boston: Little, Brown

Potter, Sulamith Heins. 1983. "The Position of Peasants in Modern China's Social Order." *Modern China* 9: 465–99

1985. *Birth Planning in Rural China: A Cultural Account*. (Working Paper on Women in International Development, No. 103, Office of Women In International Development, Michigan State University, East Lansing.)

1986. "The Position of Peasants." In *The Chinese: Adapting the Past, Building the Future*, ed. Robert F. Dernberger, Kenneth J. DeWoskin, Steven M. Goldstein, Rhoads Murphey, and Martin K. Whyte. Ann Arbor: University of Michigan, Center for Chinese Studies

1987. "Birth Planning in Rural China: A Cultural Account." in *Child Survival: Anthropological Perspectives on the Treatment and Maltreatment of Children*, ed. Nancy Scheper-Hughes. Dordrecht: D. Reidel

Radcliffe-Brown, A. R., 1952. *Structure and Function in Primitive Society*. Glencoe, Illinois: The Free Press

1964. *The Andaman Islanders*. New York: The Free Press

Rawski, Thomas B. 1980. *China's Transition to Industrialism: Producer Goods and Economic Development in the Twentieth Century*. Ann Arbor: University of Michigan Press

Redfield, Robert. 1967. "The Social Organization of Tradition." In *Peasant Society: A Reader*, ed. Jack M. Potter, May N. Diaz, and George M. Foster. Boston: Little, Brown

"Regulations on the Criteria for Defining Urban and Rural Areas." 1956. In *Collection of Legislative Documents of the People's Republic of China*. Beijing: Falu chubanshe

"Regulations for Household Registration of the People's Republic of China." 1959. In *Collection of Legislative Documents of the People's Republic of China*. Beijing: Falu chubanshe

Rice, Edward. 1972. *Mao's Way*. Berkeley: University of California Press

Rosen, Stanley, ed. 1981. *The Role of Sent-Down Youth in the Chinese Cultural Revolution: The Case of Guangzhou*. Berkeley, California: Center for Chinese Studies

Sahlins, Marshall. 1976. *Culture and Practical Reason*. Chicago: University of Chicago Press

Schurmann, Franz. 1966. *Ideology and Organization in Communist China*. Berkeley: University of California Press

Schwartz, Benjamin I. 1970. "The Reign of Virtue: Some Broad Perspectives on Leader and Party and the Cultural Revolution." In *Party Leadership and Revolutionary Power in China*, ed. John W. Lewis. Cambridge, England: Cambridge University Press

Scott, James C. 1976. *The Moral Economy of the Peasant: Rebellion and Subsistence in Southeast Asia*. New Haven: Yale University Press

Selden, Mark, ed. 1979. *The People's Republic of China: A Documentary History of Revolutionary Change*. New York: Monthly Review Press

Shue, Vivienne. 1980. *Peasant Society in Transition: The Dynamics of Development Toward Socialism 1949–1956*. Berkeley: University of California Press

Shweder, Richard A. and Edmund J. Bourne. 1984. "Does the Concept of the Person Vary Cross-Culturally?" In *Culture Theory: Essays on Mind, Self, and Emotion*, ed. R. A. Shweder and R. A. Levine. Cambridge, England: Cambridge University Press

Skinner, G. William. 1964–5. "Marketing and Social Structure in Rural China." 3 parts. *Journal of Asian Studies* 24(1): 3–44; 24(2): 195–228; 24(3): 363–399

1967. "Marketing and Social Structure in Rural China." Part 1. In *Peasant Society: A Reader*, ed. Jack M. Potter, May N. Diaz, and George M. Foster. Boston: Little, Brown

Skocpol, Theda. 1979. *State and Social Revolutions: A Comparative Analysis of France, Russia, and China*. Cambridge, England: Cambridge University Press

Solomon, Richard H. 1971. *Mao's Revolution and the Chinese Political Culture*. Berkeley: University of California Press

Stavrianos, L. S. 1981. *Global Rift: The Third World Comes of Age*. New York: William Morrow

Taussig, Michael T. 1980. *The Devil and Commodity Fetishism in South America*. Chapel Hill: University of North Carolina Press

1987. *Shamanism, Colonialism, and the Wild Man: A Study in Terror and Healing*. Chicago: University of Chicago Press

Tawney, R. H. 1966. *Land and Labor in China*. Boston: Beacon

Tax, Sol. 1953. *Penny Capitalism: A Guatemalan Indian Economy*. Washington, D.C.: Smithsonian Institution

Terray, Emmanuel. 1972. *Marxism and "Primitive" Societies: Two Studies*. New York: Monthly Review Press

Thompson, E. P. 1978. *The Poverty of Theory and Other Essays*. New York: Monthly Review Press

Tien, H. Yuan. 1983. "China: Demographic Billionaire." *Population Bulletin* 38(2): 2–42

Topley, Marjorie. 1975. "Marriage Resistance in Rural Kwangtung." In *Women in Chinese Society*, ed. M. Wolf and R. Witke. Stanford: Stanford University Press

Tu Wei-ming. 1985. "Self and Otherness in Confucian Thought." In *Culture and Self: Asian and Western Perspectives*, ed. A. J. Marsella, G. DeVos, and F. L. K. Hsu. New York: Tavistock

United States Census Bureau. 1984. *Statistical Abstracts of the United States*. Washington, D.C.

United States Department of State, Foreign Service Institute. 1970. *Cantonese*. Vols. I–III. Washington, D.C.: U.S. Government Printing Office

Urban, George. 1971. *The Miracle of Chairman Mao*. London: Tom Stacey Limited

Unschuld, Paul. 1985. *Medicine in China: A History of Ideas*. Berkeley: University of California Press

Vogel, Ezra. 1971. *Canton Under Communism:: Programs and Politics in a Provincial Capital 1949–1968.* New York: Harper and Row

Wakeman, Frederic, Jr. 1966. *Strangers at the Gate: Social Disorders in South China, 1839–1861.* Berkeley: University of California Press

Wallace, Anthony F. C. 1956. "Revitalization Movements." *American Anthropologist* 58: 264–281

Wallerstein, Immanuel. 1974. *The Modern World System.* New York: Academic Press

Watson, James L. 1975. *Emigration and the Chinese Lineage: The Mans in Hong Kong and London.* Berkeley: University of California Press

1976. "Chattel Slavery in Chinese Peasant Society: A Comparative Analysis." *Ethnology* 15: 361–375

1977. "Hereditary Tenancy and Cooperative Landlordism in Traditional China: A Case Study." *Modern Asian Studies* 11: 161–182

1980. *Asian and African Systems of Slavery.* Oxford: Blackwell

Watson, Rubie S. 1985. *Inequality Among Brothers: Class and Kinship in South China.* Cambridge, England: Cambridge University Press

Weber, Max. 1951. *The Religion of China.* Glencoe, Illinois: Free Press

1952. *Ancient Judaism.* Glencoe, Illinois: Free Press

1958. *The Protestant Ethic and the Spirit of Capitalism.* New York: Charles Scribner's Sons

Whyte, Martin K. and William L. Parish. 1984. *Urban Life in Contemporary China.* Chicago: University of Chicago Press

Willmott, Donald E. 1960. *The Chinese of Semarang: A Changing Minority Community in Indonesia.* Ithaca: Cornell University Press

Wittfogel, Karl A. 1957. *Oriental Despotism.* New Haven: Yale University Press

Wolf, Arthur P. and Chieh-shan Huang. 1980. *Marriage and Adoption in China, 1845–1945.* Stanford: Stanford University Press

Wolf, Eric. 1956. "Aspects of Group Relations in a Complex Society: Mexico." *American Anthropologist* 58: 1056–1078

1966. *Peasants.* Englewood Cliffs, New Jersey: Prentice-Hall

1982. *Europe and the People Without History.* Berkeley: University of California Press

Wright, Arthur F. 1959. *Buddhism in Chinese History.* Stanford: Stanford University Press

Xue Muqiao, ed. 1982. *Almanac of China's Economy 1981, With Economic Statistics From 1949–1980.* New York: Eurasia Press

Yang, C. K. 1944. *A North China Local Market Economy.* New York: Institute of Pacific Relations

1959. *The Chinese Family in the Communist Revolution.* Cambridge, Mass.: M.I.T. Press

Yang, Martin C. 1945. *A Chinese Village: Taitou, Shantung Province.* New York: Columbia University Press

1969. *Chinese Social Structure: A Historical Study.* Taipei: Eurasia Book Co.

Zhuang Qidong and Ye Feng. 1959. "Guanyu cheng xiang zhijian gong-nong zhijian he naoli laodong yu tili laodong zhijian benzhi chabie de suoxiao he xiaoshi wenti" ("On Reducing and Eliminating the Essential Differences Between City and Country, Worker and Peasant, and Mental and Manual Labor"). In *Woguo shehuizhuyi jianshezhong de ruogan jingji wenti* (*The Economic Problems of Socialist Construction in our Country*). Beijing: Zhongguo qingnian chubanshe (Chinese Youth Press)

# Index